FOURTH EDITION

Environmental Policy and Politics

Michael E. Kraft
University of Wisconsin, Green Bay

PEARSON
Longman

New York Boston San Francisco
London Toronto Sydney Tokyo Singapore Madrid
Mexico City Munich Paris Cape Town Hong Kong Montreal

CHAPTER **3**

Making Environmental Policy   56

CHAPTER **4**

The Evolution of Environmental Policy and Politics   85

CHAPTER **5**

Environmental Protection Policy: Controlling Pollution 111

CHAPTER **6**

Energy and Natural Resource Policies 159

CHAPTER **8**

Environmental Policy and Politics for the Twenty-First Century   241

Preface

Environmental policy today is at a critical crossroads. Since the dawn of the modern environmental era in the late 1960s, public concern and the actions of environmental groups have transformed public policy. The U.S. Congress has enacted dozens of major environmental protection and natural resource policies, as have state and local governments. Environmental issues have entered the mainstream of U.S. politics, as they have in the international arena. Yet future achievements depend on continued political support, which is less assured in the early twenty-first century than it was in earlier periods. Concern over the burdens of implementing environmental policies has dominated public discourse in recent years, and it has spurred a political backlash against environmental policies and programs that has been as evident at local and state levels as it has been in Washington, D.C.

Success in developing effective and politically acceptable policies in the next several decades depends on our collective ability to stimulate a constructive public dialogue on the issues. More than ever, we need to learn what works and what does not, and to employ that knowledge to redesign environmental policies for the next generation. Those policies and the political strategies used to advance them must command broad public support. They must also be consistent with the scarce fiscal resources that constrain all public policies today. The tasks go beyond setting budgetary priorities and fine-tuning policies. They involve building the political and institutional capacities that are essential for effective democratic governance of the environment.

The 1992 United Nations Conference on Environment and Development (the Earth Summit) and the less prominent follow-up 2002 World Summit on Sustainable Development highlighted a new array of daunting problems that all nations will face in the decades ahead. The world must learn how to respond creatively and effectively to the risks of global climate change and many other equally challenging issues. These include the destruction of forests and soils, the loss of biological diversity, and a surging human population. No responsibility of government and society will be more difficult over the next generation than accommodating the level of economic development needed to meet human needs and aspirations while simultaneously averting devastating effects on the environmental systems that sustain life.

In industrialized nations such as the United States, this new environmental agenda makes clear the imperative of integrating environmental protection with other social and economic activities, from energy use and transportation to agriculture and urban planning. We can no longer afford to think of environmental policy as an isolated and largely remedial activity of cleaning up the residue of society's care-less and wasteful habits. Emphasis must be placed on prevention of future harm through redesign of economic activities around the concept of sustainable development.

These new needs also require that governments work closely with the private sector in partnerships that can spur technological innovations while avoiding the protracted conflicts that have constrained environmental policy achievements in the past. This does not mean that tough regulation should be abandoned when it is necessary to achieve environmental goals. It does signal, however, the need to supplement regulation with other strategies and policy tools such as information disclosure, market-based incentives, and collaborative decision making that promise to speed the realization of those goals or significantly lower the costs of getting there.

Whether governments and other organizations will succeed in resolving environmental problems of the twenty-first century ultimately will depend on public understanding, support, and actions. Environmental policies require significant social and behavioral changes. These are possible only if people educate themselves about the issues and work cooperatively for environmental sustainability. Survey data confirm a high level of public concern about the environment within the United States and globally. The proliferation of thousands of grassroots organizations worldwide testifies to the public's eagerness to end environmental degradation and protect communities. At the same time, the effects of environmental and resource policies have spurred the rise of antienvironmental organizations with considerable political clout. To be effective over the next several decades, environmentalists will need to hone their political skills and forge broader alliances with new constituencies around common interests in sustainability.

Environmental Policy and Politics, Fourth Edition, seeks to contribute to these developments by offering a succinct overview and assessment of U.S. environmental policy and politics. It differs from other texts in several respects. It uses a risk-based framework for environmental policy analysis to encourage students to judge environmental problems for themselves. It summarizes an extensive collection of scientific studies, government reports, and policy analyses to convey the nature of environmental problems, their causes, progress in dealing with them, and policy implications. The problems covered include new global threats such as climate change and loss of biodiversity as well as more conventional topics such as air and water pollution, toxic chemicals, hazardous wastes, and energy use.

This book also describes major U.S. environmental and natural resource policies, their origins, the key policy actors who have shaped them, their achievements and deficiencies, and various proposals for policy change. It offers a thorough, yet concise, coverage of the U.S. policy-making process, the legislative and administrative settings for policy decisions, and the role of environmental groups and public opinion in environmental politics. The text also differs from many others in its organization. I hope the logic of its organization is both clear to readers and persuasive.

Chapter 1 introduces the subject of environmental policy and places it within the political and economic trends of the early twenty-first century that affect it. It also sets out an analytic framework drawn from policy analysis and environmental science that helps connect environmental policy to the political process. My intention is to help readers learn how to think critically about environmental problems in terms of the risks they pose to public and ecological health, and the multiple ways in which government and other actors might address those risks. Chapter 2 follows up on this introduction by reviewing scientific evidence that speaks to the severity of various environmental problems and the policy implications. The data in this chapter have been extensively updated, key Web sources are provided throughout to allow students to find current information, and new tables are used to highlight selected data. Readers are encouraged to draw their own conclusions about these problems and the need for policy action.

Chapter 3 helps set the scene for the rest of the book by describing the U.S. policy-making process in broad terms, with a focus on agenda setting and the role of policy entrepreneurs. The chapter also identifies the main features of U.S. government and politics at federal, state, and local levels. Chapter 4 uses the concepts introduced in Chapter 3 to trace the evolution of environmental policy and politics from the earliest days of the nation through the emergence of the modern environmental movement and reactions to it. The public's concern for the environment and its support for public policy actions are given special treatment, as are the activities of environmental groups in the policy process.

The core of the book, Chapters 5 and 6, turns to the basic character of U.S. environmental policies. What we call environmental policy consists of two very different collections of public policies: environmental protection or pollution control policies, such as the Clean Air Act and Clean Water Act, and natural resource policies, such as the Endangered Species Act and National Forest Management Act. Hence I cover the major environmental policies in two elaborate chapters divided along these lines. Chapter 5 discusses the leading environmental protection statutes administered by the U.S. Environmental Protection Agency (EPA) and their continuing evolution. The chapter then goes on to describe and assess the EPA's work in implementing these policies, from its staffing and budgetary resources to its relationship with the states to the intricacies of standard setting, rule making, and enforcement actions. I believe an integrated discussion of these two sets of concerns makes sense. But many instructors will probably find that several class sessions on each part of the chapter will work best.

Chapter 6 offers comparable coverage of energy and natural resource policies. The chapter outlines the history of efforts to design national energy policies in the last several presidential administrations and the adoption of a new national energy policy in 2005. It also describes the evolution of natural resource policies and the many conflicts between natural resource preservation and economic development. Here also, although these two interrelated policy topics are covered in one chapter, instructions will probably want to discuss them separately for added emphasis.

Chapter 7 revisits the major critiques of environmental protection and natural resource policies discussed in Chapters 5 and 6, and it outlines new directions for policy change in the twenty-first century. It puts this review of policy successes and failures in the context of the broad goal of sustainability, and it considers a range of policy alternatives, from market incentives and information disclosure to collaborative decision making.

Finally, Chapter 8 looks to the future and to the need for global policy action. It describes the remaining policy agenda for the early twenty-first century, explores the goal of sustainable development, and describes the leading international environmental policy institutions well as limitations on their policy-making capacity. It uses three case studies (climate change, protection of biodiversity, and population growth) to illustrate these themes.

A book like this has to cover a great deal of technical material on environmental problems and public policies. I have tried to make it all as current as possible and also faithful to the scientific literature. If in some instances the text has fallen short of these goals, I hope readers will alert me to important omissions, misinterpretations, and other deficiencies. I can be reached via e-mail at kraftm@uwgb.edu.

In preparing a book manuscript one incurs many debts. The University of Wisconsin—Green Bay and its Department of Public and Environmental Affairs supplied me with essential support. The organization of the book and its content owe much to my teaching here. I am grateful to my undergraduate and graduate students, whose interest in environmental policy and politics gave me the opportunity to discuss these issues at length with concerned and attentive people as well as the chance to learn from them. I also have benefited immeasurably from the individuals whose analyses of environmental politics and policy, and U.S. government and politics, make a book like this possible. I hope the extensive references in the text adequately convey my reliance on their scholarship and my gratitude to them.

A number of individuals offered thoughtful suggestions for previous editions of the book, and I greatly appreciate their assistance: Robert V. Bartlett, Purdue University; Christopher J. Bosso, Northeastern University; Bill Chaloupka, University of Montana; Irene Dameron-Hager, Ohio State University; Jamie Elizabeth Jacobs, West Virginia University; Leah Wilds Magennis, University of Nevada; Lisa Nelson, Bowling Green University; Philip Nyhus, Colby College; David Robertson, University of Missouri-St. Louis; Rob Sanford, University of Southern Maine; Bob Turner, Skidmore College; and Carter Whatley, Jr., Texas A & M University. I also want to thank Anne Lesser for her splendid copyediting and Maria McColligan and the editorial and production team at Nesbitt Graphics, Inc. Naturally, I assume responsibility for any errors in the text that remain.

This book is dedicated to the memory of my parents, Louis and Pearl Kraft. Their compassion, generosity, and caring for their fellow human beings embodied the social concerns that today are reflected in an environmental ethic. They also provided me and my brothers with the opportunity to grow up in a stunning environment in Southern California and experience the wonders of the desert, mountains, and ocean that exist in such close proximity in that part of the country.

MICHAEL E. KRAFT

Environmental Problems and Politics

In 2005 gasoline prices in the United States rose to near record highs, sparking public outcries and a request from President George W. Bush that citizens try to conserve gasoline by driving less. During the winter of 2005–2006, people faced another energy surprise. Their home heating bills rose sharply, reflecting higher costs for natural gas and oil. The U.S. Congress had enacted a major national energy policy only a few months earlier, but even the president conceded that it would do nothing to help with high prices in the short term. The underlying cause of rising energy costs was no puzzle. Americans have an insatiable appetite for energy to power their cars, heat and cool their homes, and enjoy the many conveniences of modern life. With a surging global demand for oil and natural gas and short-term constraints on supplies, higher prices were a given.

The energy shock of 2005 tells us much about environmental policy and politics in the early twenty-first century. Problems often are hard to identify, and taking action on them is never easy because it requires policymakers to resolve deep conflicts over what government ought to do. For example, should government provide subsidies for oil and gas companies to encourage greater energy production? Should it impose mandatory energy conservation measures to reduce demand or provide an economic incentive to achieve the same end? Should it fund scientific and technological research that could help develop new sources of energy? Each strategy has its backers among scientists, policy analysts, interest groups, and policymakers, and each group is convinced that its approach is the right thing to do.

These kinds of disagreements might suggest that no consensus at all exists about environmental problems today. Yet nearly all serious students of environmental policy recognize the abundant cause for concern and that environmental threats, if anything, are more pervasive and ominous in the early 2000s than they were when the modern environmental movement began in the late 1960s.

The problems are familiar to most people, if not always easy to understand. They include air and water pollution, public exposure to toxic chemicals and hazardous wastes, the production of large quantities of solid wastes that wind up in landfills, heavy reliance worldwide on use of fossil fuels that contribute to the risk of climate change, and the destruction of ecologically critical lands and forests, which in turn hastens the loss of biological diversity. To these problems we can add continuing growth of the human population and high levels of consumption of energy and natural resources; these two patterns can exacerbate all of the other environmental problems. Many would add to this list the deterioration of the quality of life in increasingly congested cities around the world.

Reports on these and related issues fill the airwaves and newspapers, and they provoke public apprehension over apparently unceasing environmental degradation. Individuals can see the evidence in their own neighborhoods, communities, and regions, and it clearly affects them. Not only in the United States, but worldwide, people believe the environment is in serious decline and they strongly support efforts to reverse the trend (Bosso and Guber 2006; Dunlap, Gallup, and Gallup 1993; Global Strategy Group 2004). Their fears are shared by many of the world's policymakers, who helped set the agenda for the historic Earth Summit, the United Nations Conference on Environment and Development, held in 1992 in Rio de Janeiro, Brazil, and the follow-up World Summit on Sustainable Development held in Johannesburg, South Africa, in 2002.

The Earth Summit was the largest international diplomatic conference ever held, attracting representatives from 179 nations (including 118 heads of state). More than 8,000 journalists covered the event. In addition, representatives from more than 7,000 nongovernmental organizations (NGOs) attended a concurrent Global Forum at a nearby site in Rio. The "Rio-Plus-10" summit in Johannesburg received much less attention, but it also attracted a large number of official delegates, NGO representatives, and members of the press (Speth 2003).

In the presummit planning sessions for the 1992 Earth Summit and at the conference itself, a palpable sense of urgency was felt over worsening environmental problems and their implications for economic development, especially in poor nations. There was also much evidence of public determination to deal with the problems. In a postsummit UN publication containing the conference's Agenda 21 action program, the meeting's organizer, Maurice Strong, spoke optimistically about what he termed "a wildfire of interest and support" that the Earth Summit had ignited throughout the world and that he hoped would stimulate a global movement toward sustainable paths of development (United Nations 1993, 1). Five years earlier, the report of the World Commission on Environment and Development (the Brundtland Commission), *Our Common Future* (1987), had similar effects. It sold 1 million copies in 30 languages and spurred extensive policy changes in both the government and private sectors (Starke 1990).

If they achieved nothing else, the Earth Summit and the 2002 Johannesburg conference helped to give form and substance to the concept of sustainable development, which the Brundtland Commission of the late 1980s defined as "development that meets the needs of the present without compromising the ability of future generations to meet their own needs" (World Commission 1987, 43). One prominent report released a year before the 1992 summit made the need for sustainable development clear by highlighting the astonishing world trends in population growth and consumption:

Since 1900, the world's population has multiplied more than three times. Its economy has grown twentyfold. The consumption of fossil fuels has grown by a factor of 30, and industrial production by a factor of 50. Most of that growth, about four-fifths of it, has occurred since 1950. Much of it is unsustainable. Earth's basic life-supporting capital of forests, species, and soils is being depleted and its fresh waters and oceans are being degraded at an accelerating rate. (MacNeill, Winsemius, and Yakushiji 1991, 3)

The authors looked back to social, economic, and environmental changes earlier in the twentieth century. What lies ahead in the twenty-first century, however, is equally striking and worrisome. For example, the United Nations estimates that the world's 2006 population of 6.5 billion people will grow to about 9.3 billion by 2050, with virtually all of that growth occurring in the developing nations. To feed, house, and otherwise provide for people's needs and aspirations will tax natural resources and ecological systems throughout the world. This is particularly so given the high level of economic growth that is also expected over the next half century. China, for example, expects its economic output to quadruple over the next 15 years alone. This kind of economic growth is important for increasing opportunities for billions of people around the world and advancing social justice (Friedman 2005), but it must also be compatible with the limits of natural systems.[1]

It is difficult for most of us to understand these historic trends and their effects. Yet, as biologist Jane Lubchenco noted in her 1997 presidential address to the American Association for the Advancement of Science, over the last several decades "humans have emerged as a new force of nature." We are, she argued, "modifying physical, chemical, and biological systems in new ways, at faster rates, and over larger spatial scales than ever recorded on Earth." The result of these modifications is that humans have "unwittingly embarked upon a grand experiment with our planet," with "profound implications for all of life on Earth" (Lubchenco 1998, 492).

These remarkable transformations raise fundamental issues for the study of environmental policy and politics. Will the earth be able to accommodate the kind of growth widely anticipated over the next century? If so, at what human and ecological cost? How well equipped are the world's nations to respond to the many needs created by such social, economic, and ecological trends? Will political systems around the world prove able and willing to tackle these problems? For example, will they be able to design, adopt, and implement effective policies to protect public health? Will they be able to do the same to promote sustainable use of natural resources?

This book tries to address these questions, although it can only scratch the surface. For that reason I provide extensive references and Web sites throughout to encourage you to explore many topics in more detail. The book also has a theme. It deals with the relationship of environmental policy to politics, and it argues that democratic environmental politics is essential to the development of effective public policy. I explore that theme mainly by reviewing policy actions of the U.S. federal government, but I also pay attention to state and local policy developments within the United States and to international environmental policy.

ENVIRONMENTAL POLICY AND POLITICS

Politics is about the collective choices we make as a society. It concerns policy goals and the means we use to achieve them as well as the way we organize and govern ourselves. Over the next several decades, the United States and other nations face important decisions. They can maintain current policies and practices or they can envision a better future and design the institutions and policies necessary to help bring needed change. They can rely on the invisible hand of the marketplace or they can try to accelerate and consciously direct a transition to that future in other ways. Such decisions are at least as important in the United States as they are in other nations, and the ecological consequences are probably greater here than in any other nation in the world. The National Commission on the Environment captured the choices well:

> If America continues down its current path, primarily reacting to environmental injuries and trying to repair them, the quality of our environment will continue to deteriorate, and eventually our economy will decline as well. If, however, our country pioneers new technologies, shifts its policies, makes bold economic changes, and embraces a new ethic of environmentally responsible behavior, it is far more likely that the coming years will bring a higher quality of life, a healthier environment, and a more vibrant economy for all Americans. (1993, xi)

The commission concluded that "natural processes that support life on Earth are increasingly at risk," and as a solution it endorsed sustainable development. Such development could serve, the commission said, as a "central guiding principle for national environmental and economic policy making," which it saw as inextricably linked, and thereby restore environmental quality, create broad-based economic progress, and brighten prospects for future generations. Consistent with its bipartisan composition, the commission observed that such a strategy would involve a combination of market forces, government regulations, and private and individual initiatives.

The nearly universal embrace of the idea of sustainable development is an important signpost for the early twenty-first century, even if it remains a somewhat vague term that can mask serious economic and political conflicts (Mazmanian and Kraft 1999). It was evident in the name given to the 2002 Johannesburg conference (the World Summit on Sustainable Development) and in a major report by the Clinton administration's President's Council on Sustainable Development (1996). Such widespread endorsement of the principle of sustainability would have been inconceivable a generation ago. In the early 1970s, books describing the "environmental crisis" and proposing ways to deal with "limits to growth" and "ecological scarcity" may have won over some college audiences and urged on nascent environmental organizations, but they had little discernible effect on the higher reaches of government and corporate officialdom in the United States and most other nations. In the early twenty-first century, the language of sustainability not only penetrates to that level, it has kindled promising grassroots activity both across the nation and around the world (Axelrod, Downie, and Vig 2005; Starke 2006).

These developments signal fundamental changes that have occurred in both U.S. and global environmental policy and politics over the past generation. The initial environmental agenda of the late 1960s and 1970s focused on air and water pollution control and the preservation of natural resources such as parks, wilderness, and wildlife. The problems were thought to be simple and the solutions obvious and relatively easy to put into effect. Public and congressional enthusiasm for environmental protection policy supported the adoption of innovative and stringent federal programs that would force offending industries to clean up. That was true even where policy goals appeared to exceed both available technical knowledge and the capacity of administrative agencies to take on the new responsibilities mandated by law (Jones 1975). In such a political climate, the costs of achieving new environmental standards were rarely a major consideration.

As new policies were implemented in the 1970s and 1980s, their ambitious goals proved to be far more difficult to achieve than anticipated and much more costly. By the late 1970s, policymakers and environmentalists became increasingly frustrated with the slow pace of progress, and complaints from regulated industry and state and local governments mounted. Officials in Ronald Reagan's administration frequently accentuated the deficiencies of the old policies (Durant 1992; Vig and Kraft 1984). Consensus on new directions, however, was harder to achieve as Congress and the environmental community blocked what they considered ill-informed and unwise assaults on their handiwork by White House ideologues. The evidence could be seen in years of policy gridlock in the 1980s when no agreement could be reached on renewing the major environmental statutes (Kraft 2006).

Some of the same conflicts continued in the 1990s, and yet Congress was able to enact the monumental Clean Air Act of 1990, reform the nation's pesticide control policy in 1996, and renew the Safe Drinking Water Act in the same year. For most of the past decade, however, renewal of the major federal policies, such as the Endangered Species Act and Superfund, has been mired in Congress over disputes about how to balance environmental protection and economic goals. During the mid- to late 1990s, President Bill Clinton fought repeatedly with a Republican Congress that was determined to roll back environmental policy. With the election of President George W. Bush in 2000 and again in 2004, the battles intensified as environmentalists and their supporters in Congress clashed with the Bush White House and the business community over policy priorities. Even state and local governments, weary of their struggle to comply with costly federal environmental mandates, increasingly have criticized proposed policy changes they consider too expensive (Vig and Kraft 2006).

The Earth Summit, the report of the National Commission on the Environment, and political fights both on Capitol Hill and in state capitals since the 1980s have conveyed an important message about environmental policy and politics for the early twenty-first century. Even as a consensus has been building for environmental protection and sustainable development, defining what these terms mean in practice and formulating specific policies to achieve them remain highly contentious. In this sense, we can detect continuities with the old environmental politics even as a new era is unfolding that is rich in hope and possibilities.

In many ways, environmental issues today are broader and deeper than ever before. Emerging (or reemerging) problems such as energy use, global climate change, population growth, and threats to biological diversity have extended the reach of environmentalism well beyond the old boundaries. At the same time, environmental issues, both new and old, pose deeper challenges to society as the costs and impacts of environmental policies grow, the uncertainties and complexities of the problems increase, and effective and acceptable solutions prove elusive.

The 1992 Earth Summit and the 2002 Johannesburg sustainable development summit symbolize the degree to which the environment has matured politically since the late 1960s and how it now commands broad, if not always deep, public and governmental attention and support (Bosso and Guber 2006; Guber 2003). As policy conflicts in Congress (and state legislatures) indicate, such developments do not eliminate controversies in dealing with environmental and natural resource issues at home and abroad. There will continue to be hard-fought battles over environmental policies and their implementation. The outcomes will be unpredictable and will depend on how the issues are defined, the state of the economy, the relative influence of opposing interests, and political leadership. Nothing on the horizon indicates that political conflict over the environment is likely to disappear any time soon. In fact, given the enormity of emerging global problems, many scholars believe that conflict may well increase markedly over the next few decades (Axelrod, Downie, and Vig 2005; Chasek, Downie, and Brown 2006; Pirages and Cousins 2005).

For these reasons, among others, politics and government will be indispensable to the complex process of identifying, understanding, and responding to the world's diverse environmental problems. Policy choices are inescapably political in the sense that they seek to resolve conflicts inherent in the balancing of environmental protection and other social and economic goals. They involve a struggle over whose definition of the public interest should prevail and precisely how we should reconcile environmental goals with other competing values such as economic well-being, individual rights, and social justice. Most political scientists would not dispute such assertions, but in an age of rampant political cynicism, others might well question governmental capacity to improve the environment. The role of government and politics must be assessed in the context of other leading perspectives on environmental problems and their causes and solutions.

◼ PERSPECTIVES ON ENVIRONMENTAL PROBLEMS

Even a casual review of recent commentary on the environment reveals widely disparate views of ecological problems and what ought to be done about them (Higgs and Close 2005; Huber 2000; Lomborg 2001; Vig and Kraft 2006). That should not be surprising. Definitions and understanding of any public problem are affected by political ideologies and values, education and professional training, and work or community experience. They vary greatly across society and among scientists, policymakers, and the public. At least three major perspectives in addition to those of government and politics merit brief comment here. They focus on (1) science and technology, (2) economics and incentive structures, and (3) values and ethics.

Scientific Knowledge and Its Use

Many scientists (and business leaders as well) believe that environmental problems can be traced chiefly to a lack of scientific knowledge about the dynamics of natural systems or the use of technology. They may also point to a failure to put such knowledge to good use in both the government and the private sector. That is, they have a great deal of confidence in science and engineering for solving environmental problems. For example, ecologists believe that improving our knowledge of biological diversity will highlight existing and anticipated threats; thus it may contribute to the strengthening of public policy to protect endangered species and their habitats. Better knowledge of the risks to human health posed by toxic chemicals could facilitate formulation of pollution control strategies. Knowledge of new production technologies could lead industry likewise to adopt so-called green business practices, as many have done. Or businesses may choose to market greener products, such as hybrid automobiles, because advances in technology allow them to do so (Press and Mazmanian 2006). Another example can be found in the field of nuclear energy. New technology that promises to make nuclear power reactors cheaper and safer to operate lead some to argue that the nation can rely more on nuclear power in the future.

Not surprisingly, scientists and engineers urge increased research on environmental issues, more extensive and reliable monitoring of environmental conditions and trends over time, better use of science (and scientists) in policymaking, and the development of new technologies with fewer negative environmental impacts. Government policymakers also may share this view, which explains why the federal government has invested billions of dollars a year in research on global climate change alone, and several billion dollars more on other environmental research. No shortage of recommendations is available for additional spending or for scientists playing a far more active role in communicating scientific knowledge to the public and policymakers (Lubchenco 1998).[2] In recent years, many environmental scientists also have argued for a novel approach to setting research priorities by emphasizing the need for an interdisciplinary "sustainability science" that "seeks to understand the fundamental character of interactions between nature and society" (Kates et al. 2001, 641). Advocates of this kind of scientific research believe that a much closer alignment of environmental science and the world of public policy is needed. At least one of the reasons they take this position is their concern that scientific work may not be properly appreciated or understood by the public and policymakers. Concerns of this kind were heightened during the Bush administration when many scientists inside and outside of government complained that environmental policy decisions were being made without sufficient regard for scientific evidence. The disputes ranged from the appropriate standards for mercury emissions from power plants to issues of climate change and protection of biological diversity (Andrews 2006; Rosenbaum 2006).[3]

Economics and Incentives

Another group of commentators, particularly economists, finds the major causes of environmental ills to be less a deficiency of scientific knowledge or available technologies than an unfortunate imbalance of incentives. We misuse natural resources, especially common-pool resources such as the atmosphere, surface waters, and public lands, or we fail to adopt promising new technologies such as solar power because we think we gain economically from current practices or we do not suffer an economic loss (Ostrom 1990, 1999a). In his classic essay on the "tragedy of the commons," Garrett Hardin (1968) illustrated how individuals may be led to exploit to the point of depletion those resources they hold in common. Sometimes natural resource policies have the perverse effect of encouraging the very degradation they are designed to prevent by setting artificially low market prices (e.g., for irrigation water or use of public lands for timber harvesting, mining, or grazing) through government subsidies to resource users (Burger and Gochfeld 1998; Myers and Kent 2001; Roodman 1996).

We regularly see evidence of this general phenomenon of short-sighted action. In 1994, faced with a fishery on the verge of collapse, an industry-dominated fishery management council in New England recommended a drastic cutback in allowable fishing in the Georges Bank area off Cape Cod. Previous limitations on fishing proved insufficient to prevent the exhaustion of the principal species that had supported commercial fishing in the area for generations.[4] Similar behavior is evident in urban areas. Individuals resist using mass transit and insist on driving their automobiles to work in congested and polluted cities even when they can plainly see the environmental degradation their behavior causes.

Because of such behavioral patterns, economists, planners, and policy analysts propose that we redesign the economic and behavioral incentives that current unrealistic market prices create (Freeman 2006; National Academy of Public Administration 1994). These prices send inaccurate and inappropriate signals to consumers and businesses and thus encourage behavior that may be environmentally destructive. We need, such analysts say, to internalize the external costs of individual and collective decision making and establish something closer to full social cost accounting that reflects real environmental gains and losses. It might be done, for example, with public tax policies. A steep tax on the use of gasoline and other fossil fuels could discourage their use and build demand for energy-efficient technologies. A tax credit for use of energy-efficient appliances such as refrigerators and air conditioners or hybrid vehicles could encourage individuals to make such purchases, which could save them money over time. Such a credit could also give manufacturers more reason to make products of this kind (Sawin 2004).

This argument extends to reform of the usual measures of economic accounting, such as the gross national product (GNP). Critics, such as the organization Redefining Progress (www.rprogress.org), complain that such measures fail to consider the value of environmental damage, such as loss of forest or wetland habitats. Some even call for a new paradigm of ecological economics and a fair valuing of "nature's services" to humans (Cobb, Halstead, and Rowe 1995; Costanza 1991; Daily 1997). For example, one widely discussed report in 1997 estimated the economic value of the services of all global ecological systems and the natural capital stocks that produce them at an astonishing $33 trillion a year. In comparison, the global GNP at the time was $18 trillion a year (Costanza et al. 1997). On a more concrete level, in 1997 New York City decided to spend $660 million to preserve a watershed in the Catskill Mountains north of the city because the water supply could be purified by microorganisms as it percolated through the soil. The city's alternative was to construct a water treatment plant that could have cost $6 billion or more.[5] Many other examples of this kind can be cited. It seems evident that only with accurate price signals and revised accounting mechanisms can individual and market choices steer the nation and the world in the direction of environmental sustainability.

Environmental Values and Ethics

Philosophers and environmentalists offer a third perspective. The environmental crisis, they believe, is at heart a consequence of our belief systems and values, which they see as seriously deficient in the face of contemporary ecological threats, whatever their other virtues may be. For example, William Catton and Riley Dunlap (1980) have defined a dominant social paradigm (DSP), or worldview, of Western industrial societies that includes several core beliefs: humans are fundamentally different from all other species on Earth over which they have dominion, people are masters of their own destiny and can do whatever is necessary to achieve their goals, the world is vast and provides unlimited opportunities for humans, and human history is one of progress in which all major problems can be solved. Other premises and values follow from these beliefs: the primacy of economic well-being; the acceptability of risks associated with conventional technologies that produce wealth; a low valuation of nature; the absence of any limit to economic growth; support for present social and economic structures based on competition, hierarchy, and efficiency; and support for political processes characterized by centralized authority structures and bureaucratic experts (summarized in Milbrath 1989, 189).

Environmentalists argue that the values represented by the DSP strongly affect our personal behavior and institutional priorities and constitute one of the most fundamental causes of natural resource depletion and environmental degradation (Kempton, Boster, and Hartley 1996; Milbrath 1984, 1996; Paehlke 1989).

Environmentalists thus contend that the DSP and the values related to it must change if human behavior is to be made more consonant with sustainable use of the biosphere. Such ideas are not new. Aldo Leopold, one of the most celebrated advocates of an environmental ethic, wrote in his prophetic *A Sand County Almanac* (originally published in 1949) that society would gain from adoption of an environmental ethic, which he termed a land ethic: "A thing is right when it tends to preserve the integrity, stability, and beauty of the biotic community. It is wrong when it tends otherwise" (Leopold 1970, 262).

Contemporary accounts reflect Leopold's perspective. Robert Paehlke, for example, derived a list of 13 values that constitute the "essential core of an environmental perspective." He further distilled these into three key goals: (1) protection of ecological systems, wilderness, and biodiversity; (2) minimization of negative impacts on human health; and (3) establishment of sustainable patterns of resource use (Paehlke 2000). Much environmental writing espouses similar values to achieve those broad ends (e.g., Durning 1992; Milbrath 1989; Ophuls and Boyan 1992).

The implication is that merely reforming environmental policies to improve short-term governmental actions is not enough. Instead, changes in political, social, cultural, and economic institutions may be needed. Yet environmental writers continue to debate precisely what kinds of changes are necessary. For example, political philosophers disagree about key political values and institutions, including such fundamental issues as the structure and authority of government and the role of the public in decision making (Dryzek and Lester 1995; Eckersley 2004; M. Lewis 1994; Luke 1997).

■ THE ROLE OF GOVERNMENT AND POLITICS

Each of these three perspectives offers distinctive insights into environmental problems and their solutions. All make sense, although none alone offers a complete understanding or a sufficient agenda for action. Few would question that society needs better scientific knowledge, a shift to environmentally benign technologies, or more comprehensive policy analysis and planning. Nor would many deny the need for greater economic and personal incentives to conserve energy and other resources or a stronger and more widely shared commitment to environmental values in our personal lives.

Moreover, few would disagree that diverse actions by individuals and institutions at all levels of society, in the public as well as the private sector, will be essential to the long-term goals of environmental protection and sustainable development. People may choose to live close to where they work and walk or commute on bicycles or use mass transit rather than private automobiles, or they may at least use fuel-efficient vehicles. They may also seek durable, energy-efficient, and environmentally safe consumer goods and use fewer of them, recycle or compost wastes, and adjust their air-conditioning and heating systems to conserve energy. Similarly, businesses can do much to improve energy efficiency and prevent pollution.

Government nonetheless has an essential role to play in resolving environmental problems. Public policies shape the kind of scientific research that is supported and thus the pace and character of scientific and technological developments. Governmental policies also affect the design and use of economic incentives and changes in society's environmental values (e.g., through educational programs). We look to government for such policies because environmental threats represent public or collective goods problems that *cannot* be solved through private action alone. The costs may simply be too great for private initiatives, and certain activities may require the legal authority or political legitimacy that only governments possess. Examples include setting aside large areas of public lands for national parks, wilderness, and wildlife preserves, and establishment of a range of international environmental, development, and population assistance programs.

Much the same is true of national or state regulatory and taxation policies. Such policies are adopted largely because society concludes that market forces by themselves do not produce the desired outcomes. Even free market enthusiasts admit that "imperfections" in markets (such as inadequate information, lack of competitiveness, and externalities such as pollution) may justify government regulation. In all these cases, private sector activity may well contribute to desired social ends. Yet the scope and magnitude of environmental problems, the level of resources needed to address them, and urgent public pressures for action may push the issues onto governmental agendas.

In these ways, the resultant public policies help fill the gaps created when millions of individuals and thousands of corporations make independent choices in a market economy (Ophuls and Boyan 1992; Ostrom 1990; Ostrom et al. 2002). However rational such choices are from the individual or corporate viewpoint, they are almost always guided by greater concern for personal gain and short-term profits than for the long-term social goals of a clean and safe environment or for sustainable development. Hence there is a need for establishing some limits on those choices or providing incentives to help ensure that individuals and organizations make them in a socially responsible manner. Those are the preeminent purposes of environmental policy.

The goals of environmental policies and the means chosen to achieve them are set by a variety of political processes, from the local to the international level. They are also a product of the interaction of thousands of individuals and groups that participate actively in those processes. Environmentalists are well represented in decision making at most levels of government today, if not quite on a par with business and industry groups (Bosso 2005; Duffy 2003; Kraft and Kamieniecki 2007). The presence of a multiplicity of interest groups and the visibility of environmental policies usually guarantees that policy goals and instruments are subject to intense political debate, with particular scrutiny given to their costs and effectiveness. None of that diminishes the need to have such policies even as it makes clear the necessity to evaluate them carefully and to change them as the circumstances warrant.

Specific proposals for reforming environmental policies and agencies abound. They come from individual authors, environmental organizations, industry, independent policy research groups, and a wide array of governmental agencies, advisory bodies, and commissions. Many are discussed throughout the book.

DEMOCRACY, POLITICS, AND ENVIRONMENTAL POLICY

In the chapters that follow, I argue that democratic decision making and public support are crucial to successful environmental politics. They are important as well for the formulation of environmental policy that is both technically sound and socially acceptable. Democratic politics is rarely easy, and it is made especially difficult when individuals and groups hold sharply divergent perspectives on the issues and are reluctant or unable to compromise on those views. Protracted conflict over protection of threatened northern spotted owls and old-growth forest ecosystems in the Pacific Northwest was one of the most prominent examples of environmental gridlock during the 1990s. Disagreement over climate change policy in the early twenty-first century illustrates equally well the challenge of building public and political consensus on environmental policy (Hempel 2006; Paehlke 2004). Many other cases can be cited, from nuclear waste disposal to reform of public lands policy. These conditions indicate the need to establish workable decision-making processes that offer hope of resolving such conflicts. Fortunately, successful cases at all levels of government suggest how such processes can be developed and put into effect (Mazmanian and Kraft 1999; Sabatier et al. 2005).

Not all appraisals of environmental politics reach such a positive conclusion about democracy or what some term civic environmentalism (John 1994, 2004). Critics might ask, for example, about the extent to which citizens have the capacity to make smart choices when given pertinent environmental information and the opportunity to discuss it with others. Some authors argue that democratic political systems as currently constituted are incapable of overcoming what they see as strong public resistance to the formidable social, economic, and personal changes that may well be necessary in the decades ahead. They question whether citizens will become sufficiently knowledgeable about the issues or exhibit enough foresight to support such demanding changes. They also are convinced that powerful economic and political interests (e.g., oil and chemical companies) will defeat or weaken environmental policy initiatives that threaten their privileged positions, thus preventing adequate and timely responses to environmental perils (Heilbroner 1991). Such beliefs led Ophuls and Boyan (1992, 3) to conclude that "liberal democracy as we know it, that is, our theory or 'paradigm' of politics . . . is doomed by ecological scarcity; we need a completely new political philosophy and set of political institutions."

Other scholars find public concern about the environment and support for environmental protection efforts to be relatively high and persistent, if not always well grounded in knowledge of the issues (Bosso and Guber 2006; Dunlap 1995a). Indeed, many studies have found that the public's ability to deal with difficult technical issues is greater than commonly supposed (Hager 1994; Hill 1992; McAvoy 1999). Still others conclude that policymakers can design public policies to promote citizen participation, enhance citizen capacities to deal with technical issues, improve deliberation on the issues, and increase responsiveness of government to citizen needs (Baber and Bartlett 2005; Ingram and Smith 1993; Kraft 2000). Most of these scholars are more confident than the pessimistic analysts about the capacity of democratic systems to deal successfully with environmental issues.

Whatever one's appraisal of governmental capabilities and the potential for democratic politics, obviously environmental policies adopted since the 1960s will have real and important effects in the United States and around the world. Some may be positive and some negative. It makes sense to try to understand their origins, current forms, achievements, and deficiencies. I try to do that throughout the text.

▓ DEFINING ENVIRONMENTAL POLICY

Public policy is a course of government action in response to social problems; it is what governments choose to do about those problems. Environmental policy includes a diversity of governmental actions that affect or attempt to affect environmental quality or the use of natural resources. It represents society's collective decision to pursue certain environmental goals and objectives and to use particular tools to achieve them. Environmental policy will not be found in any single statute or administrative decision. Rather, it is found in a collection of statutes, regulations, and court precedents that govern the nation, as well as in the attitudes and behavior of public officials who are responsible for making, implementing, and enforcing the law. Another way to understand environmental policy is to say that it includes not only what governments choose to do to protect environmental quality and natural resources but what they decide *not* to do; a decision not to act means that governments allow other forces to shape the environment. One example is that if governments choose not to have an energy policy, this means they leave decisions about the nation's energy use up to individuals and corporations without any governmental efforts to change how much or what kind of energy we use.

Policies may be tangible, with real consequences, or largely symbolic. That is, not all environmental policies are intended to solve problems. Some are mainly expressive in nature. They articulate environmental values and goals that are intensely held by the public and especially by key interest groups, such as environmentalists. Such statements may have little direct relationship to legally specified policy goals and objectives, although they may nevertheless bring about important environmental changes over time by influencing public beliefs and organizational values and decision making (Bartlett 1994; Cantrill and Oravec 1996).

Policy Typologies

Political scientists and policy analysts have found it useful to distinguish several basic types of policies, such as regulatory and distributive policies. Each is associated with different patterns of policymaking (Anderson 2006; Lowi 1979; Ripley and Franklin 1991). Most environmental policies fall into one category or the other, although as is the case with most typologies, the fit is imperfect.

Regulatory policies attempt to reduce or expand the choices available to citizens and corporations to achieve a social goal. They may raise the cost of, prohibit, or compel certain actions through provision of sanctions and incentives. The most common approach is the setting and enforcement of standards such as the amount of pollutants that a factory or utility may emit into the air or water. Most environmental protection policies such as the Clean Air Act and the Clean Water Act are regulatory. The politics associated with regulatory policy tend to pit environmental and health groups against industry. The former seeks benefits for the general population (such as reduced exposure to toxic chemicals), whereas the latter tries to minimize the costs and burdens imposed by government regulators. When the issues are highly visible and the public is supportive, government may impose a tough policy. If the issues are not very prominent or the public is less united, however, industry does better in getting its way (Kraft and Kamieniecki 2007; Wilson 1980).

In contrast to environmental protection efforts like this, most natural resources and conservation policies historically have been distributive. They have allocated or distributed public resources, often in the form of financial subsidies or comparable specific benefits to clientele groups. The purpose has been to achieve social goals such as providing access to public lands for mining, grazing, forestry, or recreation; protecting biological diversity; or fostering the development of energy resources such as nuclear power (Clarke and McCool 1996; Duffy 1997; McConnell 1966). The U.S. Congress traditionally has favored such distributive (critics call them "pork-barrel") policies, which convey highly visible benefits to politically important constituencies for whom the issues are highly salient. The general public usually has little interest in the issues, so its political influence is often minimal. Not surprisingly, such policies often are criticized for fostering inequitable and inefficient uses of public resources and often environmentally destructive practices (Lowry 2006; Myers and Kent 2001).

The Breadth of Environmental Policy

A wide range of social, political, and economic forces shapes environmental policy decisions, and their effect on policymaking varies, depending on the time and institutional location. As a result, the United States has a disparate and uncoordinated collection of environmental policies enacted at different times and for different purposes. It is rarely satisfactory from the perspective of ecological rationality or in terms of expectations for coherent and consistent public policy. As Dean Mann has noted, environmental policy "is rather a jerry-built structure in which innumerable individuals, private groups, bureaucrats, politicians, agencies, courts, political parties, and circumstances have laid down the planks, hammered the nails, plastered over the cracks, made sometimes unsightly additions and deletions, and generally defied 'holistic' or 'ecological' principles of policy design" (1986, 4).

Environmental policy also has an exceedingly broad scope. Traditionally, it was considered to involve the conservation or protection of natural resources such as public lands and waters, wilderness, and wildlife, and thus was concerned with recreational opportunities and aesthetic values in addition to ecological preservation. Since the late 1960s, the term has been more often used to refer to environmental protection efforts of government, such as air and water pollution control, which are grounded in a concern for human health. In industrialized nations, these policies have sought to reverse trends of environmental degradation affecting the land, air, and water, and to work toward achievement of acceptable levels of environmental quality (Andrews 1999; Axelrod, Downie, and Vig 2005; Desai 2002).

Environmental policy extends well beyond environmental protection and natural resource conservation. It includes, more often implicitly than explicitly, governmental actions affecting human health and safety, energy use, transportation, agriculture and food production, human population growth, national and international security, and the protection of vital global ecological, chemical, and geophysical systems (Deudney and Matthew 1999; Mazmanian and Kraft 1999; Starke 2006). Hence environmental policy cuts an exceptionally wide swath and has a pervasive and growing effect on modern human affairs. It embraces both long-term and global as well as short-term and local actions.

In many respects, environmental policy resembles other public policies, as do the political processes that shape it (Kraft and Furlong 2007). Yet in some important respects, environmental policy and politics are unique. There is a greater sense of urgency in addressing environmental problems, and at least some of those concerns relate to natural processes essential for human life (Daily 1997). Policy decisions also may have catastrophic or irreversible consequences that affect future generations, raising significant questions of intergenerational equity or fairness. Climate change, population growth, loss of biological diversity, and disposal of nuclear waste are good examples (Hempel 2006; Tobin 2006).

■ ENVIRONMENTAL PROBLEMS AND PUBLIC POLICY

As the preceding discussion suggests, identifying the nature of environmental problems and the solutions that may be needed to address them is rarely an easy task. Since the late 1960s, we have been bombarded with news about a multitude of threats to public health and the environment, with varying hints about the degree of scientific consensus or the extent of disagreement between environmentalists and their opponents. Sometimes the dangers are highly visible, as they are to residents of neighborhoods near heavily polluting industries. Usually, though, they are not, and citizens are left puzzled about the severity of the problems, who to believe, and what they ought to do.

Increasingly, it seems, environmental problems of the third generation, such as global climate change and loss of biodiversity, are even more difficult to recognize and solve than the more familiar issues of the first generation of environmental concerns of the early 1970s (e.g., air and water pollution) and the second generation that emerged later in the 1970s (e.g., toxic chemicals and hazardous wastes). Solutions may be very costly, and the benefits to society may be difficult to measure (Daily 1997; Hempel 2006). Thus third-generation environmental problems tend to be more politically controversial and more difficult to address than the environmental problems of earlier eras.

For all these reasons, students of environmental policy need to develop a robust capacity to sort through the partial and often biased information that is available so as to make sense of the world and the public policy choices we face. Policymakers and the public need the same skills. There is no great puzzle about the pertinent questions to ask about any public policy controversy, including those associated with the environment. They concern the nature and causes of problems (including who or what is affected and in what ways), what might be done about them, and if government intervention is called for, what kind of policy tools (e.g., regulation, public education, or market incentives) are most appropriate. Table 1.1 sets out these kinds of questions, and they are addressed throughout the book.

Defining the Problems: The Nature of Environmental Risks

One set of concerns focuses on the nature of environmental problems, that is, the prevailing environmental conditions and trends, their causes, and their consequences.

TABLE 1.1

A Framework for Evaluating Environmental Problems and Policy Responses		
Activity	*Tasks*	*Questions That Might Be Asked*
Identify the problems.	Determine which environmental and resource problems are of concern.	What are the causes of the problem and the consequences? How does the problem affect human health or environmental quality? How has the problem changed over time, and how might it change in the future?
Measure the problems or examine arguments advanced about them.	Estimate the magnitude of the problems in terms of risks posed to human and environmental health.	How severe is the problem, and how does it compare with other environmental risks or other societal problems? What forecasts are available for estimating the magnitude of the problem in the future? How much consensus or conflict exists among scientists or other experts?
Interpret and evaluate the data and arguments.	Determine the meaning of the data, assess the logic and persuasiveness of the arguments.	What conclusions do the data or the arguments suggest? Are the risks socially acceptable, or must they be lowered? Do we understand the causes of the problem well enough to determine a course of action?
Determine the policy implications.	Determine whether government intervention is needed and what policy options might be considered.	Can the problem be handled privately, or is government action warranted? Is federal action necessary, or is the problem best handled at state and local levels? What kinds of policy action are most suitable: regulation, public education, market incentives, research and development, or other alternatives?

Note: The framework emphasizes issues related to risk assessment and evaluation, as discussed in the chapter. For an elaborate treatment of this approach to studying public problems and policy analysis, see Michael E. Kraft and Scott R. Furlong, *Public Policy: Politics, Analysis, and Alternatives,* 2nd ed. (Washington, DC: CQ Press, 2007).

An enormous amount of information is available on the state of the environment, both domestic and international, and new research findings appear continually. Much of that information is available on the Internet. Especially useful are Web pages of the U.S. Environmental Protection Agency (EPA) for information on air and water quality and toxic chemicals; the Department of Interior sites for land use, parks, wilderness, wildlife, and endangered species; the Department of Energy's sites for energy production and use; and the Department of Agriculture's sites for data on some natural resources. International bodies such as the UN Environment Programme and the World Bank compile similar information for nations around the world, and their sites are listed in Chapter 8.

In addition to government sources for environmental information, some environmental groups specialize in integrating, assessing, and reporting such data. One of the most prominent is the Worldwatch Institute, which since 1984 has published an annual *State of the World* volume and now has a parallel collection of environmental indicators called *Vital Signs*. Another is the World Resources Institute, which (in cooperation with the United Nations and the World Bank) releases a biennial *World Resources* report. These and other groups, such as the World Wildlife Fund, the Union of Concerned Scientists, and academic think tanks such as Resources for the Future, also publish independent studies of environmental problems and policies. At least some of these kinds of reports include social, economic, and governmental trends as well as changes in environmental conditions (e.g., Commission for Environmental Cooperation 2001).

As useful as such information is, it can provide only a partial picture of environmental problems. The data also require careful evaluation and interpretation. The raw statistical portraits (such as how much air quality has changed in the last decade) tell us little about the causes of these conditions and trends. They also say little about what effect they have, for example, on human health. Nor do they tell us how much difference it would make for people's health or the economy if the policies were continued over time in their present form or altered in some way. Yet this is what contemporary environmental policy debate is all about.

Forecasting Environmental Effects   Some of the most difficult projections involve estimates of the probability of future environmental effects of societal or technological changes now under way. The better studies carefully set out the assumptions that underlie their projections and describe the forecasting methods they use. Even so, uncertainty and controversy are common, and some of it centers on what critics may charge are unwarranted assumptions and faulty methods. The publication of the *Global 2000 Report to the President* at the end of Jimmy Carter's administration is a good example. The report was a detailed study of "probable changes in the world's population, natural resources, and environment through the end of the century" that was to serve as "the foundation of our longer-term planning" (Council on Environmental Quality and Department of State 1980). Despite elaborate justifications offered for the forecasting methods used, the report was subject to spirited attack on methodological (and ideological) grounds (Simon and Kahn 1984). The Reagan White House also sharply criticized the study and objected to its reliance on government planning and regulation that were strongly at odds with the new administration's conservative environmental policy agenda (Kraft 1984).

A more contemporary illustration of the challenge of dealing with complex environmental problems with long-range and uncertain effects is climate change. The Intergovernmental Panel on Climate Change (IPCC), a UN-sponsored body, has reflected overwhelming scientific consensus in its projections of anticipated climate change in the twenty-first century. Such changes could raise global mean temperatures over the next 100 years as well as lead to a variety of potentially devastating environmental and economic effects (IPCC 2001). Yet scientific and political debate continues over the validity of such projections and their policy implications. Part of the reason is that questions remain about the precise relationship of greenhouse gas concentration in the atmosphere and temperature increases, the probability that temperatures will rise by a certain amount, and the location and timing of climate disturbances such as increased rainfall and the severity of storms. The complex climate change computer models that scientists use to make these projections cannot provide all the answers at this time (Hempel 2006).

In cases like this, scientific uncertainties often are exploited to strengthen particular positions on the issues. Highly vocal critics of environmentalists, from scientists such as Richard Lindzen and S. Fred Singer to conservative talk show host Rush Limbaugh, fire polemical broadsides at their adversaries on climate change and many other issues (e.g., Lindzen 1992). From their perspective, environmentalists are guilty of "inflammatory claims," "doomsday rhetoric," and "environmental overkill" (Lomborg 2001; Stevens 1993; Taubes 1993). These exchanges are intriguing but rarely enlightening, and they often confuse both the scientific and the policy issues. Unfortunately, contemporary politics has created a demand for simple ideas expressed in news conference sound bites and an impatience to work through complex scientific issues and tough policy choices. We examine many other cases of such disputes throughout the book. These tendencies are especially great when an environmental problem first becomes visible and is judged quickly and superficially. With experience, debate, and learning, ideology may give way to more thoughtful appraisals of problems and solutions.

Assessing Risks: Social and Technical Issues   As the climate change example indicates, students of environmental policy need to ask some important questions about the nature of the problems we face. A common way to do that is to use the language of risk assessment or risk analysis, a subject to which we return in later chapters. Analysts can try to estimate the magnitude of risks that are posed to public health or to the environment. These kinds of risks are by no means the only dimensions of environmental problems worthy of concern. A focus on risks does not begin to cover the social, cultural, and moral aspects of environmental problems or even practical matters of determining whether we should conserve land and other resources for recreational or aesthetic purposes. Consider the following description by an ecologist of old-growth forests in the Pacific Northwest:

> No less important [than ecological functions], ancient forests have a transcendent aesthetic and religious value in the inner landscapes of natives and newcomers alike. Their majesty inspires comparisons with the great cathedrals. Their haunting beauty and solace attract growing numbers of Northwesterners and visitors who seek connection with a wild world that is everywhere gone or going fast. Ancient forests are a national and international resource of the highest order. (Norse 1990, 42)

Few would presume to dismiss such arguments in natural resource debates, even if they speak to us in a different language than ecological risk and economic values. We can probably agree, however, that health and ecological risks are among the most widely discussed and disputed elements of environmental policy and hence merit careful consideration even if we acknowledge that other crucial issues involving moral, cultural, or social values deserve examination as well.

Risk assessment is a relatively new and evolving set of methods for estimating both human health and ecosystem risks. Controversy is endemic to use of these methods, and environmentalists have been skeptical of relying on them out of fear that the severity of the problems as they see them might be reduced when subject to formal analysis (Andrews 2006; O'Brien 2000). Equal criticism comes from the other side, with industry, political conservatives, and some members of the scientific community complaining that the EPA, as one example, has been too cautious in its risk assessment methods and related policy decisions, for instance, labeling chemicals as carcinogenic when evidence, in their view, does not support such a judgment. The result, they say, is a public that is made unnecessarily fearful of relatively minor risks, in part because of the way the media cover these controversies (Huber 2000; Lichter and Rothman 1999; Wildavsky 1995).[6]

Despite allegations of this kind that the EPA and other agencies rely on so-called junk science to reach their conclusions, risk assessment can be a useful, if imperfect, tool for systematic evaluation of many environmental problems. It also can help establish a formal process that brings into the open for public debate many of the otherwise hidden biases and assumptions that shape environmental policy (Davies 1996; National Research Council 1996; Presidential/Congressional Commission on Risk Assessment and Risk Management 1997).

The technical community (e.g., scientists, engineers, and EPA professional staff) tends to define risk as a product of the probability of an event or exposure and the consequences, such as health or environmental effects, that follow. This is expressed in the formula $R = P \times C$, where R is the risk level, P is the probability, and C is a measure of the consequences. Use of the term *risk* connotes an indefinite problem, occurrence, or exposure that can be described only in terms of mathematical probabilities rather than as a certain threat. Uncertainties may be associated with estimates of the probability, the consequences, or both.

The public, however, tends to see risks in a very different way. Ordinary citizens give a greater weight to qualities such as the degree to which risks are uncertain, uncontrollable, inequitable, involuntary, dreaded, or potentially fatal or catastrophic (Slovic 1987). On those bases, the public perceptions of risk may differ dramatically from those of government scientists, as they do most notably in the case of nuclear power and nuclear waste disposal. In these cases, experts see little risk, whereas the public is enormously fearful of the risks (Dunlap, Kraft, and Rosa 1993; U.S. EPA 1990b).[7]

Scholars describe these differences in terms of two conflicting concepts of rationality, and they argue that both are valid. Susan Hadden captures the differences well:

> "Technical rationality" is a mindset that trusts evidence and the scientific method, appeals to expertise for justification, values universality and consistency, and considers unspecifiable impacts to be irrelevant to present decision-making. "Cultural rationality," in contrast, appeals to traditional and peer groups rather than to experts, focuses on personal and family risks rather than the depersonalized, statistical approach, holds unanticipated risks to be fully relevant to near-term decision-making, and trusts process rather than evidence. (Hadden 1991, 49)[8]

These differences in understanding environmental and health risks can greatly complicate the conduct, communication, and use of risk assessments in environmental policy decisions. That is particularly so when government agencies lose public trust, a recurring problem, for example, in hazardous waste and nuclear waste policy actions (Kraft 2000; Munton 1996; Slovic 1993). Yet such different perspectives on risk do not eliminate the genuine need to provide credible risk assessments to try to get a useful fix on the severity of various environmental problems (such as air pollution, drinking water contamination, or risk of exposure to toxic chemicals) and to decide what might be done about them, that is, how best to reduce the risks.

Even without such disparities in risk perception between technical experts and the public, assessing the severity of environmental problems must take place amid much uncertainty. Consider the challenge of dealing with indoor air pollutants such as radon, a naturally occurring, short-lived radioactive gas formed by the decay of uranium found in small quantities in soil and rocks. Colorless and odorless, it enters homes through walls and foundations (and sometimes in drinking water), and its decay products may be inhaled along with dust particles in the air to which they become attached, posing a risk of lung damage and cancer. In 1987 the EPA declared that radon was "the most deadly environmental hazard in the U.S.," and in 2005 the agency labeled it the second leading cause of lung cancer in the United States, second only to smoking, and the leading cause among nonsmokers. The EPA says that radon is responsible for some 21,000 deaths a year.[9]

The best evidence of radon's effects on human health is based on high-dose exposure of uranium miners. Yet extrapolation from mines to homes is difficult. Moreover, although radon experts agree that the gas is a substantial risk at levels that are two to four times the EPA's "action level" for home exposure, it is more difficult to confirm a significant cause-and-effect relationship at the lower levels found in the typical home. EPA and other scientists, however, believe that the indirect evidence is strong enough to take action to reduce exposure to radon in individuals' homes. But critics question how aggressively the nation should attempt to reduce radon levels, in part because they think that doing so could be quite costly (Cole 1993).

Coping with Environmental Risks

As the radon example shows, another set of important questions concerns what, if anything, to do about environmental problems once we recognize them. Are they serious enough to require action? If so, is governmental intervention necessary, or might we address the problem better through alternative approaches, such as private or voluntary action? Such decisions are affected by judgments about public needs and the effects on society and the economy. For example, the Clinton administration tended to favor mandatory government regulation of many environmental risks, whereas George W. Bush's administration has favored voluntary action and market incentives. Former EPA administrator William Ruckelshaus described clearly the constraints on such policy decisions: "The difficulty of converting scientific findings into political action is a function of the uncertainty of the science and the pain generated by the action" (Ruckelshaus 1990, 125). Under such conditions, some policymakers favor a course of action that errs on the side of environmental protection, whereas others are equally inclined to lean the other way, often out of concern for the economic effects of government regulation. The latter position, for example, characterized acid rain policy under President Ronald Reagan and climate change policy under President George W. Bush.

Consensus among scientists can speed agreement on how to respond to hazards. That was the case with the decision to phase out use of chlorofluorocarbons (CFCs) and other ozone-depleting chemicals under the Montreal Protocol (Benedick 1991). It is unlikely, however, that many other environmental disputes, such as those over climate change and what to do about loss of biodiversity, can be so easily resolved because of the continuing uncertainties about their effects. What this means is that much more convincing information about the risk may be necessary to bring about agreement on action. For this reason some students of environmental risk argue for new ways of presenting risk information to the public so it can better understand what the debate is all about and even participate in discussions about what to do. Agencies that make risk decisions also need to build credibility and public trust. These points were underscored in a study by the EPA more than 15 years ago (U.S. EPA 1990b), and solid research supports such an approach. For example, numerous studies show persuasively that credibility and trust are crucial ingredients in effective assessment and management of risks (Davies 1996; Kraft 1996; Slovic 1993).

What Is an Acceptable Risk?   For the public and its political representatives, two difficult issues are how to determine a so-called acceptable level of risk and how to set environmental policy priorities. For environmental policy, the question is often phrased as "How clean is clean enough?" or "How safe is safe enough?" in light of available technology or the costs involved in reducing or eliminating such risks and competing demands in other sectors of society (e.g., education and health care) for the resources involved. Should drinking water standards be set at a level that ensures essentially no risk of cancer from contaminants, as the Safe Drinking Water Act required prior to 1996? Or should the EPA be permitted to weigh health risks and the costs of reducing those risks, within reasonable limits? In 1996 Congress adopted the latter position. Equally important are the questions of who should make such judgments and on what basis should judgments be made. Countless decisions of this kind are made every year in the process of implementing environmental policies. Over the last few years, for example, the EPA has struggled with standards on arsenic in drinking water, mercury emissions from power plants, and pesticide residues allowed in food (Andrews 2006; Rosenbaum 2006).

These judgments about acceptable risk involve chiefly policy (some would say political), not technical, decisions. That is, they call for a judgment about what is acceptable to society or what might survive a legal challenge to the agency making the decision. Even when the science is firm, such decisions are difficult to make in the adversarial context in which they are debated. Moreover, the seemingly straightforward task of setting priorities will naturally pit one community or set of interests against another. That so much is at stake is another reason to rely on the democratic political process to make these choices, or at a minimum to provide for sufficient accountability when decisions are delegated to bureaucratic officials.

Remediation of hazardous waste sites illustrates the dilemma of making acceptable risk decisions. Estimates of the costs for cleaning up the tens of thousands of sites in the United States, including heavily contaminated federal facilities such as the Hanford Nuclear Reservation in the state of Washington, have ranged from $500 billion to more than $1 trillion, depending on the cleanup standard used (Russell, Colglazier, and Tonn 1992). At the 570-square-mile Hanford site, among the worst in the nation, the federal Department of Energy (DOE) and its predecessor agencies allowed 127 million gallons of toxic liquid waste to leak into the ground. Between 750,000 and 1 million gallons of high-level nuclear waste have leaked from single-shell storage tanks, contaminating more than 200 square miles of groundwater. Cleanup of the Hanford site alone could cost $45 billion and take many decades to complete.

Historically, EPA cleanup of the average site on its National Priority List (NPL) under the Superfund program has cost about $30 million and has taken 10 years. New technologies and changes in the program, however, offer some hope of less costly and more timely cleanups in the future. There is also considerable community pressure to place local sites on the NPL and to clean them to the highest standards possible.

Yet are all these sites equally important for public health and environmental quality? Should all be cleaned up to the same standard regardless of their future use, cleanup costs, and disputed estimates of the benefits that will result? How do we consider the needs of future generations in making such judgments so that the present society does not simply pass along hidden risks to them? Is the nation prepared to commit massive societal resources to such a cleanup program? We've done a poor job historically of answering these difficult questions, but Congress did address many of them throughout the past decade as it considered renewal of the Superfund toxic waste program. That Congress could not agree on a course of action indicates the extent of the controversy.

Comparing Risks and Setting Priorities   Governments have limited budgetary resources, and the public has demonstrated a distinct aversion to raising taxes. Given these conditions, what are the priorities among the environmental risks we face? The federal EPA has issued several reports ranking environmental problems according to their estimated seriousness. They include a 1987 report, *Unfinished Business: A Comparative Assessment of Environmental Problems,* and a 1990 report, *Reducing Risk: Setting Priorities and Strategies for Environmental Protection.* One striking finding is that the American public worries a great deal about some environmental problems, such as hazardous waste sites and groundwater contamination, which the EPA accords a relatively low rating of severity. The public also exhibits much less concern about other problems, such as the loss of natural habitats and biodiversity, ozone depletion, climate change, and indoor air pollution (including radon), which are given high ratings by EPA staff and the agency's Science Advisory Board. The U.S. Congress has tended to reflect the public's views and has set EPA priorities and budgets in a way that conflicts with the ostensible risks posed to the nation (Andrews 2006; U.S. EPA 1987b, 1990b).

Critics charge, with good justification, that such legislative decisions promote costly and inefficient environmental policies. Thus they suggest that we need to find ways to compare environmental risks and to distinguish the more serious risks from the less important. Many practical ways are available to do so, and some states have launched comprehensive comparative risk projects that have included extensive citizen participation as well as expert guidance. For example, one project undertaken in California over a two-year period in the mid-1990s involved some 100 scientists as well as the public, and it separated and ranked risks dealing with human health, social welfare, and ecological health. Nonetheless, comparative risk assessment is not without its detractors, who have raised important questions regarding methodology, philosophy, ethics, and decision-making procedures (Davies 1996; Sexton 1999). Whatever the shortcomings, such efforts to compare and evaluate diverse environmental and health risks will likely play an increasingly important role in the future to help frame environmental policy issues, promote public involvement and debate over them, and assist both the public and policymakers in making critical policy choices.

■ PUBLIC POLICY RESPONSES

Finally, a third set of issues involves examination of policy alternatives. If governmental intervention is thought to be essential, what public policies are most appropriate, and at which level of government (international, national, state, or local) should they be put into effect? Governments have a diversified set of tools in their policy repertoires.

They include provision of information, education, research and other investments, regulation, use of subsidies, government purchase of goods and services, taxation, rationing, charging fees for service, and creation of public trusts. Policy analysts ask which approaches are most suitable in a given situation, either alone or in combination with others (Kraft and Furlong 2007; Schneider and Ingram 1990, 1997).

A lively debate has arisen in recent years over the relative advantages and disadvantages of the widely used regulatory approach ("command and control") as well as such competing or supplementary devices as market-based incentives, information provision, collaborative decision making, and voluntary public–private partnerships (Durant, Fiorino, and O'Leary 2004; Freeman 2006; Press and Mazmanian 2006). Such newer approaches have been incorporated into both federal and state environmental policies, from the Clean Air Act to measures for reducing the use of toxic chemicals. Both the federal and state governments also have helped spur technological developments through their power in the marketplace. Governments buy large quantities of certain products such as computers and motor vehicles. Even without regulation, they can alter production processes by buying only those products that meet, say, stringent energy efficiency or fuel economy standards. Analysts typically weigh such policy alternatives according to various criteria, including technical feasibility, economic efficiency, probable effectiveness, ease of implementation, and political and social acceptability. None of that is particularly easy to do, but the exercise brings useful information to the table to be debated.

To address questions of equity or social justice, analysts and policymakers also need to ask about the distribution of environmental costs, benefits, and risks across society, as well as internationally and across generations. Numerous studies suggest that many environmental risks, such as those posed by industrial facilities, disproportionately affect poor and minority citizens, who are more likely than others to live in heavily industrialized areas with oil refineries, chemical plants, and similar facilities or in inner cities with high levels of air pollutants (Ringquist 2006). Similarly, risks associated with anticipated climate changes are far more likely to affect poor nations than affluent, industrialized nations that can better afford to adapt to a new climate regime, even at the low to middle range of climate change scenarios. For these reasons, some of the important questions about environmental policy are who suffers the environmental risks, who pays the costs of reducing them, and who gets the benefits of public policies.

For programs already in existence, we need to ask many of the same questions. Which policy approaches are now used, and how successful are they? Would other approaches work better? Be more effective? Cost less? (Morgenstern and Portney 2004). For example, how many programs could be made more effective through higher funding levels, better implementation, institutional reforms, and similar adjustments? Some programs may be so poorly designed or so badly implemented that they fully merit cancellation. Others might be improved through careful evaluation and redesign (Coglianese and Bennear 2005; Davies and Mazurek 1998; Knaap and Kim 1998).

To offer one final example, the EPA has been the object of considerable criticism on many fronts, including the adequacy of its scientific research, its ability to supervise outside contractors properly, and various management concerns (National Academy of Public Administration 1995, 2000; Rosenbaum 2006). Reading accounts by its toughest detractors, we might think the agency is not to be trusted with any responsibilities (Schoenbrod 2005). By most measures, however, the EPA is one of the strongest federal agencies we have, and it has enjoyed remarkable success over the past three decades. It is also clear, however, that it might have accomplished even more had Congress provided it with sufficient levels of funding over the years, given it more discretion to experiment with new policy approaches, and encouraged it to adopt key management reforms. Much the same argument can be made for state environmental programs (Durant, Fiorino, and O'Leary 2004; Vig and Kraft 2006). These kind of concerns are addressed throughout the book.

CONCLUSIONS

A simple idea lies behind all these questions about the nature of environmental problems and strategies for dealing with them. Improving society's response to these problems, particularly in the form of environmental policy, requires a careful appraisal and a serious effort to determine what kinds of solutions hold the greatest promise. We will never have enough information to be certain of all the risks posed, the effects that present policies may have, and the likely effectiveness of proposed courses of action. As citizens, however, we can deal better with the welter of data and arguments by focusing on the core issues outlined in the preceding sections and acknowledging that disagreements are at least as much about different political values and policy goals as they are about how to interpret limited and ambiguous scientific information (Stone 2002). If citizens demand that policymakers do the same, we can move a lot closer to a defensible set of environmental policies that offer genuine promise for addressing the many challenges that the nation faces.

Chapter 2 focuses on an overview of contemporary environmental problems, from pollution control and energy use to loss of biological diversity and the consequences of human population growth. The intention is to ask the kinds of questions posed in the previous sections (and in Table 1.1) related to each of the major areas of environmental concern and thus to lay out a diverse range of contemporary environmental problems, the progress being made to date in dealing with them, and the challenges that lie ahead.

DISCUSSION QUESTIONS

1. How clear is the concept of sustainable development? Can it be used effectively to describe the long-term goal of environmental policy? Does doing so help to build public understanding and support for environmental policy actions?

2. What is the current relationship between environmental science and environmental policy? What should the relationship be? Should scientists do more to help inform the public and policymakers on environmental issues? If so, what would be the best way to do so?

3. How do economic incentives affect individuals' behavior with respect to the environment, such as decisions to buy a car, home, or appliance? How might such incentives be altered to help promote more environmentally positive outcomes?

4. How would a broader societal commitment to an environmental ethic affect environmental policy decisions? What might be done to improve the public's understanding of environmental issues? What might be done to increase the saliency of those issues in people's daily lives?

5. How useful is it to think about environmental problems in terms of the risks they pose to human and ecological health? Given the controversies over risk

assessment, to what extent should public policy decisions be based on scientific assessments of risk? How might citizens become more involved in judgments about the seriousness of environmental risks and what is to be done about them?

SUGGESTED READINGS

Chasek, Pamela S., David L. Downie, and Janet Welsh Brown. *Global Environmental Politics,* 4th ed. Boulder, CO: Westview Press, 2006.

Durant, Robert F., Daniel J. Fiorino, and Rosemary O'Leary, eds. *Environmental Governance Reconsidered: Challenges, Choices, and Opportunities.* Cambridge: MIT Press, 2004.

Layzer, Judith A. *The Environmental Case,* 2nd ed. Washington, DC: CQ Press, 2006.

Mazmanian, Daniel A., and Michael E. Kraft, eds. *Toward Sustainable Communities: Transition and Transformations in Environmental Policy.* Cambridge: MIT Press, 1999.

Speth, James Gustave. *Red Sky at Morning: America and the Crisis of the Global Environment.* New Haven: Yale University Press, 2004.

Vig, Norman J., and Michael E. Kraft, eds. *Environmental Policy: New Directions for the Twenty-First Century,* 6th ed. Washington, DC: CQ Press, 2006.

ENDNOTES

1. The estimate for Chinese economic growth comes from Starke 2006, p. xvi.
2. The American Association for the Advancement of Science keeps a running tab on federal spending on scientific research, and details on environmental research spending can be found on its Web site: www.aaas.org.
3. For commentary on these kinds of conflicts over the role of science and scientists in policy decisions, see Martin Kady II, Mary Clare Jalonick, and Amol Sharma, "Science, Policy Mix Uneasily in Legislative Laboratory," *CQ Weekly,* March 20, 2004, 680–88; and Union of Concerned Scientists, "Scientific Integrity in Policymaking: An Investigation into the Bush Administration's Misuse of Science" (2004), available at the UCS Web site: www.ucsusa.org.
4. For an update on the story, see Pam Belluck, "New England's Fishermen Fret for Industry's Future," *New York Times,* August 19, 2002, A9.
5. See Kirk Johnson, "City's Water-Quality Plan Working So Far, U.S. Finds," *New York Times,* June 1, 2002, A14.
6. Huber's book, *Hard Green: Saving the Environment from the Environmentalists (A Conservative Manifesto)* (2000), is described by its publisher as a "strongly-argued critique of environmentalism from the right—the conservative's answer to Al Gore's *Earth in the Balance* (1992)." In 1996 Paul and Anne Ehrlich responded to conservative critiques of this kind. See Ehrlich and Ehrlich (1996).
7. For instance, a book published in 2002, a year after the terrorist attacks of September 11, 2001, highlighted public anxiety over unfamiliar, and highly publicized, risks; see David Ropeik and George Gray, *Risk: A Practical Guide for Deciding What's Really Safe and What's Really Dangerous in the World Around You* (Boston: Houghton Mifflin, 2002). The book sold briskly at the online sites for Amazon.com and Barnes and Noble.
8. One of the most thorough reviews of the disputes over the meaning of "rationality" in risk assessment and management and the implications for citizen participation in environmental policy is by the philosopher K. S. Shrader-Frechette (1991, 1993). See also Kraft (1994b, 1996) and Slovic (1993).
9. See the EPA's Web page on the subject: www.epa.gov/radon/.

2

Judging the State of the Environment

What actions should be taken to reduce the level of pesticides in the food we eat or to ensure that our drinking water is safe? How can we reduce the nation's reliance on imported oil and encourage new sources of renewable energy? What can cities do to limit urban sprawl and help establish more sustainable and livable communities? Environmental policy can be defined simply as what governments do or do not do about environmental challenges such as these. As indicated at the end of Chapter 1, this usually means trying to determine the risks to public health posed by problems like pesticide residues in food or contaminated drinking water, and what, if anything, government—federal, state, or local—should do about them. The rest of this book concentrates on U.S. environmental policy and politics. It describes government institutions and policy actors that influence the adoption and implementation of environmental policies. It focuses on the major policies, their goals and objectives, their strengths and weaknesses, and proposals for improving them. These policies and proposals to change them can best be understood by turning first to the problems themselves and the challenges they present to government.

Which problems should be covered in such a survey? Although there is agreement that issues like air and water pollution should be included, other topics, such as energy use and population growth, might be thought to be less central. Moreover, environmental quality can be linked to other social activities as diverse as agriculture, forestry, and other land use; urban design and development; and transportation use, such as reliance on automobiles. I focus here on selected problems that are commonly addressed in reports by government agencies and other organizations. Among the most important of these are air and water pollution, toxic chemicals, hazardous wastes, consumer and solid wastes, energy use and climate change, loss of biodiversity, and population growth. All have become important concerns in recent years, and a brief assessment of them illustrates how the scope of environmental policy extends well beyond pollution control and land conservation. Such a review also shows how these problems are interrelated; that is, energy use affects air quality and population growth affects land use. So ideally we would analyze and act on all of these problems in a comprehensive and integrated manner; however, this approach is rare in public policy today (Bartlett 1990; Mazmanian and Kraft 1999).

As noted in Chapter 1, it is not always easy to understand the causes of these diverse problems and the effects they have on human health or the environment. Nor is it any easier to determine exactly what policy actions are needed to deal with them. Sometimes science can provide only partial and incomplete information, for example, about climate change or biodiversity loss. Sometimes the science is clear but there are disagreements over what to do because of the economic implications or conflicts over the role for government in acting on the problems. Sometimes all of these conflicts can be resolved, but government still finds it difficult to act because different departments and agencies, or different levels of government (federal, state, local), cannot come to an agreement. Similarly, there simply may not be enough money to fully support environmental programs in light of the ever present competition with other policies and programs, from national defense to health and education. Hence policymakers cannot do all that they would like to do. These issues are also highlighted later, and references are provided throughout the chapter to enable you to find the most recent information about both science and policy developments.

▓ AIR QUALITY

Air pollution is one of the most pervasive, salient, and long-standing environmental problems both in the United States and other nations. Its effects range from impairment of visibility to serious impacts on human health. U.S. policies on air quality date back to the late nineteenth century when cities such as Chicago, New York, and Pittsburgh began to regulate smoke emissions. Contemporary efforts, however, largely began with the federal Clean Air Act Amendments of 1970, with its focus on human health. Since then, scientific understanding of the effects of air pollutants on public health has improved greatly. Yet controversies over what to do and how much to spend to improve air quality continue unabated.

Air pollution results from myriad and complex causes, many of which have proven difficult to address, particularly with a rising population and strong economic growth. In large part, however, air pollution may be traced to the combustion of fossil fuels to generate power for manufacturing, heating and cooling of homes and offices, and transportation. Other major contributing causes are the production and use of volatile organic compounds (VOCs) such as solvents in chemical plants, refineries, and commercial establishments. Urban smog occurs when nitrogen oxides from the burning of fuel and VOCs interact with sunlight to form ground-level ozone (to be distinguished from the protective stratospheric ozone layer) and other chemicals. The use of motor vehicles powered by internal combustion engines is the major source of urban air pollution in most industrialized nations. The U.S. EPA puts these various contributions to air pollution into four categories: stationary sources (e.g., factories, power plants, and smelters), area sources (e.g., smaller stationary sources such as dry cleaners and degreasing operations), mobile sources (e.g., cars, buses, planes, trucks, and trains), and natural sources (e.g., windblown dust and volcanic eruptions).

Aside from problems of reduced visibility and mild irritation, air pollution exacts a heavy toll on public health, causing thousands of premature deaths each year in the United States and an estimated 2 to 3 million worldwide (Chivian et al. 1993; U.S.

EPA 2002a). Largely because of those concerns, the Clean Air Act requires the EPA to set national air quality standards for six principal pollutants, referred to as "criteria" pollutants: carbon monoxide (CO), lead (Pb), nitrogen dioxide (NO_2), ozone (O_3), particulate matter (PM), and sulfur dioxide (SO_2). The standards set the maximum level of human exposure to the pollutants that is to be allowed. The act and its later amendments provide the basic framework for efforts to improve air quality, which is discussed more fully in Chapter 5. Prior to passage of the act, the nation witnessed massive increases in air emissions of these chemicals. For example, between 1900 and 1970, the EPA estimates that emissions of VOCs increased some 260 percent, sulfur dioxide about 210 percent, and nitrogen oxides nearly 700 percent. The trends since the adoption of the act have been encouraging and illustrate how much public policy can accomplish over time.

Gains in Air Quality and Remaining Problems

By most measures, air quality in the United States has improved significantly since Congress approved the Clean Air Act Amendments in 1970. Between 1970 and 2004, total emissions of the six principal air pollutants decreased by 54 percent while the nation's gross domestic product increased by 187 percent, the vehicle miles traveled increased by 171 percent, energy consumption increased 47 percent, and the U.S. population grew by 40 percent (U.S. EPA 2005). Emissions of each of the six criteria pollutants decreased substantially as well in more recent time periods, for example, between 1995 and 2004. However, the nation continues to release 160 million tons of pollutants to the air each year, including 1.6 billion pounds of toxic chemicals.

As indicated in Table 2.1, national monitoring data also show substantial improvement over the past two decades in atmospheric concentrations of the six criteria pollutants, that is, in the amount found in the air as opposed to what is released by different sources. Some of these declines in air pollution might have occurred even

TABLE 2.1

Percentage Change in Air Quality Emissions and Concentrations, 1983–2002

	Air Quality Concentration	Emissions
Carbon monoxide (CO)	− 65%	− 41%
Lead (Pb)	− 94	− 93
Nitrogen dioxide (NO_2)	− 21	− 15 (NO_x)
Ozone (O_3)		
1-hr standard	− 22	− 40 (VOCs)
8-hr standard[a]	− 14	
Particulates (PM-10)[a]	NA	− 34
Sulfur dioxide (SO_2)	− 54	− 33

Source: Adapted from U.S. EPA, "*Latest Findings on National Air Quality: 2002 Status and Trends.* Washington, DC: U.S. EPA, Office of Air Quality and Standards, August 2003.

Note: The EPA is running behind schedule in releasing more recent data on air quality. But the information should be available later in 2006 at the agency's Web site: www.epa.gov/oar/.

[a]In 1997 the EPA revised the ozone and particulate standards. The data for particulates in the table reflect only the PM-10 standard.

without the push of public policy. Yet there is little question that the Clean Air Act itself has produced major improvements in air quality and thus in public health.

Despite such welcome news, some 150 million people live in counties where the air is unhealthy at times because of high levels of one of the six major pollutants covered by the act, principally ozone or fine particulates. Air quality remains unacceptable in the large urban clusters in which many Americans live (U.S. EPA 2003). As the number of cars on the road and the miles driven increase, and as the population grows, many areas will find it difficult to meet new federal air quality standards without taking action affecting the use of motor vehicles.

Ground-level ozone in particular is a major public health risk. It is capable of causing respiratory difficulties in sensitive individuals, reduced lung function, and eye irritation. It can also inflict damage on vegetation and ecosystems, reducing forest and agricultural productivity by making plants more susceptible to disease, pests, and other environmental stressors. Other major air pollutants are associated with a range of health and environmental effects, from eye and throat irritation and respiratory illness to cardiovascular and nervous system damage.

According to the EPA, fine particulate matter in air pollution from fuel combustion in motor vehicles, power generation, and industrial facilities could be responsible for perhaps 30,000 deaths a year in the United States; these occur mostly among the elderly, individuals with cardiopulmonary disease such as asthma, and children. Air pollution also contributes to hundreds of thousands of acute asthma attacks annually.[1] Following four years of scientific studies, in 1997 the EPA adopted two new PM-2.5 standards (for particles of less than 2.5 microns) to deal with the problem; revised standards were again proposed in 2005. The smaller particles have a greater effect on human health because they can evade the body's natural defenses by lodging in sensitive areas of the lung. According to the agency, some 11 million people in the United States live in counties that violate the old federal standards for particulates. Using the PM-2.5 standards, some 73 million people breathe air with particulate concentrations above the federally defined limit (U.S. EPA 2002a).

Air pollution affects even areas well removed from the nation's major urban centers. In recent years, visitors to many of the most popular national parks as well as to beach and mountain vacation areas have been warned of health-threatening levels of ozone and other pollutants (Wald 1999c). Affected parks in recent years have included Sequoia National Park, the Grand Canyon National Park, Mount Rainier National Park, the Great Smoky Mountains National Park, Acadia National Park, and Rocky Mountain National Park. In Rocky Mountain National Park, ozone levels in the 1990s frequently exceeded 80 parts per billion. At that level, ozone can cause headaches, chest pain, and labored breathing.

Indoor Air Quality

The quality of indoor air poses as high a risk for many people as does the air outside, although for years indoor air pollution was ignored by the public and government agencies alike. Recently, the EPA has expressed concern about indoor pollutants, ranking them as one of the top risks to public health. Radon (discussed in Chapter 1) and environmental tobacco smoke (ETS) are especially worrisome. In January 1993, after years of extensive investigation, two public reviews, and recommendations from its Science Advisory Board (SAB), the EPA classified ETS as a known human (group A) carcinogen and a "serious and substantial public health threat." The agency estimated that as many as 3,000 lung cancer deaths in nonsmokers a year in the United States were associated with such secondhand smoke in addition to other effects such as increased incidence of bronchitis and pneumonia in young people and of asthma attacks. The report also found that ETS has subtle although significant effects on the respiratory health of adult nonsmokers, such as reduced lung function (Browner 1993).[2]

The EPA report was instrumental in later actions by state and local governments, as well as the private sector, to restrict or ban smoking in the workplace, in college and university buildings, and in many public places. As often the case, California took the most aggressive action, eventually banning smoking in all restaurants and bars as well; many states and cities have since done the same. Studies strongly suggest that ETS is a factor in heart disease as well, potentially doubling the risk and contributing to as many as 30,000 to 60,000 deaths a year in the United States (Kawachi et al. 1997). Smokers themselves assume the greatest risk. The federal Centers for Disease Control and Prevention (CDC) reports that smoking is the single most preventable cause of premature death in the United States, accounting for more than 440,000 deaths a year.

For several reasons, indoor air quality has worsened over the past several decades, quite aside from ETS. Modern homes, schools, and office buildings that are tightly sealed to improve their energy efficiency have the distinct drawback of allowing a multitude of pollutants to build up indoors if not properly ventilated. Use of synthetic chemicals in building materials and furnishings (such as particleboard, insulating foam, and carpeting) also contributes to the problem, as does use of many household cleaning and personal care products. Important indoor pollutants in addition to tobacco smoke and radon include vinyl chloride, formaldehyde, asbestos, benzene, fine particulates, lead (from lead-based paint), combustion products such as carbon monoxide from gas stoves and inadequately vented furnaces, and biological agents such as molds, the last of which are suspected as a major factor in allergic symptoms and sinus infections (Ott and Roberts 1998; Samet and Spengler 1991).

Based on recent studies, the EPA has estimated that indoor levels of many air pollutants may be 2 to 5 times, and occasionally 100 times, higher than they are outdoors. Those studies are particularly troublesome because Americans now spend an estimated 90 percent of their time indoors. Ironically, as the air outdoors has improved, the quality of indoor air has been declining. Moreover, because most modern office buildings come equipped with permanently sealed windows, the quality of indoor air that many people breathe all day depends on the workings of fine-tuned ventilating systems that sometimes fail. In some cases, the results may be acute health effects often described as building-related illness.[3]

Acid Precipitation

Two of the major air pollutants, sulfur dioxide and nitrogen dioxide, react with water, oxygen, and oxidants to form acidic compounds. These compounds fall to the ground in either a dry or wet form and are commonly called acid rain. They can be carried for hundreds of miles by the wind, crossing both state and national boundaries. In the United States, the problem can be attributed chiefly to coal-burning electric utility plants. According to the EPA (U.S. EPA 2003), approximately 63 percent of the annual sulfur dioxide emissions in the nation and 22 percent of nitrogen oxide emissions come from such facilities. The problem is particularly acute for older utilities that operate with fewer environmental controls.

Comprehensive federal studies have found that acid precipitation adversely affects aquatic ecosystems, forests, crops, and buildings. It may also threaten the health of individuals with respiratory problems and degrade visibility (National Acid Precipitation Assessment Program 1990; U.S. EPA 2002a). As a result of such concerns, the 1990 Clean Air Act Amendments created an Acid Rain Program to sharply reduce emissions of both sulfur dioxide and nitrogen dioxide. The act established an innovative program of economic incentives through emissions trading to help meet those goals (Bryner 1995; Portney and Stavins 2000). The U.S. EPA (2003) subsequently has pointed to significant reductions in acid precipitation. Yet much remains to be accomplished, with serious and continuing effects noticeable in the Adirondacks region of New York State and elsewhere in the Northeast (Smardon and Nordenstam 1998). These and similar findings of continuing damage in Colorado's Front Range, in the Appalachians, and elsewhere have led to calls for strengthening acid rain policies (Dao 1999; Yoon 1999).

CFCs and the Stratospheric Ozone Layer

Some air emissions are more important for global atmospheric conditions than for urban air quality. With several other chemicals, chlorofluorocarbons (CFCs) have been linked to depletion of the stratospheric ozone layer, located between 6 and 30 miles above Earth, which shields life on the surface from dangerous ultraviolet radiation. Chemically stable and unreactive, CFCs rise to the stratosphere, where they are broken down by intense ultraviolet light. The freed chlorine atoms can destroy as many as 100,000 ozone molecules before being inactivated. In this way, CFCs reduce the capacity of the ozone layer to block ultraviolet radiation from penetrating to the surface of Earth. CFCs are also a major greenhouse gas, contributing to possible climate change.

Evidence of the depletion of the ozone layer has been building since the 1980s, with the loss particularly notable above the North and South Poles. As the stratospheric ozone concentration decreases, there is an increase in ultraviolet B (UVB) radiation reaching the surface of Earth (Kerr and McElroy 1993; Randel et al. 1999; U.S. EPA 2002a). The EPA reports that since 1979, there has been a 3.4 percent decrease in average total ozone over the middle latitudes in the United States. A recorded 4 to 5 percent increase in UVB radiation has also occurred since 1986 at latitudes that cover the United States.

Despite the accumulating evidence, critics continue to maintain that the ozone threat may be exaggerated, but only further scientific study can confirm these findings. Should the relationship between deterioration of the ozone layer and increased UVB radiation hold true, the EPA has projected that a 1 percent decline in stratospheric ozone could produce a 5 percent increase in cases of nonmalignant skin cancer. It could also raise by some 2 percent the number of cases of malignant skin cancer, or melanoma, which currently kills about 5,000 Americans a year. Other possible health effects include depression of immune systems, which would allow otherwise minor infections to worsen, and increased incidence of cataracts, a clouding of the eye's lens that is currently the leading cause of blindness in the world (Benedick 1991, 21). An increase in ultraviolet radiation also could adversely affect animal and plant life, and therefore agricultural productivity. Scientists have expressed concern that higher UVB radiation could severely harm oceanic phytoplankton and thus affect the food chain as well as the capacity of oceans to regulate climate. Some of these effects have been detected in Antarctica since 1987 (Schneider 1991; U.S. EPA 2002a). Scientific consensus on the risks of CFC use was great enough for the industrialized nations to agree on the phaseout of CFCs, halons, and other ozone-destroying chemicals on a fairly aggressive schedule. That agreement was embodied in the Montreal Protocol, approved in 1987 after several years of international meetings. When evidence suggested ozone depletion was more extensive than had been believed, policymakers strengthened the agreement with a series of amendments. Because of the way it integrates continuous assessment of environmental trends with policy action, the Montreal Protocol is often cited as a model of global environmental governance (Chasek, Downie, and Brown 2006; Hempel 1996).

The U.S. Congress also included a supplement to the Montreal Protocol in the 1990 Clean Air Act Amendments. The United States committed itself to a more rapid phaseout of the production and use of ozone-depleting chemicals and other measures such as recycling and disposal of such chemicals from discarded appliances. By January 1996 U.S. production of CFCs and several other ozone-depleting chemicals such as halons almost completely stopped. The same is true for most other developed nations. The chemical industry, well aware of the burgeoning new market for non-CFC refrigerants and other uses, has developed substitutes for CFCs, and it continues to search for better products. Computer makers now use ozone-safe solvents to clean circuit boards where they once used CFCs, and automobile manufacturers have switched to HFC-134a for new motor vehicle air conditioners. Taken together, these actions seem to have been effective. Scientific evidence now indicates that concentrations of ozone-depleting chemicals in the troposphere, just below the stratosphere, are beginning to decrease. Still, chlorine will continue to be released into the stratosphere, and the ozone layer is not expected to recover fully until the second half of the twenty-first century (U.S. EPA 2002a).

WATER QUALITY

The availability of water resources and the quality of that water are vital to life and to the nation's economy. Water resources support agriculture, industry, electric power, recreation, navigation, and fisheries, and they are distributed around the nation (and world) unevenly. Natural hydrologic conditions and cycles (particularly the amount of rain and snow) determine the amount of water in any given location. Its quality is affected by human uses, including so-called point discharges from industry and municipalities and nonpoint sources such as agriculture and runoff from urban areas.

The state of the nation's water quality is more difficult to measure than its air quality, in part because of the very large number of bodies of water and great variability nationwide in their condition. Hence evidence of progress since the 1970s is more limited and mixed. Most assessments deal separately with surface water quality (streams, rivers, lakes, and ponds), groundwater, drinking water quality, and the quantity of water resources available for human uses such as drinking and agriculture. Both human and ecosystem health effects of water quality have been objects of concern. Only a few key indicators of conditions and trends are reviewed here.

Pollution of Surface Waters

The state of the nation's water quality is improving only slowly despite expenditures of hundreds of billions of dollars since adoption of the Clean Water Act of 1972, mostly on "end-of-pipe" controls on municipal and industrial discharges. Lack of reliable data makes firm conclusions about the pace of progress difficult, but many studies and monitoring programs are now under way that will eventually provide a fuller accounting. In the meantime, some trends are fairly clear.

Perhaps most important is a major reduction in the raw pollution of surface waters. The percentage of the U.S. population served by wastewater treatment plants rose from 42 percent in 1970 to 74 percent in 1985, with a resulting estimated decline in annual releases of organic wastes of about 46 percent. Striking declines have also been noted since 1972 in discharge of priority toxic organic pollutants and toxic metals as regulation of point sources of pollution (such as factories) took effect. Even with such gains, many water quality problems remain. Yet this kind of control of point sources is largely responsible for the gains in water quality evident around the nation. A notable case is the Cuyahoga River, which runs through Cleveland, Ohio. The river burst into flames in 1969 as oily pollutants caught fire, one of the more spectacular images of 1960s-era environmental pollution. Yet even though fish have been returning to the river lately, warnings against eating them and also bans on swimming and boating continue (Clines 2000).

Information on water quality is collected by the states and submitted to the EPA. In previous years, the agency published a biennial *National Water Quality Inventory*. Now the same information is made available for each state.[4] In the most recent of the national summaries of this data (U.S. EPA 2002b), the states and tribes evaluated only 19 percent of rivers and streams; 43 percent of the nation's lakes, ponds, and reservoirs; and 36 percent of estuarine square miles. Moreover, several studies have found great variation in the methods used by the states to measure their water quality, as well as the frequency with which they take enforcement actions (Rabe 2006). Thus the picture of water quality is incomplete if nevertheless indicative of remaining problems.

The states reported that 61 percent of the surveyed river and stream miles fully supported all uses set by the states and tribes, with 39 percent found to be impaired to some extent as well as 45 percent of lakes. A classification as impaired means that water bodies were not meeting or fully meeting the national minimum water quality criteria for "designated beneficial uses" such as swimming, fishing, drinking water supply, and support of aquatic life. These figures from the 2002 EPA report indicate some improvement over previous years, but they also show that the nation's water quality continues to be unsatisfactory. Prevention of further degradation of water quality in the face of a growing population and strong economic growth could be considered an important achievement. At the same time, water quality clearly falls short of the goals of federal clean water acts (U.S. EPA 2002b). Further evidence can be found in the large number of fish consumption advisories issued because of contamination by toxic chemicals such as mercury, polychlorinated biphenyls (PCBs), chlordane, and dioxins, and the number of beach closings and swimming advisories related to pollution; such closings and advisories reached a record high in 2001, partly because of improved monitoring and stricter testing standards.[5] Table 2.2 summarizes some of the key findings on water quality.

TABLE 2.2

National Surface Water Quality, 2000

	Amount Assessed	Fully Supporting All Uses	Impaired for One or More Uses	Leading Sources of Impairment
Rivers and streams (miles)	19%	61%	39%	Agriculture, hydrologic modification, habitat modification
Lakes, ponds, reservoirs (acres)	43%	55%	45%	Agriculture, hydrologic modification, urban runoff and storm sewers
Estuaries (square miles)	36%	49%	51%	Municipal point sources, urban runoff and storm sewers, industrial discharges

Source: U.S. EPA, 2000 National Water Quality Inventory (Washington, DC: U.S. EPA, Office of Water, 2002).

Note: Assessments of wetlands or estuaries by the states are very limited, and criteria for meeting all uses are not well established. EPA is in the process of changing the way national water quality data are reported. Current assessments are reported by state and are available online in a national assessment database at www.epa.gov/waters/305b/index.html.

According to the EPA database, by far the biggest source of water quality problems in rivers and streams comes from agriculture in the form of nutrients (farm fertilizers and animal wastes), pesticides, and suspended solids. Large animal feedlots favored by agribusiness have been a particular target of environmentalists, forcing the EPA and the Agriculture Department to issue new rules in 2002 to reduce that source of water pollution, although the rules will likely have only a modest effect (Becker 2002).[6] Other major sources of impairment are hydrologic and habitat modification (e.g., loss of wetlands), urban runoff, forestry, municipal sewage treatment plants, storm sewers, and industry. Most of the same sources account for pollution of lakes and ponds as well, along with atmospheric deposition of chemicals. Urban runoff from rain and melting snow carries a wide assortment of chemicals into local rivers, bays, and lakes or into the groundwater. For instance, a National Academy of Science report in 2002 estimated that thousands of tiny releases of oil from cars, lawn mowers, and other dispersed sources on land equal an Exxon Valdez spill (10.9 million gallons) every eight months.[7]

Continued loss of wetlands is particularly important because of the role they play in maintaining water quality. Twenty-two states have lost more than half of the wetlands they had in the nation's early years, and seven of those—California, Indiana, Ohio, Missouri, Kentucky, Illinois, and Iowa—have lost more than 80 percent. Nationally, between the mid-1950s and the mid-1970s, an estimated 458,000 acres a year of marshes, swamps, and other ecologically important wetlands were lost to development, highways, and mining. The rate slowed to about 290,000 acres a year lost by the mid-1980s, and the EPA and the Fish and Wildlife Service maintain that the net rate slowed further, to about 58,000 acres per year, for the most recent period through 1997 (U.S. EPA 2002b). Wetland loss has not stopped, however, and other estimates of the continued rate of loss are higher than the EPA's (Gaddie and

Regens 2000). In addition, only a very small percentage of the remaining wetlands have been assessed, and analysts have found about half of those studied unable to support all the expected human and natural uses, primarily because of sediment from agriculture and development (Kusler, Mitsch, and Larson 1994). One consequence of the loss of wetlands was seen when Hurricane Katrina struck New Orleans in 2005. The effects were more devastating because the damaged wetlands could no longer offer protection against storm surges.

Regulatory water quality programs have concentrated on conventional sources of pollution such as biological waste products that can be assimilated and eventually cleaned by well-oxygenated water. Regulators are only beginning to deal with the more challenging problem of toxic chemicals that enter the nation's waters and their ecological effects. In some areas of the country, the effect of both conventional pollution and toxic contaminants on aquatic ecosystems has been severe.

Drinking Water Quality

Drinking water quality across the nation also remains a problem even though, as the EPA says, the nation has "one of the safest water supplies in the world." The agency also reminds citizens that "national statistics don't tell you specifically about the quality and safety of the water coming out of your tap." This is because drinking water quality varies from one location to another, "depending on the condition of the source water from which it is drawn and the treatment it receives" (U.S. EPA 2006). Information about each city's drinking water quality is now available, thanks to a "right-to-know" provision of the Safe Drinking Water Act Amendments of 1996. These Consumer Confidence Reports are mailed once a year with water utility bills.

What is in drinking water that may be harmful? This varies, but studies find a variety of dangerous compounds, including disease-causing microorganisms, lead, and chloroform (ironically from the chlorine used to disinfect water supplies). In part because of lax enforcement, violation of federal health standards is not as rare as it should be. An example of the effects could be seen in Milwaukee, Wisconsin, in 1993. A waterborne parasite, *Cryptosporidium*, entered the city water supply and created an epidemic of intestinal disease, affecting more than 400,000 people and contributing to the deaths of more than 100 of them. According to the local press, thousands of residents had their confidence in the safety of local water so shaken that a year later they were still boiling their tap water or buying bottled water. The outbreak cost an estimated $54 million in health care expenses and lost productivity, and it generated more than 1,400 lawsuits against the city.

Several studies indicate that such problems with city (and private) water supplies are not uncommon, particularly when groundwater is used. The EPA's water quality inventory indicates that leaking underground storage tanks are the highest priority of state water officials, with hundreds of thousands of confirmed releases. Landfills and septic systems were identified as the next most important concerns, along with agricultural practices, such as the use of pesticides and fertilizers (U.S. EPA 2002b). The agency also stated that groundwater is of good overall quality, but that many problems of contamination are reported throughout the country. Information is often too incomplete, because of limited monitoring, to draw firm conclusions about water quality. Groundwater supplies more than 50 percent of the nation's population with drinking water.

The U.S. Geological Survey (USGS) also examines water quality, and based on testing of wells around the country, it found one or more VOCs in 47 percent of the urban wells and in 14 percent of the rural wells. EPA drinking water standards were exceeded in 6.4 percent of the urban wells and in 1.5 percent of the rural wells (Saar 1999). Easily searchable data for each state can be found on the USGS Web site.[8] Leading environmental organizations also study drinking water quality, and they find a range of problems, from deteriorating waterworks to dated treatment technology. Among those that have issued such reports are the Natural Resource Defense Council and the Environmental Working Group. The latter issued a report in late 2005 on tap water quality nationwide based on the newly required testing results from water utilities. The data show what the group called "widespread contamination of drinking water with scores of contaminants for which there are no enforceable health standards."[9]

▣ TOXIC CHEMICALS AND HAZARDOUS WASTES

Modern industrial societies such as the United States depend heavily on the use of chemicals that pose risks to public health and the environment. They continue to produce vast quantities of chemicals, although some evidence indicates declining rates of production. The scope of the problem is captured in part in the quantities of chemicals produced and emitted into the environment each year, the amount of hazardous wastes produced as by-products of industrial production and other processes, and the number of contaminated sites in the nation in need of cleanup or restoration.

Toxic Chemicals and Health Effects

The nation uses tens of thousands of different chemical compounds in commercial quantities, and industry develops perhaps a thousand or more new chemicals each year. U.S. production of synthetic chemicals burgeoned after World War II, increasing by a factor of 15 between 1945 and 1985. Similarly, agricultural demand for chemical pesticides such as DDT soared in the same period because of their low cost, persistence in the soil, and toxicity to a broad spectrum of insects. Use of pesticides nearly tripled between 1965 and 1985, with more than 6 pounds applied per hectare (1 hectare is 2.47 acres) in the United States by 1985 (Postel 1988), and current EPA reports put the national total for use of all herbicides, insecticides, and fungicides at more than 1.2 billion pounds of active ingredients a year. Although the effects are disputed, consumer groups argue that U.S. fruits and vegetables contain unacceptably high levels of pesticide residues and urge citizens to inform themselves on the risks and choose foods with low levels of residues (Burros 1999; Wargo 1998).

The Risk of Toxic Chemicals   The overwhelming majority of all these widely used chemicals—exceeding 90 percent—are considered safe, although most have never been fully tested for toxicity. Toxic chemicals are usually defined as a subset of hazardous substances that produce adverse effects in living organisms. To measure such toxicity in humans, we usually look to epidemiological data on the effects of human exposures (which may occur through pesticide residues on food, contaminated water supplies, or polluted air). Researchers compare health statistics such as death rates with prevailing environmental conditions in areas around the nation.

Such data, however, are often incomplete or inconclusive, making health effects difficult to establish. Only cancer has been studied extensively, and it may be too soon to detect effects from exposures over the past several decades. Researchers have estimated that 2 to 8 percent of avoidable cancer deaths (that is, those attributable to lifestyle or environmental factors that can be modified) can be associated with occupation, 1 to 5 percent to pollution, and less than 1 to 2 percent to industrial products (Shapiro 1990). As Michael Shapiro notes, these low percentages, if correct, would translate into thousands of chemically related cancer deaths annually in the U.S. population.

Other less well documented chronic health effects add to the problem. For example, reports on so-called endocrine disrupters, or hormonally active agents such as DDT, dioxin, PCBs, and some chemicals found in plastics, suggest that in addition to cancer they may affect development of the brain and the reproductive system. These other effects may occur at very low exposure levels that are unlikely to lead to cancer.[10] Other health effects associated with toxic chemicals may include birth defects, neurotoxic disorders, respiratory and sensory irritation, dermatitis, immune system dysfunction, and chronic organ toxicity such as liver disease. Scientists are paying more attention to possible synergistic (interactive) effects, even at low levels of exposure, of diverse chemicals, including pesticides and herbicides, heavy metals such as lead and mercury, and the ubiquitous PCBs and other chlorinated organic chemicals (Shapiro 1990). An EPA rule that took effect in 2000 established or strengthened reporting requirements for 27 "persistent bioaccumulative toxics," including dioxin, PCBs, and mercury.

Ample scientific data support reducing the use of toxic chemicals to mitigate such effects and to follow the "precautionary principle" of limiting production and use of such chemicals until their effects are better understood. Congress and the states have recognized the importance of such health risks in enacting policies directed at controlling undue exposure to harmful chemicals. Those policies now give us a regular accounting of the nation's production and use of toxic chemicals, if not necessarily reliable information on their effect on human health and the environment.

The Toxics Release Inventory   Under the 1986 Emergency Planning and Community Right to Know Act, Title III of the Superfund law, manufacturers report annually to the EPA and to the states in which they have facilities the quantities of more than 650 different toxic chemicals they release to the air, water, and land. The EPA records these data in its Toxics Release Inventory (TRI), which is available at the EPA Web site and at other Internet sites that help citizens find information for their areas and communities (see Box 2.1).

In its report for the year 2003 (released in July 2005), the EPA said that 23,800 industrial facilities released or disposed of some 4.44 billion pounds of toxic chemicals. Approximately 1.6 billion pounds of those chemicals went into the air; 223 million pounds were discharged into the nation's rivers, lakes, bays, and other bodies of water; and an estimated 639 million pounds went into underground wells. Most of the off-site releases reflect transfer of chemicals to disposal facilities such as landfills and underground injection sites. None of these numbers translates easily into a public health risk, but the EPA has developed a new method that will make it easier for people to translate TRI data into such risk information for specific localities.[11]

BOX 2.1
Using the Toxics Release Inventory

The TRI database contains extensive information about the release of toxic chemicals in the United States. It can be accessed directly from an EPA Web page (www.epa.gov/tri/) or the agency's Envirofacts page (www.epa.gov/enviro/). The group Environmental Defense has made the same data available on its Web page for the program: www.scorecard.org. All of these sources are easy to use and list all major polluting industries in a community and what chemicals they release. A great deal of information is available to show how polluted a community is, the major sources of pollution, and many of the health effects of chemicals.

Aside from mining, most of these environmental releases and wastes are associated with coal-burning power plants, chemical manufacturing, and production of primary metals, petroleum and coal products, paper, rubber, plastics, and transportation equipment. The release of such data since the late 1980s had led many companies, such as Dow Chemical and Monsanto, to commit to a significant reduction of their emissions of toxic chemicals. These decreases are documented in the annual TRI reports, which show much progress since the program began in the late 1980s. Based on the chemicals that have been reported on consistently, total on- and off-site releases decreased by 59 percent between 1988 and 2003. Interpretation of progress in dealing with toxic chemicals is somewhat clouded. This is because of changing definitions of what constitutes toxicity, certain exclusions from the TRI database, and noncompliance by some of the facilities that are required to report. Environmental groups also complain that the TRI data significantly understate the problem of toxic chemicals in the nation, even with expansion of the list of covered chemicals.

State and local governments have made considerable use of the TRI data to target certain areas of concern and measure environmental achievements. In addition, the public as well as environmental organizations have been able to use the data to understand local environmental conditions better and to bring pressure to bear on industry. Box 2.1 indicates where TRI data are available and how the data can be used to provide information about local toxic chemical emissions.

Hazardous Wastes

The United States produces large quantities of hazardous waste each year, including household waste (batteries, oil, paints and solvents, and the like) and a diversity of commercial and industrial wastes. Hazardous wastes are a subset of solid and liquid wastes disposed of on land that may pose a threat to human health or the environment with improper handling, storage, or disposal.

It is difficult to describe precisely the severity of the threat of hazardous waste, but it is not a small problem. In the late 1980s, the volume of hazardous waste generated each year was estimated at 250 million metric tons, and that material came from more than 650,000 different sources (Dower 1990; Halley 1994).[12] This volume and the large number of sources make it extraordinarily hard to track where it all went, particularly before Congress enacted the Resource Conservation and Recovery

Act (RCRA) in 1976 (Dower 1990); RCRA is the nation's major hazardous waste control policy (see Chapter 5). The EPA collects current data from the states on hazardous waste generation, management, and final disposal for wastes covered by RCRA, and the agency publishes it in a National Biennial Report available at the EPA Web site. Today companies store these wastes at the point of generation and carefully track the materials sent elsewhere for disposal or some form of treatment. Industry is also more likely today to recycle and otherwise reduce the production of hazardous wastes through pollution prevention initiatives (Sigman 2000).

Much less is known about previous production and disposal of these chemicals, which is a greater problem. It is no secret that much of the waste historically was disposed of carelessly. Since 1950, for example, more than 6 billion tons of hazardous waste was disposed of on the land, usually with no treatment and with little regard for the environmental consequences (Postel 1988). Up to 50,000 sites have been used for hazardous waste disposal at some point, and thousands of these sites are thought to pose a serious risk to the environment, and possibly to public health.

The chief concern for hazardous chemicals is that they can leak from corroded containers or unlined landfills, ponds, and lagoons, and then they can contaminate groundwater. This is one reason why in 1984 Congress added underground storage tanks (USTs) to RCRA; well over a million USTs are thought to exist in the United States, and the EPA has estimated that 15 to 20 percent of tanks covered by the law are leaking or are expected to leak; if they do, they could pose a significant risk to both groundwater and human health (Cohen, Kamieniecki, and Cahn 2005).

The chemical soup found in hazardous waste sites contains a variety of dangerous compounds such as trichloroethylene, lead, toluene, benzene, PCBs, and chloroform. It is impossible to generalize about health risks at each site because of variations in waste types and exposure. Moreover, as Roger Dower (1990) observed, although the potential health risks of exposure may be substantial, "little is known about the *actual* risks to the public from past and current disposal practices" (159). In 1986 Congress required the EPA to assess the risks to human health posed by each of the Superfund National Priorities List (NPL) sites. The EPA and other federal agencies continue to study the risks, and at some potential Superfund sites they conduct elaborate risk assessments to provide such information to the public. The absence of such data in many cases, however, has fueled debate over the benefits that would accrue from the most inclusive and demanding cleanup policies.

Progress in cleaning up hazardous waste sites has been slow. The most frequently cited example is the federal Superfund program, which Congress created in 1980 following the highly publicized Love Canal chemical waste scandal near Niagara Falls, New York. The Superfund legislation required the EPA to identify and clean up the worst of the nation's abandoned hazardous waste sites. By 2005 the EPA reported that 926, or approximately 61 percent of the 1,500 sites on the NPL had been cleaned up, but the pace will likely slow because of scarce federal funds for the program.[13] Advances in scientific research and technological developments such as bioremediation are more impressive. So too are current proposals for dealing with the more than 400,000 so-called brownfields scattered across the nation, old industrial sites that may be suitable for redevelopment if federal hazardous waste laws permit and if local communities are supportive. Even with such qualifications, it is clear that these limited achievements in dealing with the most troubling of the nation's hazardous waste sites come at a high price. The nation could easily spend hundreds of billions of dollars over the next four to five decades (Probst et al. 2001; Russell, Colglazier, and Tonn 1992).

Contaminated Federal Facilities

One of the most demanding tasks facing the nation is the cleanup of federal government facilities such as military bases and former nuclear weapons production plants. Those sites, although fewer in number than Superfund sites, are generally larger and present a more complex cleanup challenge, in part because of the mix of chemical and radioactive wastes (U.S. Office of Technology Assessment 1991a). Russell, Colglazier, and Tonn (1992) estimate that over the next few decades, remediation activities by the Department of Defense (DOD) and the Department of Energy (DOE) could run between $110 billion and $430 billion, depending on the stringency of cleanup standards. Some 11,000 DOD sites may be in need of cleanup, as well as more than 4,000 that are managed by the DOE.

The cost of cleaning up the DOE's 17 principal weapons plants and laboratories alone is estimated to be $170 to $200 billion over the next half century (U.S. GAO 2005b). Much of that spending has been directed at five sites: Hanford Reservation in Washington State, Savannah River in Georgia, Rocky Flats in Colorado, Oak Ridge in Tennessee, and the Idaho National Engineering and Environmental Laboratory. At a current spending level of $6 to $8 billion per year for environmental management, cleanup of federal facilities easily dwarfs the EPA's operating budget (about $4 billion a year) and greatly exceeds annual Superfund cleanup costs. At many of the sites, large volumes of soil and groundwater have been contaminated with hazardous chemicals and radioactive wastes, and significant quantities of waste have leaked from damaged storage containers. The job of cleaning up these facilities is enormous, with more than 100 sites in 30 states around the nation. Even with extensive cleanup, hazards are likely to remain at many of the sites, thus requiring long-term stewardship (Probst and McGovern 1998). Cleanup of one major site, completed in late 2005, is illustrative: the Rocky Flats nuclear weapons plant near Denver, Colorado. It took 10 years, cost $7 billion, and is now to be converted to a wildlife refuge.

Radioactive Wastes

The disposal of high-level radioactive wastes from commercial nuclear power plants represents a comparable problem and has proved to be equally difficult to resolve. The United States has accumulated about 47,500 metric tons of high-level wastes, most of it consisting of spent fuel rods from power plants. The DOE has estimated that the nation will have about 108,000 metric tons of spent fuel alone by the year 2040. The spent fuel rods remain highly dangerous for thousands of years.

These high-level wastes have been stored since the 1950s in water-filled basins within the reactor buildings; more recently they have been stored in concrete and steel casks located on the reactor property but outside of the buildings. As of 2006, the wastes were stored at 131 civilian and military sites in 39 states. As storage space runs out, the future of the nuclear industry depends on finding more permanent locations for the waste. After the terrorist attacks of September 2001, new concerns were expressed about the vulnerability of these sites. The federal government and the nuclear industry are eager to see the proposed waste repository at Yucca Mountain, Nevada, completed, but both technical and political challenges remain.

In 2002, following a recommendation from the DOE and President George W. Bush, Congress approved establishment of a repository at Yucca Mountain. The DOE now must request a license from the Nuclear Regulatory Commission to operate the facility. The proposal still faces numerous regulatory and legal hurdles that could well delay the planned opening, including anticipated public controversy over transportation of the waste to the Yucca Mountain repository.

SOLID WASTE AND CONSUMER WASTE

An early concern of the environmental movement dealt with the by-products of the consumer society that clogged municipal landfills. The problem continues. Consumer spending increases regularly, and the amount of waste generated increases proportionately. Recycling and reusing materials helps, but reducing use of consumer goods would help even more. As noted in Chapter 1, that is the message from environmentalists on "green consumption," and many organizations and Web sites offer advice to citizens on how to change their purchasing habits to help conserve natural resources and promote sustainability.[14]

The size of the solid waste problem can be seen in figures compiled annually by the EPA's Office of Solid Waste. The agency estimated that in 2003, U.S. households, institutions, and businesses produced about 236 million tons of municipal solid waste (before recycling), more than 2.5 times the 88 million tons produced in 1960, and considerably higher than the 151 million tons in 1980. For 2003 this figure represented 4.5 pounds per person per day, or more than 1,600 pounds a year for each of us; this is twice the waste per capita generated in western European nations or Japan. These amounts have been growing at about 1 percent a year, similar to the rate of U.S. population growth. Household, institutional, and commercial wastes, however, are only the tip of the solid waste iceberg. The vast majority of solid waste comes from industrial processes, including agriculture and mining, raising the total to over 13 billion tons per year.[15]

Added increasingly to conventional wastes are millions of discarded computers, monitors, printers, cell phones, and other electronic devices or "e-wastes" that contain lead, mercury, and other toxic substances. EPA estimated that in 2003 alone about 50 million computers became obsolete (with only 6 million of them recycled). That number is likely to be at least as high in future years. An estimated 130 million cell phones will likely be discarded each year as well, many of them winding up in landfills. A large proportion of this kind of e-waste is shipped to China, India, Pakistan, and other developing nations for reuse or recycling, but with the potential for toxic contamination within those nations.[16]

Compounding the problem of disposing of such huge quantities of wastes, conventional or electronic, is the sharply declining number of municipal landfills open to receive them. The number of such landfills has fallen sharply since the 1970s, largely because they reached capacity or could not meet environmental standards. Opening new landfills (which tend to be much larger than the old ones) has proved difficult because of community opposition and stringent new requirements for construction and operation (e.g., to control air pollution and contamination of groundwater).

Recycling makes a difference in this picture. The amount of solid waste saved from landfills by recycling nearly doubled between 1990 and 2000. Many states have comprehensive recycling laws, and some innovative programs have been adopted at the municipal level. One example is the city of Seattle, which has become a model for effective curbside recycling. It uses economic incentives to promote reduction in waste and citizen cooperation. Such programs are called volume-based recycling, or "pay as you throw," with the fee reflecting the volume of waste to be collected. These programs are increasingly popular. Other actions, including enactment of the federal Pollution Prevention Act of 1990, the creation of new markets for recycled goods, and tightening restrictions on disposal of hazardous waste, should reduce industrial waste quantities as well.[17]

▪ ENERGY USE AND CLIMATE CHANGE

Energy use has a major effect on most of the environmental problems already discussed, especially air pollution, acid precipitation, and the production of greenhouse gases. These effects flow primarily from a reliance on fossil fuels—oil, natural gas, and coal. Energy use also affects both the health of the economy and national security because the United States relies so heavily on imported oil, which comes to the nation at a high cost and from politically unstable regions of the world. Despite these consequences, the United States has never found it easy to address energy problems and policy proposals (see Chapter 6).

The Nature of Energy Problems

Energy problems may be defined in part by the total amount of energy used, the efficiency of use, the mix of energy sources relied on, and the reserves of nonrenewable sources (e.g., oil and natural gas) that remain available. Among the most important considerations are the environmental costs associated with the life cycle of energy use: extraction, transport, use, and disposal. When oil is transported, spills may occur, sometimes spectacular ones like the 10.9 million gallons of crude oil that leaked from the Exxon *Valdez* supertanker in Prince William Sound off Alaska in 1989. In the aftermath of the terrorist attacks of September 11, 2001, there is also increasing concern that large oil tankers are vulnerable to acts of terrorism. The by-products of energy generation sometimes present difficult tasks of disposal; for example, as noted earlier, when the fuel rods that power nuclear plants are "spent," this highly radioactive waste needs to be isolated from the biosphere. The effect that most concerns students of energy policy is the possibility of global climate change because of the buildup of greenhouse gases, discussed briefly in Chapter 1. The most consequential greenhouse gas is carbon dioxide produced in the burning of fossil fuels. The United States releases more greenhouse gases than any other nation, with the vast majority of these emissions coming from fossil fuels that power automobiles, make electricity, run industrial processes, and heat and cool homes.

An overview of selected data on energy use conveys a simple message. It would be hard to overstate the importance of the world's choice of energy paths for the future. At the same time, energy use is so closely tied to vital industrial processes and highly valued public conveniences such as air conditioning, home heating, and automobile

TABLE 2.3

U.S. and World Energy Consumption by Source, 2004

Source	United States (in quadrillion Btu, quads, equivalent, and percentage)		World Total (in quadrillion Btu, quads, and percentage)	
Coal	22.3	(22.4%)	100.7	(24.0%)
Natural gas	23.0	(23.1%)	99.1	(23.6%)
Oil	40.1	(40.2%)	162.2	(38.7%)
Nuclear electric power	8.23	(8.2%)	26.5	(6.3%)
Hydroelectric power	2.7	(2.7%)	27.2	(6.5%)
Other renewables (geothermal, solar, wind electric power, biofuels)	3.4	(3.4%)	3.7	(0.9%)
Total	99.7	(100%)	419.5	(100%)

Source: U.S. DOE, Annual Energy Review 2004 (Washington, DC: U.S. DOE, Energy Information Administration, 2005), at www.eia.doe.gov/emeu/aer/contents.html.

Note: The world figures come from the International Energy Annual 2003 (released in July 2005).

use, it is also easy to understand the difficulty nations have in trying to alter that path in the short term.

As shown in Table 2.3, the United States derives 86 percent of its energy from fossil fuels (coal, oil, and natural gas) and 14 percent from other sources, largely nuclear (8 percent), hydroelectric, and various other renewable sources.[18] Global reliance on fuel sources is similar. Fossil fuels account for 86 percent of the total world energy use and nuclear power for 6.5 percent. Each leads to substantial adverse environmental impacts. Sources such as geothermal, solar thermal and photovoltaic generation, and wind power are still a distinctly minor part of the energy picture, although with prospects improving greatly in recent years (Hunt and Sawin 2006; Sawin 2004). Table 2.3 also shows that the United States consumes about 24 percent of the total world energy usage, with China, Russia, Japan, Germany, and Canada (in that order) among the other large energy users.

In 2006 the United States imported about 58 percent of the oil it consumed, which is twice the level that prevailed in 1973 at the time of the nation's first major energy crisis. By 2025 dependency on imports is expected to increase to 68 percent, a trend that nearly everyone thinks is harmful. In addition to creating more greenhouse gas emissions, such a high level of oil use threatens national security and worsens the nation's international trade deficit. Most of that oil is used for transportation, and reduction in its use depends on improving transportation efficiency, for example, with more fuel-efficient vehicles or greater reliance on mass transit.

Adjusted for inflation, oil and gasoline in the United States continue to be relatively inexpensive; gasoline is more than twice as costly in most European nations. But low prices over the past decade have discouraged conservation and investments in efficiency. They also have made development of alternatives, including domestic sources of oil, more difficult, although recent price increases are beginning to change that pattern.[19]

Projection of future energy use is difficult because so much depends on developments in energy efficiency (e.g., in cars, appliances, and homes), new technology, market prices, government policies, and changing consumer behavior. For example, the nuclear power industry seeks a major expansion in plants around the world. It is optimistic about new reactor designs that promise cheaper and safer nuclear energy. Yet public opposition in the United States and in other nations as well as resistance by electric utilities remain strong, costs are uncertain, and controversies over nuclear waste continue to hamper expansion of the industry. One major advantage of nuclear power, however, is that it produces no greenhouse gases, and some environmentalists are beginning to support it as one way to mitigate climate change.

Despite all these uncertainties, there are a number of contrasting long-term (20- to 40-year) scenarios for U.S. energy use. Most assume continued emphasis on fossil fuels, a major but stable role for nuclear power, and a slow transition to renewable energy sources as economic forces and technological developments permit. Over the next 25 years, the DOE projects increased demand for oil (largely imported because U.S. production is decreasing), a continued rise in coal use to keep pace with growing demand for electricity, and an increase in the use of natural gas.

Other energy scenarios indicate the feasibility of significant reductions in energy use as well as in air pollution and a shift to sustainable energy sources such as solar, geothermal, wind, and hydrogen power. Several environmental groups have estimated that the nation could lower fossil fuel use substantially over the next several decades with greater energy efficiency and conservation measures, and with more support for renewable energy (Herzog et al. 2001; Sawin 2004).[20] Even if such projections are overly optimistic, a significant shift toward nonfossil fuel energy sources has already begun, stimulated in part by concern over global climate change.

Fossil Fuels and the Threat of Climate Change

The world's scientific community and numerous independent policy studies support the basic case for major reductions in use of fossil fuels, primarily because of their contribution to climate change (Hempel 2006; IPCC 2001). Reports from the UN-sponsored Intergovernmental Panel on Climate Change (IPCC) have confirmed the seriousness of the risk of inaction. They also reached an important conclusion: human beings are influencing the global climate, a proposition previously debated at length. To date, however, proposals within the United States to reduce emissions of greenhouse gases, particularly carbon dioxide, have suffered for lack of political support.

Under the UN Convention on Climate Change approved at the 1992 Earth Summit, the United States and other developed countries that agreed to the treaty were to cut carbon dioxide and other greenhouse gas emissions significantly. Following a series of international meetings to define the detailed requirements, the United States agreed to a 7 percent cut below 1990 emission levels, to be achieved by 2012. This translates into a 30 to 35 percent reduction from what the level of greenhouse gas emissions would be under a business-as-usual scenario (Hempel 2006). The U.S. Congress, however, has been cool toward climate change policy. In addition, in early 2001 President George W. Bush rejected the international climate change agreement, the Kyoto Protocol, as "fatally flawed" based on its economic impact on the nation as well as perceptions of inequity in the lesser demands made on developing nations under the agreement. His administration preferred voluntary efforts to re-duce greenhouse gas emissions and an expanded research program in climate change. Political stalemate on climate change at the national level has stimulated innovative state-level policies, some of which may well have substantial effects on the nation as a whole. This is particularly the case with California's regulation of greenhouse gases from automobiles, which, if upheld by the courts, would force major improvements in auto fuel efficiency (Rabe 2004, 2006).

As noted in Chapter 1, without significant reductions in greenhouse gas emis-sions, scientists anticipate a doubling of carbon dioxide levels in the atmosphere over the next 100 years, primarily from fossil fuel combustion and deforestation. The con-sequences of such a change, although they continue to be disputed, likely would in-clude a climate that is warmer and wetter, with rising sea levels, significant risks of abrupt and unpredictable shifts in weather patterns, and extreme events such as droughts, floods, and more severe hurricanes. Some viewed Hurricane Katrina that struck the U.S. Gulf Coast in September 2005 as one example of what could become more common.[21] The warming range projected by recent IPCC studies is 1.4 to 5.8°C (2.5 to 10.4°F) by the year 2100. Among other effects, there could be cata-strophic consequences for agriculture, and thus for the food supply, and major risks to ecosystem integrity and biodiversity as well as to human health, particularly in de-veloping nations (IPCC 2001).[22]

Beyond the U.S. response, the global challenges are formidable and addressed in Chapter 8. Energy demand is likely to increase sharply, driven by rapid population and economic growth in the developing nations. Unless nations develop alternatives, those demands are likely to be met largely with fossil fuels. Environmentalists argue that solutions lie in a greater sharing of energy-saving technologies with those nations, removal of subsidies that encourage use of fossil fuels, and adoption of incentives for the use of renewable energy sources (Smil 2003; Sawin 2004).

■ BIOLOGICAL DIVERSITY AND HABITAT LOSS

Biological diversity, or biodiversity, refers to the variety and variability among living organisms and the ecological complexes in which they occur. Scientists generally ex-amine three types of biodiversity: genetic, species, and ecosystem diversity. The di-versity of species and the habitats that support them derive from the ecological and evolutionary processes that have shaped them over geological time spans and will continue to do so in the future.

People have long taken biodiversity for granted and have enjoyed the free ser-vices it has provided. Yet human activity, both intentional and inadvertent, has had a devastating effect on biodiversity over the past 10,000 years. People have always cleared land and have overhunted some species and caused the extinction of others. The present is distinguished from the past primarily by the magnitude of destruc-tion and rates of change. The principal causes of the new threats to biodiversity are habitat loss and modification (including fragmentation), pollution and contamina-tion, overexploitation of species and habitats, introduction of exotic and competi-tive species, and the interactive effects of these activities. There is also good reason to believe that a warming climate could rival the destruction of habitat as a cause of biodiversity loss.

Put bluntly, human beings are using an ever greater portion of the planet's natural capital and leaving less for other species. Some recent estimates suggest that human activity has transformed a third to a half of Earth's surface and that today we consume or directly use 40 to 50 percent of the land's biological production and more than half of all available fresh water. As the human population continues to grow and as the world's economy expands, these trends are likely to continue. As a result, many conservationists are growing more pessimistic about how much can be done to preserve natural areas and biodiversity. They hope to slow the human impact and to protect as many "biological hot spots" as they can, both within the United States and internationally, over the next few decades (Stein 2001).

In the broadest terms, biologists, environmentalists, and others who argue for biodiversity conservation seek to ensure the continuation, or restoration, of the full range of biological entities on Earth. From an ecological perspective, preservation of biodiversity in turn will help ensure ecosystem stability and productivity, on which human and other life depends. Ecologists also argue that it is essential to maintain the capabilities of all species to reproduce successfully, to regenerate after population losses, and to adapt in a period of significant environmental change (Barnthouse 1998; Daily 1997). An equally powerful voice in the conservation movement is based less on ecology than on philosophy and religion. It seeks on moral grounds to save "creation" and to pass along a healthy world to future generations (Stevens 2000a).

Biodiversity Loss and Implications

Between 1600 and 1900, human activities led to the extinction of perhaps 75 species of birds and mammals, or about one species every four years. A comparable number was lost in the first half of the twentieth century. Biologists estimate that in the mid-1970s, anthropogenic, or human-caused, extinctions rose to about 100 species per year (Tobin 1990). Edward O. Wilson, one of the nation's leading authorities on biodiversity, has argued that the extinction rate in the mid-1980s was accelerating rapidly and was at least 400 times the natural rate (Wilson 1990, 54). Others suggest that the rate is probably 36 to 78 times the background or historic rate—lower but still disturbingly high (Gibbs 2001). Even the congressional Office of Technology Assessment reported in a major 1987 study that the loss of biological diversity was of "crisis proportions." That view does not seem to be widely shared by the American public and its elected representatives (Tobin 1990).

The effect of such species loss is particularly acute in tropical rain forests. Although the number of species in existence is uncertain, biologists have estimated that more than half of all identified species live in moist tropical forests. Such forests cover only 6 percent of land area but are biologically rich, especially with insects and flowering plants. The forests are vulnerable ecosystems, however, and they illustrate the larger threat to biodiversity of human interventions.

From the dawn of agriculture approximately 12,000 years ago to the present, humans have eliminated about a third of the world's forest cover (Myers 1997). The loss has been especially great in tropical forests in Amazonia, Central America, and Indonesia, where more than half of the original forest cover has been lost. Current calculations put the continuing loss at an estimated 1 percent of the total rain forests annually, or nearly 25 million acres a year (Reid 1997). The United States also has experienced extensive deforestation. For example, about 90 percent of old-growth forests in the Pacific

Northwest have been lost to development. According to a comprehensive UN report in 2005, an estimated 50,000 square miles of forests worldwide, an area about the size of New York State, are cleared or logged annually. Moreover, about half of this activity occurs in areas where no significant human use took place previously. The current rate of deforestation would be higher if China were not engaged in extensive tree planting.[23]

The reasons for this loss of ecologically critical forestland are not in much dispute. Among the major factors are the clearing and burning of rain forests to make room for rapidly growing and poor populations, conversion of forests for planting of cash crops and cattle pastureland, commercial logging, overharvesting of fuel wood, and dam construction. Short-sighted government policies have encouraged many of these and similar activities (Miller, Reid, and Barber 1991; Reid 1997; Tobin 2006).

As the forest habitat is destroyed, species are lost. The Global Biodiversity Assessment (GBA), an independent analysis of the state of scientific knowledge about biodiversity commissioned by the UN Environment Programme, provides some useful data on these rates. If the current rate of loss in tropical forests continues for another 30 years, the GBA concluded that the number of species would decline by 5 to 10 percent from present levels. Some scientists have suggested a much higher rate of decline.

GBA analysts also estimated that some 5,400 species of animals and 26,000 species of plants are threatened globally. Several studies suggest that "at least 11 percent of all bird species are threatened, along with 25 percent of mammal species, 34 percent of fish species, 25 percent of amphibian species, and 11 percent of plant species" (Reid 1997, 19–20). It is easier to describe the status of well-known species than for others. For the majority of the 1.7 million known species (mostly insects) and the many millions of those not yet discovered, information for reliable assessments is lacking.

In many respects, the exact rate of species or other biodiversity loss matters less than understanding the implications of such trends for human well-being as well as for ecosystem functioning. There are many reasons to worry about biodiversity loss. Forests provide human beings with opportunities for recreation and for aesthetic enjoyment. They also are a treasure trove of medicinal drugs, oils, waxes, natural insecticides, and cosmetics, and they could contain future sources of food (World Commission on Environment and Development 1987). Of the 80,000 edible plants, humans have used an estimated 7,000 for food, but we actively cultivate only about 200 and rely heavily on only about 20, such as wheat, rye, corn, soybeans, millet, and rice (Wilson 1990, 58).

Yet as important as those ecological and agricultural values are from an anthropocentric perspective, they are not as compelling as arguments advanced from an ecocentric or ecology-centered viewpoint. Biodiversity, whether in tropical forests or elsewhere, is important because it provides irreplaceable ecological values, including the genetic heritage of millions of years of evolution. We risk damage to the functioning of ecosystems with species loss and the permanent disappearance of diverse genetic codes that could prove invaluable for species adaptation in what may be a rapidly changing environment in the future.

Ecologists continue to debate the precise relationship between biodiversity and ecosystem health or productivity, that is, how the loss of species affects ecosystem functions (Baskin 1993; Myers 1997; Tilman 1997). Yet no one disagrees that the functions put at risk with loss of biodiversity are critical. These roles include the cycling of nutrients, partial stabilization of climate, purification of air and water, mitigation of floods and droughts, decomposition of wastes, generation and renewal of soil and soil fertility, pollination of crops and natural vegetation, and control of agricultural pests (Daily 1997). The issue is not, as the press reports it, whether a single species, such as the northern spotted owl, is lost. Rather, it is that we risk the destruction of critical habitats and ecosystems, as well as the biogeochemical cycles, on which life depends. A Millennium Ecosystem Assessment released by the World Health Organization in 2005 concluded that 60 percent of critical ecosystem functions are being degraded by various human activities. The exhaustive study contains detailed information about the effects of economic development on ecosystem health.[24]

Policy Actions and Effects

Protection of biodiversity was one of the most controversial issues at the 1992 Earth Summit, which also produced an accord on protection of the world's forests. President George H.W. Bush refused to sign the proposed biodiversity treaty at the meeting. He expressed concern about the rights to commercial exploitation of biological resources and other issues. In April 1993, however, following discussion with business and environmental groups, President Clinton signed the treaty. The Convention on Biological Diversity (CBD) took effect in late 1993, with the United States among the nations supporting it, although the U.S. Senate did not ratify the agreement. The CBD is largely a framework convention that encourages governments to develop conservation strategies and action plans; see Chapter 8 for a fuller discussion.

Solutions to biodiversity challenges are not scarce even if the political will to adopt and enforce them is. Policymakers and environmental organizations have proposed a wide range of actions. These strategies include swapping international debt for preservation of natural areas, land reform that gives a local population more access to and control of the land, gaining the support of local people for conservation strategies, finding ways to derive local economic benefits from conservation, practicing conservation at the bioregional level, ending or reducing governmental subsidies (e.g., for agriculture or timber production) that encourage deforestation, and increasing investment in biodiversity research (Reid 1997; Tobin 2006). None of these actions is easy to take because the public and policymakers are not committed enough to conservation to overcome opposition from powerful economic and political forces. In his *Requiem for Nature*, biologist John Terborgh (1999) argues that the competitive nature of the global economy and "our collective obsession" with maximizing economic growth make sustainable development of this kind "currently unattainable."

In the United States, protection of biodiversity is tied closely to enforcement of the 1973 Endangered Species Act (ESA) (discussed in Chapter 6). Although the act has a broad mandate for ecosystem conservation, emphasis to date has been on protection of individual species. Even here, the act has achieved only modest success after more than 30 years. As of 2006, 1,272 U.S. plant and animal species have been listed as threatened or endangered, and several hundred others are candidates for listing. The Fish and Wildlife Service (FWS), which implements the act for terrestrial and some aquatic species, has designated over 470 critical habitats and has developed more than 500 habitat conservation plans and about 1,000 approved recovery plans. The FWS reports that 30 percent of listed species are stable, 6 percent are improving, and 21 percent are declining; the status of another 39 percent was uncertain.

Unfortunately, relatively few endangered species have fully recovered and been removed from the list. The recovered and delisted species include the peregrine falcon, brown pelican, gray whale, and the American alligator; the grey wolf has been proposed for delisting, and the bald eagle is being considered for that step as well. Increasingly, emphasis under the ESA is likely to be given to ecosystem, rather than single-species, preservation.[25]

■ POPULATION GROWTH

An increasing human population affects every environmental and resource challenge discussed in this chapter, from the generation of waste to the loss of biodiversity. Yet the environmental community has not always been attentive to these issues. Mainstream environmental organizations such as the National Audubon Society, the National Wildlife Federation, and the Sierra Club, which had long ignored population growth, rediscovered it in the 1990s. Many environmental organizations actively promoted the urgency of action on population growth in conjunction with the UN International Conference on Population and Development held in September 1994 in Cairo. They did so again in October 1999 when the world population surpassed the symbolically important level of 6 billion people, more than twice the 1950 population of 2.5 billion (Crossette 1999). Nonetheless, other environmental groups, the news media, and government policymakers often give population issues remarkably little attention. Partly for these reasons, population growth is rarely a salient issue for the public, even if it is arguably one of the most important determinants of environmental quality and human well-being.

Population and Sustainable Development

Despite wide variability in definitions of sustainability, the concept must include the enduring capacity of a given ecosystem to support the demands that its human population imposes on it. A high rate of population growth can significantly affect the environment because it requires the provision of additional food, clean water, shelter, energy, and other resources to meet the demands of additional people. The rate of growth may also affect the depletion of critical resources and threaten ecosystem integrity (Daily 1997).

Estimates vary widely, but the world's present agricultural production probably can support only about 2.3 billion people if they have a diet similar to Americans (heavy on consumption of meat), 6 billion with a Japanese diet, and perhaps as many as 15 billion if people live on a subsistence diet. Such assessments remind us that population numbers are not the only important factor to consider. They also suggest that it is inappropriate to think of the land's population "carrying capacity" in static terms. Lifestyles and the technologies that we use are equally significant (Tobin 2006). They are captured in the concept of our "ecological footprint," or the effect we have on the environment as a consequence of trying to meet our needs through use of natural resources (Wackernagel and Rees 1996). Still, it is becoming evident that the human population is currently close to many estimates of the upper range of sustainability (J. Cohen 1995). A number of Web pages allow simple calculations of ecological footprints (e.g., www.footprintnetwork.org and www.rprogress.org).

The cost in human lives attributable to population growth (and the poverty that often results) is also great. Perhaps as many as 10 million people die each year from hunger or hunger-related diseases, primarily in developing countries, with millions more harmed for life. These numbers could easily rise in the future if food supplies shrink for any reason. More than 30,000 children under the age of five die *each day* (11 million per year) in poor nations from treatable diseases such as malaria, diarrhea, measles, tetanus, and acute respiratory infections that rarely kill Americans (Tobin 2006).[26] In addition, high population growth rates may affect political stability within nations as well as conflict among them over access to scarce natural resources such as water and arable land. Sustained economic growth, national security, social peace, and human justice all depend on limiting and eventually halting human population growth. They depend as well on improving scientific knowledge and technological systems and on reallocating critical resources such as land and water to more efficient and equitable uses.

Birthrates have declined since the 1960s, but they remain well above the replacement level (slightly more than two births per woman of childbearing age) that eventually produces a stable or nongrowing population. Projections of future population, both globally and in the United States, provide little basis for complacency, either for economic development in poor nations or for protection of critical environmental resources worldwide. The impact on habitats and biodiversity, air and water quality, energy and water use, and other aspects of environmental quality is likely to be enormous but also geographically quite varied. Some nations and regions of the world will be affected far more than others by food and water shortages, poor health, environmental degradation, and economic dislocations, including widespread unemployment. The World Bank estimated in 2001 that nearly 1.1 billion people in the world lived in severe poverty and a total of 2.7 billion lived on less than $2 per day.

We can hardly place all the blame on the poor nations, where nearly all of the future growth in human numbers will occur. The industrialized nations consume a far greater proportion of the world's resources and have a much higher per capita effect on the environment. For example, the richest quarter of the world's nations controls about 75 percent of the global income, consumes a large share of the world's meat and fish, and uses most of its energy, paper, chemicals, iron, and steel. It also is responsible for more than 90 percent of the industrial and hazardous wastes produced and for about two thirds of greenhouse gases (Tobin 2006). The United States, with less than 5 percent of the world's population, consumes 25 percent of its commercial energy and produces a fifth of all global greenhouse gas emissions. Because of these patterns of intensive resource consumption, the United Nations estimates that a child born today in an industrialized nation will consume more and pollute more in his or her lifetime than between 30 and 50 children born in a developing nation. Residents of rich countries have a large ecological footprint.

These numbers suggest what the future might hold if high global population growth rates are combined with intensive economic development based on the technologies currently in use in the developed nations. They also indicate a moral imperative for developed nations to lower energy and materials consumption and to assist the developing nations as they attempt to improve their lot. Those expectations have been made plain at a series of UN meetings since the 1992 Earth Summit, including the 2002 Johannesburg Summit on Sustainable Development.

TABLE 2.4

U.S. and World Estimated Populations and Growth Rates

Region or Country	Estimated Population (millions)			Rate of Increase (2005)
	Mid-2005	2025	2050	
World total	6,477	7,972	9,262	1.2%
Developed nations	1,211	1,251	1,249	0.1
Developing nations	5,266	6,701	8,013	1.5[a]
United States	296.5	349.4	419.9	1.0

Source: Population Reference Bureau, *2005 World Population Data Sheet* (Washington, DC: Population Reference Bureau, 2005), www.prb.org.

Note: The United States has a "natural rate of increase" listed in this and similar databases of 0.6 percent. The estimated rate included in the table, however, reflects the addition of substantial immigration that does not exist for most other nations. Current estimates of U.S. and world population can be found at the Census Bureau's population clock display at www.census.gov.

[a]The rate for developing nations if China is not counted in this category is much higher: 1.8 percent.

Growth Rates and Projected Population Increases

According to the United Nations, in 2005 the world's human population was growing at 1.2 percent annually, adding about 80 million people every year to its base of 6.5 billion. This is a net increase in the world's population (not the number born) of nearly 215,000 people per day. The population of the poorest nations is expected nearly to double over the next 40 years. Although fertility rates continue to decline slowly, the UN's most likely projection for the year 2025 is 8 billion people and for 2050 is about 9.3 billion people (United Nations 2005).[27] Table 2.4 summarizes some of the most notable figures and trends for the United States and the world.

All such projections depend critically on assumptions about economic and social development, the availability of family planning programs, and the extent of contraceptive use. Social development, such as improved education, a higher status for women and improved gender equity, better reproductive health care and nutrition, adoption of old-age security programs, and economic reform are all as important as provision of family planning services. The United Nations has recognized both the continuing need for family planning and the imperative of social and economic development. These kinds of measures were strongly endorsed at the 1994 UN International Conference on Population and Development held in Cairo, Egypt, and at the Johannesburg Summit on Sustainable Development in 2002.

The combination of such efforts has produced striking declines in fertility levels in some nations, including Bangladesh, Kenya, Mexico, South Korea, Thailand, Tunisia, and China. Many nations have made much less progress toward lower growth rates. An added factor for developing nations is rapid urbanization of the population, often leading to overcrowded and severely polluted megacities. The World Health Organization estimates that outdoor air pollution is responsible for more than 800,000 deaths a year, most of which occur in the developing world's large cities.

In contrast to the world average of 1.2 percent, the population of developed nations is growing by an average of only 0.1 percent per year, creating a demographically divided world. The U.S. rate, however, is about 10 times the average for developed nations, or about 1 percent a year counting immigration. The U.S. population (298 million by early 2006) increases by nearly 3 million people a year. Moreover, growth is likely to continue throughout the twenty-first century even if the fertility rate remains below the replacement level. According to a 1997 National Academy of Sciences study, about 60 percent of this growth is attributable to the nation's high level of immigration. The U.S. Census Bureau projects that the nation is likely to reach 420 million by 2050 and an astonishing 571 million by 2100. These estimates are the middle-level projections; the actual results could be lower or higher.[28]

The effect of such changes in selected areas of the nation, such as Florida, Arizona, Colorado, Nevada, and California, or in rapidly growing cities elsewhere, such as Atlanta, is often dramatic. During the 1990s Florida was gaining more than 6,000 residents every week. Phoenix, the fasting growing of America's large cities, surged by more than 20 percent in the late 1990s. Colorado is expected to grow by 50 percent over the next two decades. The Las Vegas metropolitan area, which has experienced explosive growth in recent years, is now home to more than 1.6 million people and continues to add more than 6,000 residents each month, putting enormous demands on area water supplies.

Such growth also exacts a toll on farmland and tree and forest cover in urban areas, especially as cities spread out to distant suburbs. Urban sprawl and development in the form of housing, shopping malls, and roadways consume more than 3 million acres a year of forest, cropland, and other open space; between 1992 and 2002, the United States lost more than 13 million acres of cropland.[29]

Cities and states will have to plan carefully to minimize adverse impacts on land, water supplies and water quality, air quality, critical habitats, urban infrastructures, and the overall quality of life as population grows and congestion increases. Given these trends, rising public support for growth management and the preservation of green spaces and increasing local efforts to build sustainable communities are both welcome news (Mazmanian and Kraft 1999; Portney 2003).

CONCLUSIONS

This selected overview of U.S. and global environmental problems provides at least some indication of the scope and severity of current threats to public and ecosystem health as well as to the quality of our lives. As always, debate continues on how to interpret available data, leaving plenty of room for environmentalists and their opponents to disagree. Government agencies and both domestic and international environmental organizations recognize the inadequacy of present monitoring of environmental trends and the need to improve data collection, its integration, and its assessment. Progress on these fronts is evident across the board compared with past decades. Yet even the best scientific information cannot eliminate disagreements over environmental policy that are rooted more in politics, economics, and cultural values than in science.

The rate of environmental change threatens to outstrip our capacity to assess and respond to it. Thus we need more accurate modeling of environmental trends and improved forecasts of what may lie ahead. Just as important, however, is providing adequate opportunities for citizens to discuss the information and participate in any decisions on what actions to take, from individual communities to state, national, and international levels. The movement toward creating sustainable communities in many areas of the nation indicates a strong potential for such integrated assessment of local and regional environmental data as well as for citizen involvement in decision making (Mazmanian and Kraft 1999; Portney 2003).

Partly because of the paucity of reliable scientific information, disputes continue over the extent of progress being made in dealing with air and water quality, toxic chemicals and hazardous wastes, and most of the other environmental challenges summarized in this chapter. As will be made clear in later chapters, there are also frequent conflicts over what role government should play in dealing with these problems, in part because policymakers and other policy actors have sharply conflicting views of just how severe the problems are. Disagreement is particularly intense over how much more should be done, with what policy instruments (regulation, market incentives, public education), and at what cost.

There is another message for all students of environmental policy. We need to improve our individual and collective capacities to review and judge the scientific facts and the various political assertions tied to them. This is increasingly difficult to do because partisan debate over environmental policy sometimes brings diametrically opposed analyses of the problems as each side "frames" the issues to suit its case (Bosso and Guber 2007; Layzer 2007). Citizens can jump into these battles, but they will do better if they understand the issues and learn how to sort out reasonable from unreasonable claims.

DISCUSSION QUESTIONS

1. For any of the environmental problems reviewed in the chapter, how severe is the risk to public health or the environment? What is the basis for your conclusions? For example, how severe is the problem of contaminated drinking water? How serious is global climate change? The loss of biological diversity? Population growth, either in the United States or worldwide? For any of these issues, what do you see as the implications for public policy?

2. Based on improvements in air quality since 1970, how would you evaluate the federal Clean Air Act? Has it been successful? What changes might make it more effective in the future? What about the Clean Water Act? The Endangered Species Act?

3. What kind of government policies might help address environmental risks such as indoor air quality for which a conventional regulatory approach would not work? What about the similar challenge of dealing with nonpoint source water pollution? Public education? Economic incentives? Something else?

4. The Toxics Release Inventory (TRI) provides an enormous amount of information about toxic chemicals released to the local environment, yet the public is not well informed about community risks. What actions might make TRI information more visible and more useful to the public?

5. What might be done to make community and state recycling programs more effective? To increase the national recycling rate for solid waste and consumer electronic goods?

6. Why has the United States not been more effective in reducing its energy use, particularly the use of fossil fuels? What actions might increase energy conservation and efficiency?

SUGGESTED READINGS

Brown, Lester R. *Plan B 2.0: Rescuing a Planet Under Stress and a Civilization in Trouble.* New York: W. W. Norton, 2006.

Daily, Gretchen C., ed. *Nature's Services: Societal Dependence on Natural Ecosystems.* Washington, DC: Island Press, 1997.

Paehlke, Robert, ed. *Conservation and Environmentalism: An Encyclopedia.* New York: Garland, 1995.

Starke, Linda, ed. *State of the World 2006.* New York: W. W. Norton, 2006.

United Nations Development Programme, United Nations Environment Programme, World Bank, and World Resources Institute. *World Resources 2005—The Wealth of the Poor: Managing Ecosystems to Fight Poverty;* available online at http://multimedia. wri.org/worldresources2005.cfm. See also the World Resources Institute's Environmental Information Portal: http://earthtrends.wri.org/.

Worldwatch Institute. *Vital Signs 2005.* Washington, DC: Worldwatch Institute, 2005.

ENDNOTES

1. See Jocelyn Kaiser, "Evidence Mounts That Tiny Particles Can Kill," *Science* 289 (July 7, 2000): 22–23. The original estimate was 60,000 deaths a year, but the estimates were revised downward by about half when scientists adopted a new method of calculation. See Andrew C. Revkin, "Data Revised on Soot in Air and Deaths," *New York Times,* June 5, 2002, A19.

2. The EPA report is entitled *Respiratory Health Effects of Passive Smoking: Lung Cancer and Other Disorders.* The EPA's staff strongly defended its 530-page health risk assessment against tobacco industry charges of inadequate science. Nonetheless, the report was challenged by tobacco interests in federal district court in North Carolina, and they won a partial victory in 1998. The EPA appealed the ruling and continued to defend its scientific studies. Of interest as well is a 1997 study by the California Environmental Protection Agency that found secondhand smoke nationally causes up to 2,700 cases of sudden infant death syndrome, 62,000 deaths from heart disease, and 26,000 new cases of asthma in children annually.

3. For a recent review of the problem, see Michelle Conlin, "Is Your Office Killing You?" *Business Week,* June 5, 2000, 114–30.

4. The EPA is in the process of changing this system and has yet to provide national summaries of the most recent data. However, each state report is available at the agency's Web site in its National Assessment Database: www.epa.gov/waters/305b/index.html.

5. See Barbara Whitaker, "Beach Closings and Advisories Reach Record, Report Shows," *New York Times,* August 9, 2001, A14. The study was released by the Natural Resources Defense Council and is available at the group's Web site: www.nrdc.org. Some states, such as California, have comprehensive monitoring of beaches, whereas others, such as Louisiana and Oregon, have no regular monitoring or lack sufficient procedures to

warn swimmers if safety standards are not met. Little federal money has been spent on monitoring despite unanimous congressional approval of the Beach Act in 2000 (the Beaches Environmental Assessment and Coastal Heath Act). The main concern with water quality at beaches is bacterial contamination.

6. Becker reports that the new rules are expected to reduce the major pollutants from animal feedlots by approximately 25 percent. The rules apply only to the very largest animal feeding operations, each farm is allowed to write its own pollution control plans, and they may keep them secret from the public, although they also must file an annual report that will be made public. Citizens groups had filed dozens of lawsuits in recent years to try to control or stop such feedlots because of their odor and impact on both drinking and surface water.

7. See Andrew C. Revkin, "Offshore Oil Pollution Comes Mostly as Runoff, Study Says," *New York Times*, May 24, 2002, A14.

8. The USGS National Water Quality Assessment Program is designed to describe the status and trends in the quality of the nation's groundwater and surface water resources. Its Web page contains a wealth of data on the nation's water quality: http://water.usgs.gov/. To complicate matters, the Government Accountability Office has identified 72 different federal programs and initiatives that directly or indirectly deal with water quality protection. Accessible and consolidated information is hard to find.

9. The report can be found at http://ewg.org/tapwater/findings.php. The NRDC Web site, www.nrdc.org, also has a number of studies of drinking water quality.

10. A general overview of the problem can be found in Colborn, Dumanoski, and Myers, *Our Stolen Future* (1996), and in a symposium in the journal *Forum for Applied Research and Public Policy* (Fall 1998). A panel of the National Research Council reported in 1999 that it found evidence of the chemicals' effects inconclusive, particularly at low levels of exposure. The report can be found at www.national academies. org.

11. This is the agency's Risk Screening Environmental Indicators (RSEI) model. It has been available only on a CD-ROM database, but should be an online source in the future. For a history of the TRI program and its effects, see Hamilton (2005).

12. In recent years, the number of generators covered by RCRA has increased enormously, largely because of the reduced threshold for waste quantities for inclusion in this category. Historically and currently, the vast majority of hazardous waste comes from a small percentage of generators; 2 percent of them generate 95 percent of the waste. But there are still some 13,000 large generators, and many of the small ones are still important for their local environment.

13. The EPA reports current achievements and challenges at its Web site for the Superfund program: www.epa.gov/superfund/index.htm.

14. See Alan Durning's *How Much Is Enough?* (1992). John C. Ryan and Alan Thein Durning's *Stuff: The Secret Lives of Everyday Things* (Seattle, WA: Northwest Environment Watch, 1997) offers a sobering view of the environmental effects of the daily consumer products we use, from coffee to automobiles.

15. The EPA's Office of Solid Waste compiles such data: www.epa.gov/msw/facts.htm.

16. For a comprehensive study of e-waste, see Government Accountability Office, Electronic Waste: Observations on the Role of the Federal Government in Encouraging Recycling and Reuse (Washington, DC: GAO-05-937T, July 2005). The result can be found at the GAO Web site: www.gao.gov.

17. Extensive information on the "pay as you throw" or unit pricing programs can be found at the EPA Web site: www.epa.gov/epaoswer/non-hw/payt/index.htm.
18. The Energy Information Administration in the Department of Energy publishes a comprehensive *Annual Energy Review* that surveys the nation's production and consumption of all major energy sources. It is available online: www.eia.doe.gov/. A comparable international survey is the annual *World Energy Outlook*, published by the International Energy Agency.
19. For a discussion of how higher oil prices are stimulating a search for new fuels, see Joan Lowy, "An Exploration of Alternatives," *CQ Weekly*, September 12, 2005, 2396–2409.
20. For example, see the Alliance to Save Energy Web site, www.ase.org/, and the Natural Resources Defense Council's site, www.nrdc.org. The NRDC argued strongly against the Bush energy proposal of 2001 and in favor of a greater reliance on energy efficiency, conservation, and renewables. See also the site for the American Council for an Energy Efficiency Economy: www.aceee.org/.
21. See Juliet Eilperin, "Katrina May Be Just the Beginning," *Washington Post National Weekly Edition*, September 26–October 2, 2005, 35.
22. The EPA maintains a global climate change site with key information, extensive links to current studies, and about three dozen links to other organizations that follow climate change, reflecting a broad cross section of debate on the issues: www.epa.gov/globalwarming/. See also the IPCC Web site: www.ipcc.ch/. References to regional and national climate change assessments can be found in Thomas M. Parris, "Downscaling Climate Change Assessments," *Environment* 43 (May 2001): 3.
23. The UN report is available at www.fao.org/forestry. The Web page for the UN Convention on Biological Diversity provides a wealth of information on scientific assessments and policy actions related to biodiversity loss: www.biodiv.org
24. The reports are available at www.millenniumassessment.org/en/index.aspx. Another valuable compilation of such ecosystem changes within the United States was released by the John Heinz III Center for Science, Economics and the Environment (2002).
25. The Fish and Wildlife Service Web site provides extensive data on threatened and endangered species and habitat recovery plans: www.fws.gov/.
26. UNICEF, the United Nations Children Fund, provides a biennial report on children's welfare, the latest of which is *The State of the World's Children 2002*: www.unicef.org/sowc02/. Estimates on deaths from hunger are taken from the Food and Agriculture Organization (FAO) Web page. The estimate for 2003 was about 10 million per year. This figure is down sharply from a decade earlier when as many as 40 million died each year from hunger. A 2005 FAO study estimated that 6 million children die each year from hunger and malnutrition, or about half of all childhood deaths. See its report, The State of Food Insecurity in the World 2005: www.fao.org/.
27. There is much uncertainty in these kinds of projections, and the longer the time frame, the more uncertainty there is. See the UN Web sites, www.unfpa.org/and www.un.org/popin, for updates on population projections and reports. The Population Reference Bureau (www.prb.org) also has a wealth of population data in easily readable form.
28. In addition to the UN Web site, see the U.S. Census Bureau site for reports on U.S. population trends: www.census.gov/. See also Kent and Mather (2002).
29. The data are reported in the National Resources Inventory released in April 2004 (for the year 2002) by the U.S. Department of Agriculture's Natural Resources Conservation Service. See www.nrcs.usda.gov/technical/land/nri02/nri02lu.html.

3

Making
Environmental Policy

Environmental problems now occupy a prominent position on national and international political agendas. Yet debate continues over their severity, the extent of governmental intervention needed, and the policy approaches that promise to be the most effective, efficient, or fair. These conflicts are evident in just about every policy area, from action on global climate change to the Endangered Species Act (Vig and Kraft 2006). It was not always so. Prior to the 1960s, environmental issues were barely mentioned in the national media, and most policymakers took little interest in them. That pattern continued even as evidence of environmental degradation mounted during the 1960s. The importance of the environment as an issue rose rapidly in the late 1960s, however. Since then, it has ebbed and flowed in response to shifts in the economy and the political climate and to changing perceptions of environmental, natural resource, and energy problems.

These fluctuations speak to an important aspect of environmental policymaking. The mere existence of detrimental environmental conditions and dire warnings about the future provide no guarantee that the public will pay attention or that governments will act. Public concern and government action require that the problems achieve a sufficient level of visibility and make it onto the policy agenda (Kingdon 1995). Even after reaching the agenda, the problems may return to obscurity or at least to a lower level of attention if prominent events push them off, as occurred following the terrorist attacks of September 11, 2001. For six months after the attacks, major environmental policy actions by the Bush administration received negligible coverage in most national news outlets (Bosso and Guber 2006).

When governments do act, the policies considered and chosen may or may not be the best way to address a problem. Much depends on available scientific information and how policymakers appraise the situation, including the anticipated cost of action and its impacts on society. Politics has a great deal to do with such policy choices. Among the most central factors in the politics of the environment are the extent of public concern and involvement; the activities of major environmental, business, and other interest groups; and the beliefs, attitudes, and values of public officials. The striking difference between environmental policy decisions of the Clinton administration in the 1990s and the Bush administration in the 2000s makes clear that the views of a president and his top advisers matter a great deal (Vig and Kraft 2006).

This chapter focuses on the policy-making process and the general features of U.S. government that influence environmental politics and policy. In Chapter 4, the concepts developed here are used to assess the evolution of natural resource and environmental policy. Special emphasis is given there to the rise of the modern environmental movement, the diversity of interest groups that are active on the issues, and public support for environmental policy actions. Taken together, these two chapters speak to the capacity of the U.S. political system to deal effectively with environmental problems. As indicated in Chapter 1, it is important to ask how well the U.S. government has responded to environmental problems to date and how well it is likely to deal with new problems faced in the future. To answer these questions requires an understanding of the policy-making process, including the factors that may inhibit appropriate government action as well as those that may foster the development of innovative and effective public policies.

■ UNDERSTANDING ENVIRONMENTAL POLITICS

In January 2006 the federal government reported what many would consider to be a bizarre development. As energy prices remained at record highs and the oil and gas industries reported soaring profits, federal officials said they collected no more royalties from those companies than five years earlier for their right to extract oil and gas from publicly owned lands and coastal waters. The companies extracted more than $60 billion worth of oil and gas from these areas, but paid only $8 billion to the government in royalties. How could this be? One press account explained the outcome as the result of "an often byzantine set of federal regulations, largely shaped and fiercely defended by the energy industry itself." The result was that "the nation's taxpayers, collectively, the biggest owner of American oil and gas reserves, have missed much of the recent energy bonanza." After a scandal over similar pricing of oil royalties five years earlier, major oil companies paid a fine of $438 million to settle charges of fraud, and the government tightened the rules for oil payments of this kind. However, for natural gas the Bush administration chose to loosen the rules and also to ease the way audits are conducted, so it is more difficult to uncover corporate misbehavior; the administration had been trying to increase the incentives for oil and gas production.[1]

As this example shows, the U.S. policy-making process is often complex and sometimes utterly mystifying. Policy decisions may focus on narrow and highly technical issues understood only by those who are intimately involved with the specific policy or program. Moreover, the same people may be responsible for writing the rules and regulations that govern those decisions, including those who benefit financially from them. This is the case for many environmental and resource policies. For example, few people have the time or inclination to follow the intricacies of nuclear waste policy, such as the way that standards are set and scientific assessments are conducted for potential waste repository sites, or comparable aspects of clean air policy, drinking water policy, the handling of hazardous wastes, or pesticide regulation. Yet these decisions can affect people's health and the quality of the environment significantly. Fortunately, the overall character of policymaking and the stages through which most environmental policies move are more comprehensible.

Political scientists use several different models and theories that help explain how the policy-making process works and how it results in the policies on which we rely. A few of these bear mentioning. Some, such as elite theory, emphasize the role of economic or governing elites (such as corporate leaders), who may hold values and policy preferences that differ substantially from those of the public at large (Gonzalez 2001); the oil and gas rules just described seem to be an example of such elite dominance in policymaking that serves the public interest poorly. Others, such as group theory, see public policy as the product of a continuous struggle among organized interest groups, such as business and environmental groups (Kraft and Kamieniecki 2007). Compromises reached on pesticide policy, for example, may reflect a balance between preferences of agricultural chemical companies and environmental and health groups. Institutional theory emphasizes the formal and legal aspects of government institutions, for example, the way they are structured or arranged, their legal powers, and procedural rules that they follow; among these are how much public involvement is allowed in government decisions and how much authority is given to state governments to act on their own under the principle of federalism (Ostrom 1999b). One common approach, called rational choice theory, draws heavily from economics. It assumes that in making decisions individuals try to maximize their self-interest. Thus it seeks to explain public policy in terms of the actions of individual policy actors who are motivated in this way, whether they are voters, interest group leaders, legislators, or agency officials (Anderson 2006; Moe 1980; Rothenberg 2002). The example about oil and gas leasing rules reflects the profit-maximizing behavior of energy companies as well as the desire of elected officials to respond to their interests, especially when the decisions are of low visibility and they are unlikely to suffer politically for rewarding special interests.[2]

Each one of these perspectives is helpful for explaining some aspects of environmental politics and policy. That is, each can identify some element of policymaking that is important, such as the role that elites, or interest groups, or rules and procedures may play. Each can help as well in explaining why policymaking in the U.S. political system is often difficult. Yet no one theory or model by itself is completely satisfactory because it tends to miss other factors that also are important. Another approach, however—the policy process or policy cycle model—incorporates most of the valuable elements from each of these other approaches. It also has the distinct advantages of clarity and flexibility. For these reasons, this chapter and the rest of the book make extensive use of the policy process model.

■ THE POLICY PROCESS MODEL

The policy process model proposes a logical sequence of activities that affect the development of public policies. It depicts the policy-making process and the broad relationships among policy actors within each stage. The model can also be helpful in understanding the flow of events and decisions within different cultures and institutional settings.[3] The discussion that follows focuses on the national level of government, but similar activities are just as evident at state and local levels (Lowry 1992; Rabe 2006; Scheberle 2004) or at the international level (Chasek, Downie, and Brown 2006). As indicated in Table 3.1, the model distinguishes six distinct, if not entirely separate, stages in policymaking.

TABLE 3.1

The Policy-Making Process

Stage of the Process	What It Entails	Illustrations
Agenda setting	How problems are perceived and defined, command attention in the media, and are taken seriously by interest groups, the general public, and policymakers.	Energy problems that rose on the agenda in 2001. Defined by the Bush administration as a problem of insufficient supply that required more oil and gas drilling rather than conservation to reduce demand.
Policy formulation	The design and drafting of policy goals and strategies for achieving them. Usually involves the use of environmental science and policy analysis, such as economic analysis.	Attempts to develop a U.S. policy on global climate change have floundered because of conflicts over the meaning of scientific data and concern about economic effects.
Policy legitimation	Justifying and authorizing government action. Involves mobilization of support by the public, interest groups, and elected officials.	Approval of the Clean Air Act Amendments of 1990, including new provisions for control of acid rain and stronger actions on urban air pollution. Had broad political support.
Policy implementation	Provision of institutional resources for putting the programs into effect within a bureaucracy.	Implementation of the federal Endangered Species Act by the Interior Department. Shortages of budgetary resources and shifting administrative priorities have reduced its effectiveness.
Policy and program evaluation	Measurement and assessment of policy and program effects, including success or failure.	The Clean Air Act of 1970 is widely viewed as a success because urban air quality has improved significantly. Many policies are less successful.
Policy change	Modification of policy goals and means in light of new information or shifting political environment.	Pesticide regulation, largely unchanged for decades, was finally modified by adoption of the Food Quality Protection Act of 1996.

Sources: Adapted from Kraft and Furlong (2007). Similar models can be found in Jones (1984) and Anderson (2006). The original policy process model can be traced to Harold Lasswell's early work on the policy sciences.

Agenda Setting

Agenda setting is one of the most critical stages for environmental policymaking. It includes how environmental problems are perceived and defined, the development of public opinion on them, and the organization of public concerns and new policy ideas to demand action by government. Agenda setting comprises all those activities that bring environmental problems to the attention of both the public and political leaders and also shape the ideas and policy alternatives that get serious consideration in government (Anderson 2006; Baumgartner and Jones 1993; Stone 2002). This includes scientific research and government studies and reports of the kind discussed in Chapter 2, prominent environmental accidents, media coverage of environmental events, and the promotional activities of environmental advocacy groups and their adversaries.

In one effort to explain the rise and fall of issues on both the larger societal agenda and what is usually called the institutional or governmental agenda, John Kingdon (1995) proposed an intriguing model. It is useful for understanding how environmental problems come to be objects of public concern or not, how they gain or fail to gain the attention of public officials, and how environmental policy takes the form it does. It can also serve as a guide to developing political strategies for influencing the future development of environmental policy. In addition, it provides some concepts that are helpful for reviewing, if only briefly, the history of environmentalism and environmental policy in the United States, the subject of Chapter 4.

Problems, Policies, and Politics   Kingdon argues that three separate but interdependent "streams" of activities (related to problems, politics, and policies) flow continuously through the political system. They sometimes converge, with the assistance of policy entrepreneurs or political leaders, and create windows of opportunities for policy development. Much of this activity occurs within policy communities of specialists and interested parties, such as the environmental and industry groups that focus on air and water pollution, pesticide use, energy use, or population issues.

Kingdon defines the agenda as "the list of subjects or problems to which government officials, and people outside of government closely associated with those officials, are paying some serious attention at any given time" (1995, 3). The governmental agenda may be influenced by the larger societal agenda, the problems that most concern people, as would be expected in a democracy when the public is mobilized around salient issues. It may also be shaped by the diffusion of ideas among policy communities (or policy elites) or by a change in the political climate. Good examples of the latter include the election of President Ronald Reagan in 1980, which inaugurated an unprecedented period of antienvironmental rhetoric and action and the Republican capture of the House of Representatives in the 1994 elections for the first time in 40 years. The latter began another round of antienvironmental policy actions, this time from Capitol Hill. The way in which the government's agenda is set depends on the flow of those problem, policy, and politics streams.

The *problem stream* influences the agenda by providing data about the state of environmental conditions and trends, as reviewed in Chapter 2. The information may come from government reports and program evaluations such as EPA studies of air or water quality, assessments by the National Academy of Sciences and other scientific bodies, reports by presidential commissions and task forces, and studies sponsored by environmental groups, industry, and others. The data and assessments circulate among policy specialists, affecting their perceptions and understanding of the problems regardless of whether or not they produce any immediate effects on policy decisions.

The problem stream is also affected by other variables such as environmental crises or disasters, technological developments, and ecological changes. Accidents such as the chemical plant explosion at Bhopal, India, in 1984, the Exxon *Valdez* oil spill off Alaska in 1989, and the Chernobyl nuclear reactor disaster in Ukraine in 1986 often receive extensive media coverage. Such reporting may prompt people to pay greater attention to the problems of dangerous chemicals, transportation of oil in vulnerable supertankers, and potential nuclear power plant accidents. Catalytic or focusing events like these accidents increase the credibility of studies and reports that document the environmental problem at issue, and they help ensure they will be read and debated and thus influence policy decisions (Birkland 1997).

The *policy stream* concerns what might be done about environmental problems. Proposals are developed by analysts, academics, legislators, staffers, and other policy actors, as noted earlier. These proposals are floated as trial balloons and become the objects of political speeches, legislative hearings, and task forces. They get tested by the policy community for technical acceptability and political and economic feasibility. They are endorsed or rejected, revised, and combined in new ways, somewhat like a process of biological natural selection.

Ideas that are inconsistent with the current political mood may be dropped from consideration and relegated to the policy back burner for warming or incubation until the climate improves. Such was the fate in the early 1990s of proposed stiff carbon taxes to discourage consumption of fossil fuels. Conventional policy alternatives such as "command and control" regulation may drop from favor, as they did during the 1990s and early 2000s, while other ideas, such as market-based incentives, public–private partnerships, and collaborative decision making, are viewed more positively. In this way, a short list of acceptable policy alternatives emerges at any given time, reflecting the prevailing sense of what kinds of government activity are deemed to be legitimate.

The language used and symbols evoked in these debates can make the difference between acceptance and rejection (Cantrill and Oravec 1996; Edelman 1964). This is sometimes called the *framing* of issues or, in the popular press, the "spinning" of issues. For instance, policy actors may avoid population "control" policies as coercive while they embrace voluntary family planning as consistent with cultural values of individual choice. Similarly, policymakers may reject higher fuel efficiency standards for automobiles because they think about them as an extension of government regulation, which they dislike. They might be more sympathetic if such standards were linked with a goal they support, such as reduced reliance on imported oil or a stronger economy. Some of the harshest criticism of such issue framing has been directed at large coal and oil companies, such as ExxonMobil, for their persistent attempts to convince the public and policymakers that global climate change is not really a problem and no government action is needed (Gelbspan 2004; Layzer 2007).

The political game of issue framing can be seen in almost every environmental and energy dispute of recent years. Consider the long-standing debate over drilling for oil in the Arctic National Wildlife Refuge (ANWR). To environmentalists the core issue was one of protecting a pristine wildlife refuge, and they emphasized energy conservation as an alternative to drilling in ANWR. To pro-drilling forces, it was a matter of exploiting a domestic source of energy to meet rising demand for oil. The latter group, which included the Bush administration, knew that drilling in ANWR would be more acceptable to the American public if it were framed as a national security need—a way to increase domestic production of oil. Among other strategies, supporters in Congress attached an ANRW bill to a defense spending measure to make the connection clear. The vote margins in Congress were extremely close, and any advantage of this kind was viewed as important (Bosso and Guber 2007; Kraft 2006).

Finally, the *politics stream* refers to the political climate or national mood as revealed in public opinion surveys, election results (particularly a change in presidential administrations), and the activities and strength of competing interest groups. The political mood is never easy to decipher, and sometimes judgments are well off the mark, as was the case with the reputed Reagan election mandate in 1980. Many Reagan supporters and political analysts assumed that the public became more conservative on environmental issues during the 1980s. The evidence suggests that this assessment was seriously in error (Dunlap 1987; Kraft 1984). Much the same political misjudgment characterized the Republican electoral victory of 1994 and the subsequent congressional efforts to cut environmental program budgets and enforcement actions. That is why the Clinton administration and environmentalists were able to block most of those initiatives. Once publicized, it became evident that little public support existed for such weakening of environmental policy (Bosso and Guber 2006). Most elected officials develop a well-honed ability to detect important shifts in public attitudes, at least in their own constituencies. Thus environmentalists and other advocacy groups try to mobilize the public around their issues by stimulating a sense of public outrage over existing problems or actions by policymakers with which they disagree. It has often been a highly effective political strategy.

Policy Entrepreneurs and Policy Change   Environmental policy entrepreneurs—leaders inside and outside of government who devote themselves to the issues and their advancement—often help bring these three streams together. By doing so they facilitate the process of policy change. Normally the three streams of activities (problems, policy ideas, and politics) flow through the political system independently; that is, each is affected differently and unrelated to the others. But sometimes these activities come together, or, to use the water metaphor, the streams combine into a river of action; at that time public policy breakthroughs can occur. Often this is no accident. The entrepreneurs act when they see windows of opportunity open, as they do when a major accident or crisis occurs or at the beginning of a new presidential administration. For example, after more than 10 years of congressional inaction on oil spill legislation, the Exxon *Valdez* spill prompted Congress to enact the Oil Pollution Act of 1990 (Birkland 1997).[4] It required companies to submit oil spill contingency plans to the Coast Guard and the EPA and to train their employees in oil spill response. Similarly, enactment of the Superfund reauthorization act of 1986 and its section creating the public's right to know about toxic chemicals in their communities was a direct result of the disastrous chemical plant accident in Bhopal, India. The accident raised fears of the possibility that similar accidents and loss of life might occur in the United States (Hadden 1989). The experience with Bhopal and the subsequent enactment of "right-to-know" policies such as the Superfund Amendments and Reauthorization Act (SARA) of 1986 stimulated many related enactments of information disclosure policies, including the 1996 revision of the Safe Drinking Water Act discussed in Chapter 2.

Policy entrepreneurs are prepared to take advantage of the opportunities created by such accidents and other focusing events. In the meantime, they continue to stimulate interest in the problems, educate both the public and policymakers, circulate new studies, and otherwise "incubate" the issues; that is, they keep them warm until they are ready to be hatched, when the political climate is favorable. Entrepreneurs are not equal in their ability to perform those essential tasks. Environmental and other public interest groups have greatly increased their political clout since the 1960s. Nonetheless, according to several recent surveys, they still lack the financial and other resources common among business and industry groups (Bosso 2005; Furlong 1997; Kraft and Kamieniecki 2007; Schlozman and Tierney 1986).

This kind of convergence of the three streams helps explain some peculiar patterns of environmental attention and inattention. Energy issues, for example, were at the top of the political agenda in the late 1970s as President Jimmy Carter sought (but largely failed) to enact a comprehensive national energy policy. Carter did much to promote energy conservation and efficiency, symbolized by placing solar panels on the roof of the White House. Energy issues, however, disappeared from sight in the 1980s as the White House and members of Congress lost interest in the subject when energy prices fell and public concern dissipated. The Reagan administration had the Carter solar panels removed, a fitting indicator of the administration's view that energy problems required no government intervention in the marketplace beyond the conventional subsidies for nuclear energy and fossil fuels that had existed for years (see Chapter 6).

Attention to energy issues increased again in 1988 as a hot, dry summer stirred fears of global warming. That concern was aided by the activism of scientists such as James E. Hansen, director of Goddard Institute for Space Studies of the National Aeronautics and Space Administration (NASA), and the noted climatologist Stephen Schneider. They spoke out frequently (unusual for scientists) about the risks of climate change and the need for governmental action. By 2001 national concern over a short-term energy crisis in California and weaknesses in the electric power grid in the East led to a Bush administration proposal for a national energy policy that focused heavily on increasing energy supplies. After four years of intense debate and negotiation in Congress, parts of it were finally approved in 2005 amid concern about high energy costs.

Policy Formulation

The formulation of environmental policy involves the development of proposed courses of action to resolve the problem identified. It often involves the use of scientific research on the causes and consequences of environmental problems, including projections of future trends, such as rising energy use or population growth. Typically, formulation includes analysis of the goals of public policy (such as improved energy efficiency) and various policy options to reach them (e.g., regulation or use of market incentives). Ordinarily, such assessment of policy options includes consideration of economic, technical, political, administrative, social, ethical, and other issues.

Increasingly, public policy scholars have underscored the importance of policy design in selecting a course of action that is likely to be successful. That means careful assessment of the characteristics of target populations (i.e., the groups at which policy actions are directed, such as chemical manufacturers, automobile companies, or the general public) as well as trying to figure out what policy tools or mechanisms will likely bring about the intended behavior. For example, if a state wanted to encourage energy conservation among the public, it would want to know whether that goal can best be achieved through public education campaigns or provision of financial incentives (Schneider and Ingram 1990, 1997). In 2001 California found that financial incentives worked remarkably well as substantial energy conservation among the public helped avert an energy crisis.[5]

A multiplicity of policy actors play a role in policy formulation, from environmental and business groups to think tank policy analysts and formal policymakers and their staffs in legislatures and executive offices (of the president, governors, county executives, mayors, and city managers). Even the courts get involved as they attempt to resolve environmental disputes by issuing legally binding policy decisions (Vig and Kraft 2006). Given the technical nature of policy action on climate change, protection of biodiversity, or pollution control, it is not surprising that the scientific community (both within and outside of government agencies) is often important as well, even if not as active as many scientists would like to see (Harrison and Bryner 2004; Lubchenco 1998). As noted in Chapter 1, scientists also sometimes protest that politicians give their views insufficient weight. This complaint was common during the George W. Bush administration when national scientific groups, including many Nobel Prize winners, complained that the president was ignoring or distorting science on many environmental issues (Andrews 2006; Rosenbaum 2006).[6]

International policy actors are also important in U.S. environmental policy decisions (Chasek, Downie, and Brown 2006; DeSombre 2000). U.S. policymakers are pressured by their European allies on issues ranging from climate change to population assistance policies. In the early 2000s, for instance, European Union leaders were highly critical of the U.S. refusal to support the Kyoto Protocol on climate change (Hempel 2006). International nongovernmental organizations (NGOs), which number in the tens of thousands, similarly try to influence press coverage of environmental issues such as energy use, biodiversity protection, and agricultural subsidies, and thereby alter American public opinion. Especially in formulating international environmental policy positions, U.S. policymakers are likely to hear from a diversity of multinational corporations, environmentalists, scientific organizations, and officials at the leading international organizations, such as the World Bank and the United Nations Development Programme (Axelrod, Downie, and Vig 2005; Vig and Faure 2004).

Even under the best of circumstances, the various actors involved in environmental policymaking are rarely equal in their political resources or influence, as noted earlier. The business community, for example, has far more resources for lobbying legislators and administrative agencies than do environmental groups. Indeed, some theorists worry that policymaking can be dominated by one set of interests or another (the business community or environmentalists) and thus distort the nation's ability to devise effective and equitable environmental policies (Dryzek 1987, 2005; Kraft and Kamieniecki 2007, Chap. 1; Lindblom and Woodhouse 1993).

A related issue is the extent of influence by technical experts such as environmental scientists and engineers in policy formulation. Some theorists worry that such specialists may dominate the policy-making process, creating a kind of technocratic decision making that can drive out democracy (Fischer 1990; Sclove 1995). Such concerns are widely shared, sparking interest in the various ways in which the public might participate in environmental decisions, from the local to the international level (Baber and Bartlett 2005; Beierle and Cayford 2002; Ingram and Smith 1993). On the other side of this dispute, at least some environmental theorists have warned of the risks of democracy when the public is not well informed on the issues or stoutly resists policy actions that arguably are in its own interests. These theorists tend to prefer an even greater role for scientists and experts in the belief that they can devise technically superior public policies (Ophuls and Boyan 1992).

Policy analysts and other experts both within the government and outside clearly do play a significant role in policy formulation. Indeed, ad hoc policy task forces or commissions may do much of the work before a proposal is modified and formally endorsed by elected officials. Yet unlike western European nations, in the U.S. system elected officials and their appointed top-level assistants, rather than permanent professional staff in the agencies, make the final policy decisions. The National Energy Strategy that President George H. W. Bush proposed to Congress in early 1991, for example, followed 18 months of study by a policy task force in the Department of Energy (DOE). The task force held extensive public hearings, consulted closely with other federal agencies, and ultimately endorsed strong energy conservation initiatives as a core element in its recommendations. In this case, the Bush White House significantly modified the energy strategy before sending it to Capitol Hill. In particular, Bush's top economic and political advisers persuaded the president to eliminate virtually all the important energy conservation proposals.

An interesting contrast is provided by the secretive energy task force established by President George W. Bush at the beginning of his administration in 2001. Vice President Dick Cheney was put in charge of the national energy task force, which was coordinated by Secretary of Energy Spencer Abraham. Considerable controversy developed over the emphasis the task force gave to the views of energy industry leaders, who in many cases were also large contributors to the Bush-Cheney election campaign. Democrats in Congress tried repeatedly, but largely unsuccessfully, to force the vice president to reveal the names of the energy officials who were consulted. In an unprecedented action, the investigative arm of Congress, the Government Accountability Office, even sued the administration to try to get the information. Based on a review of the energy secretary's calendar, however, the *New York Times* concluded that he met with more than 100 energy industry officials in preparing the administration's energy report but not with any representatives of environmental or consumer organizations.[7] The task force report and the president's recommendations to Congress were highly favorable to the energy industry. But the Bush White House maintained the energy report was the product of a balanced process that solicited advice from a diversity of interests.

Comprehensive environmental policy analysis would seem a prerequisite for policy formulation. Yet, as is common in the U.S. policy-making process and illustrated by the work of the Bush energy task force, such analysis faces substantial intellectual, institutional, and political barriers (Bartlett 1990). It is hard to engage in comprehensive analysis when the requisite information is not always available, the process may be hindered by competition among different government agencies and offices, and political pressures from affected interest groups may push the process toward a more narrow examination of the issues than might be desirable. The result is that policy formulation typically proceeds incrementally, slowly and in small steps.

Policy Legitimation

Policy legitimation is usually defined as giving legal force to decisions, or authorizing or justifying policy action, such as through a majority vote in a legislature or a formal bureaucratic or judicial decision (Anderson 2006; Jones 1984). It also includes the legitimacy of action taken (i.e., whether it is viewed as a proper exercise of governmental authority) and its broad acceptability to certain publics. Legitimacy or acceptability can flow from several conditions. The action is consistent with constitutional or statutory specifications, or it is compatible with U.S. political culture and values, and it has demonstrable popular support. It may also be approved through a decision-making process where relevant publics and policy officials interact extensively. That interaction would be expected to involve an elaborate debate on the issues and some effort to resolve difference among the policy actors. Of course, there is always a chance that some legitimate interests (e.g., the poor or minority groups) may be excluded from the decision-making process, either intentionally or because they lack the time, expertise, knowledge of the opportunities, or adequate finances to participate.

Public participation is a significant part of policymaking and particularly important for the policy legitimation stage. From the national to the local levels, such participation often means that environmental interest groups, and those who oppose them, try to speak for the public, or at least for their members, within legislative and bureaucratic settings. Such action might involve lobbying for the passage of new laws or trying to affect their implementation by influencing decisions within agencies such as the EPA or the Interior Department, a state environmental protection agency, or a local land use planning agency (Kraft and Kamieniecki 2007).

At local and regional levels, public involvement may be far more direct and extensive, with citizens taking part in public meetings and hearings, sitting on task forces and planning groups, and working directly with policymakers to ensure that decisions reflect their concerns (John 2004; Meadowcroft 2004; Sabatier et al. 2005; Weber 2003). The growth of the sustainable communities movement is a case in point. It has provided citizens in hundreds of communities nationwide the opportunity to affect significant local decisions on transportation, land use, urban sprawl, and the quality of life (John and Mlay 1999; Mazmanian and Kraft 1999; Portney 2003).

The mere passage of legislation or adoption of a regulation at any level of government is no guarantee that policy legitimation has occurred. In some cases, such as the National Environmental Policy Act (NEPA), legislation may be enacted with little serious consideration of the likely effects. NEPA sailed through the House and Senate in 1969 with virtually no opposition and few members asking what difference the new law actually would make; this is remarkable in light of how controversial the act later became. Much the same was true of the demanding Clean Air Act Amendments of 1970 (Jones 1975). Concern over costs and other impacts of environmental policies has been so great in recent years, however, that such oversight is far less likely to occur today; yet it still happens on occasion. For instance, rapid action by Congress in 1995 on the Contract with America provided few opportunities to consider its effects on the environment and public well-being (Kraft 2006).

Like policies that are carelessly formulated (e.g., using poor data, unreasonable assumptions, or questionable forecasting), policies adopted or changed without legitimation run some important risks. They may fail because of technical misjudgments or inaccurate appraisals of public acceptability. Such was the fate of the Nuclear Waste

Policy Act of 1982. Congressional proponents of the act seriously misjudged the public's willingness to accept nuclear waste repositories and its trust and confidence in the Department of Energy, the bureaucracy in charge of the program (Flynn et al. 1995; Kraft 2000). Similar criticisms have been directed at the Endangered Species Act for failing to consider the effect on property owners and at the Superfund program for insufficient attention to its economic costs and the inequities of its legal liability provisions. As a result, all three of these programs have been adversely affected and have achieved much less than they otherwise might have. Risks of policy failure or ineffectiveness of this kind may be minimized by ensuring participation by all key interests ("stakeholders" in government reports), including citizens, opportunities for careful review of policy proposals, and maintenance of political accountability for decision makers.

Policy Implementation

Policy implementation refers to activities directed toward putting programs into effect. These activities include interpretation of statutory language, organization of bureaucratic offices and efforts, provision of sufficient resources (e.g., money, staff, and expertise), and the details of administration such as provision of benefits, enforcement of environmental regulations, and monitoring of compliance. Those activities occur at all levels in the United States—federal, state, and local—as well as internationally. Most federal environmental protection policies are implemented routinely at the state level through delegation of authority to the states equipped to assume the responsibility (Rabe 2006; Ringquist 1993; Scheberle 2004).

Implementation is rarely automatic, however, and it involves more than a series of technical and legal decisions by bureaucratic officials. It is deeply affected by political judgments about statutory obligations, priorities for action, provision of resources, and selection of implementation tools, such as the imposition of fines and other penalties. For example, the Bush administration, like the Reagan administration before it, focused heavily on quietly rewriting administrative rules and regulations to achieve environmental policy goals that would have been unattainable had it sought congressional approval; debate in Congress would have been more visible and aroused far more opposition (Vig 2006).[8] Implementation is also influenced by the responses or expected responses of target groups and other publics. Variables such as the commitment and administrative skills of public officials in charge of the program make a difference as well (Mazmanian and Sabatier 1983). In later chapters I explore all these issues in detail as they apply to the major environmental protection and natural resource policies and their implementation by both federal and state bureaucracies.

Policy and Program Evaluation

Once implemented, analysts and policymakers need to ask whether environmental policies and programs are working well or not. This is usually taken to mean the extent to which they are achieving their goals and objectives. Policies also may be judged against other standards, such as the extent of public involvement, fairness or equity in environmental enforcement actions, or efficiency in the use of resources. Despite extensive criticism directed at environmental programs over the past several decades, formal evaluation of this kind is surprisingly rare. It is also not easy to do. Yet there is little question that we will see far more evaluations in the future. The costs and effects of environmental policies are creating new demands for better appraisal of how well the policies are working and whether alternative approaches might work better (Coglianese and Bennear 2005; Morgenstern and Portney 2004; Portney and Stavins 2000).

Environmental policies may be evaluated in several different ways, but the most common is to ask whether they produce the expected outcomes. For example, does the Clean Air Act result in cleaner air? Does the Endangered Species Act save threatened and endangered species and habitats? Evaluations may be rigorous attempts to measure and analyze specific program outcomes and other effects. As is the case with other public policies, however, they may also be far less systematic assessments by congressional committees, internal agency review bodies, or environmental and industry interest groups (Anderson 2006). As is true of all stages in the policy cycle, political pressures and judgments affect whether, and to what extent, policymakers consider such information when they decide to continue or alter environmental policies and programs.

Policy Change

The last stage in the cycle is policy change. Particularly if the results of public policies are not satisfactory, they may be revised in an attempt to make them more successful, or they may be terminated or canceled. Revision may involve establishing new policy goals, granting different authority to an agency, spending more money on the program, using new approaches (such as market-based incentives), or setting new priorities for implementation. Termination itself is a rare form of policy change, but environmentalists and many others have suggested taking exactly this action for some natural resource policies that they view as wasteful and harmful to the environment. Examples include some western land and water use policies that are nonetheless stoutly defended by politically powerful constituencies that benefit from their continuation; these include ranchers, farmers, miners, and logging interests (Myers and Kent 2001; Roodman 1996, 1997). By the same token, many business organizations have argued that some environmental protection policies do more harm than good (Superfund is often mentioned, as are some sections of the Clean Air Act) and should be terminated.

Although analytically distinct and logically arranged, this sequence of activities in the policy process may follow a different order, the stages may overlap one another, and the actions may take place in more than one institutional setting—for example, at the state level. As discussed later, state governments are intimately involved in implementing federal environmental protection policies. They are often well ahead of the federal government in policy developments. A notable example is California's adoption in 2002 of state regulations on greenhouse gas emissions by automobiles, the first such effort in the nation.[9]

As should be clear from the preceding discussion, the overall policy process is also highly dynamic. It can change greatly over time as specific policy actors come and go, new data and arguments are advanced, problems are defined and redefined, and new policy solutions, such as market incentives and public education, are put forth and judged. That should be good news to environmental activists as well as to their opponents. The process of policymaking never really ends. Defeat in one venue or at one time (e.g., in Congress in the early 2000s) may mean that the battle is fought again at a later time or that it shifts to a different location, such as the states.

The Republican victory in the 2004 congressional elections, for instance, pushed even more environmental policymaking to the state and local level as gridlock prevailed in Washington. Environmentalists and their adversaries found that the policy process at the state and local level better suited their purposes than focusing exclusively on Washington (Brick and Cawley 1996; Cawley 1993; Rabe 2004). The key players in the environmental policy game understand this pattern well and adjust their strategies accordingly. These topics are covered more fully later in the chapter.

Box 3.1 highlights key sources of information about institutions and policy actors that are influential in environmental policy processes. These include Web site references for the most significant departments and agencies of the federal government, the 50 states, and policy think tanks that are often active on environmental policy issues.

BOX 3.1
Finding Information About Environmental Policymaking on the Web

Government Web sites provide a vast quantity of environmental data, such as EPA reports on air and water quality and toxic substances and Fish and Wildlife Service accounts of threatened and endangered species. Similarly, both government and nongovernmental Web sites are essential sources for information about current environmental policies and programs, proposed policies and evaluations of them, and the process of policy development and implementation. These sites are cited throughout the text as major policies and their implementing agencies are discussed. Some of the most general and useful portals to those sites are listed here.

FEDERAL EXECUTIVE AGENCIES AND THE LEGISLATIVE BRANCH

The best Web portal for access to the range of federal environmental agencies and programs and Congress is FirstGov: www.firstgov.gov. Either programs or agencies are easily located. Among the leading federal government sites are the following:

- www.epa.gov (U.S. Environmental Protection Agency)
- www.doi.gov (U.S. Department of the Interior)
- www.energy.gov (U.S. Department of Energy)
- www.usda.gov (U.S. Department of Agriculture)
- www.nrc.gov (U.S. Nuclear Regulatory Commission)
- www.whitehouse.gov/ceq (Council on Environmental Quality)
- http://thomas.loc.gov (the official portal for the U.S. Congress)
- www.gao.gov (U.S. Government Accountability Office)

FEDERAL COURTS

Information about the courts can be found at www.uscourts.gov. The site has links to the Supreme Court, the courts of appeals, and the district courts as well as to the administrative offices that help run the court system. The Supreme Court page (www.supremecourtus.gov) offers access to details about the Court's docket, or

(Continued)

cases up for review, the current schedule of cases being heard, oral arguments made before the Court and briefs submitted, Supreme Court rulings, and the full text of opinions.

STATE AND LOCAL GOVERNMENTS

The Web site for the Council of State Governments (www.csg.org) provides links to all 50 state government home pages, which in turn have links to the major policy areas, including environmental protection and natural resources. The council also has extensive news reports on policy activities within the states, such as environmental policy innovation. Another top site is the Environmental Council of the States (www.ecos.org), a national and nonprofit organization of state and territorial environmental administrators that collects invaluable state data on policy actions, including environmental innovations, delegation of national authority to the states, spending and regulatory enforcement actions, and state agency organization.

INTEREST GROUPS

Major interest groups provide a variety of pertinent policy information, from news accounts of policy developments to studies and reports on environmental issues. A comprehensive list of both environmental groups and their adversaries is provided in Table 4.3 in Chapter 4.

POLICY RESEARCH GROUPS

Among the leading sites for policy analysis groups (think tanks) active on environmental policy are the following:

- www.rff.org (Resources for the Future)
- www.brook.edu (Brookings Institution)
- www.ucsusa.org (Union of Concerned Scientists)
- www.wri.org (World Resources Institute)
- www.worldwatch.org (Worldwatch Institute)
- www.aei.org (American Enterprise Institute)
- www.heritage.org (Heritage Foundation)
- www.cato.org (Cato Institute)
- www.cei.org (Competitive Enterprise Institute)

■ PATTERNS IN ENVIRONMENTAL POLICYMAKING

A general description of the policy-making process such as the preceding conveys little of the high stakes involved in environmental policy decisions. It also can seem to miss the role of powerful interest groups and individuals, the opportunities for citizen influence, and the unpredictability of the policy results. Only by examining particular environmental issues and their politics can these factors be fully appreciated. We will see more of this in later chapters. The policy-making process also may strike some as seriously deficient. It is true that policymaking in the U.S. political system is almost never an orderly or tidy process. Indeed, Dean Mann has argued that the outcomes of the process fall well short of conventional models of problem solving in part because of the character of U.S. politics:

> That the politics of environmental policymaking is a process of dramatic advances, incomplete movement in the "right" direction, frequent and partial retrogression, sometimes illogical and contradictory combinations of policies, and often excessive cost should come as no surprise to students of American politics. (Mann 1986, 4)

As might be expected, however, the pattern of policymaking varies significantly from one problem area to another. This means that the overall governmental structure is not the only factor that matters. The nature of the issue also is important. The politics of western water use, for example, is quite different from the politics of controlling toxic chemicals, which in turn has little to do with national energy policymaking. What else makes a difference? Ingram and Mann (1983) argue that the types of environmental policies adopted, such as regulatory or distributive policy, reflect variables such as the structure of demand (e.g., conflict or consensus among interest groups), the structure of decision making (e.g., integrated or fragmented government institutions), and the structure of impacts (e.g., the actual effects on society of the policies, including costs and other burdens and on whom they fall). We review many examples later in the text.

Other important variables that help explain why we get the environmental and natural resource policies we do include the perception of policy impacts, particularly the concentration or dispersal of costs and benefits. The distribution of costs and benefits can strongly affect the incentives that are created for different actors to participate in the policy-making process (Wilson 1980). Narrow economic interests (e.g., automobile manufacturers, ranchers, loggers, and mining companies) adversely affected by proposed environmental policies, for example, have a good reason to organize and fight them, and they are often successful in doing so (Kraft and Kamieniecki 2007). The public receiving the broadly dispersed benefits of environmental protection, however, is not usually so stimulated to rise in their defense. What James Q. Wilson calls "entrepreneurial politics" may alter the usual logic of collective action, where the public has little incentive to organize or actively support actions that benefit society as a whole (Moe 1980; Olson 1971). Policy entrepreneurs in environmental groups and Congress mobilize latent public sentiment on the issues, capitalize on well-publicized crises and other catalytic events, attack their opponents for endangering the public's welfare, and associate proposed legislation with widely shared values (e.g., clean air and public health). This kind of politics helps explain how the nation came to adopt policies such as the Clean Air Act and Superfund.

Quite a different situation exists when the benefits of environmental, energy, or resource policies flow to narrow economic interests (e.g., oil and natural gas interests, the nuclear power industry, the highway construction industry, ranchers, miners, loggers, or sugarcane growers in Florida) and the costs are borne by the public at large. Here the beneficiaries are likely to organize and lobby fiercely to protect their interests, whereas environmental groups find it hard to mobilize the general public. Most of us are likely to consider such natural resource subsidies or "giveaways" to such economic interests to be improper or unfair. Yet, typically, these policies are also low-salience issues for us, as they are for the nation's media. The same is true for most policymakers not directly affected by the programs. Hence the majority of us do little about the situation, allowing the beneficiaries to maintain their preferred status. Opponents of such programs may mount campaigns against what they term "corporate welfare" (Myers and Kent 2001; Roodman 1996), but they face significant political obstacles to success. Thus whether we get what Wilson calls "client politics" under such circumstances depends on how visible the policies are and the extent to which the public and environmental groups are able to challenge the beneficiaries effectively.[10] The case of oil and natural gas profits discussed early in the chapter is a good example of this kind of client politics.

As these various examples illustrate, the salience and complexity of the issues and the degree of conflict that exists over them are important factors in shaping policy outcomes (Gormley 1989). These qualities affect whether the public and policymakers take a strong interest and choose to get involved or not. Elected officials may prefer not to engage complex issues of low salience and high conflict because they consume valuable time to acquire the necessary expertise. There also are few political benefits given the low visibility of the issues and significant political risks because of conflict among opposing interests. Thus politicians may ignore the issues altogether or allow those with expertise and strong interest in the outcome to dominate the process.

CHARACTERISTICS OF U.S. GOVERNMENT AND POLITICS

Some unique characteristics of the U.S. political system shape the policy process outlined here and the environmental policies that emerge from it.[11] Formal institutional structures, rules, and procedures are never neutral in their effects. Some groups gain advantages from certain institutional arrangements while others may lose. One of the most persistent concerns, identified long ago by the political scientist E. E. Schattschneider (1960), is that some ideas and some groups may be excluded from the decision-making process as a result. For example, poor and minority groups may have little to say about the location of polluting factories that can affect their health (Ringquist 2006). Another example is that efforts to limit uncontrolled urban growth or sprawl could gain no footing for years; they were kept off the agenda in many cities (Portney 2003). Generalizing about such phenomena, Schattschneider said that all organizations "have a bias in favor of the exploitation of some kinds of conflict and the suppression of others because *organization is the mobilization of bias.* Some issues are organized into politics and others are organized out" (p. 71; emphasis in original). We study the details of government institutions in part because they channel political conflict and thus affect the policy process and its results.

Constitutional and Political Features

The U.S. Constitution sets out the basic governmental structure and establishes an array of individual rights that have been largely unchanged for well over 200 years. Government authority is divided among the three branches of the federal government and shared with the 50 states and some 80,000 local units of government. The logic of the tripartite arrangement of the federal government was to limit its authority through creation of separate and countervailing powers in each branch and to protect individual rights.

Additional guarantees of freedom for individuals (and corporations) were pro-vided in various sections of the Constitution. Most notable is the due process clause of the Fifth Amendment, which puts a premium on the protection of property rights and thereby creates significant barriers to governmental action.[12] Decentralization of authority to the states likewise reflected public distrust of the national government in the late eighteenth century and a preference for local autonomy. At that time, the na-tion's small population of 4 million lived largely in small towns and rural areas, and the activities of the federal government were minuscule compared with its present size and scope of responsibilities. Yet the constraints placed on government authority to act, majority rule, and prompt policy development continue today.

Other constitutional dictates and political influences also have important implica-tions for environmental policy. They include staggered terms of office for the presi-dent, senators, and representatives, which tend to make members of Congress inde-pendent of the White House. That motivation is reinforced by the geographic basis of representation and an electoral process that induces members to pay more attention to local and regional interests directly related to their reelection than to the national concerns that preoccupy presidents and executive branch officials. To this inherent legislative parochialism, we can add a preoccupation with individual political goals. Members of Congress assumed almost complete responsibility for their own political fundraising and reelection campaigns as political parties weakened and the number and political influence of narrowly focused interest groups surged. The interest group "explosion" from the 1970s to the present has severely eroded the broader and more integrative forces of political parties and the presidency (Berry 1996).

Competition between the two major parties also inhibits coalition building and the development of comprehensive and coordinated environmental policies. An ex-tensive scholarly literature confirms a strong association between partisanship and en-vironmental policy support among elected officials. Democrats are far more support-ive of environmental protection policy than are Republicans (Calvert 1989). The differences are clearly evident in congressional voting scores compiled by the League of Conservation Voters (LCV) and in most years are also seen in national party plat-forms. The second session of the 108th Congress (2003–2004) was typical of recent years. During 2004 Senate Democrats averaged 85 percent support for the positions the league and the environmental community favored. Senate Republicans averaged 8 percent. In the House, Democrats averaged 86 percent, and Republicans 10 percent. Of course, there are members of each party who are more or less "green" in their voting than the averages, but the difference between the parties is still striking. A clear trend can also be discerned over time. Analysis of LCV scores over nearly 30 years indicates that the two parties show increasing divergence from the early 1970s through the late 1990s. On average they have differed by nearly 25 points on a 100-point scale. The differences grew during the 1980s and 1990s and reached the wide gap evident in the scores for the 108th Congress.[13]

Institutional Fragmentation and Policy Stalemate

These formal constitutional and informal political forces have led some scholars to question whether the U.S. government is capable of responding in a timely and co-herent way to environmental challenges (Ophuls and Boyan 1992). There is good reason to be concerned. Constitutionally created checks and balances may constrain abuses of authority by either Congress or the president, but they also can lead to policy stalemate or gridlock, that is, where environmental problems cannot be addressed quickly or adequately. Sometimes the reason is a lack of public consensus on the issue, which seems to be the case with climate change (Bosso and Guber 2006). Sometimes it can be found in the intense competition among organized interest groups, and sometimes in the inability of the two major parties to reach agreement. But the structure of government, such as fragmentation of authority within Congress and the executive branch, is also a contributing cause of policy inaction, even when solid scientific evidence is available about the severity of the problem (Kraft 2006).

Dispersal of Power in Congress   The congressional committee system is a good example of the tendency to fragment authority in the U.S. political system and to make policymaking difficult. Most of the policymaking in Congress takes place in the committees, not on the floor of the House or Senate. But no single committee on the environment exists in either the House or Senate. Rather, seven major committees in the House and five in the Senate are responsible for different aspects of environmental policy, as shown in Table 3.2. Each of these committees also has several semiautonomous subcommittees that can be involved. Sometimes the committees work cooperatively, especially in the House when the party leadership favors action (Davidson and Oleszek 2006). Yet sometimes they disagree on what course of action is best. Moreover, a committee that creates or authorizes government programs (such as Superfund and the Endangered Species Act) may find that the appropriations committees choose to supply less money than needed to run them effectively.

In some respects, the dispersal of power in Congress is even greater than suggested by looking only at the activities of the major environmental committees. For example, one study of the EPA found that 13 committees and 31 subcommittees in the 103rd Congress had jurisdiction over some portion of the agency's activities (National Academy of Public Administration 1995). Different committees also have quite varied agendas, and some are more supportive of the EPA's activities than others. One consequence of this fragmentation of authority is that the agency is subject to unclear and inconsistent instruction from Congress about the preferred direction of environmental policy. Combined with the inability of Congress to revise the major statutes or to set priorities among programs, the EPA is therefore limited in what it can do to reform environmental policy (Durant, Fiorino, and O'Leary 2004; Rosenbaum 2006).

The committee system changes from time to time but with little real alteration in its dispersal of power. Upon winning control of the House in 1995, for example, the Republican Party eliminated one environmental committee, Merchant Marine and Fisheries, and slightly altered the jurisdictions (and names) of several others. In the 104th Congress, power was also somewhat more concentrated in the party leadership, particularly under Speaker of the House Newt Gingrich (R-Georgia); committees played a less independent role. That made it easier for the majority party to influence the flow of legislation, especially bills related to the party's Contract with America agenda. This legislation included the Unfunded Mandates Reform Act of 1995, bills to reform the Clean Water Act, and various regulatory reform measures (Davidson and Oleszek 2006; Kraft 2006). By the 106th Congress, however, under Speaker Dennis Hastert (R-Illinois), power in the House became decentralized once

TABLE 3.2

Major Congressional Committees with Environmental Responsibilities

Committee	Environmental Policy Jurisdiction
House of Representatives	
Agriculture	Agriculture, forestry, pesticides and food safety, soil conservation.
Appropriations[a]	Appropriations for all programs.
Energy and Commerce	All energy sources, the Department of Energy and the Federal Energy Regulatory Commission, nuclear energy industry and nuclear waste, air pollution, safe drinking water, pesticide control, Superfund and hazardous waste disposal, toxic substances control.
Resources	Public lands and natural resources; mineral resources on public lands; national parks, forests, and wilderness areas; fisheries and wildlife; coastal zone management; Geological Survey.
Science	Environmental research and development; energy research and development; research in national laboratories; NASA, National Weather Service, and National Science Foundation.
Transportation and Infrastructure	Transportation, including civil aviation, railroads, water transportation, and transportation infrastructure; water resources and the environment.
Senate	
Agriculture, Nutrition and Forestry	Agriculture, soil conservation and groundwater, forestry, nutrition, pesticides, food safety.
Appropriations[a]	Appropriations for all programs.
Commerce, Science and Transportation	Interstate commerce and transportation; coastal zone management; marine fisheries; oceans, weather, and atmospheric activities; surface transportation.
Energy and Natural Resources	Energy policy; mines, mining, and minerals; national parks and recreation areas; wilderness areas; wild and scenic rivers; public lands and forests.
Environment and Public Works	Environmental policy in general; air, water, and noise pollution; safe drinking water; fisheries and wildlife; Superfund and hazardous wastes, solid waste disposal and recycling.

Source: This is a shorter version of a similar table developed for Norman J. Vig and Michael E. Kraft, eds., *Environmental Policy*, 6th ed. (Washington, DC: CQ Press, 2006).

[a]Both the House and Senate Appropriations Committees have Interior and Environment subcommittees that handle all Interior Department agencies as well as the Forest Service and the EPA. Other environmental agencies fall under different subcommittees.

again, and the fragmentation of environmental responsibilities remained largely unchanged.

One other effect of this kind of dispersion of power within Congress is important. Building a consensus on policy goals and means is often unattainable because of the diverse policy actors and the multiplicity of committees involved. Action may be blocked even when public concern about the environment is high and consensus exists on broad policy directions. The reason is that it is much easier for opponents to stop legislative proposals from going forward than it is for those favoring action to build broad coalitions in support of them. One of the best examples is that the Clean Air Act could not be reauthorized between 1977 and 1990 because of persistent controversies over acid rain and other issues. Much the same has been true in recent years for the Clean Water Act and the Superfund program, as discussed in Chapter 5. Still, one message is that, as Barbara Sinclair (2001) has argued, lawmaking in Congress is often "unorthodox" or unusual today. It is not as straightforward as civics books suggest, and party and committee leaders sometimes find creative ways to get around the many obstacles to action on environmental and other policy issues.

Divided Authority in the Executive Branch   A similar division of authority characterizes the executive branch, where it is often difficult to act quickly and effectively on environmental problems. Figure 3.1 indicates the large number of executive branch agencies with environmental responsibilities. The EPA has authority for the major environmental protection statutes. As is evident from the agency's organization chart, however, its work is divided among separate offices dealing with specific environmental media such as air and water. There are assistant administrators for air and radiation, water, solid waste, and pollution prevention and toxics. The result is that it is often difficult to encourage comprehensive and cross-media environmental planning and decision making. Staff in each office tend to pursue their single-medium responsibilities despite the obvious need for more integrated decision making. The agency has been unable to change despite wide criticism of this arrangement and many suggestions for a more integrative administrative structure (Durant, Fiorino, and O'Leary 2004; Rosenbaum 2006). As we see later, Congress is also largely to blame for many of the EPA's failures in environmental policymaking. It has given the agency mixed signals about what it should do and what priorities it should set. Significant improvements in environmental policy require that Congress do a better job in sorting out the EPA's responsibilities and giving the agency the resources and flexibility it needs to implement the laws.

In addition to the EPA, 12 cabinet departments have significant roles in environmental policy. Four departments have major responsibilities for either environmental protection or natural resources: Interior, Agriculture, Energy, and State (the last for international policies). Others, such as Commerce and Transportation, arguably have a comparable effect on the environment through their implementation of research and management programs dealing with mass transit, highways, oil pollution, and coastal zones. Independent agencies such as the Nuclear Regulatory Commission and selected offices in the executive office of the president [the Council on Environmental Quality (CEQ), Office of Management and Budget, Council of Economic Advisors, and Office of Science and Technology Policy] are also regular participants in formulating and implementing environmental policies. The CEQ, for example, is charged with oversight of the important National Environmental Policy Act and its environmental impact statement process. As might be expected, the various agencies and departments sometimes find it difficult to work cooperatively; for example, the EPA and the Department of Energy have clashed frequently on a range of issues because the former emphasizes environmental quality and the latter the production of energy.

Under the conditions prevailing in both Congress and the executive branch, policymaking depends on bargaining among power wielders to frame compromises that are acceptable to most policy actors. In turn, as discussed earlier, the process of bargaining and compromise means that environmental policies ordinarily change incrementally rather than dramatically or quickly, although exceptions occur. As

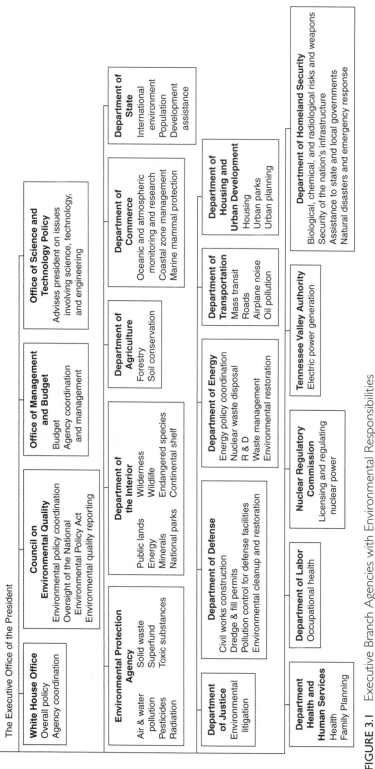

FIGURE 3.1 Executive Branch Agencies with Environmental Responsibilities

Sources: Council on Environmental Quality, *Environmental Quality: Sixteenth Annual Report of the Council on Environmental Quality* (Washington, DC: Government Printing Office, 1987); *United States Government Manual 1998/99* (Washington, DC: Government Printing Office, 1998); and author. A similar figure is used in Norman J. Vig and Michael E. Kraft, *Environmental Policy: New Directions for the Twenty-First Century,* 6th ed. (Washington, DC: CQ Press, 2006).

suggested earlier in the discussion of policy formulation and agenda setting, successful policymaking in the U.S. political system also requires skillful and determined political leadership. Policy entrepreneurs and other leaders must be capable of assembling coalitions of stakeholders, fashioning legislative and executive compromises, and shepherding the resultant measures through Congress or an executive agency. Former Senate Majority Leader George Mitchell's (D-Maine) leadership on the Clean Air Act of 1990 exemplified those qualities, as made clear in Richard Cohen's (1995) insider account of the act's passage.

The Benefits of Dispersed Power

Would more centralized or integrated political institutions produce a better outcome than the decentralized and loose policymaking apparatus we now have? The answer is not entirely clear. Despite criticism of the present institutional arrangements in government, a decentralized and competitive political process has some attractive and often overlooked qualities. Among them are the many opportunities created for interest groups and policy entrepreneurs, including environmentalists, to promote issues of concern to them. There are also innumerable points of access in the highly permeable U.S. system for those who wish to oppose the policies promoted by the president, members of Congress, or others.

Congressional Committees   The decentralization of the congressional committee system, for example, virtually guarantees that environmental advocacy groups (and their opponents) can find a friendly audience somewhere to publicize and promote their cause. Environmentalists discovered the attractiveness of this strategy during Ronald Reagan's presidency (1981–1989) when they became highly adept at stimulating public and congressional opposition to the president's efforts to weaken environmental policies. Between May 1981 (when she was confirmed as administrator of the EPA) and July 1982, Anne M. Gorsuch (later Burford) was forced to testify 15 times before congressional committees. Other EPA officials appeared more than 70 times between October 1981 and July 1982, and between 56 and 79 times each year from 1984 to 1986 (U.S. EPA 1987a). During the Republican Congress of the mid- to late 1990s, the tables were turned. In the words of one journalist, the "more ideologically committed House conservatives" became "increasingly aggressive in their use of oversight powers to jam the gears of Clinton's bureaucracy" (Simendinger 1998, 1732). The EPA was a major target of these inquiries.

More positively, the existence of some 200 congressional committees and subcommittees means that almost any organized group can find a member of Congress who is willing to introduce legislation and perhaps to move the issue to a committee hearing or investigation. In this way, members of Congress can help set the agenda by providing a forum for raising an issue's visibility. Historically, for instance, some members of Congress have been willing to promote environmental and resource issues that were of little interest to either the president or party leaders within Congress, such as population growth and its effect on the environment, or climate change. Congress is nearly a perfect setting for such entrepreneurial behavior because of the freedom and flexibility that members have to define their jobs and set their priorities, and their continuing search for activities that will bring them some attention and political credit (Kraft 1995).

The Role of the Courts   Similarly, the federal courts offer a rich opportunity for groups that seek to influence environmental policy, particularly when they wish to challenge the prevailing sentiment in Congress or in the executive agencies. Even before President Reagan assumed office, for instance, environmentalists had come to rely heavily on using the federal courts to pressure reluctant executive agencies to implement the tough new statutes adopted during the 1970s. Much of the bitter fight over protection of old-growth forests in the Pacific Northwest, for example, has taken place in the federal courts, with either environmentalists or the logging industry challenging administrative plans that sought to balance competing interests (Yaffee 1994). Environmental groups have become adept at playing a kind of watchdog or oversight role, keeping a close eye on administrative decision making that is often obscure to the general public. Industry groups are likely to do the same to guard against what they see as burdensome and costly actions by the EPA, the Interior Department, or other agencies. Both groups make their case in the courts when they cannot succeed in Congress or in executive agency proceedings (Kraft and Kamieniecki 2007; O'Leary 1993, 2006).

Courts shape environmental policy in many ways. One is that they serve a kind of gatekeeper function by deciding who has standing to sue, or the right to appeal to the federal courts, and whether a dispute is ready for review. Environmentalists won an important victory in early 2000 when the U.S. Supreme Court voted 7 to 2 in the case of *Friends of the Earth v. Laidlaw* to uphold "citizen suit" provisions of environmental laws such as the Clean Air Act and Clean Water Act that business and conservative interest groups had long opposed. By permitting such a "standing to sue," the Court kept the door open for citizen groups trying to pressure federal agencies into more aggressive enforcement of environmental laws (Greenhouse 2000). Such a lawsuit filed by environmental groups in 1989 to force the development of water pollution standards for large animal feedlots (increasingly important in rural areas) met a degree of success when new rules were announced in 2002 to reduce such pollution (Becker 2002).

The courts also set standards for review, including whether they will defer to the expert judgment of administrative agencies or instead review an agency's decisions more critically. The EPA, for instance, sets environmental quality standards that are one of the first steps in regulating pollution (see Chapter 5). The agency is frequently sued over the standards that it chooses, putting the decision into the federal courts. Where a statute is silent or ambiguous on a given issue, the courts usually defer to the expert judgment of an agency as long as it is reasonable and not arbitrary or capricious.

One important example of this process concerns the EPA's decision in 1997 to tighten standards for fine particulates and ozone (supported by the Clinton White House). The decision was contested by the American Trucking Association, which represented a coalition of industry groups opposed to the new standards. The group argued that the EPA did not consider the costs of the new standards nor did it conduct a cost–benefit analysis to support them. It also argued that the decision by Congress to delegate such broad rule-making authority to the EPA was unconstitutional. In February 2001, in one of the most important environmental law rulings in years, the Supreme Court unanimously upheld the EPA's action. It said that the Clean Air Act required only the consideration of public health and safety, and that it "unambiguously bars cost considerations" from the standard-setting process. The Court also defended the congressional delegation of authority to the agency as a legitimate exercise of congressional lawmaking power, rejecting a ruling by a federal appeals court to the contrary. The decision constituted a major victory for environmental groups and for the EPA.[14]

Frequently the courts must interpret the Constitution, statutory language, administrative rules, regulations, executive orders, treaties, and prior court decisions that may serve as a precedent or standing judicial policy. The policy language in these various documents may be ambiguous or vague, or new situations arise that the architects of that language failed to anticipate. For instance, in 1995, in a major victory for supporters of the Endangered Species Act, the Supreme Court upheld (in a 6–3 decision) a Clinton administration interpretation of the act's prohibition on the "taking" of a species. Secretary of the Interior Bruce Babbitt promulgated a regulation that defined the act's prohibition of such taking as including "significant habitat modification or degradation where it actually kills or injures wildlife." A group called the Sweet Home Chapter of Communities for a Great Oregon (representing small landowners, logging companies, and families who depend on the forest products industry) filed suit. They asserted that the secretary of the interior exceeded his authority under the act in issuing such an interpretation. A series of judicial rulings turned on how to interpret the word *harm* in the ESA, culminating in the Supreme Court ruling (O'Leary 2006).[15]

As this example illustrates, the courts have the final say on what the law means, although Congress always has the right to revise the law to make its meaning clearer if it disagrees with court rulings. Court decisions on "regulatory taking" of property (when government regulations deprive property owners of some rights to use their property), for instance, have led conservative property rights groups to press state legislatures and Congress to change the law to make it more difficult for regulatory agencies to affect property rights in this way (see Chapter 6).

State and Local Governments   Environmentalists also look increasingly to state and local governments when they are stymied in Congress or executive agencies. In many ways state and local policy action is easier, in part because there is much less of the ideological and partisan wars that so often are found at the national level of government. Moreover, state officials may be able to play the role of policy entrepreneur discussed earlier. That is, they can follow an issue closely, build coalitions of support, and take advantage of windows of opportunity to advance their policy initiatives (Rabe 2004). For these reasons, some of the most innovative environmental policies recently can be found at the state level, the "laboratories of democracy"; this includes the use of "green taxes" and other economic incentives, public disclosure of information on toxic chemicals, pollution prevention programs, and even climate change policies (John 1994, 2004; Rabe 2006).

Using such measures, some states—including California, Michigan, Minnesota, Wisconsin, New Jersey, Oregon, Washington, and New York—have ranked consistently among the most innovative and committed to environmental protection goals. Yet a state's willingness to innovate or take strong enforcement action depends on a number of factors that can change over time. Among them are the partisan alignments at the state level, the strength of the state's economy, public support, and the relative influence of environmental and industry interest groups.

The importance of the states' role in environmental policy is easily demonstrated. According to the Council of State Governments, the states together issue more than 90 percent of all environmental permits and are responsible for more than 75 percent of all enforcement actions. They rely on the federal government for only about 25 percent of their budgets for these activities; that is, the states raise 75 percent of the money they need for environmental programs. Nearly all the states have gone beyond the minimum federal requirements in at least some ways. The states also compile the vast majority of the data in six of the largest federal environmental databases and virtually all the data on air pollution and drinking water quality (Rabe 2006; Scheberle 2004).

Consistent with these patterns, the number of federal programs delegated to the states increased from 45 percent in 1993 to 75 percent in 2001. Not surprisingly, the states have greatly increased the size of their environmental staffs in recent years. By 1998 those staffs collectively stood at some 65,000 people, or over 2.5 times the number of federal EPA employees (Brown 2000). Stringent budgetary constraints in many states in the early 2000s, however, may well mean stagnant or declining staffs over the next few years.[16] Even if budgetary crises constrain state actions, taken together these developments at the state level constitute a remarkable shift in U.S. environmental politics and policy since the 1980s.

Something of the same pattern can be found in local and regional environmental policy developments. For example, states in the Great Lakes Basin have cooperated in developing regional initiatives to promote environmental sustainability, particularly as it affects water quality (Rabe 1999). Across the nation, but particularly in the Pacific Northwest, local and regional watershed councils and similar grassroots organizations have demonstrated the promise of collaborative and participatory decision making that brings together citizens, key stakeholder groups, and government agencies in a search for acceptable solutions to long-standing conflicts over environmental protection and economic development. These ad hoc and voluntary processes have helped foster consensus on habitat conservation plans for protecting endangered species, restoration efforts for degraded ecosystems, smart growth strategies for suburban communities, and redevelopment of contaminated lands (Paehlke 2006; Portney 2003; Sabatier et al. 2005; Weber 2003).

Many local governments, particularly in progressive communities and university towns, such as Davis, California, have adopted their own distinctive policies on issues as diverse as recycling programs, land conservation, and use of alternative energy sources. Along with the newly expanded state actions on the environment, these local activities have created a richness and diversity in environmental policy that would not be possible in a more centralized and unified system (Mazmanian and Kraft 1999; Press 1999). Some of these efforts have been so successful that the EPA itself has made Community-Based Environmental Protection (CBEP) an agency priority. The actions are taken locally and remain a "bottom-up" form of environmental protection and resource conservation. The EPA, however, provides both technical and financial assistance through a variety of federal grant programs. The agency maintains Web sites devoted to this purpose and to encourage citizen action at the local level. It also has indicated in recent years that some 20 percent of the EPA's resources in its 10 regional offices should be directed toward CBEP programs (John and Mlay 1999; U.S. EPA 1997a).[17]

■ CONCLUSIONS

This chapter has reviewed some of the key features of the policy-making process. It has also highlighted certain characteristics of U.S. government and politics that shape the way environmental issues are defined and acted on by policymakers. Critics are correct to say that the U.S. political system suffers from serious institutional deficiencies when weighed against the imperatives of contemporary environmental policy needs (Ophuls and Boyan 1992). The U.S. system, however, also has important strengths that environmentalists and other political activists know well. There are some reasons to be optimistic about the potential for policy development, particularly at the state and local levels of government where policy gridlock is less a problem than it is in Washington. Yet formulating and adopting effective environmental policies that can be broadly supported is not easy at any level of government.

Chapters 5 through 7 discuss the way U.S. government and politics affect environmental decisions. Another way to judge governmental performance is to take a brief retrospective look at the development of environmental policy since the 1960s, which is the focus of Chapter 4. Such an examination offers persuasive evidence that government has been responsive to changing public concerns about the environment, which is particularly the case when the issues are politically salient, thus giving policymakers a reason to take seriously the public's environmental views. It is no exaggeration to say that public opinion has been the driving force in modern environmental policy.

What is less evident is whether that influence will continue at a time when many environmental policy decisions are increasingly technical, when they are made largely in administrative agencies and the courts rather than in legislatures, and when few who are not active participants in issue networks can easily understand them. Whether at the national level or at community, regional, and state levels, the message should be clear to environmentalists and to their opponents. Whatever the broad preferences of the public—which is highly sympathetic to environmentalists—political influence depends on building a strong understanding of the issues, organizing supportive publics or constituencies, and persistently advocating one's case when opportunities present themselves.

DISCUSSION QUESTIONS

1. Should environmental scientists and other experts play a greater role in the policy-making process, as some suggest? What might the consequences be if they did so? Would it improve public and policymaker understanding of the issues? Would it facilitate the adoption of more effective policies?

2. Many analysts and policymakers call for further devolution of environmental responsibilities to state and local governments, although their record has been mixed. What are the major advantages of such a redistribution of authority for environmental protection? The most important disadvantages?

3. Environmental policy gridlock in Congress has become common. What are the major causes of such a policy stalemate? What might be done to overcome it?

4. Environmental policy responsibilities are widely distributed in government, particularly in the federal executive branch and between the federal government

and the states. What are the major disadvantages of such fragmentation of authority? What are the major advantages of it?

5. Would the quality of environmental policy decisions be improved with greater public participation, particularly at the state and local levels of government? Why do you think so? What actions or events might encourage the public to take a greater interest in and to participate more in the policy process?

SUGGESTED READINGS

Kingdon, John. *Agendas, Alternatives, and Public Policy*, 2nd ed. New York: Longman, 1995.

Layzer, Judith A. *The Environmental Case: Translating Values into Policy*, 2nd ed. Washington, DC: CQ Press, 2006.

Lazarus, Richard J. *The Making of Environmental Law*. Chicago: University of Chicago Press, 2004.

Lester, James P., ed. *Environmental Politics and Policy: Theories and Evidence*, 2nd ed. Durham, NC: Duke University Press, 1995.

Soden, Dennis L., ed. *The Environmental Presidency*. Albany: State University of New York Press, 1999.

Sussman, Glen, Byron W. Daynes, and Jonathan P. West. *American Politics and the Environment*. New York: Longman, 2002.

Vig, Norman J., and Michael E. Kraft, eds. *Environmental Policy: New Directions for the Twenty-First Century*, 6th ed. Washington, DC: CQ Press, 2006.

ENDNOTES

1. Edmund L. Andrews, "As Profits Soar, Companies Pay U.S. Less for Gas Rights," *New York Times*, January 23, 2006, 1, A17.

2. The various models and theories are reviewed briefly in Kraft and Furlong (2007). See also Anderson (2006).

3. The policy process model is not without its critics. Some argue that it should be replaced by a more accurate and genuinely causal model of policy activities that lends itself both to empirical testing and to incorporation of a broader variety of policy actors and behavior (Sabatier 1999; Sabatier and Jenkins-Smith 1993). I disagree with much of this critique. The policy process model can be useful for describing the diversified players in the policy game and for alerting us to pertinent actions that contribute to our understanding of environmental politics and policy.

4. The full title of the act is the Oil Pollution Prevention, Response, Liability, and Compensation Act. Birkland (1997) offers a history of how federal oil spill policy was altered by the Exxon *Valdez* accident.

5. See Timothy Egan, "Once Braced for a Power Shortage, California Now Finds Itself with a Surplus," *New York Times*, November 4, 2001, A17.

6. The Union of Concerned Scientists was especially active in documenting concerns about the lack of scientific integrity; its reports are available at its Web site: www.ucsusa.org. See also James Glanz, "Scientists Say Administration Distorts Facts," *New York Times*, February 19, 2004, A21; and Andrew C. Revkin, "Bush's Science Aide Rejects Claim of Distorted Facts," *New York Times*, April 3, 2004, A9.

7. See Don Van Natta Jr. and Neela Banerjee, "Documents Show Energy Official Met Only with Industry Leaders," *New York Times*, March 27, 2002, A1–20. See also Van Natta Jr. and Banerjee, "Top G.O.P. Donors in Energy Industry Met Cheney Panel," *New York Times*, March 1, 2002. The reporters concluded from interviews and task force correspondence that 18 of the energy industry's top 25 financial contributors to the Republican Party advised the Cheney energy task force.

8. For an account of such efforts, see Bruce Barcott, "Changing All the Rules," *New York Times Magazine*, April 4, 2004, 39–44, 66, 73, 76–77.

9. See Danny Hakim, "At the Front on Air Policy: California Is Moving to Set U.S. Standard," *New York Times*, July 3, 2002, 1, A12.

10. The literature on the role of "subgovernments" in the policy process helps clarify such political relationships and why they continue even after more than three decades of the modern environmental movement. See, for example, McCool (1990) and the earlier but still insightful work by Grant McConnell (1966) and E. E. Schattschneider (1960).

11. For a detailed analysis of U.S. government institutions and environmental policy, see the edited collection by Lester (1995). Leading environmental policy scholars assess the characteristics and performance of Congress, the bureaucracy, the courts, and state government as well as public opinion, interest groups, and political parties. Chapters in Vig and Kraft (2006) also offer appraisals of how Congress, the presidency, the courts, the EPA, and the states have dealt with environmental policy challenges in recent years.

12. The Fifth Amendment states, among other provisions, that no person shall "be deprived of life, liberty, or property, without due process of law; nor shall private property be taken for public use, without just compensation."

13. The LCV national scorecard is available at its Web site: www.lcv.org. The league has compiled these voting scores since 1970. For an assessment of how the two parties have diverged over time in support for environmental policy, see Shipan and Lowry (2001). See also Kamieniecki (1995).

14. The case is *Whitman v. American Trucking Association* 531 U.S. 457 (2001); it was previously called *Browner v. American Trucking Association*. See Linda Greenhouse, "E.P.A.'s Authority on Air Rules Wins Supreme Court's Backing," *New York Times*, February 28, 2001, A1, A18.

15. The case is *Babbitt v. Sweet Home Chapter for a Great Oregon* 515 U.S. 687 (1995).

16. Current information on such state activity can be found at the Environmental Council of the States (ECOS) Web site: www.ecos.org.

17. The EPA Web site on community-based approaches can be found at www.epa.gov/ecocommunity/. A further contribution to the diversity represented by state and local environmental activities is made by the 280 reservation-based tribal governments. They too have moved increasingly to assume control of actions affecting their territories (Chaffey 1999). An excellent example is the Menominee Indian Tribe's unique sustainable forestry efforts (Davis 2000).

4

The Evolution of Environmental Policy and Politics

During the election campaign of 2004, the national League of Conservation Voters made two important decisions. One was to give President George W. Bush a grade of "F" on his environmental policy record. The other was to shift from the league's historic concentration on Congress to a focus on the presidential race. The league was convinced that the American public would repudiate President Bush's environmental policies if it was made aware of his actions. To that end the league spent some $6 million on the election campaign, in addition to millions spent by the Sierra Club and a group of former Clinton environmental officials organized as Environment 2004.[1] Bush won his reelection bid against Senator John Kerry by 50.7 percent to 48.3 percent, but the environment never emerged as a significant issue in a campaign dominated by voter concern about terrorism, the war in Iraq, and the economy (Bosso and Guber 2006; Vig 2006).

The league's political strategy in 2004 illustrates well the striking change in environmental politics over the last three decades. In the late 1960s and 1970s, environmental policy was embraced by both political parties, if not with the same enthusiasm. The American public was strongly supportive of policy action, and elected officials competed with one another to claim political credit for their environmental actions. The policies adopted at that time remain in force today, but the political mood of the nation has changed, as has the policy agenda.

The concepts of policymaking introduced in Chapter 3 are helpful for understanding the history of U.S. environmental policy. They are especially useful in explaining the emergence of the modern environmental movement, the role and effect of environmental interest groups, and the influence of public values and attitudes toward the environment. This chapter explores that history, particularly the impact of the environmental movement and public opinion on contemporary environmental politics and policy. The influence of public opinion is a theme revisited in Chapters 5 and 6 when we turn more directly to the substance of environmental protection and natural resource policies.

▨ NATURAL RESOURCES AND ENVIRONMENTAL POLICIES IN HISTORICAL PERSPECTIVE

Modern environmental policy emerged in the 1960s and became firmly established on the political agenda during the so-called environmental decade of the 1970s when Congress enacted most of the major environmental statutes. Actions at state and local levels paralleled these developments. Senator Gaylord Nelson of Wisconsin organized the first Earth Day held on April 22, 1970. It was widely celebrated across the nation and signaled the arrival of a mass political movement dedicated to ending environmental degradation (Nelson 2002). Politicians responded eagerly to what many at the time considered to be a motherhood issue that posed little political risk and offered many electoral dividends.

Yet concern about the environment and the value of natural resources arose early in the nation's history and periodically sparked the adoption of preservation, conservation, economic development, and public health policies that continue to shape the environmental agenda today. Most of those policy actions coincided with three periods of progressive government in which other social and economic issues also advanced: the Progressive Era from about 1890 to 1915, the New Deal of the 1930s, and the era of social regulation of the 1960s and 1970s. Within each period, perceived environmental or health crises, catalytic or focusing events, and the leadership of policy entrepreneurs heightened public concern and kindled policy innovation. Broader social, economic, and technological changes also contributed to recognition of looming environmental and resource problems and created the political will to deal with them. As suggested in the model of agenda setting introduced in Chapter 3, these developments helped set the intellectual, scientific, aesthetic, moral, and political foundations of contemporary environmentalism (Shabecoff 1993).[2]

The Settlement and "Conquest" of Nature

In the early seventeenth century, in one of the first conservation actions in the new nation, New England colonists adopted local ordinances protecting forestland and regulating timber harvesting (Andrews 1999; Nash 1990). Such actions did not prevent the colonists from attempting to subdue the wilderness they faced and fundamentally altering the landscape and ecology of New England as the population grew and the land was cleared for agriculture and settlements (Cronon 1983). That behavior was an early indication of the limits of policy intervention in the face of profound pressures for expansion and a culture that favored exploitation of the nation's rich natural resources.

By the middle of the nineteenth century, new trends were emerging. The study of natural systems was gaining stature within the scientific community, and in 1864 George Perkins Marsh published his influential treatise, *Man and Nature*. The book documented the destructive effects on nature from human activity. Literary figures contributed as well to the sense that industrialism and technology were not entirely beneficent in their effects. Henry David Thoreau's *Walden*, a poignant account of his two years in the wilderness at Walden Pond, reflected many of the same concerns as today's "deep ecology" writing.

The late nineteenth century brought significant advances in conservation policy as the consequences of human activities began to attract more attention, although by present standards the effects of the policies were modest. Discoveries of vast areas of unsurpassed beauty in the newly explored West led to the establishment of Yosemite Valley, California, as first a state park (1864) and later as a national park (1891). In 1872 Congress set aside 2 million acres in Wyoming, Montana, and Idaho to create Yellowstone National Park as a "pleasuring ground for the benefit and enjoyment of the people," the first of a series of national parks.

During this same period, however, the federal government sought to encourage rapid development of its vast holdings in the West. It adopted public policies toward that end that reflected prevailing beliefs in Congress and elsewhere that the West was an immense frontier promising "limitless opportunities" for resource exploitation and creation of wealth. Chief among those actions were classic distributive policies: the generous distribution of public lands (free or at token prices) to private parties, such as railroad companies and homestead settlers.

For example, the Homestead Act of 1862 allowed individuals to acquire 160 acres of public land by living on it and working it as a farm. More than 250 million acres were converted to farms through this act. The federal government transferred over 94 million acres to railroad corporations and an additional 800 million acres to the states, veterans, and other groups under various programs. Over 1 billion acres of the 1.8 billion in the original public domain were privatized in these ways between 1781 and 1977, leaving about 740 million acres of public land, of which 330 million acres are in Alaska (Wengert 1994).[3] A number of government actions also gave large subsidies to ranchers, farmers, and mining companies, all with the same objective of encouraging development of the West by providing access to public lands and waters. For example, the 1872 General Mining Law gave miners virtually free access to rich mineral deposits on public land with no obligation to pay royalties on the minerals extracted. The Reclamation Act of 1902 provided for public construction of dams and other projects to make cultivation of desert lands possible. The West did indeed gain population and the economy prospered, but at a high cost to the environment.

Another important effect was more political. Those who received the subsidies came to believe they were entitled to them indefinitely. The legacy affects natural resource policy even today. For years, powerful western constituencies (e.g., the mining industry, ranchers, large farming operations, and timber companies) dominated these natural resource policies; they did so by forming protectionist subgovernments in association with members of key congressional committees and executive agencies. Such alliances operate autonomously with little political visibility, and conflict over policy goals typically is minimal. Disputes that do arise are resolved through logrolling, or mutually beneficial bargaining, in which each party may gain its goals (McCool 1990). The existence of these political arrangements allowed the natural resource subgovernments to ward off significant policy changes sought by conservationists and others until the mid-twentieth century. Some of them, such as the mining industry, continue to fight successfully against reform of the old laws (Foss 1960; Lowi 1979; McConnell 1966).

The Conservation Movement and Advances in Public Health

By the late nineteenth century, winds of change began to blow as the Progressive Era unfolded. Reflecting the growth of concern about preservation of natural resources and public lands in response to reckless exploitation in earlier decades, John Muir founded the Sierra Club, the first broad-based environmental organization, in 1892. Muir led the preservationist wing of the incipient environmental movement, with a philosophy of protecting wilderness areas, like his beloved Yosemite Valley, from economic development. Such areas, Muir argued, should be preserved for their own sake and used exclusively for recreational and educational purposes.

A countervailing conservationist philosophy took hold under Gifford Pinchot, a Yale graduate trained in forestry in Germany who became the first professional forester in the United States. In 1898 Pinchot, who emphasized efficient use (or "wise management") of natural resources for economic development, became chief of the Division of Forestry, the forerunner of the modern U.S. Forest Service. Pinchot's approach to conservation soon became the dominant force in twentieth-century natural resource policy in part through his close association with President Theodore Roosevelt. In 1908 Pinchot chaired a White House Conference on Resource Management that firmly established his brand of conservation as the nation's approach to natural resources. The heritage can be seen in key doctrines of what historian Samuel P. Hays (1959) called the "progressive conservation movement," among them "multiple use" and "sustained yield" of the nation's resources.

Despite the differences between Muir and Pinchot, the conservation movement achieved early successes in the creation of national parks and forest reserves, national monuments such as the Grand Canyon (1908) and government agencies such as the Forest Service (1905), National Park Service (1916), and Bureau of Reclamation (1902). Many of the prominent national conservation groups also emerged at this time or shortly thereafter. In addition to the Sierra Club in 1892, the National Audubon Society was founded in 1905 and the National Parks Conservation Association in 1919. Other environmental organizations emerged between the world wars, including the Izaak Walton League in 1922, the Wilderness Society (founded by ecologist and writer Aldo Leopold) in 1935, and the National Wildlife Federation in 1936.

None of these developments posed a serious challenge to prevailing values regarding the sanctity of private property, individual rights, and economic growth. Rather, they represented a somewhat inconsistent and awkward accommodation of new social forces in twentieth-century America that eventually would provoke a more spirited opposition. The actions taken, however, did establish the important principle that resources in the public domain should be used equitably for the benefit of all citizens.

Environmental protection efforts focusing on public health did not appear for the most part until the 1960s. There was, however, a Progressive Era parallel to the conservation movement in the establishment of urban services such as wastewater treatment, waste management, and provision of clean water supplies, along with broader societal improvements in nutrition, hygiene, and medical services. Such gains were spurred by concerns that developed in the late nineteenth century over the excesses of the Industrial Revolution and a system of private property rights that operated with virtually none of the restraints common today.

Consistent with the new emphasis on urban public health, the first air pollution statutes in the United States were designed to control heavy smoke and soot from furnaces and locomotives. They were approved in Chicago and Cincinnati in the 1880s, and by 1920 some 40 cities had adopted air pollution control laws. Although a few states such as Ohio took action as early as the 1890s, no *comprehensive* state air pollution policies existed until 1952, when Oregon adopted such legislation (Portney 1990; Ringquist 1993).

From the New Deal to the Environmental Movement

The environmental agenda during President Franklin Roosevelt's 12-year tenure emphasized the mitigation of natural resource problems, particularly flood control and soil conservation, in response to a series of natural disasters. The most memorable of these was prolonged drought and erosion in the Dust Bowl. Activities such as the creation in 1933 of the Tennessee Valley Authority (TVA) were intended to stimulate economic development and employment to pull the nation out of the Depression. Yet the TVA also was important for demonstrating that government land use planning could be used to benefit the broad public in a region. Other actions—for example, the establishment of the Civilian Conservation Corps and the Soil Conservation Service—were directed at repairing environmental damage and preventing its recurrence. Notable among the many New Deal policies was the Taylor Grazing Act of 1934, which was intended to end the abuse from overgrazing of valuable rangelands and watersheds in the West by authorizing the Department of the Interior to issue grazing permits and regulate rangeland use. Congress created the Bureau of Land Management in 1946 and ended the massive privatization of public lands (Wengert 1994).

During the 1950s and 1960s, a third wave of conservation focused on preservation of areas of natural beauty and wilderness, stimulated in part by increased public interest in recreation and the efforts to stem the tide of economic development threatening key areas. The Wilderness Act of 1964 was intended to preserve some national forest lands in their natural condition through a National Wilderness Preservation System. The Land and Water Conservation Fund Act, enacted in 1964, facilitated local, state, and federal acquisition and development of lands for parks and open spaces. In addition, Congress created the National Wild and Scenic Rivers System in 1968. Its purpose was to preserve certain rivers with "outstandingly remarkable" scenic, recreational, ecological, historical, and cultural values. At the request of President Lyndon B. Johnson, Lady Bird Johnson, and the President's Commission on Natural Beauty, Congress approved legislation to "beautify" federal highways by, among other actions, reducing the number of unsightly billboards to promote aesthetic values (Gould 1999). Stewart Udall, secretary of the interior under both Presidents John F. Kennedy and Johnson, was a forceful advocate of conservation policies.

This latest "wilderness movement" eventually evolved into the modern environmental movement, with a much broader policy agenda. Congress adopted the first federal water and air pollution control laws in 1948 and 1955, respectively, and gradually expanded and strengthened them. The federal government gingerly approved its first international population policies in the early 1960s several years after congressional policy entrepreneurs held hearings and incubated the controversial measures. In his 1965 State of the Union address, President Johnson called for federal programs to deal with "the explosion in world population and the growing scarcity in world resources." The following year Congress authorized the first funds for family planning programs abroad (Kraft 1994b).

The successes of conservation efforts and the nascent environmental movement depended fundamentally on long-term changes in social values that began after

World War II. These value changes accelerated as the nation developed economically and the production and consumption of consumer goods escalated dramatically in the 1950s and 1960s. The United States slowly shifted from an industrial to a postindustrial or postmaterialist society. An increasingly affluent, comfortable, and well-educated public placed new emphasis on the quality of life (Hays 1987; Inglehart 1990). Concern for natural resource amenities and environmental protection issues was an integral part of this change. By the 1970s it was evident across all groups in the population, if not to the same degree. Similar factors help account for the growth of the global environmental movement at the same time (McCormick 1989).

Scientific discoveries brought new attention to the effects of pesticides and other synthetic chemicals on human health and the natural environment. These were documented in Rachel Carson's influential *Silent Spring* (1962), Murray Bookchin's *Our Synthetic Environment* (published about six months before Carson's book under the pseudonym Lewis Herber), and Barry Commoner's *The Closing Circle* (1971), a trenchant analysis of ecological risks inflicted by use of inappropriate technologies. Paul Ehrlich's *The Population Bomb* (1968) underscored the role of human population growth in resource use and environmental degradation. Rapid growth in the capacity of the nation's media to alert the public to such dangers heightened public concern, and policy entrepreneurs like consumer activist Ralph Nader helped tie environmental quality to prominent health and safety issues.

The effect of these developments was a broadly based public demand for more forceful and comprehensive governmental action to protect valued natural resources and to prevent environmental degradation. New environmental organizations quickly arose and adopted the tactics of other 1960s social movements, using well-publicized protests and university-based teach-ins to mobilize the public to press for policy change (Nelson 2002). A variety of political reforms, including congressional redistricting and easier access by public interest groups to the courts and legislatures, and changes in the mass media facilitated their success.

■ THE MODERN ENVIRONMENTAL MOVEMENT AND POLICY ACHIEVEMENTS

The environmental movement of the late 1960s and 1970s represented one of those unusual periods in U.S. political history when the problem, policy, and politics streams—as discussed in Chapter 3—converged. This convergence set the stage for a dramatic shift in environmental policies. In an unprecedented fashion, a new environmental agenda rapidly emerged. It sought to expand and strengthen early conservation programs and to institute new public policies organized around the integrative and holistic concept of environmental quality. Environmental quality could bring together such otherwise distinct concerns as public health, pollution, natural resources, energy use, population growth, urbanization, consumer protection, and recreation (Caldwell 1970). That agenda drew from new studies of health and environmental risks and from widespread dissatisfaction with the modest achievements of early federal air and water pollution control policies and equally limited state efforts (Davies and Davies 1975; Jones 1975). The legacy of this period includes the major federal environmental protection statutes, a host of important natural resource measures, and countless state and local initiatives that established environmental concerns firmly on the governmental agenda.

Contributing to the building of this new environmental policy agenda was an extraordinary bipartisan group of policy entrepreneurs on Capitol Hill. They and their staffs had been patiently incubating these issues for years before public demand had crystallized and the media (and the White House) discovered the environment. They included such influential environmental lawmakers as Henry Jackson, Edmund Muskie, and Gaylord Nelson in the Senate and Paul Rogers, John Saylor, Paul McCloskey, Charles Mosher, Morris Udall, John Blatnik, and John Dingell, among many others, in the House (Kraft 1995).

By early 1970 there was abundant evidence of the problem stream changing quickly and influencing members of Congress who dealt with environmental policy. Indeed, the 92nd Congress (1971–1972) was the most productive in history for environmental protection and natural resources. It enacted measures on water pollution control, restrictions on ocean dumping, protection of sea mammals and coastal zones, regulation of pesticides, and noise control. Within a few years, other legislation followed on endangered species, drinking water quality, disposal of hazardous waste, control of toxic substances, and management of federal lands and forests. Table 4.1 lists most of these federal laws. With a rapid rise in public concern about the environment, extensive coverage of the issues in the media, and lobbying by new environmental groups, it is not surprising that the key statutes received strong bipartisan congressional support.

The key features of environmental and natural resource policies are discussed in Chapters 5 and 6. It is worth noting here, however, that the major federal environmental protection statutes adopted in the 1970s departed sharply from previous efforts even if members of Congress were not always certain of their likely effectiveness or cost. Environmental policy was "nationalized" by adopting federal standards for the regulation of environmental pollutants, action-forcing provisions to compel the use of particular technologies by specified deadlines, and tough sanctions for noncompliance. Congress would no longer tolerate the cumbersome and ineffective pollution control procedures used by state and local governments (especially evident in water pollution control). Nor was it prepared to allow unreasonable competition among the states created by variable environmental standards.

To some critics, these distinctly nonincremental (some might even say radical) changes in environmental policy were risky. The new policies attempted to hasten technological developments and went beyond the government's short-term capabilities. They invited administrative delays and imposed heavy burdens on industry and state and local governments that were ill prepared to respond to the new demands (Jones 1975). The political attractiveness of these new policies in the warm glow of the early 1970s, however, was obvious to all who followed their formulation and approval not only in Congress but among the 50 states.

These policy developments coincided with a massive third wave of broader social regulation in the 1970s. It focused on health and safety issues as well as environmental quality, and it resulted in the formation of new federal agencies, including the Occupational Safety and Health Administration, the Consumer Product Safety Commission, and the EPA itself. The EPA was established not by a law of Congress but through an executive order issued by President Richard Nixon that consolidated into

TABLE 4.1

Major Federal Environmental Laws, 1964–2005	
1964	Wilderness Act, PL 88-577
1968	Wild and Scenic Rivers Act, PL 90-542
1969	National Environmental Policy Act, PL 91-190
1970	Clean Air Act Amendments, PL 91-604
1972	Federal Water Pollution Control Act Amendments (Clean Water Act), PL 92-500
	Federal Environmental Pesticides Control Act of 1972, PL (amended the Federal Insecticide, Fungicide and Rodenticide Act [FIFRA] of 1947, PL 92-516)
	Marine Protection, Research, and Sanctuaries Act of 1972, PL 92-532
	Marine Mammal Protection Act, PL 92-522
	Coastal Zone Management Act, PL 92-583
	Noise Control Act, PL 92-574
1973	Endangered Species Act, PL 93-205
1974	Safe Drinking Water Act, PL 93-523
1976	Resource Conservation and Recovery Act (RCRA), PL 94-580
	Toxic Substances Control Act, PL 94-469
	Federal Land Policy and Management Act, PL 94-579
	National Forest Management Act, PL 94-588
1977	Clean Air Act Amendments, PL 95-95
	Clean Water Act (CWA), PL 95-217
	Surface Mining Control and Reclamation Act, PL 95-87
1980	Comprehensive Environmental Response, Compensation, and Liability Act (CERCLA or Superfund), PL 96-510
1982	Nuclear Waste Policy Act of 1982, PL 97-425 (amended in 1987 by the Nuclear Waste Policy Amendments Act of 1987, PL 100-203)
1984	Hazardous and Solid Waste Amendments (RCRA amendments), PL 98-616
1986	Safe Drinking Water Act Amendments, PL 99-339
	Superfund Amendments and Reauthorization Act (SARA), PL 99-499
1987	Water Quality Act (CWA amendments), PL 100-4
1988	Ocean Dumping Act of 1988, PL 100-688
1990	Clean Air Act Amendments of 1990, PL 101-549
	Oil Pollution Act, PL 101-380
	Pollution Prevention Act, PL 101-508
1991	Intermodal Surface Transportation Efficiency Act (ISTEA), PL 102-240
1992	Energy Policy Act, PL 102-486
	The Omnibus Water Act, PL 102-575
1996	Food Quality Protection Act (amended FIFRA), PL 104-120
	Safe Drinking Water Act Amendments, PL 104-182
1998	Transportation Equity Act for the 21st Century (also called ISTEA II or TEA 21), PL 105-178
2002	Small Business Liability Relief and Brownfields Revitalization Act, PL 107-118
2005	Energy Policy Act of 2005, PL 109-58

Note: A fuller list with a description of the key features of each act can be found in Vig and Kraft (2006), Appendix 1. Chapters 5 and 6 of this text provide brief descriptions of the major environmental protection and natural resource policies.

one agency programs dealing with environmental protection or pollution control that previously were scattered among many federal bureaucracies.

The new social regulation differed from the old in several important respects. It reflected a deep distrust of establishment organizations (especially the business community) and a determination to open the administrative process to public scrutiny. It led to a more activist or reformist orientation within the agencies, depending on the administration in power, and to extensive participation by new public interest groups such as consumer organizations and environmentalists (Berry 1977; Eisner, Worsham, and Ringquist 2000; Harris and Milkis 1996). By the 1980s these very qualities contributed to efforts in the Reagan presidency to reverse policy advances of the 1970s, particularly in response to complaints of excessive and needlessly expensive regulation. Environmental regulations were prime targets of this criticism and retrenchment (Vig and Kraft 1984).

The new environmental movement that was so critical to bringing about the innovative policy changes of the 1970s drew much of its political strength and moral force from the American public itself, which has continued to be one of the most important determinants of U.S. environmental politics and policy. Anthony Downs (1972) captured the new power of environmental public opinion in comments about the "issue-attention cycle," referring to the cyclical nature of the rise and fall of attention to environmental issues. Downs postulated that prior to the upsurge in public concern in the late 1960s, the nation was in a "pre-problem stage" on the environment. Such a stage exists when highly undesirable social conditions may exist but attract little public attention, even if a few experts, public officials, or interest groups are alarmed by them. As a result of a series of catalytic events (e.g., an oil-rig blowout off the coast of Santa Barbara, California, in 1969) and the publicity they receive, the public "suddenly becomes both aware of and alarmed about" the problem.

The dramatic rise in public concern over environmental quality in the late 1960s was confirmed by survey research, as was its slow decline during the 1970s to a lower but still substantial level and its striking resurrection in the 1980s during the Reagan administration (Dunlap 1992). Hazel Erskine (1972) described the initial rise as a "miracle of public opinion" because of the "unprecedented speed and urgency with which ecological issues have burst into American consciousness. Alarm about the environment sprang from nowhere to major proportions in a few short years" (120). Coverage of the environment by both print and electronic media followed a similar pattern, as did congressional agenda-setting activity such as hearings held on the subject (Baumgartner and Jones 1993). Despite a decline in their salience by the mid-1970s, environmental issues had become part of mainstream American values and were viewed almost universally as a positive symbol, with few negative images attached to it (Bosso and Guber 2006; Dunlap 1992, 1995; Mitchell 1984, 1990).

Environmental Interest Groups

Both the older and the newer environmental groups found such a supportive public opinion to be an invaluable political resource in their lobbying campaigns in Washington and in state capitals. Many of the established conservation groups saw their membership soar between 1960 and 1970. For example, the Sierra Club grew from 15,000 members in 1960 to 113,000 in 1970, more than a sevenfold increase. The newer

TABLE 4.2

Membership and Budgets of Selected National Environmental Organizations, 1960–2004

		Membership					
Organization	Year Founded	1960	1970	1980	1990	2004	2003 Revenue ($ million)
Sierra Club	1892	15,000	113,000	181,000	630,000	736,000	83.7
National Audubon Society	1905	32,000	148,000	400,000	600,000	550,000	78.6
National Parks Conservation Association	1919	15,000	45,000	31,000	100,000	375,000	20.9
Wilderness Society	1935	10,000	54,000	45,000	350,000	225,000	18.8
National Wildlife Federation	1936	NA	540,000	818,000	997,000	650,000[a]	102.1
Environmental Defense	1967	[b]	11,000	46,000	200,000	350,000	43.8
Natural Resources Defense Council	1970	[b]	[b]	40,000	150,000	450,000	46.4

Sources: Christopher J. Bosso and Deborah Lynn Guber, "Maintaining Presence: Environmental Advocacy and the Permanent Campaign," in Norman J. Vig and Michael E. Kraft, eds., *Environmental Policy,* 6th ed. (Washington, DC: CQ Press, 2006), 89; and Christopher J. Bosso, "After the Movement: Environmental Activism in the 1990s," in Norman J. Vig and Michael E. Kraft, eds., *Environmental Policy in the 1990s,* 2nd ed. (Washington, DC: CQ Press, 1994). Membership figures are notoriously hard to pin down because of conflicting data and varying definitions of what constitutes membership. All figures reported here should be considered estimates and used only to illustrate growth over time. Much more extensive information on the groups' sources of revenue and spending can be found in Bosso (2005).

[a]The NWF used to distinguish between regular and affiliated members, but it consolidated the two in the mid-1990s and now reports only the combined figure. For 2000 this figure was 4 million. Bosso and Guber, however, estimate that in 2004 regular, dues-paying members constituted 650,000.

[b]In 1960 neither Environmental Defense nor the Natural Resources Defense Council existed, and in 1970 NRDC was not a membership organization.

environmental organizations grew rapidly as well (Mitchell, Mertig, and Dunlap 1992). The trend continued through the 1970s and then accelerated in the 1980s as environmental groups mounted highly successful membership recruitment campaigns in response to the antienvironmental agenda of Ronald Reagan's presidency. The groups' budgets and staffs grew in parallel with membership rolls (Baumgartner and Jones 1993, 189; Bosso 2005). The results can be seen in Table 4.2, which reports memberships over time and recent budgets for selected national environmental groups. One recent estimate puts the total membership of U.S. environmental groups at more than 14 million people and their combined operating budget at over $600 million a year.

One other set of figures on the groups' financial strength bears mentioning. The National Center for Charitable Statistics reports that in 1999, thanks to a surging stock market, individuals, corporations, and foundations together contributed an astonishing $3.5 billion to environmental groups, double the level of 1992. That's nearly $9.6 million per day. The Nature Conservancy, easily the favorite of donors, netted $402 million that year (Duffy 2003). Such donations declined in the aftermath of the stock market crash and new concerns about global terrorism. Yet the incredible success of environmental groups in attracting this kind of money speaks to the appeal of their message.

Despite their many shared values and political goals, however, by the 1980s environmentalists began to splinter visibly into factions with often sharply conflicting styles and political strategies. The differences became so great that some analysts wondered whether the groups could be subsumed under the same label at all. For example, writing in 1991, Robert Mitchell noted that the unity of environmental groups was "tempered by a diversity of heritage, organizational structure, issue agendas, constituency, and tactics." They competed with one another, he said, "for the staples of their existence—publicity and funding" (Mitchell 1989, 83). Some of these divisions were noticeable even in the early 1970s, but they became even more evident by the early twenty-first century (Bosso and Guber 2006).[4]

At least three major categories of environmental groups should be distinguished: mainstream, greens, and grassroots. The mainstream organizations, such as the Natural Resources Defense Council, Sierra Club, National Audubon Society, and the National Wildlife Federation, have evolved into highly professional and Washington-based organizations that focus on public policy issues (Bosso 2005). In the 1990s the National Wildlife Federation, for example, had 35 people in its Washington office assigned to tracking legislation. Most of these organizations engage in the full range of activities common to interest groups active in the policy process. They collect and disseminate information on environmental problems and policy proposals, lobby members of Congress and their staffs, mobilize their members to contact public officials through grassroots lobbying campaigns, participate in the often detailed administrative processes of executive agencies such as rule making, and defend or challenge environmental decisions of those agencies through the judicial process (Kraft and Wuertz 1996; Schlozman and Tierney 1986). Increasingly, the major environmental groups make extensive use of the Internet for distributing a vast array of information to their members and in facilitating indirect or grassroots lobbying of policymakers (Bosso and Collins 2002; Duffy 2003).

Even small groups can be influential by using an Internet-based strategy. In one striking example in 2002, the Environmental Working Group (EWG) was widely credited with altering national debate on the fairness of agricultural subsidies by posting critical information on its Web site. The group built a farm subsidy database over six years by prying the crucial information out of reluctant government agencies. During the Senate debate on the agriculture bill, senators referred repeatedly to the EWG Web site, which allowed them to see which farmers were getting most of the federal money. The group succeeded in raising fundamental issues of equity because its data revealed that most of the subsidies were going to wealthy farmers and agribusinesses; in the end, however, Congress chose to continue the subsidies.[5]

The more radical greens (including groups like Greenpeace, the Earth Liberation Front, and Earth First!) tend to emphasize public education, direct action, and social change far more than lobbying or administrative intervention. The greens are distinguished from the mainstream groups chiefly by their dedication to more eco-centric philosophies and a conviction that basic changes in human values and behavior are required to deal with environmental problems. At least some of the radical groups have advocated eco-sabotage or "eco-terrorism" to highlight destructive industrial practices and gain visibility for their cause. In one notable action, for instance, the Earth Liberation Front (ELF) claimed credit in 1998 for burning down a Colorado ski resort as part of its campaign to protect wildlife habitat. According to the *New York Times*, it was "the most expensive act of eco-terrorism in the nation's history" (Cushman 1998d, A11).[6] Such acts caught the attention of the Federal Bureau of Investigation. For years it considered the ELF and the Animal Liberation Front (ALF) one of the bureau's "highest domestic terrorism priorities." By early 2006 a federal grand jury in Oregon indicted 11 people affiliated with either ELF or ALF for various acts of eco-terrorism. The indictment prompted Senator James M. Inhofe, chair of the Senate Environment and Public Works Committee, to compare ELF and ALF to the international terrorist group al-Qaeda.[7] His comments are an example of a tendency of critics of environmentalism to label all activists as extremist whether or not they share ELF's political strategy.

Finally, grassroots groups have sprung up in great numbers around the nation. They deal chiefly with local environmental issues such as threats from hazardous waste sites, urban sprawl, or loss of ecologically important lands (Bosso 1991). Such groups sometimes are affiliated with local chapters of the major national organizations such as the National Audubon Society or the National Wildlife Federation. Often, however, the grassroots groups reflect the concerns of local citizens who organize on their own to deal with community and regional environmental problems. Many of the independent grassroots groups also have their own Web pages and often are able to circulate environmental studies and reports and other information to concerned citizens in the area.

Not all environmental organizations fit easily into these three categories. Some focus far more on education, policy analysis, and scientific research than policy advocacy; indeed, many of them reject advocacy as unsuitable for their mission. Here too is a great diversity of organizations. Among the most visible of these groups that often have an effect on environmental policy are Resources for the Future (a highly regarded research organization specializing in economic analysis), the Union of Concerned Scientists, the Worldwatch Institute, and the World Resources Institute. Table 4.3 lists some of the most prominent national environmental organizations and their Web sites, along with their leading adversaries in the business community and among conservative policy research groups.

The environmental movement today is in the throes of change, and some critics even speak of the "death of environmentalism."[8] Environmental groups do face a daunting array of new challenges and dilemmas that flow from their very success since the 1960s, but they are far from dead. The mainstream groups, for instance, are now a political fixture in Washington and in many state capitals; many of them have substantial memberships and budgets to facilitate their work. Yet in some respects these groups, such as the Sierra Club, are losing ideological fervor and the capacity to

TABLE 4.3

Web Sites for Leading Environmental Organizations and Their Adversaries

Organization	Major Issues or Orientation	Web Address
Sierra Club	Broad environmental education and policy action	www.sierraclub.org
National Audubon Society	Diversified conservation of resources	www.aubudon.org
National Parks Conservation Association	Parks and land conservation	www.npca.org
Wilderness Society	Wilderness protection	www.tws.org
National Wildlife Federation	Wildlife and land conservation	www.nwf.org
Environmental Defense	Diversified environmental education, policy, law	www.environmental defense.org
Natural Resources Defense Council	Diversified environmental education, policy, law	www.nrdc.org
League of Conservation Voters	Congressional voting and elections	www.lcv.org
Union of Concerned Scientists	Science and environmental protection	www.ucsusa.org
Greenpeace International	International environmental action	www.greenpeace.org
Izaak Walton League	Land and water conservation	www.iwla.org
Nature Conservancy	Land conservation	http://nature.org
World Wildlife Fund	Wildlife conservation and global environment	www.worldwildlife. org
Earth First!	Direct action, ecosystem protection	www.earthfirst.org
Rainforest Action Network	Rain forest protection	www.ran.org
American Farmland Trust	Farmland conservation	www.farmland.org
Population Connection	Population growth	www.population connection.org

Groups and Policy Research Institutes Often in Opposition to Environmentalists

U.S. Chamber of Commerce	Represents business interests	www.uschamber.com
National Association of Manufacturers	Represents manufacturing interests	www.nam.org
National Federation of Independent Businesses	Represents interests of small businesses	www.nfib.com
American Chemistry Council	Represents chemical manufacturers	www.american chemistry.com
Competitive Enterprise Institute	Conservative research institute focusing on regulation	www.cei.org
Cato Institute	Libertarian policy institute	www.cato.org
Heritage Foundation	Conservative think tank	www.heritage.org
American Council on Science and Health	Critical of environmental science and health reports considered unbalanced	www.acsh.org

Note: For a broader list of groups, see www.webdirectory.com (organized by subject area, such as pollution and sustainable development); www.environlink.org (also organized by subject area); or the comprehensive and searchable Conservation Directory prepared by the National Wildlife Federation, available at www.nwf.org/conservationdirectory/. Other organizations that generally oppose environmental groups may be found through an Internet search.

attract and hold public support to the greens and especially to emerging grassroots and regional environmental groups. Their activities in Washington and in state capitals may be important for achieving the environmentalist policy agenda, but increasingly that agenda is too narrowly defined to capture the public's attention and mobilize its energies. The green groups and grassroots organizations have a greater capacity to appeal to the public's identification with local and regional environmental issues—such as local land use and pollution disputes, transportation choices, environmental justice concerns, and community sustainability—even if they often lack the funding and technical expertise to succeed entirely on their own. The success of these groups suggests a substantial potential for a robust and broadly supported civic environmentalism organized around such issues, especially when groups can effectively blend environmental, social, and economic concerns in urban settings (Gottlieb 2001; Paehlke 2006; Portney 2003; Shutkin 2000).

All the leading environmental groups face difficult choices as well over organizational priorities and strategies if they are to continue to thrive and represent their positions well in the political process at all levels of government. Disagreements over goals, strategies, and political styles—as well as competition for members and funds—have divided the environmental community for well over a decade (Bosso 2005; Gottlieb 1993; Shaiko 1999). In addition, during the early to mid-1990s, most of the national groups struggled to stem declining memberships and dwindling financial contributions. The Nature Conservancy, a group devoted to private land conservation efforts, was one major exception. In 1995 its membership reached 800,000, its highest level ever, and its fundraising rose to an all-time high. It has done even better since that time, with a membership total in 2006 of more than 1 million; it also has enough resources to hire a staff of over 3,200 people, including 720 scientists. Some other groups, such as NRDC, have recovered as well; NRDC membership rose from 185,000 in 1995 to 450,000 by 2004 (see Bosso and Guber 2006 and Table 4.2). This kind of improvement may be difficult to sustain in the years ahead, though, unless the salience of environmental issues increases enough to rekindle public enthusiasm.

As has been evident over the past decade and more, environmentalists have been confronted at local, state, and national levels by a newly energized opposition in the property rights and wise use movements. Those groups represent timber, mining, ranching, and other land development interests, particularly in the West, and they reflect rising local concern over the impact of environmental and resource policies such as the Endangered Species Act (Brick and Cawley 1996; Cawley 1993; Switzer 1997). The land rights movement activists and other opponents of environmentalists have failed to win most of the policy contests in which they have engaged. They have succeeded, however, in altering the rhetoric of public debate through increased emphasis on adverse economic effects of environmental and resource policies. Their influence can be seen in the prolonged policy gridlock in Congress and state legislatures over renewal of major environmental programs (Bosso and Guber 2006; Kraft 2006) as well as in a new skepticism toward environmental regulation (Higgs and Close 2005).

In addition, environmentalists continue to face strong opposition by business groups that traditionally have criticized environmental policies for their costs and other burdens they impose. The Bush administration has been very supportive of business interests and their concerns. The result is that the reelection of President

Bush in 2004 has not been good news for environmentalists, as suggested at the beginning of the chapter. Indeed, a prominent environmental journalist observed after the 2004 elections that national environmental groups "have less political clout today than they've wielded at any other time since their movement sprang up in the late 1960s." She concluded that the next several years are expected to be "the toughest in decades for environmental activists seeking to block Bush's initiatives."[9]

Public Opinion and the Environment

The American public has long expressed concern about the environment, and it has strongly supported public policy actions for environmental protection and resource conservation. Public opinion surveys from the 1970s to the present offer abundant evidence of that concern and support, particularly as it applies to public health threats (Dunlap 1995). In this section we consider some of the findings.

Large majorities of the public (61 percent) say they are either active in or sympathetic to the environmental movement. Similar results can be found in surveys dating back to 1980 (Bosso and Guber 2006; CEQ 1980). Most of these surveys, old and new, find a surprisingly small percentage of the public is *un*sympathetic, generally about 2 to 4 percent (Ladd and Bowman 1995). Other evidence of public concern is easy to find. For example, when a Gallup survey taken in March 2004 asked people how they would rate "the overall quality of the environment in this country today," 46 percent rated it as "only fair," and 11 percent said it was "poor" (Bosso and Guber 2006). People express even more concern when they look to the future. A Yale University survey taken about the same time found that far more people thought the environment was getting worse (50 percent) than better (16 percent); the public also rated the environment as one of the top concerns over the "next twenty years" (Global Strategy Group 2004). Surveys find that support for environmental protection is a consensual issue that generates little overt opposition among the general public. As one major study concluded, "most Americans share a common set of environmental beliefs and values" (Kempton, Boster, and Hartley 1996, 211). Consistent with this picture, more recent polls have found that strong majorities (55 to 67 percent) think the government is doing "too little" to deal with environmental problems and should do more; only a small minority (5 to 11 percent) believes it is doing "too much" (Bosso and Guber 2006; Global Strategy Group 2004). As these numbers imply, a majority of Americans disagrees with decisions of the George W. Bush administration to pull back from environmental protection efforts (Kriz and Barnes 2002).[10] Yet these results also tell us there is a permissive consensus on the environment that leaves room for public officials to act as they prefer. The political risk they may face rises when the issues gain extensive media coverage and environmental groups are able to mobilize their supporters. A good example is the success of environmental groups in late 2005 in defeating congressional proposals to drill for oil in the Arctic National Wildlife Refuge.

Surveys of the kind summarized here are informative but also misleading. They almost never ask about the depth of public concern or how well informed the public is about environmental problems, and they do not point to inconsistencies in the public's beliefs and attitudes or document the saliency of these issues for the average person. Yet these characteristics are all important for understanding public opinion on the environment and its implications for policy action (Guber 2003).

Consistency of Opinions and Depth of Concern   On many policy issues the public's views are inconsistent and sometimes contradictory. Environmental opinions are no different. For example, people say that they favor greater environmental protection in the abstract, but over the past decade they have also indicated they prefer less government, less regulation, and lower taxes, again in the abstract. Similarly, people say that they support energy conservation, but they are unwilling to pay even modest sums in increased gasoline taxes to further that goal. Politicians are so convinced of the public's hostility to increased fuel taxes that such proposals have rarely been given serious consideration in the United States. The public's general preference for environmental protection also may weaken when people face real and intense local or regional conflicts in which environmental measures are believed to affect employment or economic well-being adversely. Thus the level of public support for environmental protection depends heavily on the way issues are framed in any given controversy.

One way to judge public preferences is to ask whether people act on their pro-environmental opinions. As a journalist once put it, "tree talk" is cheap, but it creates a "lip-service gap" when the public is unwilling to make the necessary personal sacrifices to clean up the environment. Survey data speak to this point and tend to confirm Everett Ladd and Karlyn Bowman's 1995 description of the American public as "Lite Greens"; they are generally favorable toward environmental protection activities but exhibit little depth or personal commitment (see also Guber 2003). A 2005 survey of college freshmen in the United States, for example, reported that 77 percent agreed that "the federal government is not doing enough to control environmental pollution." But when asked about goals they consider to be essential or very important, only 20 percent of the freshmen selected "becoming involved in programs to clean up the environment"; the choice landed among the bottom five of activities and goals.[11] Other evidence points to much the same pattern. For example, despite general public concern for the environment, half of new passenger vehicles sold in the United States in recent years have been vans, light trucks, and sport utility vehicles, most with poor fuel economy. So there is a disconnect between the environmental beliefs and attitudes people profess to hold and their personal behavior.

Moreover, people tend not to be politically active. Fewer than 5 percent claim they regularly contribute money to environmental groups, write to public officials about environmental issues, or write to specific companies about their environmental concerns. This is closer to the finding in many surveys that peg the hard-core environmental activists among the public at between 1 and 5 percent, and the attentive public (those who are interested and relatively well informed) at perhaps 5 to 10 percent. Of course, even 1 percent of the population is a lot of people, and they may influence many others.

Environmental Knowledge and Opinion Saliency   There are also reasons to question the public's knowledge about environmental issues and about environmental policy actions. Annual surveys commissioned by the National Environmental Education and Training Foundation (NEETF) and conducted by the Roper Starch survey firm have found consistently that relatively few people are knowledgeable about environmental problems. In a September 2005 summary of 10 years of such "environmental literacy" surveys, the organization says there has been "a persistent pattern of environmental ignorance even among the most educated and influential members of society" (Coyle 2005). Just 12 percent of Americans, it says, can pass a basic quiz on energy topics (see also Smith 2002), and only a third can pass a comparable test of environmental knowledge. These results led the organization to conclude that Americans are "unprepared to respond to the major environmental challenges we face in the 21st century."[12] To cite one example of the public's limited understanding of such issues, a 2005 survey found that only 52 percent agreed there is "a consensus among the great majority of scientists that global warming exists and could do significant damage," even though this is indeed the position of the Intergovernmental Panel on Climate Change (discussed in Chapter 2). However, an equal percentage were willing to take significant steps to reduce greenhouse gas emissions if they were convinced that an overwhelming majority of scientists agreed global warming posed a significant threat.[13]

An Earth Week 2004 survey of public views about the Bush administration's environmental policy actions found a similar lack of awareness, in this case of presidential policy actions. Riley Dunlap (2004) reports that a majority of Americans thought that Bush's policies were about the same as in previous presidential administration; that is, they did not see that President Bush was any different from Bill Clinton on the environment. Moreover, despite all the press coverage of controversies over criticism of the Bush administration by scientists, two thirds of Americans said they had heard either nothing at all or not much about the charges leveled by the scientists. From these results, Dunlap concluded that Bush was likely "not especially vulnerable on the environment at this point." As made clear in the discussion of electoral politics at the chapter's beginning, Dunlap's analysis was indeed correct.

These findings are consistent with what may be the most important attribute of public opinion on the environment. Environmental issues are rarely considered to be important by the American public except for major catastrophes. This is especially so in the face of other problems considered to be more pressing, such as the global war on terrorism, health care, and the economy. That is, the environment generally is not among the issues that people consider the most important to their lives or to their communities, at least in the immediate future. Surveys do suggest that environmental issues rise to the top of the list of issues that people think will be most important some 25 years from now.[14] According to a March 2006 Gallup poll, Americans claim to be most concerned about water pollution, pollution of drinking water, contamination by toxic waste, and air pollution. They are less concerned about more remote issues such as acid rain and global warming. The results were identical to a similar survey conducted in 2002.

Given the generally low salience of the environment, people usually are not motivated to invest the time and energy needed to keep up with the issues and to become informed about them. Nonetheless, the importance of environmental issues can change abruptly if a local problem—such as contaminated drinking water—becomes unusually visible or controversial or if environmental groups or their opponents successfully mobilize the public. Opponents of environmental protection have sometimes fallen into the "salience trap" of believing that the low salience of these issues implies a low level of public concern (Bosso 2000). Little evidence, however, suggests that public concern for the environment is likely to wane anytime soon.

An intriguing question remains. How readily would people change their behavior if given the necessary information, encouragement, and incentives? It is not fair to fault people for failing to act on their views if there are too many barriers to doing so. Similarly, it is easy to disparage the public's rather low level of civic involvement, but this may be a consequence of limited opportunities for getting involved. A continuing high level of cynicism toward government, politics, and politicians further diminishes the likelihood of public participation in the political process and in community affairs (Putnam 2000; Skocpol and Fiorina 1999). The success of many local environmental initiatives, however, indicates that considerable potential may exist to improve public knowledge and to foster involvement in community and regional decision making.

Despite its limited knowledge of environmental problems, the public believes that environmental conditions from the local to the global level have worsened and that they will continue to decline in the future. People also believe that such expected deterioration in the environment poses a direct threat to their health and well-being. Such findings suggest a powerful new depth to environmental concern in recent years that was largely absent during the 1970s (Dunlap 1992). Thus people in the United States and elsewhere may be ready to respond to political and community leaders who learn how to appeal to their concerns, fears, and hopes for the future. The rise of the sustainable community movement over the past several years and new expressions of public concern across the nation over urban sprawl are two recent indicators of that potential (Mazmanian and Kraft 1999; Paehlke 2006; Portney 2003).

Beyond U.S. borders, most of the same issues arise. International surveys have found an equivalent level of concern for environmental quality around the world in both developed and developing nations. The Gallup Health of the Planet survey of 1992 covered two dozen nations, from low income to high income, and it found "little difference in reported levels of environmental concern between people of poor, less economically developed nations and those of the richer, highly industrialized nations." Majorities in 21 of the 24 nations surveyed reported either a "great deal" or a "fair amount" of concern (Dunlap, Gallup, and Gallup 1993, 11). More remarkably, residents of poor nations were only slightly more willing than those in rich nations to accept environmental degradation in exchange for economic growth. As is true in the United States, however, the pursuit of the worldwide sustainable development goals endorsed at the 1992 Earth Summit and the 2002 Johannesburg conference will require that a generally sympathetic and concerned public become better informed and be encouraged to play an active role in environmental and development decisions at local, regional, and community levels.

Environmental Issues in Election Campaigns

One way that environmental organizations reach new constituencies and broaden public support is to promote environmental issues in election campaigns. Environmental issues only rarely have been a decisive factor in elections, even though they have long been prominent in selected contests in Oregon, Washington, California, New Jersey, Colorado, and other states. Moreover, there is little evidence to date of the existence of a reliable "green" vote in most areas of the United States.

The Green Party itself has attracted sustained support only within a few regions of the country, unlike in Europe. Yet the U.S. electoral system is strongly biased against third or minor parties, which accounts for the challenges they face in national elections.

Local election are somewhat different. For example, in 1996 in Arcata, California, voters elected a Green Party majority to the city council, the first time the party had won control of a city government in the United States. Arcata is close to the Headwaters Forest, an old-growth redwood stand at the center of a major controversy over continued cutting of redwood groves in the Pacific Northwest.

When Green Party candidate Ralph Nader ran in the 2000 presidential election, he managed to win 2.8 million votes, or 2.7 percent of votes cast (3.8 percent in California). Gore won the popular vote, but Nader drew enough votes in the exceedingly close campaign between Bush and Gore to cost Gore the Electoral College votes in several states, including the hotly contested election in Florida. Nader received over 97,000 votes in Florida, far more than the thin margin that separated Gore and Bush in the state. The election results were both good news and bad news for the Green Party. Nader demonstrated his nationwide appeal (and the frustration of many voters with the two major parties). Yet his very success demonized him within the Democratic Party, which had otherwise become the nominal home for environmentalists. As the Bush administration sought to pull back from many of the environmental policy achievements of the previous three decades (Vig 2006), many Democrats became even more disenchanted with Nader and the Green Party. In the 2004 elections, the Greens chose a less prominent presidential candidate and received only a tiny fraction of the vote; the result suggests that Nader's support had more to do with his personal appeal than support for the party.

Several environmental groups have tried to influence elections through candidate endorsements, financial support for candidates, and voter mobilization. The League of Conservation Voters (LCV) has engaged in such electioneering actions since 1970, and the Sierra Club has long had a political action committee for this purpose. Both have done well in these efforts, but they face the obstacles just discussed, especially the low salience of environmental issues in most campaigns. In 1998, for example, the Sierra Club spent $7 million when it fought hard against the Republican Congress's "war on the environment." Much of that money was devoted to voter education efforts and attempts to activate some 250,000 of the club's members in 20 states through issue advocacy advertisements (Berke 1998). The effort appeared to pay off. The Sierra Club said that its efforts "contributed to the victories of pro-environment candidates in 38 out of 43 (88 percent) priority races" (Bosso 2000, 66). The club spent similar amounts of money in later election cycles (Duffy 2003).

For its part, the LCV has spent similar amounts of money on congressional races and enjoyed considerable success. One of its most noteworthy efforts was in Wisconsin's 1998 Senate race. The league spent $420,000 to fend off Representative Mark Neumann's challenge to Democratic senator Russell Feingold by emphasizing Neumann's votes against cleanup of toxic chemicals in waterways, protecting wetlands, and protection of drinking water. The league said that some 40 percent of voters cited these three issues combined in explaining their vote, more than any other single concern. The league placed a full-time campaign manager in Milwaukee, put a field organizer in Madison, and ran an extensive television and advertising campaign in the state, including over 400 television spots in the state's largest cities (Duffy 2003).

The environment could play a greater role in future elections. When voters are asked whether a candidate's positions on the environment will be important in their voting decision, large majorities say yes (Kriz and Barnes 2002; LCV 1999). In one survey in 2004, 84 percent of Americans said a candidate's stance on the environment would be a factor in how they voted (Global Strategy Group 2004). Whether people really do think about the environment during election campaigns is likely to depend on the efforts made by groups such as the LCV and the Sierra Club to inform and mobilize the public, the extent of media coverage of environmental issues in campaigns, and the willingness of candidates to speak out on their environmental records or positions. In one pertinent study, Ringquist and Dasse (2004) found that statements made by candidates for the House of Representatives are usually an accurate guide to what they try to do in office. That is, campaign promises are meaningful. So if voters pay attention to the differences, they can learn a lot. The authors expressed one caveat, however. Republicans, they found, were "far more likely" to break those campaign promises, and "pro-environmental campaign promises are more likely to be broken." So it pays to look beyond simple campaign statements.

Further positive news about the electoral potential for environmental issues can be found in voting on ballot measures for land conservation and other environmental actions. In the November 2004 election, for example, of 161 conservation ballot measures, voters approved 120, or 75 percent. These votes authorized spending $3.25 billion dollars on land conservation. These kinds of measures did well even in states and counties that voted heavily for President Bush.[15] Another kind of ballot measure did well in Colorado. After the state legislature refused three times to pass a bill requiring utilities to generate more electricity from renewable sources such as wind turbines, voters approved a state referendum in 2004 mandating that 10 percent of the state's electricity must come from renewable sources by 2015. Colorado was the 18th state to set such standards but the first to do by a direct citizen action (Rabe and Mundo 2007). The result was particularly striking in light of the generally conservative voting record in the state and intense opposition by most energy companies there.[16]

▓ POLITICAL REACTION TO ENVIRONMENTALISM

So far in the chapter we have examined the evolution of environmental policy through the 1970s and have focused on the rise of a powerful environmental movement and a supportive public opinion that together helped establish and maintain a remarkable array of national and state environmental policies. As indicated in the preceding discussion, however, environmental issues have divided the U.S. public despite the generally positive attitudes toward a strong government role. Before turning in the next two chapters to the details of environmental policies and the politics associated with them, we should pay at least some attention to this political reaction to environmentalism that began in the late 1970s, was vividly apparent during Ronald Reagan's presidency, and emerged again both in U.S. Congress in the mid-to late 1990s and in the administration of George W. Bush in the early 2000s.

If the 1970s reflected the nation's initial commitment to environmental policy, by the early 1980s there was at least some ambivalence about how far to go in pursuit of policy goals and at what price. Such concerns had surfaced in both the Nixon and Ford administrations and again in the late 1970s in the Carter administration, partly because of the effect of the Arab oil embargo of 1973 and other energy and economic shocks of the decade (Vig 1994; Whitaker 1976). Industry had complained about the financial burdens of environmental regulation, and some labor unions joined in the chorus when jobs appeared to be threatened.

Environmental Policy in the Reagan and Bush Administrations

These criticisms reached full force in Ronald Reagan's presidency (1981–1989) and returned in the 104th Congress (1995–1996) when a Republican majority governed. Reagan and his advisers brought with them a dramatically different view of environmental issues and their relationship to the economy than had prevailed, with bipartisan support, for the previous decade. Virtually all environmental policies were to be reevaluated, and reversed or weakened, as part of Reagan's larger political agenda. That agenda included reducing the scope of government regulation, cutting back on the role of the federal government, shifting responsibilities where possible to the states, and relying more on the private sector.

Set largely by the right wing of the Republican party and western ranchers and others associated with the Sagebrush Rebellion (see Chapter 6), Reagan's agenda was the most radical in half a century (Kraft 1984). The major problem he faced was that Congress and the American public continued to favor the programs he was so anxious to curtail. Reagan tried as much as he could to bypass Congress in pushing his agenda through an administrative strategy of deregulation, defunding of regulatory agencies, and appointment of high-level personnel more in tune with his own conservative ideology. That strategy was only moderately effective and soon backfired.

Although initially successful in gaining congressional support for deep budgetary cuts that he justified largely on economic grounds, Reagan soon found his deregulatory actions sharply criticized and blocked by Congress. EPA administrator Anne Burford was forced to resign after less than two years in office. Reagan replaced her in March 1983 with William D. Ruckelshaus, who had served as the first EPA administrator between 1970 and 1973. Secretary of the Interior James G. Watt, the administration's controversial point person on environmental policy, lasted only a little longer before resigning in October 1983. He was replaced by William P. Clark, who, like Ruckelshaus, was more moderate and sought to repair some of the political damage Watt had caused (Vig and Kraft 1984).

Congress went on to renew and fortify every major environmental statute that came up for renewal in the 1980s. These statutes included the Resource Conservation and Recovery Act (RCRA) in 1984, Superfund amendments and the Safe Drinking Water Act in 1986, and the Clean Water Act in 1987. RCRA in particular was markedly strengthened in direct response to the political turmoil at the EPA and congressional distrust of the agency. By 1990 even the Clean Air Act, the nation's most important environmental law, was expanded and enhanced with the support of Reagan's vice president and successor, George H. W. Bush. The reasons could be found in public opinion and the capacity of environmental leaders to capitalize on the public's favorable stance toward environmental policy and its distrust of both industry and government. Early in 1990, for example, public opinion surveys indicated that more than 70 percent of the U.S. public favored making the Clean Air Act stricter, over 20 percent favored keeping it about the same, and only 2 percent wanted it less strict (National Journal 1990).

In retrospect, the remarkable turmoil over environmental policy under Ronald Reagan can be seen as short-term retrenchments in a striking evolutionary advance toward stronger environmental policies both in the United States and globally. As already noted, public support not only continued in the 1980s and 1990s, but it increased considerably. Environmental groups saw their memberships grow to new heights, and media attention was mostly favorable to environmentalists.

The message was not lost on George Bush's political advisers. During his run for the presidency in 1988, he broke openly with the Reagan environmental agenda. In a remarkable speech on the shore of Lake Erie in late August 1988, he promised to be "a Republican president in the Teddy Roosevelt tradition. A conservationist. An *environmentalist*" (Holusha 1988). Bush's record on the environment was decidedly mixed, although it clearly was different from Reagan's in many respects. His administration suffered from deep internal divisions over the direction of environmental policy that contributed to the president's inability to live up to his initial promise to depart sharply from Reagan's agenda. He ended his presidency openly critical of "environmental extremists" and of vice-presidential candidate Al Gore in particular. Bush did not convince the American public. A Gallup poll in June 1992 indicated that the public disapproved of his handling of the environment by a 2-to-1 margin (Vig 1994).

Clinton and Gore Reform Environmental Policy and Battle Congress

During the Clinton administration, many of the same conflicts became evident, only this time it was the Republican Congress that sought to pull back from the environmental commitments of the 1970s and 1980s. The Democratic White House assumed the role of defender of the status quo in environmental policy. The administration also pushed strongly for "reinventing environmental regulation" that would help address some of the most persistent criticisms of environmental policy, such as its high cost, burdens on industry and state and local governments, inflexibility, and inefficiency (Kraft and Scheberle 1998). Clinton was generally praised by environmentalists for his appointments, most notably Carol Browner as EPA administrator and Bruce Babbitt as secretary of the interior. The president sharply increased spending on environmental programs, and he earned praise from environmental groups for speaking out forcefully against the attempts within Congress to weaken environmental protection legislation (Kraft 2006). More significantly, the administration took important steps toward shifting the environmental agenda in the direction of sustainable development and more integrative policy action. Clinton ended his term as president with numerous measures to protect public lands, including executive orders that established 19 new national monuments and enlarged 3 others (Vig 2006). The Clinton administration policy initiatives receive detailed consideration in the rest of the text.

George W. Bush and the Environment

The administration of George W. Bush took a dramatically different stance on most environmental and resource issues. Bush entered office with the weakest of mandates, having lost the popular vote to Al Gore. Yet it was clear from the election campaign and from Bush's record as governor of Texas that he would depart significantly from the Clinton administration's environmental, energy, and resource policies. During the campaign, for instance, Bush argued for increasing oil and gas production on public lands, including the Arctic National Wildlife Refuge (ANWR), and he criticized the Kyoto Protocol on global climate change. He also made clear that he opposed the Clinton land preservation efforts as too rushed and inconsiderate of state and local interests. The policy differences became apparent with Bush's appointments and his actions as president.

Bush appointed the moderate former governor of New Jersey, Christine Todd Whitman, as EPA administrator, and he named conservative Gail Norton, a protégé of James Watt, as secretary of the interior. After frequently disagreements with the White House, Whitman resigned in 2003 and was replaced first by Michael Leavitt, former governor of Utah, and then in May 2005 by Stephen Johnson, a career EPA employee. Almost all the other high-level executive appointees in offices dealing with the environment and natural resources were probusiness advocates who came to the administration from corporate posts or from positions with conservative ideological groups.[17] Virtually no environmentalists were named to White House or agency positions.

In short order, President Bush charted a new direction in environmental policy, both domestic and international. He withdrew the United States from the Kyoto Protocol and exhibited far less concern with climate change than the Clinton administration had. He proposed a national energy policy grounded in increased oil and gas drilling, including in ANWR. And in numerous decisions on water quality standards, clean air rules, energy efficiency standards, protection of national forests and parks, and mining regulations, the administration sided with industry and economic development over environmental protection (Vig and Kraft 2006). Those decisions are discussed throughout the remainder of the text.

Unlike the Reagan administration, with which the president's environmental policy actions were widely compared, Bush kept a low profile on controversial decisions of this kind and defended them as balanced and in the public interest. Even where the polls indicated public disapproval of his environmental policies, the president did not appear to suffer politically from them. His popularity, which soared in the aftermath of the terrorist attacks of September 11, 2001, and the global war on terrorism, helped minimize criticism from environmental groups and the media (Bosso and Guber 2006; Kriz and Barnes 2002). In 2001 and 2002 a Democratic Senate blocked many of Bush's antienvironmental initiatives, including proposals to cut the EPA's budget and to drill for oil and gas in ANWR, but after the 2002 elections the Republican Party held majorities in both the House and Senate that gave the president freer rein. Whether the U.S. public will continue to support the president's environmental initiatives depends on the way the media cover the issues, how effective environmental groups are in opposing Bush, and the extent to which the Democrats are able to elevate environmental issues to a higher status on the political agenda.

CONCLUSIONS

In at least one respect, the Reagan administration's efforts during the 1980s to curtail environmental policy actions and the controversies that reappeared in the Congress in the mid- to late 1990s and in the administration of George W. Bush left an important legacy. Environmental policy must be judged by many of the same standards applied to other public policies today, such as effectiveness, efficiency, and equity. Good intentions are not enough, and agencies must offer demonstrable evidence of success. When programs fail to measure up, alternatives should be examined. If environmental standards are to be set at high levels, some indication of positive benefits needs to be offered to justify the costs and burdens imposed on society. All these considerations lie at the heart of current efforts to appraise and reform environmental policy and to set it on a more defensible and enduring path for the future (Durant, Fiorino, and O'Leary 2004; Morgenstern and Portney 2004; Vig and Kraft 2006).The next two chapters turn to the goals and chosen instruments of U.S. environmental protection policy and natural resource and energy policy and to debate over issues of this kind. Chapter 7 then takes an even more direct tack by assessing three decades of U.S. environmental policy and the promise of policy alternatives such as market incentives, privatization, information disclosure, and other approaches.

The record of policy evolution reviewed in this chapter points to an important paradox of U.S. environmental policy and politics. Policy achievements of the 1960s and 1970s withstood a severe challenge during the 1980s and again in the 1990s in large part because the American public strongly favored prevention of further environmental degradation and protection from environmental and health threats. In this sense, the U.S. political system proved to be fairly responsive to public demands despite its institutional fragmentation and other barriers to majority rule. The paradox is that government may be too responsive to short-term public *demands* and insufficiently attentive to long-term public *needs*.

In response to public concern over environmental threats from air and water pollution to hazardous waste sites, Congress has mandated that the EPA and other agencies take on many more tasks than they can handle with their budgets and staffs. Environmental interest groups have lobbied effectively for adoption of those policies and their strengthening over time. Understandably, they also resist the many recent efforts in Congress and the states to alter them. Yet in many respects the policies are very much in need of reform to bring them into the twenty-first century and to help launch a more sustainable era of environmental policy both domestically and internationally (Mazmanian and Kraft 1999).

As discussed in Chapter 1, this tendency to reflect public fears about the environment and to overload and underfund administrative agencies translates into significant inefficiencies in U.S. environmental policy (Portney and Stavins 2000; Rothenberg 2002). As a nation we spend a lot of money and time dealing with problems that pose relatively little risk to public and ecological health, such as many hazardous waste sites, but not nearly enough on other problems, such as climate change, loss of biological diversity, and indoor air quality, arguably of far greater consequence (U.S. EPA 1990b). So democracy appears to be working well in representing public concerns, but it is failing the public in protecting its health as well as ensuring ecological integrity and sustainable development. An important question is how environmental politics and policy can better serve the public's long-term needs by building a sustainable and just society both within the United States and the rest of the world.

DISCUSSION QUESTIONS

1. What factors best explain the rise of the environmental movement in the 1960s and 1970s? Similarly, what accounts for the outpouring of federal and state environmental policies during the 1960s and 1970s?
2. The environmental movement today is much less cohesive than often supposed. Why do environmental organizations find it so hard to cooperate in pursuit of common goals? What difference does that make for achieving environmental policy goals?
3. Most survey research finds the U.S. public both concerned about environmental problems and supportive of strong public policies. Yet the public is not well informed on the issues and they are not usually salient to the average person. Why? What actions might raise the public's awareness of environmental issues and their salience?
4. Only a few national environmental groups, such as the League of Conservation Voters and the Sierra Club, have been active in the electoral process. Why is that? If more environmental organizations were active in campaigns and elections, what do you think the effect would be on environmental politics and policy?
5. The adversaries of environmental groups, or the "environmental opposition," have become more active since Ronald Reagan's administration in the 1980s. Given the broad public support for environmental policy, how did these groups become so politically influential? How have they been able to remain so in recent years, for instance in the administration of George W. Bush?

SUGGESTED READINGS

Andrews, Richard N. L. *Managing the Environment, Managing Ourselves: A History of American Environmental Policy.* New Haven, CT: Yale University Press, 1999.

Bosso, Christopher J. *Environment, Inc.: From Grassroots to Beltway.* Lawrence: University of Kansas Press, 2005.

Duffy, Robert J. *The Green Agenda in American Politics: New Strategies for the Twenty-First Century.* Lawrence: University of Kansas Press, 2003.

Guber, Deborah Lynn. *The Grassroots of a Green Revolution: Polling America on the Environment.* Cambridge, MA: MIT Press, 2003.

Lacey, Michael J., ed. *Government and Environmental Politics: Essays on Historical Developments since World War II.* Baltimore: Johns Hopkins University Press, 1989.

Shabecoff, Philip. *A Fierce Green Fire: The American Environmental Movement.* New York: Hill and Wang, 1993.

ENDNOTES

1. See Margaret Kriz, "A Green Spotlight on Bush's 'F'," *National Journal*, January 17, 2004, 184–85. The league also published elaborate analyses of each of the Democratic candidates for the presidential nomination. All are available at its Web site: www.lcv.org. The full assessment of President Bush, with the report card, runs to about 30 pages and is called "The Bush Environmental Record: Putting Corporate Interests over America's Interests."

2. In addition to Philip Shabecoff's history of the environmental movement, many recent volumes on U.S. conservation history provide a full account of what can only be summarized briefly here. See Lacey (1989), Nash (1990), Hays (1959, 1987), and especially Andrews (1999).

3. These public lands are managed chiefly by the National Park Service, now responsible for about 83 million acres; the U.S. Forest Service, about 190 million acres; and the Bureau of Land Management, about 264 million acres (CEQ 1998). The balance of land outside of Alaska consists of desert, rangeland, and mountain land.

4. Although most groups today have their own Web sites and many sites include an alphabetical listing of links to environmental groups, the National Wildlife Federation has long published a comprehensive and elaborately indexed annual directory, the current edition covering more than 4,000 groups. It includes not only environmental interest groups but federal and state agencies and university programs. See its most recent *Conservation Directory*, available online at www.nwf.org/conservationdirectory.

5. See Elizabeth Becker, "Web Site Helped Change Farm Policy," *New York Times*, February 24, 2002, 22.

6. One inventory of such acts by the *Portland Oregonian* identified at least 100 major cases of such violence since 1980 and put the total cost at $43 million for 11 western states. The study was cited in a news report on MSNBC, "Eco-terrorism Escalating, Study Finds," November 9, 1999.

7. Michael Janofsky, "11 Indicted in Cases of Environmental Sabotage," *New York Times*, January 21, 2006, 1, A9.

8. The phrase comes from a provocative essay with that title by Michael Shellenberger and Ted Nordhaus that was circulated via the Internet in October 2004, stimulating widespread reaction, pro and con.

9. See Margaret Kriz, "Out of the Loop," *National Journal*, February 5, 2005, 344–49. See also Mary Clare Jalonick, "After November Elections, Change Could Be in the Air—and Water," *CQ Weekly*, October 23, 2004, 2520–22.

10. See also Richard L. Berke and Janet Elder, "Bush Loses Favor Despite Tax Cut and Overseas Trip," *New York Times*, June 21, 2001, A1, 16.

11. Eric Hoover, "Freshman Survey: More Students Plan to Lend a Hand," *Chronicle of Higher Education*, February 3, 2006, A40–41.

12. The studies are available at the group's Web page: www.neetf.org/roper/roper.shtm.

13. Steven Kull, principal investigator, "Americans on Climate Change: 2005," released by the Program on International Policy Attitudes, University of Maryland, available online at www.pipa.org.

14. A Gallup poll in April 2000, for instance, found that 14 percent of the U.S. public chose the environment as likely to be "the most important problem facing our nation 25 years from now." That score put the environment ahead of every other issue mentioned by the public. An additional 6 percent identified "overpopulation" as a problem of concern. The poll was summarized in *National Journal*'s Poll Track section, June 17, 2000, 1941.

15. See Will Rogers, "It's Easy Being Green," *New York Times*, November 20, 2004, A31.

16. Kirk Johnson, "Coloradans Vote to Embrace Alternative Sources of Energy," *New York Times*, November 24, 2004, A13.

17. Katharine Q. Seelye, "Bush Picks Industry Insiders to Fill Environmental Posts," *New York Times*, May 12, 2001, 1.

Environmental Protection Policy: Controlling Pollution

The American public has made clear its desire for clean air, clean water, and a healthy environment free of toxic substances and hazardous wastes. Yet it has been ambivalent about its willingness to pay higher taxes and product costs or to tolerate regulatory activities at the federal and state levels to achieve these environmental quality goals. Congress has responded to public opinion by enacting and, over time, strengthening seven major environmental protection, or pollution control, statutes: the Clean Air Act; Clean Water Act; Safe Drinking Water Act; Toxic Substances Control Act; Federal Insecticide, Fungicide, and Rodenticide Act; Resource Conservation and Recovery Act; and Comprehensive Environmental Response, Compensation, and Liability Act (Superfund). The first six statutes look primarily to the future. The U.S. EPA develops regulations that affect the current and future generation, transportation, use, and disposal of chemicals and pollutants that pose a significant risk to public health or the environment. The last statute is largely, although not exclusively, remedial. It aims to repair damage from careless disposal of hazardous chemicals in the past. Superfund also affects present and future pollution control efforts.[1]

Separately and collectively, these acts mandate an exceedingly wide array of regulatory actions that touch virtually every industrial and commercial enterprise in the nation and increasingly affect the lives of ordinary citizens. Routine implementation decisions as well as the periodic renewal of the acts by Congress invariably involve contentious debates over the extent of the risks faced, the appropriate standards to protect public and ecological health, and the policy strategies used to achieve those standards. Policymakers and interest groups argue as well over the degree to which environmental and health benefits should be weighed against the costs of compliance and other social and economic values.

As shown in Chapter 2, these policies have produced substantial and well-documented gains, particularly in urban air quality and in control of point sources of water pollution.

It is equally true, however, that the policies have fallen short of expectations, and in some cases distressingly so, as actions on toxic chemicals, pesticides, and hazardous wastes clearly illustrate. Existing policy barely touches some major risks, such as indoor air quality, and others, such as surface water, groundwater, and drinking water quality, have proved far more difficult to control than originally expected. As welcome as they are, the achievements to date also have not been cheap. The U.S. General Accounting Office (GAO) estimated that between 1972 and 1992 the cumulative expenditures for pollution control were in excess of $1 trillion (U.S. GAO 1992). By the early 2000s, the continuing cost to government and the private sector of these same policies was probably about $200 billion per year.[2]

The nation remains committed to the broad policy goals of controlling pollution and minimizing public health risks. Yet implementation and compliance costs and the intrusiveness of environmental regulation will test its resolve over the next decade. Tight budgets at all levels of government, as well as growing impatience with ineffective and inefficient public policies, are creating new demands that programs either produce demonstrable success or be changed. In particular, the federally driven command-and-control approach to pollution control adopted during the 1970s is increasingly viewed as only one component in a larger policy arsenal that may be directed at environmental problems in the twenty-first century (Durant, Fiorino, and O'Leary 2004; Mazmanian and Kraft 1999; Sexton et al. 1999).

This is quite a long chapter that covers both the substance of the major pollution control policies and their implementation by the EPA and the states. The relationship of the two parts is important, and I try to make that connection clear throughout the chapter. Those who prefer may read each part independently.

■ THE CONTOURS OF ENVIRONMENTAL PROTECTION POLICY

The first part of the chapter reviews the configuration of current environmental protection policy to provide some perspective on the developments just cited and on contemporary debates about the future of pollution control efforts. Each policy has different goals, uses distinctive means to achieve them, and sets out its own standards for balancing environmental quality and other social goals. Yet policies may also be grouped together for present purposes. All focus on environmental protection or pollution control, and all seek primarily to protect public health even when ecological objectives are included as well. All of these policies also rely on national environmental quality standards and regulatory mechanisms, and all are implemented primarily by the EPA, in cooperation with the states. Attention is paid here to the institutions and policy actors that shape policy decisions, the political and administrative processes that affect the outcomes, and competing policy approaches and solutions. Some questions about how well these programs are working are saved for Chapter 7, which deals broadly with issues of policy and program evaluation.[3] Table 5.1 provides an overview of these seven policies and their key provisions.

The Clean Air Act

The Clean Air Act (CAA) is one of the most comprehensive and complex statutes ever approved by the U.S. government. It is the premier example of contemporary

TABLE 5.1

Major Federal Environmental Protection Policies

Statute	Key Provisions and Features
Clean Air Act Amendments of 1970, PL 91-604. Revised in 1977 and 1990.	Requires the EPA to set primary and secondary national ambient air quality standards and emission limits, and the states to develop implementation plans. Regulates motor vehicle emissions and fuels. The 1990 amendments sought to limit acid deposition, to phase out CFCs, and to regulate major sources of toxic and hazardous air pollutants.
Federal Water Pollution Control Act (Clean Water Act) Amendments of 1972, PL 92-500, amended in 1977 and 1987.	Sets national water quality goals, establishes a pollution discharge permit system for dischargers of waste into U.S. waters. The 1987 amendments established a state revolving loan fund to help build wastewater treatment plants and urged states to develop nonpoint source pollution management plans.
Safe Drinking Water Act of 1974, PL 93-523, amended in 1986 and 1996, the latter as PL 104-182.	Sets standards to safeguard the quality of public drinking water supplies and to regulate state programs for protecting groundwater sources. Provides loans and grants to assist localities with meeting standards. The 1996 amendments require local water systems to distribute annual reports on drinking water safety.
Resource Conservation and Recovery Act of 1976, PL 94-580, amended in 1984.	Sets federal regulations for hazardous waste treatment, storage, transportation, and disposal, and provides assistance for state programs. The 1984 amendments prohibited land disposal of certain hazardous liquid wastes and mandated state consideration of recycling programs.
Toxic Substances Control Act of 1976, PL 94-469.	Authorizes premarket testing of chemical substances and allows the EPA to ban or regulate the manufacture, sale, or use of chemicals presenting an "unreasonable risk of injury" to health or the environment.
Federal Insecticide, Fungicide, and Rodenticide Act of 1972, PL 92-516. Amended in 1996 as the Food Quality Protection Act, PL 104-170.	Requires registration of all pesticides in U.S. commerce and allows the EPA to cancel or suspend registration when needed to protect public health or the environment. Amendments of 1996 created a new "reasonable risk" approach for raw and processed foods and required the EPA to adopt a 10-fold margin of safety to protect children.
Comprehensive Environmental Response, Compensation, and Liability Act (Superfund) of 1980, PL 96-510. Revised in 1986.	Authorizes the federal government to respond to hazardous waste emergencies and to clean up chemical dump sites through use of a Superfund supported by taxes on the chemical and petroleum industries. Also sets liability for cleanup costs. The 1986 amendments (SARA) added the Emergency Planning and Community Right-to-Know Act, which established the Toxics Release Inventory program.

environmental regulation. Unsurprisingly, since the early 1970s the act has been a frequent target of critics even while environmentalists and public health specialists have sought to fortify and expand it. The battles continued throughout the 1990s and remain evident today. Congress approved the 1990 amendments to the CAA with President George H. W. Bush's active support. Yet Bush's own White House Council on Competitiveness tried repeatedly to weaken EPA regulations for implementing the act in an effort to reduce its economic effects on industry and local governments (Bryner 1995). The Clinton White House resisted similar economic arguments when in 1997 it supported the EPA's recommendation to tighten air pollution standards for ozone and fine particulates (Cushman 1997). Yet George W. Bush's administration leaned the other way. It sought to give greater weight to economic effects of clean air policies and thus pull back from Clinton administration initiatives, particularly for older industrial facilities. Both decisions are discussed later.

Federal air pollution control policy dates back to the original and modest Clean Air Act of 1963, which provided for federal support for air pollution research as well as assistance to the states for developing their own pollution control agencies. Prior to the 1963 act, federal action was limited to a small research program in the Public Health Service authorized in a 1955 act. The 1970 amendments to the Clean Air Act followed several incremental adjustments in federal policy, including the 1965 Motor Vehicle Air Pollution Control Act and a 1965 amendment to the CAA that began the federal program for setting emissions standards for new motor vehicles. A 1967 Air Quality Act provided funds to the states to plan for air pollution control, required them to establish air quality control regions (i.e., geographic areas with shared air quality problems), and directed the federal government to study health effects of air pollution to assist the states in their control strategies.

Congress adopted the radically different 1970 Clean Air Act both in response to sharply increased public concern about the environment, as discussed in Chapter 4, and because it saw little progress in cleaning the air under the previous statutes. The states as well as the federal government had been slow in responding to worsening air quality problems, states were reluctant to use the powers they were given, and the automobile industry displayed little commitment to pollution control. With near unanimity, Congress approved a far stronger act despite intense industry pressure to weaken it. It also did so in the face of significant doubts about both available technology and governmental capacity to implement the law (Bryner 1995; Jones 1975).

The new policy mandated National Ambient Air Quality Standards (NAAQS), which were to be set by the EPA and be uniform across the country with enforcement shared by the federal and state governments. As discussed in Chapter 2, these standards deal with permissible concentrations of chemicals in the air. The primary standards were to protect human health, and secondary standards, where necessary, were to protect buildings, forests, water, crops, and similar nonhealth values. The EPA was to set the NAAQS at levels that would "provide an adequate margin of safety" to protect the public from "any known or anticipated adverse effects" associated with six major, or criteria, pollutants: sulfur dioxide, nitrogen dioxide, lead, ozone, carbon monoxide, and particulate matter. The standard for lead was added in 1977. A standard for hydrocarbons issued by the EPA under the 1970 act was eliminated in 1978 as unnecessary.

The act also required that an "ample margin of safety" be set for toxic or hazardous air pollutants such as arsenic, chromium, hydrogen chloride, zinc, pesticides, and radioactive substances. Congress assumed that a safe level of air pollution existed and standards could be set accordingly for air toxics as well as the criteria pollutants. The act has been interpreted as requiring the setting of the crucially important NAAQS without regard to the costs of attainment (Portney 1990). If control technologies were not available to meet these standards, Congress expected them to be developed by fixed deadlines. The goal was to reduce air pollution to acceptable levels.

The 1970 CAA and subsequent amendments also set national emissions standards for mobile sources of air pollution: cars, trucks, and buses. Congress explicitly called for a 90 percent reduction in hydrocarbon and carbon monoxide emissions from the levels of 1970, to be achieved by the 1975 model year, and a 90 percent reduction in the level of nitrogen oxides by the 1976 model year. Yet it gave the EPA the authority to waive the deadlines, which it did several times. Similarly, the act set tough emissions standards for stationary sources such as refineries, chemical companies, and other industrial facilities. New sources of pollution were to be held to New Source Performance Standards to be set industry by industry and enforced by the states. The standards were to be based on use of state-of-the-art control technologies (best available technology, or BAT), with at least some recognition that economic costs and energy use should be taken into account. Existing sources (e.g., older industrial facilities) were held to lower standards set by the states, a decision that became highly controversial by the 2000s.

To deal with existing sources of air pollution, each state was to prepare a State Implementation Plan (SIP) that would detail how it would meet EPA standards and guidelines. States have the primary responsibility for implementing those sections of the act dealing with stationary sources; the EPA retains authority for mobile sources. The 1970 act called for all areas of the nation to be in compliance with the national air standards by 1975, a date later extended repeatedly. The EPA could reject a SIP if it could not be expected to bring the state into compliance, and the agency could impose sanctions on those states, such as banning construction of large new sources of air pollution, including power plants and refineries, or cutting off highly valued federal highway and sewer funds.[4]

The 1977 Amendments In the 1977 amendments to the Clean Air Act, Congress backtracked in some respects from its early uncompromising position, such as on the dates by which compliance was to be achieved. Yet it left the major goals of the law intact and even strengthened the act on requirements for nonattainment areas and provisions for prevention of significant deterioration (PSD) in those areas already cleaner than the national standards.

Congress established three classes of clean areas. In Class I (national parks and similar areas), air quality would be protected against any deterioration. In Class II, the act specified the amount of additional pollution that would be permitted. Finally, in Class III, air pollution was allowed to continue until it reached the level set by national standards. Congress further provided for protection and enhancement of visibility in national parks and wilderness areas affected by haze and smog. A new and controversial provision in the 1977 amendments called for the use of so-called scrubbers to remove sulfur dioxide emission from new fossil-fuel-burning power plants whether those plants used low- or high-sulfur coal. The action was widely understood to be an effort to protect the high-sulfur coal industry (Ackerman and Hassler 1981).

Substantial progress in meeting policy goals was made during the 1970s, and the results were evident in cleaner air in most U.S. cities. Nevertheless, unhealthy levels of air pollution continued, and control of toxic air pollutants called for in the 1970 act proved difficult to achieve. Newer problems, such as acid rain and the contribution of greenhouse gas emissions to climate change, demanded attention. At the same time, criticism mounted over the EPA's implementation of the Clean Air Act, particularly its inconsistent, inflexible, and costly regulations and inadequate guidelines for state action. Technical obstacles to meeting the act's goals and deadlines also became apparent. Conflicts over reformulation of the act were so great that Congress was unable to fashion a compromise acceptable to all parties until 1990.

The 1990 Amendments   The 1990 amendments to the Clean Air Act further extended the act's reach to control of the precursors of acid rain (sulfur dioxide and nitrogen oxides) emitted primarily by coal-burning power plants and to the chlorofluorocarbons (CFCs) that damage the ozone layer. Among the most innovative provisions in Title IV of the 1990 amendments was the use of an emissions trading program for reducing sulfur dioxide emissions. Title II of the amendments called for further reductions (of 35 to 60 percent) in automobile tailpipe emissions between 1994 and 1996, and it mandated development of cleaner fuels for use in selected areas of the nation. Oxygen-containing additives were to be used in fuels in communities with high levels of carbon monoxide (chiefly in the winter when carbon monoxide is more of a problem). Reformulated, or cleaner, gasoline was to be used in cities with severe ozone problems. The reformulated fuels require more refining and cost slightly more. They burn more thoroughly and evaporate more slowly, and they contain much lower concentrations of toxic compounds such as toluene and benzene. These fuels also have oxygen-containing additives.

Because residents of many metropolitan areas are still forced to breathe polluted air, Title I of the act set out an elaborate and exacting multitiered plan intended to bring all urban areas into compliance with national air quality standards within 3 to 20 years, depending on the severity of their air pollution. The amendments invited private lawsuits to compel compliance with those deadlines.

Unhappy with the EPA's dismal progress in regulating hazardous air pollutants, Congress departed sharply from the 1970 act. It required the agency to set emission limits for all major industrial sources of hazardous or toxic air pollutants (e.g., chemical companies, refineries, and steel plants). These rules were intended to reduce emissions by as much as 90 percent by the year 2003 through technology-based standards. Title III listed 189 specific toxic chemicals that were to be regulated as hazardous air pollutants. Within eight years of setting emission limits for industrial operations, the agency was required to set new health-based standards for those chemicals determined to be carcinogens representing a risk of one cancer case in 1 million exposed individuals.

In Title V of the act, Congress established a new permit program to facilitate enforcement of the act. Major stationary sources of air pollution are now required to have EPA-issued operating permits that specify allowable emissions and control measures that must be used (Bryner 1995).

As attention has shifted from Congress to the intricacies of the EPA's rule making and state implementation efforts, controversy over the 1990 Clean Air Act Amendments has continued. The broad scope and demanding requirements of the 1990 act guarantee that conflict is not likely to fade anytime soon.[5]

Proposed Reforms   Recent years have brought many proposals to change the Clean Air Act in incremental ways, through both legislation and administrative rules. For example, the Bush administration in 2002 proposed a Clear Skies Initiative that would use market incentives to control emissions of mercury, nitrogen dioxide, and sulfur dioxide from power plants but not, as Bush had indicated during the 2000 presidential campaign, carbon dioxide. Much like the Clean Air Act's acid rain provisions, the proposal called for mandatory emissions caps to be placed on the three pollutants. Plant emissions would be governed through a market-based system to achieve cost-effective reductions. The administration argued that the new approach would cut emissions faster and more cheaply than conventional regulatory approaches.[6] Environmentalists and other opponents disagreed with the White House estimates. They asserted that the current Clean Air Act could achieve better results and more quickly if properly implemented. They also were adamant about including controls on carbon dioxide, the most important greenhouse gas.

Through 2005, Bush pressed Congress to act on his Clear Skies proposal. Environmental groups and most Democrats remained strongly opposed to the legislation, however, and they were able to block it in the Senate in March 2005 by a one-vote margin. At that time, Sen. James Jeffords (I-Vermont), ranking minority member of the Senate Environment and Public Works Committee, proclaimed that "we must strive to build upon the success of the Clean Air Act, not gut it." The Bush bill, he said, "allows giant corporate utilities to avoid compliance and stops enforcement of our existing clean air laws." Sen. James Inhofe (R-Oklahoma), chair of the committee, saw matters differently. The bill, he said, was "killed by environmental extremists who care more about continuing the litigation-friendly status quo and making a political statement on CO_2 than they do about reducing our pollution." The exchange between the two says much about current environmental politics in Congress. Following its loss in the Senate, the Bush administration then chose to pursue its goals through a change in administrative rules that it hoped would provide many of the same advances in clean air policy; these rules, however, were certain to be challenged in court, and they would fall short of what a change in the law itself would have achieved.[7]

Environmentalists, among many other critics, were even more strongly opposed to a related Bush initiative to ease the Clean Air Act's new source review (NSR) requirements. Long a point of contention, the NSR standards were intended to force older, coal-fired power plants, oil refineries, smelters and steel mills, pulp and paper mills, and other industrial facilities to install new emissions controls when their plants undergo certain major renovations rather than mere "routine maintenance, repair, and replacement." Many facilities attempted to modernize their equipment but avoid the added expense of pollution control by describing their work as maintenance only. Those plants faced aggressive enforcement of the NSR rules under the Clinton administration. New Bush administration rules adopted in 2003 allowed plants to undertake extensive changes without invoking the NSR standards as long as the total cost was below a specified level (20 percent of the cost of rebuilding the production facility). EPA officials argued that the older plants and factories needed the flexibility that the Bush rules would provide. Yet as one press account put it, the new rules "triggered a storm of criticism from environmentalists, Democrats, and some Republicans."[8] An assessment by Resources for the Future analysts, however, argued that the NSR standards did indeed need reform because they had been both ineffective and inefficient. The standards were, they said, excessively costly and environmentally counterproductive because they kept old and dirty plants operating and held back investments in newer and cleaner plants (Gruenspecht and Stavins 2002). Dozens of federal and state lawsuits were filed to challenge the EPA's new NRS rules, and the administration struggled to find a way to ease controls on aging power plants that would survive legal challenge. Among other solutions, in March 2005, the administration issued a new Clean Air Interstate Rule (CAIR) that it argued would achieve the "largest reduction in air pollution in more than a decade." CAIR is designed to use emissions trading to reduce releases of sulfur dioxide and nitrogen oxides in the eastern United States. The administration said that it would do so at lower cost than the NSR guidelines for modernization of power plants. Environmental groups and many states disagreed, and further legal challenges are likely.[9]

The Clean Water Act

The Federal Water Pollution Control Act Amendments of 1972, now known as the Clean Water Act (CWA), is the major federal policy regulating surface water quality. As was the case with the Clean Air Act, the CWA dramatically altered the original and very limited Water Pollution Control Act (1948), which emphasized research, investigations, and surveys of water problems.[10] Under the 1948 act, there was no federal authority to establish water quality standards or to restrict discharge of pollutants. Amendments adopted in 1956 also failed to establish any meaningful control over discharge of pollutants. The 1965 Water Quality Act went much further by requiring states to establish water quality standards for interstate bodies of water and implementation plans to achieve those standards, and by providing for federal oversight of the process. Yet the 1965 law was widely viewed as administratively and politically unworkable and ineffective, in part because of significant variation among the states in their economic resources, bureaucratic expertise, and degree of commitment to water quality goals.

The 1972 Clean Water Act was intended to correct these deficiencies by setting a national policy for water pollution control. It established deadlines for elimination of the discharge of pollutants into navigable waters by 1985 and stated that all waters were to be "fishable and swimmable" by 1983. It also encouraged technological innovation and areawide planning for attainment of water quality (Freeman 1990). The 1972 act was itself revised and strengthened in 1977 and again in 1987 without fundamentally altering the goals or means to achieve them. Congress, however, postponed several deadlines for compliance and established new provisions for toxic water pollutants, the discharge of which in "toxic amounts" was to be prohibited. Throughout the 1990s Congress was deeply divided over how to revise the act.

The goals of the 1972 act may have been admirable, but they proved to be wildly unrealistic. The tasks were of a staggering magnitude, industry actively opposed the act's objectives and frequently challenged the EPA in court, technology proved to be costly, and planning for control of nonpoint sources (i.e., those with no specific point of origin) was inadequately funded and difficult to establish. Thus deadlines were postponed and achievement of goals suffered.

For example, in 1992 the International Joint Commission reported that the United States had yet to eliminate completely the discharge of any persistent toxic chemical. The achievement of fishable and swimmable waters is supposed to mean, as stated in the 1977 act, that the water quality provides for "the protection and propagation of a balanced population of shellfish, fish, and wildlife" as well as recreation in and on the water. As noted in Chapter 2, the EPA reported in 2002 that 39 percent or more of the rivers, lakes, ponds, and estuaries assessed failed to meet those standards. Nevertheless, as the first sentence of the Clean Water Act states, it aspires to "restore and maintain the chemical, physical, and biological integrity of the nation's waters." Elaborate efforts are under way to move toward those challenging objectives, and signs of progress are evident.

Much like the Clean Air Act, the Clean Water Act gives the states primary responsibility for implementation as long as they follow federal standards and guidelines. Dischargers into navigable waterways must meet water quality standards and effluent limits, and they operate under a permit that specifies the terms of allowable discharge and control technologies to be used. The EPA has granted authority to most states to issue those permits, which operate under the National Pollutant Discharge Elimination System (NPDES). The NPDES applies to municipal wastewater treatment facilities as well as to industry. Compliance with the permits is determined by self-reported discharge data and on-site inspections by state personnel. Studies suggest, however, that underreporting and weak enforcement of the law are common (Hunter and Waterman 1996). For example, an environmental group in Los Angeles (joined by the EPA) sued the city for a "chronic, continuing, and unacceptable number" of spills from the sewage collection system into area waters in violation of the Clean Water Act. The EPA pursued similar cases in Atlanta, Baltimore, Miami, and New Orleans.[11] The Clean Water Act permits private citizens to file lawsuits against polluters to help enforce the law; any financial penalties are paid to the federal government. The U.S. Supreme Court upheld that provision of the law in early 2000 in *Friends of the Earth v. Laidlaw Environmental Services*.[12]

The states also establish Water Quality Criteria (WQC) that define the maximum concentrations of pollutants allowable in surface waters. In theory, the WQC concentrations would be set at levels posing no threat to individual organisms, populations, species, communities, and ecosystems (including humans). States do so using EPA guidelines that take into account the uses of a given body of water as defined by the states (e.g., fishing, boating, and waste disposal). The purpose is to prevent degradation that interferes with the designated uses. States may consider benefits and costs in establishing water quality standards.

Effluent limitations specify how much a given discharger, such as a manufacturing facility, is allowed to emit into the water and the specific treatment technologies that must be used to stay within such limits. The EPA has defined such effluent limitations for different categories of industry based on available treatment technologies. Economists and industry leaders have long objected that the requirements are irrational: "To put it simply, standards are set on the basis of what can be done with available technology, rather than what should be done to achieve ambient water quality standards, to balance benefits and costs, or to satisfy any other criteria" (Freeman 1990, 106). Critics also object to what they consider to be vague statutory language such as "best practical," "best available," and "reasonable costs," which grant enormous discretion to administrative agencies to interpret complex and varied scientific, engineering, and economic information. In response, defenders of the CWA argue that use of approaches that call for best available technology (BAT) is a major reason the nation has achieved the degree of progress it has under the act.

A politically attractive feature of the Clean Water Act was federal funding to assist local communities to build modern municipal wastewater treatment facilities. The federal government initially assumed 75 percent of the capital costs, and for several years in the 1970s it subsidized such construction to the tune of $7 billion per year. Later called "water infrastructure" and "state and tribal assistance" grants, the percentage of federal assistance was reduced in the 1980s; in recent years it stood at about $2.0 billion per year. The 1987 revision of the CWA authorized creation of a state revolving loan fund program to help local governments build wastewater treatment facilities; the communities later repay the states. All 50 states have such funds. Between 1987 and 1996, Congress spent about $11 billion on the loan program as it phased out the earlier nationally funded construction grant program.

The discharge of toxic chemicals has proved to be much more difficult to regulate than conventional pollutants. Although bodies of water may assimilate a certain amount of biologically degradable waste products, the same cannot be said for toxic chemicals, which often accumulate in toxic hot spots in river and lake sediments. By the late 1990s, a consensus was emerging that the best course of action was to identify and end the use of the most toxic, persistent, and bioaccumulative pollutants. For example, this position was a cornerstone of the EPA's Great Lakes Five-Year Strategy. The agency's Great Lakes Water Quality Initiative called for the "virtual elimination" of discharges of persistent toxic substances throughout the Great Lakes Basin.

Unlike conventional, or "point," sources such as industry discharge pipes, nonpoint sources of water pollution such as agricultural runoff have proved to be exceptionally difficult to manage. The 1987 Clean Water Act amendments required the states to develop an EPA-approved plan for control of nonpoint sources such as urban stormwater runoff, cropland erosion, and runoff from construction sites, woodlands, pastures, and feedlots. Before implementation of the CWA, these sources constituted between 57 and 98 percent of total discharges of phosphorus, nitrogen, suspended solids, and biological oxygen demand in the nation's surface waters (Freeman 1990, 109). As discussed in Chapter 2, even by 2005 they remained responsible for the majority of stream pollution.

So far, most states have chosen voluntary approaches using "best management practices" to deal with nonpoint sources. In 1998, however, the Clinton administration proposed and Congress approved a new Clean Water Action Plan that provided $1.7 billion over five years to help state and local governments deal with nonpoint source water pollution. In addition, in August 1999 the EPA proposed a new rule that would require states to regulate water pollution by focusing on the quality of a body of water as well as the actions of individual dischargers. The new rule would have established a quota system for overall discharges and permitted a form of emissions trading among polluters, among other innovations to encourage state cooperation. The new action, stimulated by lawsuits filed by environmentalists and others, in effect tried to enforce an existing but neglected provision of the Clean Water Act (Kriz 2000).[13] Congress, however, objected to the Clinton rule, and in late 2002 the Bush administration dropped it as unworkable, implying it would continue to seek an alternative.

It remains to be seen how well new regulations, economic incentives, and public education programs can reduce this continuing and difficult contribution to water pollution (Pope 2000). Much may depend on the ability of state and local governments, industry, and environmental scientists to formulate and implement watershed management plans that can improve water quality through comprehensive measures taken over a broad geographical area.

Water quality should improve eventually. But it will require more effective efforts to control nonpoint sources, stronger water quality controls, requirements for use of new technologies, and the alteration of industrial practices through pollution prevention programs. A key question is how much the development of such control technologies should be pushed. The very threat of higher standards, and thus higher costs, has persuaded many companies to concentrate on pollution prevention. With preventive approaches, a toxic chemical is eliminated through substitution of a less toxic or nontoxic one, or the industrial process itself is changed, as, for example, through wastewater recycling and filtration.

The way in which Congress will change the Clean Water Act also remains uncertain. Over the past decade, different advocacy coalitions fought over the act's provisions. Business groups have organized as the Water Quality Task Force (chemicals, oil, and durable goods), the Clean Water Industry Coalition (agriculture and manufactures), and the Clean Water Working Group (agricultural chemicals), among others. Environmentalists marched under the banner of the Clean Water Network (www.cwn.org), including over a thousand public interest groups. In 2004 the Clean Water Network released an extensive report entitled the *National Agenda for Clean Water* that called for sweeping reforms in the act. Environmentalists also mounted a forceful grassroots lobbying effort to try to win the day. State and local governments concerned about the high costs of water policies formed their own coalition, which included the National Association of Counties, National Governors Association, National Conference of State Legislators, National League of Cities, and U.S. Conference of Mayors. Through the end of 2005, Congress was unable to agree on significant reforms of the Clean Water Act.

The Safe Drinking Water Act

The 1974 Safe Drinking Water Act (SDWA) was designed to ensure the quality and safety of drinking water by specifying minimum public health standards for public water supplies. The act authorized the EPA to set National Primary Drinking Water Standards for chemical and microbiological contaminants for tap water. The act also required regular monitoring of water supplies to ensure that pollutants stayed below safe levels.

The EPA made slow progress in setting standards. Only 22 standards for 18 substances had been set by the mid-1980s. In 1986 a Congress frustrated with both the EPA's pace of implementation and insufficient action by state and local governments strengthened the act. Congress required the EPA to determine maximum contaminant levels for 83 specific chemicals by 1989 and set quality standards for them, set standards for another 25 contaminants by 1991, and set standards for 25 more every three years. Congress was highly prescriptive in detailing what contaminants would be regulated, how they would be treated, and the timetable for action. The standards were to be based on a contaminant's potential for causing illness and the financial capacity of medium- to large-size water systems to foot the bill for the purification technology.

States have the primary responsibility for enforcing those standards for the more than 50,000 public water systems in the United States. Water systems were to use the best available technology to remove contaminants and monitor for the presence of a host of chemicals. Even the EPA acknowledges that the states receive far less funding than needed to comply. The problems are especially severe for the thousands of small water systems that can ill afford the cost of expensive new water treatment technologies.

For those reasons, the nation's governors and mayors pressed Congress in the mid-1990s to ease regulatory red tape by focusing on tests for contamination and monitoring of only those chemicals posing the greatest risk to human health. The drinking water law symbolized a broader complaint about so-called unfunded federal mandates that require states and localities to spend their scarce local funds on environmental programs over which they have no say. The SDWA also reflected concern over the high marginal costs of further improvements in environmental quality after the gains of the previous 20 years.

When the SDWA came up for reauthorization, the Safe Drinking Water Act Coalition, representing a dozen organizations of state and local officials, lobbied aggressively for reducing the regulatory burden on states. It sought the use of less expensive and slightly less effective technologies, less strict water quality standards when public health would not be endangered, and a new federal revolving loan fund to defray the cost for smaller water systems. Environmentalists were equally as determined to keep stringent public health protections in place (Kriz 1994a).

Groundwater contamination is of special concern for municipalities that rely on well water and for the nation's rural residents. As discussed in Chapter 2, aquifers may be contaminated by improper disposal of hazardous wastes and leaking underground storage tanks, and from agricultural runoff (e.g., nitrates and pesticides), among other sources. By 2000, for example, the EPA was urging the phaseout of the gasoline additive MTBE out of concern that it had already contaminated several thousand groundwater sites around the nation, and in early 2006 it urged Congress to drop the Clean Air Act requirement for using additives such as MTBE in gasoline. Groundwater historically has been governed chiefly by state and local governments. Yet it is affected by the Safe Drinking Water Act, the Clean Water Act, and many other federal statutes, with no consistent standards or coordination of enforcement.

In one of the important exceptions to the rule of environmental policy gridlock in the mid- to late 1990s, Congress in 1996 was able to agree on renewal of the Safe Drinking Water Act. Both the House and the Senate voted overwhelmingly for the act, which established a new, more flexible approach to regulating water contaminants based on their risk to public health; the act also permitted the consideration of costs and benefits of proposed regulations. The 1996 act ended the previous requirement for setting standards for 25 additional contaminants every three years. Instead, every five years the EPA is to publish a list of unregulated contaminants found in drinking water and then use that list when it proposes to regulate a new contaminant. The act also authorized federal support for state-administered loan and grant funds to help localities meet federal drinking water standards. States are allowed to transfer funds between the clean water and drinking water revolving funds. Under pressure from the environmental community, the act also created a new right-to-know provision that requires community water systems to provide their customers with annual consumer confidence reports on the safety of local water supplies. Small water systems face reduced standards out of concern for the cost of compliance (Freedman 1996; Hosansky 1996a).

The Resource Conservation and Recovery Act

Although the federal government had dealt earlier with solid waste in the 1965 Solid Waste Disposal Act (SWDA), by the 1970s concern was shifting to hazardous waste. In 1976 Congress enacted the Resource Conservation and Recovery Act (RCRA) as amendments to the SWDA and to the 1970 Resource Recovery Act. RCRA (pronounced "rick rah") was to regulate existing hazardous waste disposal practices as well as promote the conservation and recovery of resources through comprehensive management of solid waste. Congress addressed the problem of abandoned hazardous waste sites in the 1980 Superfund legislation discussed later.

RCRA required the EPA to develop criteria for the safe disposal of solid waste and the Commerce Department to promote waste recovery technologies and waste conservation. The EPA was to develop a cradle-to-grave system of regulation that would monitor and control the production, storage, transportation, and disposal of wastes considered hazardous, and it was to determine the appropriate technology for disposal of wastes.

The act delegated to the EPA most of the tasks of identifying and characterizing such wastes (the agency counts more than 500 chemical compounds and mixtures) and determining whether they are hazardous. That judgment is to be based on explicit measures of toxicity, ignitability, corrosivity, and chemical reactivity. If a waste is positive by any one of these indicators, or is a "listed" hazardous waste, it is governed by RCRA's regulations (Dower 1990).

RCRA also established a paper trail for keeping track of the generation and transportation of hazardous wastes that was intended to eliminate so-called midnight or illegal dumping. Eventually, the EPA developed a national manifest system (the paperwork that accounts for transport of the waste) for that purpose. However, because most hazardous waste never leaves its site of generation, the manifest system governs only a small portion of the total. More important is that RCRA called for the EPA to set standards for the treatment, storage, and disposal of hazardous wastes that are "necessary to protect human health and the environment." As is the case for the air and water acts, the EPA over time delegated authority to most states to implement RCRA.

Initially, the EPA was exceedingly slow in implementing RCRA, in part because of the unexpected complexity of the tasks, lack of sufficient data, and staff and budget constraints. In addition, environmentalists, EPA technical staff, the chemical industry, and the White House (especially in the Reagan administration) battled frequently over the stringency of the regulations (Cohen 1984). The EPA took four years to issue the first major regulations and two additional years to issue final technical or performance standards for incinerators, landfills, and surface storage tanks that had to be met for licensed or permitted facilities. In the meantime, public concern had escalated because of publicity over horror stories involving disposal of hazardous waste at Love Canal, New York, and soil contaminated with dioxin-tainted waste oil at Times Beach, Missouri. EPA relations with Capitol Hill were severely strained in the early 1980s during Anne Burford's tumultuous reign as administrator, and the Reagan administration ultimately had no legislative proposal for renewal of RCRA that would allow the EPA to put forth its own vision of a workable policy.

As a result of these developments, Congress grew profoundly distrustful of the EPA's "slow and timid implementation of existing law," and it sharply limited administrative discretion in its 1984 rewrite of RCRA, officially called the Hazardous and Solid Waste Amendments (HSWA). The 1984 RCRA amendments rank among the most detailed and restrictive of environmental measures ever enacted, with 76 statutory deadlines, 8 of them with so-called hammer provisions that were to take effect if the EPA failed to act in time (Halley 1994). Congress uses this hammer language in environmental and other acts to impose a legislative regulation if an agency fails to adopt its own regulations by the stated deadline. Such provisions are intended to force agency compliance with the law, but they may also interfere with sound policy implementation, particularly when agency budgets are tight and much technical uncertainty surrounds the problems being addressed.

The 1984 act sought to phase out disposal of most hazardous wastes in landfills by establishing demanding standards of safety and expand control to cover additional sources and wastes (particularly from small sources previously exempt). In addition it extended RCRA regulation to underground storage tanks (USTs) holding petroleum, pesticides, solvents, and gasoline, and moved much more quickly toward program goals by setting out a highly specific timetable for various mandated actions. The effect of all that was to drive up the cost of hazardous waste disposal dramatically. Although economists question the economic logic of these provisions (Dower 1990), Congress helped bring about an outcome long favored by environmentalists: the internalization of environmental and health costs of improper disposal of wastes. If disposal of wastes is extraordinarily expensive, a powerful incentive to produce less of them exists, thus leading (eventually) to source reduction, recycling, and new treatment technologies, which the 1984 amendments ranked as far more desirable than land disposal. At least that is the idea.

Congress struggled in the 1990s with reauthorization of RCRA without resolving continuing conflicts. Through 1992 the George H. W. Bush administration opposed revamping the act, saying it was unnecessary. Members of Congress, however, heard warnings of impending solid waste crises because most of the nation's remaining landfills were to close over the next 15 years. Environmentalists pressed for higher levels of waste reduction and waste recovery through recycling and tighter controls on waste incineration. Local governments worried about what to do with incinerator ash that may be classified as hazardous under a 1994 U.S. Supreme Court decision, and some states fought the solid waste industry over efforts to restrict interstate transport of solid wastes. As was often the case over the past decade, environmental gridlock prevailed as each side fought for its preferred solutions and no consensus emerged on a comprehensive revision of RCRA (Kraft 2006).

The Toxic Substances Control Act

After five years of development and debate, Congress enacted the Toxic Substances Control Act (TSCA) in 1976. The EPA was given comprehensive authority to identify, evaluate, and regulate risks associated with the full life cycle of commercial chemicals, both those already in commerce as well as new ones in preparation. TSCA (pronounced "toss kah") aspired to develop adequate data on the effect of chemical substances on health and the environment and to regulate those chemicals posing an "unreasonable risk of injury to health or the environment" without unduly burdening industry and impeding technological innovation.

The EPA was to produce an inventory of chemicals in commercial production, and it was given authority to require testing by industry where data are insufficient and the chemical may present an unacceptable risk. Exercise of that authority was made difficult and time consuming, however. An Interagency Testing Committee, with representatives from eight federal agencies, was established to recommend candidates and priorities for chemical testing. Where data are adequate, the EPA may regulate the manufacture, processing, use, distribution, or disposal of the chemical. Options range from banning the chemical to labeling requirements, again with demanding, formal rule-making procedures required (Shapiro 1990).

Congress also granted to the EPA the authority to screen new chemicals. The agency must be notified 90 days before manufacture of a new chemical substance, when the manufacturer must supply any available test data to the agency in a Premanufacturing Notice. If the EPA determines that the chemical may pose an unreasonable risk to health or the environment, it may ban or limit manufacture until further information is provided. The requirements here are more easily met than for existing chemicals, and the EPA can act more quickly.

Although the meaning of "unreasonable risk" is not formally defined in the act, Congress clearly intended some kind of balancing of the risks and the benefits to society of the chemicals in question (Shapiro 1990). TSCA was modified by amendments in 1986, by the Asbestos Hazard Emergency Response Act, and in 1992 by the Residential Lead-Based Paint Hazard Reduction Act. The asbestos legislation required the EPA to develop strategies for inspecting schools for asbestos-containing material and controlling the risk appropriately. The paint hazard legislation called for a variety of actions to reduce public exposure to lead from paint. Such actions include inspection and abatement of lead hazards in low-income housing, disclosure of the risks of lead-based paint prior to the sale of homes built before 1978, and development by the EPA of a training and certification program for lead abatement contractors.

Like the other major acts, the implementation of TSCA has not gone smoothly. The EPA encountered resistance from industry in getting the necessary information, had difficulty recruiting sufficient trained personnel for the regulatory tasks, and made very slow progress in achieving TSCA's objectives. The EPA's job was made more difficult than it otherwise might have been by forcing the agency to prove that a chemical was unsafe or posed an unreasonable risk. As a result of these stipulations in the law and the other constraints the agency faced, only a handful of chemicals have been banned under TSCA.

The Federal Insecticide, Fungicide, and Rodenticide Act

Federal regulation of pesticides is much older than laws dealing with other chemical risks. It dates back to a 1910 Insecticide Act designed to protect consumers from fraudulent products. In 1947 Congress enacted the Federal Insecticide, Fungicide, and Rodenticide Act (FIFRA), authorizing a registration and labeling program, and it gave authority for its implementation to the Department of Agriculture. Concern focused chiefly on the efficacy of pesticides as agricultural chemicals. By the 1960s, following the publication of Rachel Carson's *Silent Spring*, public attention shifted to environmental consequences of pesticide use. Congress amended FIFRA (pronounced "fif rah") in 1964, 1972, and 1978, establishing a new regulatory framework. Jurisdiction over the act was given to the EPA in 1970. A 1996 amendment discussed later pertains especially to pesticide levels in food.

FIFRA requires that pesticides used commercially within the United States be registered by the EPA. It sets as a criterion for registration that the pesticide not pose "any unreasonable risk to man or the environment, taking into account the economic, social, and environmental costs and benefits of the use" (Shapiro 1990). The law is less stringent than other environmental statutes of the 1970s, and critics assert that the government has given greater weight to economic arguments than to the effects on public health. The EPA is required to balance costs and benefits, with the burden of proof of harm placed on the government if the agency attempts to cancel or suspend registration of an existing pesticide. For a new pesticide, the burden lies on the manufacturer to demonstrate safety. Procedures under the law historically have been cumbersome, however, making regulatory action difficult.

These statutory provisions reflected the still considerable power of the pesticide lobby despite the many gains environmental, health, and farmworker groups have made against the long-influential agricultural subgovernment (Bosso 1987). Because of its origins in the agricultural policy community, FIFRA differs in many respects from other environmental laws. Indeed, environmentalists have referred to it as an "anachronistic statute" that is "riddled with loopholes and industry-oriented provisions." Although reauthorized in 1988 after years of political controversy and legislative stalemate, the act reflected only modest changes, leading critics to dub it "FIFRA Lite."

The EPA is also required under the Food, Drug, and Cosmetic Act to establish maximum permissible concentrations of pesticides in or on both raw agricultural products (e.g., fresh fruits and vegetables) and processed foods. Those standards are then enforced by the Food and Drug Administration (FDA) and the Department of Agriculture. Until the 1996 amendments, the EPA was governed in part by the Delaney clause in the act that prohibited any food additive shown to cause cancer in laboratory animals. Of the roughly 400 kinds of pesticides used on food crops, more than 70, including the most commonly used, cause cancer in laboratory animals. In a long-awaited 1993 report, the National Academy of Sciences indicated that children may be at special risk from exposure to trace levels of pesticides from foods as well as from lawn care products and household insect sprays. Rep. Henry Waxman (D-California), chair of the Health and the Environment subcommittee in the House, termed the report a "wake-up call to all of us" about the "unnecessary risk from pesticides in food" (Michaelis 1993).

Most of the debate in the mid- to late 1990s over FIFRA concerned whether, and in what way, to modify the Delaney clause. To bring the law into conformity with practice and with contemporary views of the relatively minor risks to public health posed by minute pesticide residues in food, the Clinton administration proposed in 1993 a more realistic "negligible risk" standard. It would have allowed no more than one additional case of cancer for every 1 million people. The food and chemical industries supported such an easing of the Delaney policy, but many environmental groups opposed the action.

By 1994 national environmentalists joined with a diversity of grassroots organizations to form the National Campaign for Pesticide Policy Reform. These groups proposed speeding up the renewal or cancellation of pesticide registration, strengthening the law to help control contamination of groundwater, limiting pesticide residues in food, protecting farmworkers from exposure to harmful chemicals, and improving public access to health and safety information. Industry groups, organized as the National Agricultural Chemicals Association (which in 1994 changed its name to the American Crop Protection Association), protested that such changes would cost millions of dollars, yield no appreciable benefits, and jeopardize trade secrets.

The impasse continued until 1996, at which point an agreement on pesticide policy emerged rapidly and unexpectedly. Court decisions required the EPA to act aggressively to enforce the Delaney clause barring trace amounts of chemicals in processed foods. The agency would have been forced to begin canceling the use of some common pesticides. Industry fear of such potential and costly EPA action set the stage for a remarkable agreement to support the Food Quality Protection Act of 1996. In addition, Republican lawmakers were eager to vote for an election-year environmental bill after having suffered politically throughout 1995 and 1996 in battles with the Clinton White House over environmental policies. The act passed both the House and Senate without a single dissenting vote and in record time. It was hailed by both major parties as a key achievement of the otherwise conflict-ridden 104th Congress. The act essentially reflected proposals made by the Clinton administration in 1994, although without much support at that time by the leading players in pesticide policy (Hosansky 1996c).

The Food Quality Protection Act replaced the decades-old Delaney clause, requiring the EPA to use a new uniform "reasonable risk" approach to regulating pesticides used on food, fiber, and other crops. The EPA would set a tolerance level to ensure that people who eat both raw and processed foods face a "reasonable certainty of no harm." Such language is generally interpreted to mean no more than a 1-in-1-million lifetime chance exists that the chemical could cause cancer. The agency is required to review all tolerances within 10 years. The act also required that special attention be given to the many different ways in which both children and adults are exposed to these chemicals, such as through drinking water, pest-control sprays used in the house, and garden products. Doing so is an enormous challenge given the state of scientific knowledge. Yet it also makes sense to assess all health risks, not just for cancer, and to consider the cumulative risks of exposure to multiple pesticide residues on food, not just a single chemical. The EPA was to take unusual precaution to protect children against such risks, establishing up to a 10-fold margin of safety. State agencies generally cannot impose pesticide standards tighter than those of the federal government without petitioning the EPA for permission to do so, but states could refuse to follow an EPA action to relax a standard to below the 1-in-1-million risk level.

In its first decisions under the act, the EPA not surprisingly was subject to intense pressure from agricultural interests on one side and public health and environmental groups on the other. Farm interests were concerned they would lose the use of long-standing pesticides that they believed were essential to an economical practice of agriculture. They questioned the adequacy of the EPA's science used to support pesticide withdrawals. Environmentalists and health groups worried that the EPA was giving insufficient attention to children's health needs (Freedman 1998). The delicate balancing of interests required under the law will likely continue to produce such conflicts. As one example, in 2002 the EPA was embroiled in legal and scientific disputes over its efforts to write new rules to regulate use of atrazine, one of the nation's most widely used herbicides (Cushman 2002).

The act also mandated that the EPA consult with the FDA and the Agriculture Department and publish pamphlets that would be displayed publicly in large retail grocery stores. The pamphlets are to be in language that is easily understood by a layperson, describe the risks and benefits of pesticide residues in or on food purchased by consumers, and provide a kind of consumer alert when the risks are high. Consumers are also to be advised on how to reduce their exposure to pesticide residues (Hosansky 1996b). The language used in the EPA's drafts was hotly contested. Food industry groups called the brochures unduly alarmist, whereas environmental and consumer advocacy groups complained that the agency did not take a hard enough line, for example, in referring to pesticides as poisons (Cushman 1998c).

In addition to amending the Delaney clause, the new act amended FIFRA with respect to the EPA's role in registration, or approval, of pesticides. The agency is to establish procedures to ensure that each pesticide registration is reviewed every 15 years. The law gives broader power to the EPA to suspend or change the use of a suspect pesticide immediately through an emergency order; it would have 90 days to follow through by issuing a formal notice of cancellation. The act also establishes procedures to speed up EPA review of what are called "minor use pesticides" used on many fruits, vegetables, and specialty crops (as distinguished from those used on major crops such as wheat, corn, soybeans, cotton, and rice). Reviews are to take place within one year. Because the EPA has faced long delays in reviewing such registration applications, the act authorizes the agency to collect additional fees from pesticide registrants to help avoid such delays. Finally, the 1996 law mandates research, demonstration, and education programs to support integrated pest management and other alternatives to pesticide use.

The Comprehensive Environmental Response, Compensation, and Liability Act

Congress enacted the Comprehensive Environmental Response, Compensation, and Liability Act (CERCLA), better known as Superfund, in 1980 and revised it in 1986 with the Superfund Amendments and Reauthorization Act (SARA). The act is a partner to RCRA. Whereas RCRA deals with current hazardous waste generation and disposal, Superfund was directed primarily at the thousands of abandoned or uncontrolled hazardous waste sites. Little was known about the number, location, and risks associated with these sites, and existing law was thought to be insufficient to deal with the problem. With Superfund, Congress gave the EPA responsibility to respond to the problem by identifying, assessing, and cleaning up those sites. Where necessary, the EPA could use a special revolving fund (originally $1.6 billion), most of which was to be financed by a tax on manufacturers of petrochemical feedstocks and other organic chemicals and crude oil importers. The act put both responsibility for the cleanup and financial liability on those who disposed of hazardous wastes at a site, a "polluter pays" policy.

Unhappy with the pace of cleanup and the Reagan administration's lax implementation of Superfund, in 1986, with SARA (pronounced "Sarah"), Congress authorized an additional $8.5 billion for the fund and mandated stringent cleanup standards using the best available technologies. SARA also established an entirely new Title III in the act, stimulated by the 1984 chemical plant accident in Bhopal, India, which killed more than 3,000 people and injured hundreds of thousands. Within three months of the Bhopal accident, bills in Congress merged the right-to-know concept with the Superfund reauthorization legislation. Title III, also called the Emergency Planning and Community Right-to-Know Act (EPCRA), provided for public release of information about chemicals made by, stored in, and released by local businesses (published each year as the Toxics Release Inventory). It also required the creation of state and local committees to plan for emergency chemical releases (Hadden 1989; Hamilton 2005).

Superfund Provisions and Controversies   Superfund gives the EPA authority to identify the parties responsible for inactive or abandoned hazardous waste sites and to force cleanup. It may also clean up sites itself and seek restitution from the responsible parties. Such actions are governed by complicated "strict, joint, and several liability" provisions of the act that can be especially burdensome on minor contributing parties. The parties responsible may be sued as a group or individually for all the cleanup costs even if they are not fully at fault. Settlement of Superfund cases, however, often is based on an allocation of liability related to the amount of hazardous substances contributed by each party. The act's retroactive liability provision also holds companies liable for wastes disposed of legally prior to 1980.

In addition, Superfund requires that sites be identified and ranked according to their priority for cleanup. The EPA and the states nominate sites for a National Priorities List (NPL), and the EPA uses a hazard ranking system to measure the severity of risks at each site and thus set priorities for cleanup. The rankings do not reflect actual human or environmental exposures but rather potential health and environmental risks as judged by EPA project officers and technical consultants (Dower 1990; Mazmanian and Morell 1992, 31). Only sites listed on the NPL qualify for long-term cleanup under Superfund and for use of the federal dollars associated with the program.

The EPA has evaluated tens of thousands of sites (both government and privately owned) for possible inclusion on the NPL. These sites include pesticide plants, landfills, small industrial sites, rivers and harbors with contaminated sediments, and former nuclear weapons production facilities such as the Hanford Reservation in Washington State where soil has been poisoned with chemical and radioactive wastes. Although critics often have pointed to the modest number of NPL sites that have been fully cleaned up at any given time (see Chapter 2), defenders of the program, including the EPA itself, offer a far more positive assessment (De Saillan 1993; Rahm 1998). The Clinton administration gave Superfund cleanups a high priority and pressed Congress to supply the funds necessary to improve the program's effectiveness. The federal government spent about $1.4 billion a year on Superfund during the late 1990s, and private parties spent another $1 billion a year. Critics, however, have complained that in recent years a large percentage of the funds have gone toward "support activities" (including litigation and administration) rather than to cleanup actions themselves.[14]

The full process—from identification and preliminary assessment of a site to hazard ranking, listing, remedial design, and remediation itself—is complex and time consuming. It can take as long as 15 years (some state cleanups take only two or three years), which helps explain the relatively slow pace of actual cleanup. Groundwater cleanup can be especially difficult and costly. Other reasons for the limited progress have included extensive litigation among potentially responsible parties and insurance companies and the enormous difficulty in locating hazardous waste treatment and disposal sites because of community opposition (Hird 1994; Mazmanian and Morell 1992; U.S. Office of Technology Assessment 1988, 1989).

Controversy over the Superfund program has centered on the degree of cleanup needed for any given site (and hence the cost). Cleanup costs historically have averaged about $30 million per NPL site but with wide variability of costs depending on the nature of the risks at the site and the cleanup standard used. Total costs for all expected Superfund sites could be as high as $350 billion if standards are stringent or as "low" as $90 billion under less demanding standards. Annual costs in recent years have been around $1.5 billion (Probst and Konisky 2001; Russell, Colglazier, and Tonn 1992). These costs are paid chiefly by the responsible parties (about 70 percent of costs) rather than the federal government. Of special note is that cleanup of former nuclear weapons production sites is far more difficult and costly. These cleanups are likely to cost $150 to $200 billion in public funds and take seven decades or more (Probst and Lowe 2000).

Beginning in 1995 Congress chose not to reauthorize the taxes needed to replenish CERCLA's (pronounced "serk la") trust fund, which declined from $3.8 billion in 1996 to a projected $28 million in 2003. Chemical and oil industry representatives had long sought to end the taxes, which they viewed as unfair to them. Through 2005 President Bush did not recommend reauthorization of the taxes. The effect is to shift to taxpayers the cost of cleaning up the remainder of the sites on the NPL for which responsible parties cannot be charged.[15]

Proposed Reforms   Since its reauthorization in 1986, Superfund has in many ways epitomized environmental policy gridlock. Despite the work of numerous special commissions and congressional committees over the years, agreement on reform of the widely criticized Superfund program has proved elusive (Cushman 1994a).

Industry has complained that returning all sites to pristine or "greenfield" conditions is unnecessarily burdensome if such sites are intended for further industrial use, as many are. Business groups also have objected to being forced to clean up trace amounts of chemicals that pose little or no measurable health risk. In contrast, throughout much of the 1990s, environmentalists wanted uniform standards for all sites nationwide and generally opposed the flexibility that industry sought in these standards. They were more favorably inclined toward industry's position, however, if local communities could be given a significant say in cleanup decisions. Grassroots groups associated with the environmental justice movement actively sought early citizen participation in these decisions to ensure that minority communities were ranked high in priority for cleanup actions (Kriz 1994b, 1994c).

Although agreement seemed close on most of the key issues, including the allocation of liability for cleanup costs among responsible parties, Congress was unable to renew the program. When the Republicans gained control of the House and Senate following the 1994 elections, polarization on Superfund renewal and most other environmental policies increased. Republicans proposed sweeping reforms of Superfund to reduce liability for the business community and to free responsible parties from litigation, but they failed to gain sufficient support for passage of a renewed law.

In the 1990s the EPA itself agreed that the program's liability provisions needed to be revamped to reduce the burden on small businesses and to ensure that funds went to cleanup rather than litigation. Indeed, the agency instituted reforms of its own that "significantly changed how the Superfund program operates," making it a "fairer, more effective, and more efficient program," according to former EPA administrator Carol Browner (Mullins 1999, 3140). EPA officials argued that overhauling the act was no longer necessary and could even erode many of the improvements the agency instituted administratively. Partly as a result, Republicans scaled back their ambitious reform bill, and Democrats similarly began to focus on cleaning up some 500,000 so-called brownfields (contaminated areas) that could be used to bolster economic development in urban areas. The EPA started to assist cities in redevelopment of such urban industrial land by removing thousands of such sites from possible inclusion under Superfund and by funding demonstration cleanup projects. States also began to adopt laws that eased the threat of liability and adjusted pollution standards for such sites (Holusha 1995). In early 2002 President Bush signed a bipartisan brownfields bill that authorized $250 million per year for five years to help states clean up and redevelop such sites. The measure also limited the liability of some small businesses, and the EPA would be restrained from seeking additional cleanup of a site if the state certifies it to have been restored.[16]

In 2005 the Bush administration also proposed reforms of the Toxics Release Inventory program, which it said would reduce the burden on companies that must report their chemical releases each year. It wanted to relax the reporting requirements under the law, although its proposal was challenged by many environmental groups and state attorneys general. They argued that such a weakening of the requirements could impede the ability of citizens and local governments to gain access to critical information. By early 2006 the administration highlighted another challenge related to chemical plants: their vulnerability to terrorist attacks. Homeland Security Secretary Michael Chertoff urged Congress to approve changes in the law that could improve security at the nation's 15,000 chemical plants and other facilities where substantial quantities of dangerous chemicals are stored or used.[17]

In part because of limited federal resources and the rising demand for cleaning up contaminated sites around the nation, the Bush administration has called for fundamental changes in the Superfund program. As many as 355,000 sites may require cleanup over the next three decades, with cost estimates running to $250 billion. However, the administration, facing the reality that such funds will not likely be available, sought to reduce public expectations for the program. It also suggested that cleanup costs might be borne by businesses that have an economic stake in using restored sites.[18] Passage of a broad Superfund reform bill will depend on a shift in the political climate that can bring the various policy actors closer together on this highly contentious program. In the meantime, cleanup activities are proceeding across the nation, as already discussed, making reform of the program appear less urgent than in earlier years.

■ THE INSTITUTIONAL CONTEXT OF POLICY IMPLEMENTATION

As the preceding discussion makes clear, these seven core statutes present the EPA with an astonishingly large and bewildering array of administrative tasks that are essential to meet congressional mandates for environmental protection. It would be truly remarkable if the agency could pull it all off, and especially if it could keep Congress and the multitude of constituency groups happy with the results. That the EPA shares responsibility for implementing these statutes, and about a dozen others, with the states is a mixed blessing that creates supervisory headaches even while it relieves the agency of some of the routine burdens of administration (Scheberle 2004).

Critics of regulatory policy often lump all agencies together. Yet they are a highly varied lot, and their individual characteristics must be considered to understand why they operate as they do. The EPA's success or failure in policy implementation is affected by most of the usual factors shaping administrative decision making and some that are distinctive to the agency (Bryner 1987). Some of these are largely beyond the control of agency officials, such as the intractability of many environmental problems, changing economic conditions and technology, constrained budgetary resources, statutory specifications (e.g., sanctions and incentives provided for inducing compliance), and political judgments made by Congress and the White House. Others are influenced to at least some extent by agency behavior. The administrative and leadership skills of agency officials, for instance, significantly affect staff recruitment and expertise, internal organization and priorities, cooperation elicited from other federal agencies, and the political support received from the White House and Congress. Through their policy choices and public outreach efforts, EPA officials can also shape the public's attitudes toward environmental issues and the agency's legitimacy and competency in the eyes of important policy actors such as the environmental community, business, and state and local governments.

The EPA's Organization, Budget, and Staff

The EPA's organizational structure, budgetary resources, and staff characteristics are especially important for policy implementation. President Richard Nixon created the agency by executive order on December 2, 1970, following submission of a reorganization plan to Congress. The order transferred most (although not all) of the existing federal environmental programs to the EPA, which was established as an independent executive agency. Its administrator and other top officials are nominated by the president and confirmed by the Senate. Unlike environmental ministries in other Western democracies, the EPA has not enjoyed cabinet rank, although the administrator is the only head of a regulatory agency reporting directly to the president. Proposals to convert the agency into a Department of the Environment, with cabinet status, have languished in Congress, a victim of persistent controversies over environmental policy.

For years, the physical location of the agency in a remote corner of southwest Washington, D.C., in two converted apartment buildings had symbolized the EPA's uncertain status in the universe of federal agencies. In 1997, however, the EPA staff began moving into its impressive new headquarters in the palatial Ronald Reagan Building and International Trade Center in the center of the city, not far from the White House. Whether the new offices portend an improved era for the agency and for its environmental policies remains to be seen. If nothing else, the agency's new surroundings testify to its growing responsibilities and unquestioned importance.

Organizational Structure   As shown in Figure 5.1, the EPA's organization reflects its media-specific responsibilities, with separate program offices for air and radiation; water; pesticides, toxic substances, and pollution prevention; and solid waste and emergency response. Each of these program offices has operated independently even though many studies have recommended that pollution control efforts across the different media (air, water, and land) would be more effective if they were better integrated (Davies and Mazurek 1998; National Academy of Public Administration 1995). The Clinton administration's Common Sense Initiative (CSI) and its other efforts to reinvent environmental regulation included a modest move toward cross-media pollution control. The CSI was intended to work with selected industries (e.g., auto manufacturing or computers and electronics) through a consensus approach that engaged various stakeholders to look at all aspects of an industry's actions on a cross-media basis. The idea was to better coordinate rules and regulations, simplify the process, and reduce the cost of compliance. The EPA's formal structure and its administrative culture, however, have been significant obstacles in moving away from the old single-medium approach and conventional regulation (Coglianese and Allen 2004; Kraft and Scheberle 1998; Rosenbaum 2006). Time will tell if the agency is able to make the transition, but without congressional willingness to alter the basic statutes that have created the present EPA organizational structure, the change will be difficult.

In one promising development late in 1999, the EPA created a new Office of Environmental Information at the assistant administrator level. It is expected to play a key role in the agency's collection, management, integration, and dissemination of environmental information. The idea is to consolidate the enormous diversity of environmental data now collected in different EPA programs and help improve the quality of the data.[19] Equally important is making the data more useful in a range of activities, from measuring program success to enhancing public access and understanding.

As is the case with many federal agencies, much of the EPA's routine policy implementation takes place in its 10 regional offices. Two thirds of the agency's staff are employed in those offices or in other facilities outside of Washington, D.C., where they work closely with state governments (Rabe 2006; Scheberle 2004). Rule making and policy development, however, remain the responsibility of the headquarters staff.

Resources and Staff   In its first full year in 1971, the EPA had a staff of about 5,700 and a total budget of $4.2 billion (Portney 2000). It has grown much larger over time, as have its responsibilities. It is now far and away the largest federal regulatory agency. By 2004 the staff had increased to nearly 18,000 and the overall budget to about $8 billion. However, the budget declined significantly after 2004 and is projected to be only about $7.3 billion in the president's proposed fiscal year 2007 budget. The agency's operating budget (the funds used to run agency

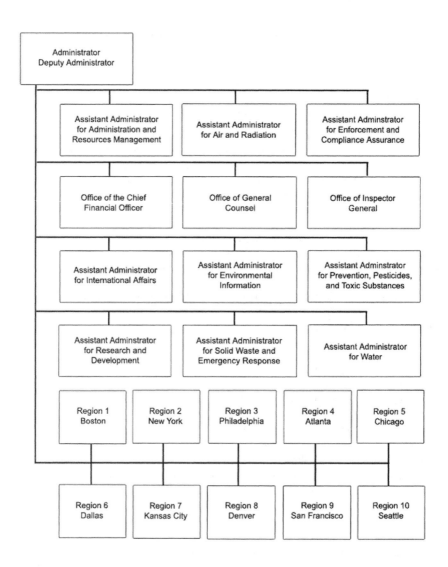

FIGURE 5.1   Organizational Structure of the U.S. Environmental Protection Agency
Source: U.S. Environmental Protection Agency Web page: www.epa.gov/epahome/
organization.htm (March 24, 2006).

programs) has been about $4.3 billion in recent years. In constant dollars, however, the agency's operating budget grew by only about 5.7 percent between 1980 and 2000 despite the many new responsibilities given to it by Congress during this period (Vig and Kraft 2006). Congress increased the budget between 2000 and 2004 but then allowed it to fall well below the level reached in 2000. As these figures suggest, for much of its existence, and even today, the EPA has not had the full resources needed to implement environmental protection policies successfully.

The agency's current budget would be in far worse shape, however, had it not been raised substantially during the 1990s under Presidents George Bush and Bill Clinton.

The EPA tends to recruit a staff strongly committed to its mission but with a diversity in professional training and problem-solving orientations that can breed conflict over implementation strategies (Landy, Roberts, and Thomas 1994). The staff consists predominantly of scientists and engineers who are assisted by a multitude of lawyers, economists, and policy analysts. By one count in the late 1990s, the agency employs some 4,000 scientists, 2,700 engineers, and more than 1,000 lawyers. Among its political appointees at the policy-making level in the agency, a background in law is the most common; six of the seven EPA administrators through the end of the Clinton administration held law degrees (Morgenstern 1999). With the notable exception of Anne Burford in the early 1980s, the EPA has attracted talented and respected administrators: William Ruckelshaus (twice), Russell Train, Douglas Costle, Lee Thomas, William Reilly, Carol Browner, and, under President George W. Bush, Christine Todd Whitman, Michael Levitt, and Stephen Johnson.[20]

Science at the EPA   As might be expected for an agency dealing with demanding technical problems, the EPA has developed a reputation for expertise even while the quality of its science is often disparaged by its critics. Over the past decade, the agency has relied on about a dozen research labs and another 28 facilities to provide technical support for its regulatory efforts. Following a consolidation of the laboratories and research centers during the Clinton administration, work is now concentrated in several specialized laboratories that operate under the various media offices such as the Office of Air and Radiation and another five facilities that operate under the Office of Research and Development.[21]

The EPA also makes extensive use of outside scientists. Its Science Advisory Board (SAB), created by Congress in 1978, has been, according to a former director, the "principal ongoing, institutionalized mechanism by which the scientific community interacts with all levels of EPA on many issues" (Yosie 1993, 1476–77). The SAB advises the agency as requested through a series of specialized committees, conducts an annual review of the scientific adequacy of EPA's research and development (R&D) work, and reviews the technical quality of proposed criteria documents, standards, and regulations.

Numerous studies in previous years have found the agency's scientific work to be inadequately staffed and insufficient. They have also faulted the EPA for lacking a strategy for long-term environmental research essential to its mission (Carnegie Commission 1992, 1993; Powell 1999). The reorganization of its science laboratories just discussed was one effort to improve EPA research capabilities. Equally important is improving the capacity of EPA administrators to apply uncertain environmental science to policy decisions.

Despite widespread calls in Congress and elsewhere for grounding rules and regulations in "sound science," the EPA has lacked the level of funding to improve the scientific basis of environmental regulation. Support for environmental research has recovered from its low point in the Reagan administration, but it remains a small portion of the $137 billion federal R&D budget for fiscal year 2007. EPA's share was about $560 million, an amount that, adjusted for inflation, has not changed since 1990. The rest is allocated among some 20 other federal agencies, with NASA and the Department of Energy receiving the lion's share of the total federal R&D funds for the environment. Science budgets in general have been rising in recent years.[22]

Despite its large staff, the EPA has been forced to rely heavily on outside scientific consultants and contractors for some of its most visible activities, such as implementation of the Superfund program. In fiscal year 2005, the EPA reported that it spent more than a billion dollars for contractor services in areas ranging from environmental assessments and cleanup of contaminated sites to information management services. The EPA is not alone in this regard. The Department of Energy's Office of Environmental Management oversees some 36,000 contractors working on cleanup of the nation's former nuclear weapons complexes. By many accounts, both the EPA and the DOE have done a poor job of supervising the contractors, who handle about a third of the EPA's work (Probst and Lowe 2000; U.S. GAO 1992). The EPA also cooperates with other federal agencies such as the FDA, Occupational Safety and Health Administration (OSHA), DOE, and National Oceanic and Atmospheric Administration. This dependence, however, adds to the administrative complexity and uncertainty of implementation.

Working with the States

Beyond its relation with other federal agencies, the EPA has developed an elaborate program, both formal and informal, to share environmental protection activities with the 50 states. As discussed in Chapter 3, about 75 percent of the major environmental protection program functions have been delegated to the states, a rate that has increased significantly over the past decade (Brown 2000). Many of the states have program requirements that exceed the minimum federal standards, and states also operate many of their own programs that are separate from federally mandated activities. Indeed, as noted earlier, the Council of State Governments has estimated that about 70 percent of significant legislation approved by the states has been initiatives unrelated to federal policy. The states are also responsible for most of the enforcement actions taken under federal environmental laws for delegated programs.

When the states operate their programs under authority delegated to them by the EPA, they are supervised in part by the agency's Washington headquarters but chiefly by the regional offices. Those offices keep in close contact with state officials and other environmental policy actors at the state and local levels. Among the most important of those local actors are citizen activists and environmental watchdog groups who monitor and review key implementation actions such as the issuance of air and water pollution permits and new regulations.

In some of the more environmentally progressive states, a kind of symbiotic relationship has developed between the state agency and citizen groups. Agency employees need the citizen groups to bring sufficient political pressure on sometimes reluctant state governments to push for more aggressive implementation than might otherwise occur. Citizen groups also turn to the state agencies (and the EPA itself) for financial assistance through various grant programs designed to promote public education and pollution prevention initiatives. Citizens may serve as well on local, regional, and state stakeholder advisory committees on which both the states and the

EPA increasingly rely. In many states, business and industry groups may have the dominant influence in such decision-making processes.

In addition to the delegated programs, the federal government offers a variety of voluntary programs to the states, generally by making available funds to establish state programs to deal with particular environmental problems. The Indoor Radon Abatement Act, for example, encourages states to adopt radon programs and to inform the public about health risks related to radon. In a third type of action, states may be under direct federal mandates to establish a program; examples are a State Implementation Plan under the Clean Air Act and wellhead protection programs under the Safe Drinking Water Act (Scheberle 1998).

As might be expected in such a system of intricate and politically delicate federal— state relations, the respective roles of the federal government and the states have varied significantly over time.[23] Among the most salient issues of the 1990s were the adequacy of federal financial assistance, the extent of federal micromanagement of state programs, and the degree to which states were given flexibility to set policy priorities that reflected problems of local importance. Congressional concern over the imposition of costly programs on the states led to approval of the Unfunded Mandates Reform Act of 1995 as part of the Republican's Contract with America. The act requires that new legislative proposals (including major revisions of existing laws) imposing costs of more than $50 million annually on state and local governments be accompanied by a cost estimate prepared by the Congressional Budget Office. Sponsors also must specify how the programs would be financed. The law erects new procedural barriers to enacting statutes that are likely to lead to unfunded federal mandates. Although the act is not likely to have a major effect on state environmental programs, it did signal the need for a new era of cooperation between the EPA and the states.

In this emerging political climate, the Clinton EPA experimented with several new environmental program initiatives that aspired to improve relations with the states as well as make environmental policies more effective and efficient. Among these were the Common Sense Initiative (CSI) noted earlier, Project XL, and the National Environmental Performance Partnership System (NEPPS). Most were widely considered to have fallen short of the goal of finding "cleaner, cheaper, smarter" ways to reduce or prevent pollution (Durant, Fiorino, and O'Leary 2004; Marcus, Geffen, and Sexton 2002; Scheberle 2004). The Bush administration has emphasized another initiative begun by the Clinton administration in 2000, called Performance Track. The idea is to give businesses more incentives to improve their environmental performance by granting them increased regulatory flexibility in return; participating companies file annual reports with the EPA that measure their improvement over time.[24]

The EPA also has experimented with a variety of programs to encourage local environmental initiatives through what it has called Community-Based Environmental Protection (CBEP), discussed in Chapter 3. CBEP is a kind of catch-all category for EPA grant programs and demonstration projects that are designed to assist new, more cooperative environmental initiatives at the local level (John and Mlay 1999). The EPA argues that by being sensitive to local environmental and social conditions and employing "multi-level, cross-sector partnerships to achieve results," it can help "lay the foundation for a new generation of environmental protection" (U.S. EPA 1997b, 1, 6–7).[25]

Even if some of the recent efforts to improve federal–state relations and local environmental action have yet to prove themselves, there is reason to be optimistic about the future role of the states and also of local governments. Many states, such as California, Minnesota, Wisconsin, Oregon, Washington, and New York, already have demonstrated a strong commitment to environmental protection goals. As discussed in Chapter 3, hundreds of highly innovative state, local, and regional policy initiatives on pollution prevention, use of economic incentives, and public disclosure mandates also testify to the potential for innovation at these levels of government (John 1994; Mazmanian and Kraft 1999; Rabe 2006). At the same time, caution is warranted because some states and localities are likely to lack either the commitment to such environmental quality goals or the resources to put programs into effect. In addition is the challenge of dealing with transboundary pollution (where pollutants move across state and national boundaries), the need to ensure that local economic and other interest groups do not exert undue pressure on state governments to weaken environmental protection, and the reality that states and localities will continue to depend on federal research and technical support that cannot be duplicated at the state level.[26]

Political Support and Opposition

All the factors discussed here affect the EPA's ability to perform its many statutory tasks. Both political support for the agency and opposition to it are equally important. Over time, the EPA has benefited from strong support for environmental protection goals in Congress (most notably among Democrats, but also from Republicans such as Rep. Sherwood Boehlert of New York and Sen. Lincoln Chafee of Rhode Island), among the public at large, and among the well-organized environmental community. That support has allowed it to fend off critics and for the most part to prevent weakening of its statutory authority. Members of Congress consider the EPA, like other federal regulatory agencies, to be a creature of their own making, and they keep close watch over its operation. They also defend it from presidents critical of its mission, as they did during the 1980s, although they frequently engage in EPA bureau bashing themselves to score political points about burdensome regulations. Congress may grant or withhold administrative discretion to the EPA depending on the prevailing trust of the agency's leadership and confidence in the president. As it demonstrated with its reauthorization of RCRA in 1984 and with the Clean Air Act in 1990, Congress may choose to specify environmental standards and deadlines in great detail so as to compel the EPA to do what it wants (Bryner 1995; Halley 1994; Kraft 2006).

The critics of EPA decision making have not been without considerable political clout. Industry, state and local governments concerned about the cost of environmental protection, and ideological conservatives opposed to government regulation have found receptive ears in Congress in recent years among both Democrats and Republicans. In addition, since the EPA's creation, presidents have taken a keen interest in its activities, and each has devised some mechanism that allows close White House supervision of the agency's regulatory program (Harris and Milkis 1996; Shanley 1992; Vig 2006).

The EPA has at best a mixed record of success, which reflects both the scope and complexity of the environmental problems it addresses and its organizational features.

After a period of institutional growth and development in the 1970s, the agency suffered severe budget and personnel cuts in the early to mid-1980s, which took a toll on staff morale. Since then, the EPA has struggled to redefine its mission, improve its capabilities for risk assessment and environmental management, and cope with the enormously difficult jobs given it by Congress.

Many students of environmental policy are convinced that the agency still has a long way to go (Davies and Mazurek 1998; Landy, Roberts, and Thomas 1994; Rosenbaum 2006). If its responsibilities continue greatly to exceed the resources provided to it, and if the agency and Congress are unable to institute needed reforms, it will continue to disappoint the environmental community as well as the regulated parties. A review of environmental rule making and enforcement helps illuminate some of the many challenges the agency faces in implementing environmental policy in the twenty-first century.

SETTING ENVIRONMENTAL STANDARDS

Under the general command-and-control, or direct regulation, approach that prevails in environmental policy today, implementation involves the setting and enforcing of environmental standards. The process involves a number of distinct scientific, analytic, and political tasks that cut across the different policy areas discussed earlier. These tasks include the determination of overall environmental policy goals and objectives; the setting of environmental quality criteria, quality standards, and emissions standards; and the enforcement of the standards through the various incentives and sanctions provided in the statutes. Table 5.2 summarizes these components of command-and-control regulation, which are discussed in detail later.

Environmental Goals and Objectives

Environmental policy goals and objectives are set by elected public officials, especially Congress, and reflect their conception of how environmental quality is to be reconciled with other social and economic values. Goals and objectives historically have been general rather than specific (e.g., "fishable and swimmable waters" under the Clean Water Act). They also have been highly ambitious, especially in light of available technologies and resources. They have emphasized important symbolic values and emotionally charged images (e.g., clean air, clean water, public health, safe drinking water) to maintain public support, even when the statutory language has embodied inevitable compromises over competing values. Congress grants authority to the EPA to fill in the details by providing for administrative discretion in developing rules and regulations (Bryner 1987, 1995; Furlong 2007; Kerwin 2003). By the 1980s, however, as we saw earlier, Congress grew impatient with the EPA and set highly specific goals and objectives and tighter deadlines, often with hammer clauses meant greatly to reduce agency discretion. Nonetheless, Congress is rarely clear in establishing priorities among the environmental policy goals it sets for the EPA and other agencies. It seems content to say "do it all" even when it fails to appropriate the funds necessary for the job (National Academy of Public Administration 1995, 2000).

TABLE 5.2

Steps Involved in Command-and-Control Environmental Regulation

Steps in the Process	Activities
Establish environmental goals and objectives	Sets general policy goals and objectives. Usually a legislative decision that balances environmental quality goals against social and economic considerations. Grants discretion to administrative agency to develop necessary rules and regulations.
Determine environmental quality criteria	Uses experimental and public health data as well as modeling exercises to establish the relationship between pollution and health or ecological effects. Essentially requires health and ecological risk assessments, largely technical decisions.
Set environmental quality standards	Determines the level of pollution that is acceptable in light of health and ecological effects and other considerations as allowed by law (such as economic costs). Quality standards reflect the maximum amount of pollution deemed to be socially tolerable. They are the result of an agency risk evaluation and reflect a policy judgment as well as technical analysis.
Set emissions standards	Sets a maximum amount of pollutants that individual sources such as power plants, manufacturing facilities, or automobiles, buses, and trucks are allowed to release without exceeding the capacity of the environment as reflected in the quality standards. Such agency decisions reflect a judgment about environmental science, technology, public health, and, as permitted, economic effects of regulation.
Enforce the standards and other requirements	Uses the methods as specified in the pertinent statute to monitor compliance with environmental quality and emissions standards and to enforce legal requirements. Normally penalties or sanctions exist for noncompliance, and they are imposed through legal and administrative mechanisms spelled out in the law. Much compliance is achieved through negotiation with the regulated parties.

The EPA has no statutory charter or organic law that defines its mission and explicitly sets out its policy objectives. That omission is a major liability and can be traced to the agency's establishment by executive order rather than by legislative action. The consequence is that the EPA administers about a dozen major environmental statutes adopted at different times by different congressional committees for different reasons.[27] It is not a comprehensive environmental agency, and it would not be even if it were made into a cabinet department. That is because significant environmental and natural resource responsibilities have been given to other agencies scattered across the executive branch. These deficiencies make the EPA more vulnerable than other agencies to short-term forces such as changes in public opinion, shifting legislative majorities, and varying presidential agendas. It also complicates the job of setting agency priorities and allocating scarce resources without congressional specifications about which program should take precedence.

Environmental Quality Criteria

Unlike the political process that sets broad environmental policy goals and objectives, environmental quality criteria lie chiefly in the scientific realm. They spell out what kinds of pollutants are associated with adverse health or environmental effects. In making such determinations, the EPA and other agencies such as the FDA and OSHA draw from experimental and epidemiological studies and modeling exercises both from within and outside of government. Setting environmental criteria requires some kind of risk assessment to answer key questions. What is the relationship between pollution and health? For example, how do fine particulates affect the lungs? How do specific pollutants affect the functioning of ecosystems? At what level of contamination for toxic chemicals such as PCBs or dioxin can we detect either human health or ecosystem effects? Studies of such relationships eventually allow government agencies to set environmental protection criteria.

Health Risk Assessment   Because these determinations set the stage for regulatory action (or inaction), risk assessment has been at the center of disputes over environmental protection policy for well over two decades. Scientific controversies abound over the most appropriate models, assumptions, and measurements even in areas in which there has been extensive experience with these methods, such as testing potential carcinogens (Andrews 2006; Rushefsky 1986). No one approach to conducting assessments can completely resolve these arguments. Therefore users of such assessments have to be alert to their limitations and rely on open debate over risk studies, and on adversarial processes, to detect and compensate for their weaknesses.

Health risk assessments normally involve a series of analytic procedures: identifying a given hazard, determining whether and how exposure to it can have adverse health effects, determining how many people (and which groups of people) are likely to be exposed to the substance; and describing the overall health risk, such as the increased chances of developing cancer or respiratory illness.[28] None of these activities is easy, and a good deal of uncertainty characterizes the whole process. At each step, myriad scientific and policy judgments are required to determine which methods to use and how to infer human health risk from limited epidemiological evidence or data drawn from animal exposures. The data gathering itself is complex, time consuming, and expensive, and the potential for misinterpretation is always there.

A major EPA study of dioxin released in 1994 in draft form illustrated all these problems, and it has been extensively debated, much as has the EPA's study of the effects of secondhand smoke discussed in Chapter 2. In the case of dioxin, a family of persistent bioaccumulative toxic chemicals that share a similar chemical structure and toxicity, the EPA concluded that it leads to "worrisome" health problems. These problems included an increased likelihood of cancer, damage to reproductive functions, stunted fetal growth, and weakened immune systems, even at extremely low exposure levels. Based on those findings, the EPA was prepared to take steps to reduce exposure to the chemical. The dioxin risk assessment took three years to complete, involved about 100 scientists within and outside of government, and ran to some 2,000 pages (Lee 1994; Schneider 1994a). In late 2000, after six years of scientific debate, reanalysis of the data, and redrafting of the conclusions, an outside group of scientists convened by the EPA's Science Advisory Board concluded that the massive report was "by and large a very fair and balanced description" of health risks.[29] Although not very visible to the public, such exhaustive analysis and extended regulatory decision making is by no means uncommon.

Risk assessments of this kind have tended to concentrate on individual pollutants and on cancer risks, but such an approach is not sufficient to detect health risks. Synergistic effects of multiple pollutants are also important, but they are hard to determine, as are long-term risks of exposure. Moreover, less adequate information is available about a host of health concerns other than cancer, such as the effects of environmental exposure on nervous systems, reproduction, and immune systems (Misch 1994). Many have argued persuasively that new approaches are needed. A major study in 1997, for example, called for a more comprehensive effort to examine multiple contaminants and sources of exposure as well as the value perspectives of diverse stakeholders (Presidential/Congressional Commission on Risk Assessment and Risk Management 1997). Congress did not act on the recommendations.

Ecological Risk Assessment   Much of the debate over risk assessment has focused on health risks. Increasingly, the concepts are being extended to ecological risks (U.S. EPA 1992b). Because knowledge of ecosystem functioning is even less well developed than knowledge of how pollutants affect public health, the nation needs to ensure that environmental science research can address such questions. Whether the issue is the effects of toxic chemicals on the nation's surface water quality, the effects of acid precipitation on aquatic ecosystems, or the probability of climate change related to the buildup of greenhouse gases, regulatory decisions depend critically on improving environmental science and bringing it to bear more effectively on policy decisions (Carnegie Commission 1993).

Setting Quality Standards

After risk assessments permit at least tentative answers to the question of how pollutants affect health and the environment, the EPA and other agencies have to determine the tolerable level of contamination based on the defined criteria. These levels are called *environmental quality standards*. Setting them involves not only risk assessment but risk evaluation. The latter is a policy judgment about how much risk is acceptable to society or to the particular community or groups at risk, including sensitive populations (such as children, pregnant women, or the elderly) and disadvantaged or minority groups. For example, what is the maximum level of ground-level ozone acceptable in light of its adverse health effects? What is the permissible level of lead or arsenic in drinking water? What level of pesticide residue on food is tolerable? For years, critics have urged the EPA and other agencies to distinguish clearly between the scientific basis of such choices and their policy judgments and to educate the public and policymakers on the issues. To illustrate how environmental quality criteria and standards are developed, Table 5.3 lists the major effects, primarily health effects, of the six major ambient air pollutants regulated under the Clean Air Act. Table 5.4 indicates the quality standards, the National Ambient Air Quality Standards (NAAQS), for the same six pollutants.

TABLE 5.3

Effects of Ambient Air Pollutants Regulated by the Clean Air Act

Pollutants	Effects
Carbon monoxide	Impairs the blood's ability to carry oxygen to the body's organs and tissues; can damage cardiovascular system, impair vision, reduce work capacity, and reduce learning ability.
Nitrogen dioxide	Can irritate the lungs and lower resistance to respiratory infections such as influenza. Long-term exposure can increase acute respiratory disease in children. Also a precursor to both ozone and acid precipitation.
Ozone	Repeated exposure can cause respiratory infection and lung inflammation, aggravate preexisting respiratory diseases such as asthma, and cause premature aging of the lungs. Short-term exposure may decrease lung function, cause eye irritation and nasal congestion, and reduce resistance to infection. May also damage trees and crops.
Lead	Accumulates in the blood, bones, and soft tissues and can adversely affect the kidneys, liver, nervous system, and other organs. Can cause seizures, mental retardation, and behavioral disorders. Most seriously affects fetuses and children; may be a factor in high blood pressure and heart disease in adults.
Particulate matter	May cause eye and throat irritation, bronchitis, lung damage, decreased lung function, and cancer. Such effects are more pronounced among sensitive groups, including children, the elderly, and those with cardiopulmonary disease such as asthma. Most serious health risks are related to fine particulates (PM-2.5). May also decrease visibility and cause soiling and materials damage.
Sulfur dioxide	Affects breathing and respiratory illness and may alter the defenses of the lungs and aggravate existing cardiovascular disease. Effects are greatest for asthmatics, children, and the elderly. Also a precursor of acid precipitation.

Source: U.S. Environmental Protection Agency, Office of Air and Radiation, *Latest Findings on National Air Quality: 2002 Status and Trends.* Available at www.epa.gov/air/airtrends/reports. html (released August 2003).

A revealing example of the mix of science and politics in environmental quality standards concerns the setting of drinking water quality standards for arsenic. The Clinton administration had proposed a new rule that would have set the acceptable level at 10 parts per billion beginning in 2006, an 80 percent reduction over prevailing U.S. standards but identical to the standards of the European Union and the World Health Organization. The mining industry and some municipalities had lobbied hard for a weaker standard out of concern for the costs of compliance. In March 2001 the Bush EPA announced it would withdraw the Clinton rule on the grounds that it was not supported by scientific research; that decision was widely condemned as inappropriate, and it caused significant political harm to a Bush White House eager to demonstrate its environmental protection credentials. Six months later, a National

TABLE 5.4

National Ambient Air Quality Standards in Effect in 2002		
Pollutant	Standard Value	Standard Type
Carbon monoxide (CO)		
8-hour average	9 ppm (10 mg/m^3)^a	Primary
1-hour average	35 ppm (40 mg/m^3)^a	Primary
Nitrogen dioxide (NO$_2$)		
Annual (arithmetic mean)	0.053 ppm (100 μg/m^3)^a	Primary and secondary
Ozone (O$_3$)		
8-hour average	0.08 ppm	Primary and secondary
Lead (Pb)		
Quarterly average	1.5 μg/m^3	Primary and secondary
Particulate matter less than 10 micrometers (PM-10)		
Annual (arithmetic mean)	50 μg/m^3	Primary and secondary
24-hour average	150 μg/m^3	Primary and secondary
Particulate matter less than 2.5 micrometers (PM-2.5)		
Annual (arithmetic mean)	15 μg/m^3	Primary and secondary
24-hour average	65 μg/m^3	Primary and secondary
Sulfur dioxide (SO$_2$)		
Annual (arithmetic mean)	0.03 ppm (80 μg/m^3)^a	Primary
24-hour average	0.14 ppm (365 μg/m^3)^a	Primary
3-hour average	0.50 ppm (1,300 μg/m^3)^a	Secondary

Source: U.S. Environmental Protection Agency, Office of Air and Radiation: www.epa.gov/air/criteria.html (July 29, 2005). The Clean Air Act established two kinds of air quality standards. Primary standards set limits designed to protect public health, which includes the health of sensitive populations such as asthmatics, children, and the elderly. Secondary standards set limits designed to protect public welfare, which includes protection against decreased visibility, damage to animals, crops, vegetation, and buildings. The table lists the National Ambient Air Quality Standards (NAAQS) set by the EPA's Office of Air Quality Planning and Standards for six principal pollutants, which are called criteria pollutants. The units of measure for the standards are parts per million (ppm) by volume, milligrams per cubic meter of air (mg/m^3), and micrograms per cubic meter of air at 25°C (μg/m^3).
^{a}Parenthetical value is an approximately equivalent concentration.

Academy of Sciences panel, asked to update an earlier report on arsenic in drinking water, concluded that, if anything, the Clinton administration had underestimated the risk of cancer. The Bush EPA then decided to leave the Clinton standards in place.[30]

These crucial decisions about acceptable risk levels are never easy to make, even if some analytic tools are available to estimate the public's general risk preferences or tolerances or if the public is able to participate directly in the process. Whatever the basis for decisions, the consequences are important. If environmental and health risks are exaggerated and if unnecessary or excessive regulations are imposed, the nation (or state or community) pays a price in added costs of compliance and possibly wasteful diversion of economic resources. If, however, risks are ignored or underestimated, we may fail to protect human health and environmental quality sufficiently, and as a result, severe or irreversible damage may occur.

As discussed earlier, risk-based priority setting has become a kind of mantra in commentary on reform of environmental policy. The EPA's 1990 study *Reducing Risk* set the tone for this ongoing debate, which is now heard at the state level as well. The EPA has tried to help the states identify and respond to their most pressing environmental risks, recognizing that they lack the financial resources to do everything required by the welter of federal environmental statutes (Davies 1996; Stone 1994). If the comparative risk strategy is to work, methodologies for both human health and ecological risk assessments will need improvement, as will our capacity to evaluate scientific findings and to ensure they are integrated with policy judgments. Risk assessments alone cannot determine policy. They also should not replace careful judgment by scientists, regulators, and the public about proper levels of safety, trade-offs between risks and benefits, or priorities for regulatory efforts. They can, however, bring much needed information to participants in those decisions.

Emissions Standards

Emissions standards follow from the environmental quality standards. They regulate what individual sources (e.g., factories, refineries, automobiles, and wastewater treatment plants) are allowed to emit into the air, water, or land without exceeding the overall capacity of the environment reflected in the quality standards. In most cases, decisions on air and water permits are made by state agencies using federal standards and guidelines. Such agency decisions reflect judgment about environmental science, public health, available emission control technologies, and, where permitted, economic repercussions of regulatory decisions.

■ BALANCING STATUTORY GOALS AND COSTS

The costs of environmental regulation are high enough that most of the decisions described here have become intensely controversial, whether the issue is automobile emissions standards or water quality criteria. The battles often reach the evening news and the front pages of the newspapers. Several cases illustrate the disputes that arise and also how they have been resolved.

The EPA's decision in 1997 to tighten air quality standards for fine particulates and ozone is a notable case. The EPA is required by law to review the scientific evidence and to update the regulations every five years. It missed a 1992 deadline, was sued by the American Lung Association, and was under a court order to issue new particulate standards. It chose to update the ozone standards at the same time. The agency conducted four years of scientific studies, many of them challenged by industry. Even though the EPA's only obligation under the Clean Air Act is to protect public health with an "adequate margin of safety," it also conducted cost–benefit analyses for the new standards. It concluded that the health benefits of reducing exposure to fine particles greatly outweighed the costs, in part because such fine particles may be responsible for 15,000 deaths a year in addition to widespread hospitalization for respiratory disorders (Cushman 1997).[31] The fine particles are especially dangerous because they are inhaled deep into the lungs where they do considerable damage. The cost–benefit ratio for the new ozone standard was more debatable (Freeman 2006; Portney 1998).

In the end, the Clinton White House supported both of the new EPA standards, despite concern expressed by the president's economic advisers and industry over the anticipated costs. The administration tried to soften the economic blow and opposition by the states, industry, and Congress by allowing up to 15 years for the states to comply. Nonetheless, as discussed in Chapter 3, industry groups challenged the EPA standards in federal court. They won at the appeals court level (Wald 1999a) but lost at the Supreme Court in the case of *Whitman v. American Trucking Association* (2001). The case then returned to the D.C. Circuit Court of Appeals to have several issues resolved, and the EPA won again as industry challenges were rejected by the court (Wald 2002).

In a related move in late 1999, the Clinton administration issued tougher vehicle emissions standards to begin taking effect in 2004 and described the action as the most ambitious antipollution initiative of Clinton's presidency. For the first time both cars and light trucks (including sport utility vehicles) would be governed by the same national emissions control system. The administration proposed cleaner fuel standards as well, part of an integrated approach designed to reduce urban smog. At least one auto company, Ford, announced that it anticipated no difficulty in meeting the new rules. The EPA estimated that automakers and oil companies would spend $5.3 billion complying with the new regulations over the next several years. Yet it also argued that the benefits of the rules would total some $25 billion over the same period (Bradsher 1999a).

In a decision strongly condemned by the long-haul trucking industry, the Bush administration in 2002 also sided with those favoring more stringent auto and truck emissions, in this case from diesel engines. It was one of the few Bush environmental rulings applauded by environmentalists. Diesel emissions contribute to thousands of cases of asthma, heart disease, and premature deaths each year. The rule is intended to cut emissions by 90 percent by 2007, and it could prevent 8,300 premature deaths annually, according to the EPA. Engine manufacturers argued that the new rule would cost billions of dollars a year and would create havoc in their industry (Seelye 2002). The new rule emerged as part of a 1998 settlement between the Clinton EPA and truck engine manufacturers (see Box 5.1 later in the chapter). Bush administration officials also announced their intention to adopt rules to cut pollutants sharply from diesel-powered construction equipment, some farm and mining equipment, and other off-road vehicles, which are projected to save 8,000 additional lives each year. Those regulations were announced in 2004 and reflected an unusual degree of collaboration among environmental groups, public health groups, engine manufacturers, and fuel refineries, all of whom praised the EPA for listening to the concerns they had with the rules.[32]

As these examples illustrate well, environmental protection is definitely costly. As noted earlier, public and private sector spending totals about $200 billion a year for the seven statutes covered in this chapter. To judge from one estimate from the mid-1990s, private industry bears about 57 percent of that amount, local governments 24 percent, the federal government 15 percent, and state governments 4 percent (Portney and Probst 1994). The cost is especially striking when viewed historically. The EPA estimates that U.S. spending on pollution control and abatement increased almost fourfold from its 1972 level of $30 billion (in 1990 dollars), or 0.9 percent of the gross domestic product (GDP), through 1990, when it reached $115 billion, or

1.9 percent of the GDP. The trend is projected to continue although at a slower rate of growth (U.S. EPA 1990a).

As these amounts suggest, compliance costs are a far larger portion of the total than the direct costs of running government programs. Yet their measurement is not as simple and straightforward as industry or state and local governments suggest. The cost of complying with environmental regulations depends on technological developments that cannot always be foreseen accurately. Annual costs may well decline over time as manufacturing and other industrial processes change. For obvious political reasons, industry tends to use estimates at the high end of the range to argue against additional regulations, whereas environmental groups and government agencies invariably use lower estimates. Estimates of public health and environmental benefits are harder to come by. They also receive less attention than costs in debates over the economics of environmental protection.

ADOPTING AND ENFORCING REGULATIONS

Implementing statutes requires more than setting environmental standards. Agency officials must interpret often vague statutory language and develop the means to achieve policy goals. That typically requires drafting guidelines and regulations that are legally binding. The 1990 Clean Air Act, for example, is more than 400 pages long and required the EPA to write hundreds of new regulations, 55 of them within two years of enactment. It is scarcely surprising that the EPA falls behind in meeting such expectations and is often compelled to act when environmentalists and others file suit in federal court. Such suits have an important drawback. Judicial decisions can force the agency to concentrate on the disputed issues to the detriment of other statutory provisions (Melnick 1983; O'Leary 1993).

Administrative Rule Making

The federal Administrative Procedure Act, specifications in individual environmental statutes, and judicial rulings all have sought to make the exercise of administrative discretion transparent, or visible, and accountable to the public. In addition, agencies are not to engage in arbitrary and capricious actions. That is, they must base their decisions on the record or docket for any given issue and must stay within the guidelines for such decisions that are set out in the statutes or pertinent judicial rulings. Such stipulations, however, cannot guarantee well-designed or effective regulations, only adherence to the law. They also provide only minimal assurance of agency responsiveness to public preferences because the administrative process cannot easily accommodate full and regular participation by environmental and citizen groups, nor by the general public. Whether at the federal or state level, it is not surprising that the access to administrative agencies afforded to competing interest groups and their influence on decision making is not equal. By any measure, industry groups have a major advantage over environmentalists, and particularly in Republican administrations that ideologically tend to be more probusiness than Democratic administrations, although this does not mean that business groups always win the policy battles (Furlong 2007; Kamieniecki 2006; Kraft and Kamieniecki 2007).

The administrative rule-making process is straightforward in its basic outline, even if its execution is not. When agencies such as the EPA determine that a rule is needed, they may publish an advance notice of proposed rule making in the *Federal Register* to signal their intent to consider a rule (although this is unusual). They assemble the requisite scientific, economic, and other data and then begin formulation of a draft rule or regulation. When a draft is ready, another published notice in the *Federal Register* invites public comment. The agency submits the draft rule to the White House Office of Management and Budget (OMB) for review and clearance, which at times has been done prior to public notice. In late 2002 the OMB announced that, as an element in the new "E-Government Initiatives" in the Bush administration, it would launch a centralized Web portal that would allow any citizen to view and submit comments on federal regulations (www.regulation.gov). After consideration of public comments, data, studies, and other material submitted to the agency by interested parties, the agency publishes the final rule in the *Federal Register*, accompanied by agency responses to the major issues raised during the public participation stage (Bryner 1987; Furlong 1995b). A roughly analogous process exists for state agency rule making.

The EPA and other agencies have to defend their work carefully, and they assemble the evidence in an elaborate rule-making docket. This includes agency planning documents and studies, legal memoranda, advisory committee reports, public comments, summaries of meetings and hearings, scientific and economic analyses, the proposed and final rules, and more. The entire rule-making process can easily take three or more years to complete, not counting the time needed for judicial or congressional review (Furlong 1995b; Kerwin 2003).

These complicated processes are difficult to avoid, however, given the nation's dedication to due process and protection of individual rights. The high stakes involved in environmental policy compound the problem as numerous parties seek to participate in and influence the administrative process. The larger and better financed trade associations, industries, and other organizations employ an army of law firms and technical consultants to help them make their case. Although environmental and citizen groups are rarely as well endowed as business interests (Furlong 1997), they often have significant opportunities to shape the outcome, especially at state and local levels. Even at the federal level, however, the EPA has tried to encourage citizen participation through a new Public Involvement Policy that it adopted in 2003.[33]

Participants in rule making bring with them diverse and conflicting perspectives on environmental problems (scientific, legal, administrative, economic, and political), which are inherently difficult to reconcile. Unfortunately, the adversarial U.S. political system encourages seemingly endless disputation among them, particularly where procedural delays benefit one or more parties. The disappointed losers have additional options, including suing the agency and making their case again in the federal courts. Over the past several decades, EPA officials have asserted that some 80 percent of major EPA regulations have been contested in court because of their significance and economic impact. Others have disputed those figures as far too high. In recent years, the EPA has been sued about 100 times a year by environmental or business groups or the states. The result can be protracted legal proceedings, long delays in implementing the laws, and excessive costs.

These effects have motivated critics to seek "regulatory reform" measures in Congress that would further constrain the EPA's regulatory process by requiring additional economic and other studies to support proposed regulations (Andrews 2006; Freeman 2006). Partly in response to congressional criticism, the Clinton administration in 1995 initiated its "regulatory reinvention" programs described earlier. The Common Sense Initiative, Project XL, and various other agency programs focused on a more cooperative, consensus-building approach to environmental regulation. Similarly, EPA administrators have experimented over a longer period with a form of consensus-based rule making called regulatory negotiation (Weber 1998, 1999). The idea is that the various stakeholders will come together and work cooperatively to negotiate and agree on regulatory changes in a way that will limit subsequent legal challenges.

Although promising, and encouraged by the government since adoption of the Negotiated Rulemaking Act of 1990, regulatory negotiation is of limited use. It is most appropriate when rule making involves only a few parties who are prepared to negotiate in good faith and who have no incentive to obstruct the proceedings, when the issues do not involve compromise of fundamental principles, and when no great inequities in resources or political power exist among participants (Amy 1987). A major study of the EPA's use of negotiated rule making, in fact, concluded that not only did it not save the agency any time, but it actually stimulated more, not less, litigation. The reasons for these outcomes seem to be that such negotiation added new sources of conflict and raised expectations about the benefits of participation in rule making that could not be met (Coglianese 1997; see also O'Leary and Bingham 2003).

Enforcement and Compliance

Environmental policies mean little without monitoring of regulated parties and enforcement actions that can ensure a high level of compliance. Yet one of the acknowledged weaknesses of the command-and-control approach to environmental regulation is that such close monitoring of compliance is rare because of the difficulty of the task and the lack of sufficient resources (Davies and Mazurek 1998; Russell 1990). Instead, the EPA and the states rely heavily on self-monitoring by industry and other regulated parties, who then report their results to regulatory authorities. Despite the public impression to the contrary, visits and inspections of industrial facilities by regulatory officials are infrequent. The effect is further diminished by the common practice of announcing such inspections in advance (Russell 1990).

Perhaps as a consequence of the weak incentives this approach creates for complying with the law, recent studies have found high rates of violation of environmental standards. In 1998, for example, the EPA's own inspector general found widespread enforcement failures at the state and local levels for both air and water pollution control. Some wastewater treatment plants were operating with obsolete permits or none at all. In one state, half of the major air pollution sources were not inspected between 1990 and 1996, and in 1995 and 1996, the state stopped reporting significant violation of air quality regulations to the federal government. The report faulted both federal and state officials for falling short of goals (Cushman 1998b). Similarly, a GAO study in 1994 found that one in six of inspected major industrial and municipal sources were in significant violation of their permits (Freeman 2006).

Considerable variation in enforcement activity also exists across the 50 states, explainable in part by public perceptions of environmental problems, state economic conditions, and interest groups' strength (Hunter and Waterman 1996). Moreover, the aggressiveness of enforcement efforts may make a difference in achieving environmental quality goals. For example, states with strong and consistent enforcement actions, at least in air pollution control, are more likely to improve environmental quality (Ringquist 1993).

If environmental regulation in practice often appears to be less strict than we might assume, it has not reduced the level of criticism. Industry and state and local governments have complained frequently about environmental regulations that they see as burdensome, costly, and inflexible. The critics often suggest that the effectiveness and efficiency of environmental policy could be improved through greater use of cooperation, negotiation, and financial incentives to promote achievement of environmental goals (Sexton et al. 1999).

It is hard to say who is right. Surprisingly little empirical evidence speaks definitively to the question of which approach produces the best results. It may well be that collaborative and cooperative approaches work better than conventional regulation, at least for some kinds of environmental protection actions. At a minimum, their use can help bring the stakeholders together and review both the scientific evidence and policy alternatives (Kraft and Johnson 1999). Many environmentalists, however, remain skeptical of moving too far from the relative certainty of direct or conventional regulation.[34] Given this state of affairs, it would be useful for agencies to experiment with a variety of policy tools, old and new, and to evaluate programs carefully to see which strategies produce the best results.

Even when the laws appear to be coercive and invite adversarial relations between government and industry, the reality is that the enforcement process is fundamentally one of self-compliance and negotiation. Agencies at both the federal and state levels encourage compliance through informal means, using meetings, telephone conversations, letters, and other exchanges. Only when such efforts fail do more formal means of enforcement come into play. Agencies may then turn to an increasingly severe series of formal actions. These start with what are called Notices of Violation, where the agency indicates it has found a failure to comply with regulatory law. The agency may then proceed to an Administrative Order, where it stipulates action that must be taken by the party out of compliance (e.g., a state agency or an industrial facility). It may also list companies as ineligible for federal contracts, grants, and loans, as allowed by the statute. As a last resort, when all these actions fail to yield compliance, the EPA can move to civil and criminal prosecution with the aid of the Justice Department's Environment and Natural Resources division (Hunter and Waterman 1992, 1996). Even here, however, most cases are settled out of court, clearly signaling that the EPA is reluctant to use the courts in routine enforcement actions.

Because of their visibility and symbolism, civil and criminal actions are sometimes used to signal the government's intent to enforce the law and thus spur voluntary compliance. Early in 2000, for example, the Clinton EPA announced it had achieved a record in enforcement actions taken during 1999. The agency referred 403 civil cases to the U.S. Department of Justice and filed 3,935 civil and administrative actions. It also referred 241 criminal cases for prosecution and assessed $52 million in criminal fines as well as $167 million in civil penalties.[35] Upon taking office in 2001, EPA officials in the Bush administration argued that their overall record was comparable to Clinton's, but Democrats in Congress insisted that enforcement of environmental laws had declined appreciably under Bush. Lending credence to the Democrats' charge,

BOX 5.1
Enforcing Environmental Law: Unusual Penalties

Four relatively recent cases illustrate both the scope of violations of environmental law and what enforcement efforts can achieve through use of fines and other penalties.

- In October 1998 diesel truck engine manufacturers agreed to pay $83 million in fines and spend $1 billion on environmental improvements to settle EPA accusations that they cheated on engine performance tests, resulting in far more pollution than legally allowed. It was the most expensive settlement ever for a clean air case and involved the world's leading manufacturers of such engines, including, among others, Mack Trucks Inc., Cummins Engine Co., and Caterpillar Inc. (Cushman 1998e).

- In July 1999 Royal Caribbean Cruises Ltd., the world's second-largest cruise line, pleaded guilty to dumping oil and hazardous chemicals routinely from nine ships into U.S. coastal waters and then lying about the practice to the U.S. Coast Guard. It promised to pay $18 million in fines, subject to judicial approval (Wald 1999b). Many other cruise ships engaged in similar practices and also have been heavily fined.

- In December 2001 the ExxonMobil Corporation agreed to pay a fine of $11.2 million in one of the largest settlements for violating environmental laws. The company had illegally discharged hazardous waste in Staten Island, New York, and lied about its activities, according to the EPA. ExxonMobil placed the blame on the complexity of the regulations (Stewart 2001).

- In January 2005 ConocoPhillips, the largest oil-refining company in the nation, settled with the federal Justice Department over violations of the Clean Air Act. The government said the settlement would lead to annual reductions of some 47,000 tons of dangerous emissions. The company is to pay civil fines of $4.5 million and invest a much larger sum, $525 million, in technological improvements at nine refineries in seven states to comply with the new source review sections of the federal Clean Air Act. It is to spend an additional $10 million on related environmental projects that also will lead to lowered emissions (Janofsky 2005).

Eric Schaeffer, director of the Office of Regulatory Enforcement, resigned his EPA position in early 2002, citing both declining enforcement actions and weakening of the Clean Air Act's new source review program under the Bush administration.[36]

Box 5.1 summarizes notable cases in which the EPA has imposed substantial fines for egregious violations of environmental law. As discussed in Chapter 3, most enforcement actions take place at the state level, with considerable variation from state to state. Data on enforcement activities, however, are not as complete or accurate as they should be, making comparisons among the states and assessments of their effectiveness very difficult (National Academy of Public Administration 2002).

Even as it announces settlements of the kind illustrated in Box 5.1, the EPA highlights its continuing use of "incentives to achieve industry compliance with environmental laws" through a variety of new mechanisms, such as opening Compliance Assistance Centers that offer interactive Web sites. These new activities were said to be part of the Clinton administration's "sweeping efforts to reinvent government," and they were continued in the Bush administration. A visit to the EPA's compliance and enforcement Web page provides many examples of this new orientation.[37]

White House Oversight

Concern over the costs and burdens of environmental and other regulations have led all presidents since Gerald Ford to institute some form of centralized White House oversight of agency rule making as part of their broader effort to control the federal bureaucracy. EPA rules have been a major target of the reviews (National Academy of Public Administration 1987; Shanley 1992; Vig 2006). For ideological and political reasons, these efforts were particularly wide reaching under Ronald Reagan and George H. W. Bush. The procedure was modified by the Clinton administration, but under George W. Bush it once again became a vehicle for rolling back environmental regulation.

Both the Reagan and Bush administrations operated under two executive orders (EOs) from 1981 and 1985—12291 and 12498, respectively—that guided the White House regulatory review process. One required a formal cost–benefit analysis, or Regulatory Impact Analysis (RIA), prior to formal proposal of major regulations, which were defined as having an annual impact on the economy of at least $100 million. No regulatory action was to be undertaken by an agency "unless the potential benefits to society for the regulation outweigh the potential costs to society." Moreover, the EPA and other agencies were to select the "alternative involving the least net cost to society." The order authorized an Office of Information and Regulatory Affairs (OIRA) in the White House Office of Management and Budget to review the documents and enforce the policy. The second executive order required the EPA and other federal agencies to develop an annual regulatory agenda for submission to OIRA and to indicate how their programs were consistent with the president's own agenda.

Critics faulted the Reagan review process on many grounds, including closed decision making, poor documentation, bias in discussing issues with regulated interests, lack of technical expertise, and regulatory delays (Eads and Fix 1984). Even after some reforms, scholars continued to question OIRA's capacity for judging agency proposals, its ability to review as many as 2,400 regulations a year, and the use of cost–benefit analysis in the manner required by EO 12291, which was biased against approval of new regulations (Cooper and West 1988).

In addition to the use of the executive orders from the Reagan era, President George H. W. Bush established a White House Council on Competitiveness, headed by Vice President Dan Quayle. The council quickly became known in the business community for providing a secret "back door" in government for industries displeased with agency regulators. It operated largely in secret and independently of the OIRA review (Berry and Portney 1995). Environmental regulations were a favorite target of the council. It is not entirely clear what effect the antiregulatory fervor of the Reagan and Bush years had on the agencies, including the EPA. Industry gained short-term regulatory relief but achieved little in the way of basic reform of environmental policy (Furlong 1995a). On the whole, political rhetoric and symbolism were probably more important than substantive policy impacts. Yet the Reagan and Bush White House review process institutionalized the idea of centralized oversight of regulation and helped legitimize the use of economic analysis by the agencies.

The day after taking office, President Bill Clinton announced the termination of the Council on Competitiveness. Yet he too recognized the imperative of having some form of White House oversight. On September 30, 1993, Clinton replaced Reagan's executive orders with a new executive order (12866) on regulatory planning and review. These guidelines clearly instructed agencies to seek balance among a variety of goals in their implementation of environmental statutes. They differed from the parallel orders in the Reagan and Bush administrations, though, by avoiding a narrow focus on economic costs.

George W. Bush continued the process of White House review under the Clinton executive order (slightly amended), but he signaled his intention to view proposed agency rules far more skeptically than Clinton's administration did. As director of OIRA, Bush selected John Graham, a noted critic of regulatory policy, who made clear his intention to require cost–benefit analyses as well as rigorous risk assessments in support of proposed agency regulations. Early evaluations of the Bush record of agency oversight concluded that the new review process was likely to tip the balance of power toward the regulated business community (Adams 2002b; Vig 2006). For instance, the independent OMB Watch stated that under Graham's leadership, OIRA was "increasingly using its regulatory review authority to weaken or block health, safety, and environmental standards."[38]

More concerns about OIRA's role are likely to arise in the future as it implements new congressionally imposed requirements in the Data Quality Act of 2000. The act was designed to ensure the accuracy of data on which agencies base their regulations, but it did not go through a full process of policy legitimation of the kind discussed in Chapter 3. Press accounts indicate that the law's provisions were written largely by business and industry groups and that they were approved by Congress as a little-noticed rider in 2000: 27 lines of text buried in a massive budget bill that President Clinton had to sign. The same groups indicated that they would use the law to challenge regulations they believe to be burdensome or unfair (Revkin 2002), and they have.[39]

CONCLUSIONS

With all the criticism directed at it, we might be tempted to conclude that hardly anything is right with the present environmental regulatory regime and that only wholesale policy and management change would improve the situation. Such appraisals ignore important, if uneven, improvements in environmental quality over the past three decades that are directly and indirectly tied to environmental policies, including command-and-control policies. They also ignore major shifts now under way in industry and government such as pollution prevention, green technology development, and environmental research that arguably are related to federal environmental policy efforts over this time period and strong public support for them.

The problems with environmental policies and with the EPA are real enough, although not without solutions. Some of the blame for the present state of affairs surely lies with EPA and other federal officials who could have done a better job of managing their programs. Congress is equally, if not more, responsible, however, for the deficiencies of environmental protection policy. It has burdened the EPA with far more tasks than it can possibly handle with its budgetary resources. It also has deprived the agency of the discretion and tools it needs to set priorities among its varied programs and to spend money effectively and efficiently. In addition, the EPA has long received mixed signals about what it is expected to do from Capitol Hill, the White House, the courts, other federal agencies, state and local governments, environmentalists, and industry (Rosenbaum 2006).

Thoughtful assessments of what might be done to improve environmental policy are not hard to come by (Davies and Mazurek 1998; Fiorino 2006; National Academy of Public Administration 1995, 2000; Sexton et al. 1999); some of these are discussed in Chapter 7. Solutions depend on policymakers developing a broader and clearer understanding of environmental goals than we have seen to date. They also require the political will to pursue those goals with a diversity of strategies (e.g., regulation, market incentives, public education, information disclosure, and public–private partnerships) that can meet the varied expectations the nation has for environmental protection policy. Included here are not only policy effectiveness and efficiency, but also other values such as social equity and environmental justice. Dealing with a new generation of environmental problems, such as nonpoint pollution and urban sprawl, requires rethinking which policies will work best. Even the effective policies of the past must be judged by their suitability for the future. There is all the more reason today, then, to evaluate environmental programs more frequently and more rigorously to determine just how successful they are or can be. That goal in turn speaks to the need to improve the quality and dissemination of environmental data.

The most essential requirement is taking a far more comprehensive approach to environmental policy and concentrating on the long-term goal of sustainable development. That means trying to integrate the pursuit of environmental, economic, and social values at all levels of government. The public must be part of any dialogue toward these ends, from the community to the national and international levels. Admittedly, it is a challenge at a time of substantial cynicism toward government and the political process. Yet success in working toward sustainable communities across the United States indicates a great potential for these innovative efforts (Mazmanian and Kraft 1999; Portney 2003). Effective public participation in these critical decisions requires that citizens become far better informed about the nature of environmental problems and risks, how they compare with one another, the costs of dealing with them, the trade-offs involved, and the policy choices we face as a nation.

DISCUSSION QUESTIONS

1. What would you propose for reforming the federal environmental protection laws reviewed in this chapter or the processes for implementing them? Why do you favor the kinds of policy changes you propose?
2. The EPA is frequently criticized by the business community and its other adversaries, but it seems not to have as much political support as one would guess based on favorable public attitudes toward environmental policy. Why is that? What might the agency do to increase its visibility to the public and build such support?
3. In implementing environmental protection laws, the EPA and the states usually try to balance the benefits of environmental protection against the costs imposed on society, at least to the extent allowed by law. What are the major advantages of such a balancing approach to environmental protection? What are the major disadvantages?
4. Decision making within administrative agencies such as the EPA and comparable state agencies is often subjected to intense lobbying, particularly by regulated

parties. Would greater public participation in such decision making be desirable? If so, how would you encourage or facilitate such participation?

5. Most of the major federal environmental protection laws are administered largely by the states under federal supervision. Are the states doing a good job in handling their responsibilities? How would you determine that? Where would you go to find pertinent information on state activities?

SUGGESTED READINGS

Bryner, Gary C. *Blue Skies, Green Politics: The Clean Air Act of 1990 and Its Implementation*, 2nd ed. Washington, DC: CQ Press, 1995.

Davies, J. Clarence, and Jan Mazurek. *Pollution Control in the United States: Evaluating the System*. Washington, DC: Resources for the Future, 1998.

Durant, Robert F., Daniel J. Fiorino, and Rosemary O'Leary, eds. *Environmental Governance Reconsidered: Challenges, Choices, and Opportunities*. Cambridge, MA: MIT Press, 2004.

Fiorino, Daniel J. *The New Environmental Regulation*. Cambridge, MA: MIT Press, 2006.

Portney, Paul R., and Robert N. Stavins, eds. *Public Policy for Environmental Protection*, 2nd ed. Washington, DC: Resources for the Future, 2000.

Scheberle, Denise. *Federalism and Environmental Policy: Trust and the Politics of Implementation*, 2nd ed. Washington, DC: Georgetown University Press, 2004.

ENDNOTES

1. I focus in this chapter on these seven key acts. By any measure they are the most important ones dealing with pollution control. Others, though, also merit attention, such as the Pollution Prevention Act of 1990 and the Oil Pollution Act, also of 1990.

2. In the late 1990s, the U.S. EPA put the cost at $170 billion each year, which some analysts (e.g., Portney 1998) considered to be too high. The $200 billion is an estimate for the early 2000s. The EPA no longer calculates the cost.

3. To read a fuller treatment of the statutes and some of the issues raised here, explore the sources cited in the chapter and the edited collection by Paul Portney and Robert Stavins (2000). Another good site for the complete laws and pertinent regulations is the EPA itself: www.epa.gov/epahome/laws.htm. The agency site offers both summaries and full texts of the laws.

4. The far-reaching and innovative Southern California clean air plan resulted from precisely such a rejection. The formally submitted California SIP openly admitted that it would not bring the state into compliance with national standards. Local environmentalists sued the EPA, arguing that under the provisions of the Clean Air Act, it could not accept such a plan. A federal appeals court agreed. For the details, see Mazmanian (1999).

5. For more discussion of the Clean Air Act, see Bryner (1995) and Portney and Stavins (2000).

6. In proposing the Clear Skies initiative, the Bush White House chose a less stringent approach to air pollution reform than recommended by the EPA. The decision was one of many indications that the EPA was less influential in the Bush White House than it was in the Clinton administration. See Katharine Q. Seelye, "White House Rejected a Stricter E.P.A. Alternative to the Clear Skies Plan," *New York Times*, April 28, 2002, 24.

7. See Michael Janofsky, "Bush-Backed Emissions Bill Fails to Reach Senate Floor," *New York Times*, March 10, 2005, A21; Janofsky, "E.P.A. Sets Rules to Cut Pollution," *New York Times*, March 11, 2005, 1, A14; and Matthew L. Wald, "New Rules Set for Emission of Mercury," *New York Times*, March 16, 2005, online edition. Jeffords' statement is taken from the committee Web page: http://epw.senate.gov. Inhofe's remarks appear in Janofsky's March 10 article.

8. Matthew L. Wald, "E.P.A. Says It Will Change Rules Governing Industrial Pollution," *New York Times*, November 23, 2002, 1, A16. The announcement of the relaxed NSR rules was made quietly by an assistant administrator of the EPA in a briefing with no cameras allowed and with President Bush out of the country. EPA administrator Christine Todd Whitman did not appear at the press briefing. The 628-page rule is available at www.epa.gov/nsr/. Press accounts made clear that the EPA was at odds with the DOE, which favored weaker NSR standards to keep costs of U.S. energy production low. See Katharine Q. Seelye, "E.P.A. and Energy Department War over Clean Air Rules," *New York Times*, February 19, 2002, A15. See also Seelye, "9 States in East Sue U.S. over New Pollution Rules," *New York Times*, January 1, 2003, 1, A12.

9. Juliet Eilperin, "New Rules Could Allow Power Plants to Pollute More," *Washington Post*, August 31, 2005, A1. For a statement of the administration's view of CAIR's potential, see www.epa.gov/cair/. For a review of the arguments advanced by critics of the rule, see Shankar Vedantam, "Clearing the Air? The EPA's Ruling on Mercury Prompts Sharp Criticism," *Washington Post National Weekly Edition*, March 21–27, 2005, 29. In March 2006 a three-judge federal appeals court overturned one element of the NSR rule, the stipulation that routine maintenance of less than 20 percent of the plant's cost would not trigger the NSR requirement for pollution control upgrading. It remained uncertain whether the Bush administration would appeal the ruling. See Michael Janofsky, "Judges Overturn Bush Bid to Ease Pollution Rules," *New York Times*, March 18, 2006, 1, A11. The same court had unanimously approved the central provisions of the NSR rules in June 2005, ruling against states and environmental groups that had challenged it. See Janofsky, "U.S. Court Backs Bush's Changes on Clean Air Act," *New York Times*, June 25, 2005, 1, A8.

10. The history of federal water pollution control dates back to the Refuse Act of 1899, which was intended to prevent constraints on navigation. The act prohibited the discharge or deposit of "any refuse matter" into "any navigable water" of the United States. The volume of waste products such as fiber and sawdust from paper mills and sawmills was so great in some rivers and channels that it threatened to block navigation. Administered by the U.S. Army Corps of Engineers, the Refuse Act had little or no effect on most industrial and municipal water pollution (Freeman 1990).

11. Barbara Whitaker, "Federal Judge Rules Los Angeles Violates Clean Water Laws," *New York Times*, December 24, 2002, A14.

12. There are similar citizen suit provisions in other environmental laws, most notably the Clean Air Act, the Resource Conservation and Recovery Act, and the Emergency Planning and Community Right-to-Know Act.

13. For an assessment of the Total Maximum Daily Load provisions of the Clean Water Act and the proposed EPA rule, see Jim Boyd, "Unleashing the Clean Water Act: The Promise and Challenge of the TMDL Approach to Water Quality," *Resources* 139 (Spring 2000): 7–10, available at www.rff.org.

14. Many of those support activities may be essential to cleanup (the EPA argues that 70 percent of the Superfund budget is used for "cleanup response"), but the critics

have long argued that far too much of the money spent on Superfund goes to litigation, an argument that found a receptive home in the Republican Congress. See an Associated Press release published in the *New York Times*, "Toxic Waste Fund Criticized for Its Noncleanup Spending," June 13, 1999, 33. A General Accounting Office study found that about half of public and private funds expended under Superfund went to administrative and support activities, and the rest went to contractors for cleanup work. A good summary of debates over Superfund can be found in Steve Schapiro and Cat Lazaroff, "Time Is Not on the Side of Superfund Reform Effort," National Journal's *CongressDailyAM*, March 24, 1999, 10–15.

15. See Raymond Hernandez, "Political Battle Looming over Superfund Plan," *New York Times*, April 15, 2002, A22; and Margaret Kriz, "Superfund Slowdown," *National Journal*, June 1, 2002, 1623–26.

16. The measure is the Small Business Liability Relief and Brownfields Revitalization Act, PL 107–118 (2002).

17. Eric Lipton, "Chertoff Seeks a Chemical Security Law, Within Limits," *New York Times*, March 22, 2006, A18.

18. Michael Janofsky, "Changes May Be Needed in Superfund, Chief Says," *New York Times*, December 5, 2004, 24. See also Rebecca Adams, "Superfund at 25: Time for a Makeover?" *CQ Weekly*, November 14, 2005, 3039–41.

19. The EPA has a single point of access to its diversified databases through its extensively used Envirofacts Web page: www.epa.gov/enviro/html/.

20. Whitman left office in June 2003 and subsequently published a critique of her service in the Bush administration: *It's My Party Too: The Battle for the Heart of the GOP and the Future of America* (New York: Penguin Press, 2005).

21. For a current list, see the EPA Web site: www.epa.gov/epahome/locate3.htm.

22. Details about the federal environmental research budgets can be found at the Web site for the National Council for Science and the Environment: www.ncseonline.org.

23. Among the major complaints during the 1980s were late issuance of regulations and inflexibility in the detailed federal grant conditions and mandatory policy guidelines that wasted state resources, stifled initiative, and added unnecessary costs. Other frequently cited problems during this period included delayed program grants, excessive paperwork that diverted limited state staff, unclear regulations and guidelines, and friction between the EPA and state staff related to program deadlines and priorities. See Hamilton 1990; Kraft, Clary, and Tobin 1988; and Tobin 1992.

24. For an overview of the program, including criticism of it, see Rebecca Adams, "EPA Program Offers Too Much Carrot, Not Enough Stick," *CQ Weekly*, February 27, 2006, 528–31. Details about the program can be found on the EPA Web page: www.epa.gov/performancetrack/.

25. See the EPA Web page for CBEP for links to the various projects and activities: www.epa.gov/ecocommunity/.

26. Extensive data on the environmental conditions and policies in the 50 states can be found in Hall and Kerr (1991). Because that report is now somewhat dated, newer information can be found at the Web site for the Environmental Council of the States, a national nonpartisan association of state and territorial environmental commissioners: www.ecos.org.

27. In addition to the seven statutes discussed in this chapter, the EPA is also charged with administration of the Pollution Prevention Act, the Ocean Dumping Act, the Oil Pollution Act, the Solid Waste Disposal Act, the Emergency Planning and

Community Right-to-Know Act (part of Superfund), and parts of the National Environmental Policy Act and the Endangered Species Act, among others.

28. For a comprehensive review and assessment of how this process works, see the report of the Presidential/Congressional Commission on Risk Assessment and Risk Management (1997). The commission's reports and other studies and commentary on risk are available at www.riskworld.com.

29. See Jocelyn Kaiser, "Panel Backs EPA Dioxin Assessment," *Science* 290 (November 10, 2000): 1071. For a description of dioxins and furans, see the EPA Web page on the subject: www.epa.gov/opptintr/pbt/dioxins.htm.

30. See Douglas Jehl, "E.P.A. to Abandon New Arsenic Limits for Water Supply," *New York Times*, March 21, 2001, 1, A20; and Jocelyn Kaiser, "Second Look at Arsenic Finds Higher Risk," *Science* 293 (September 21, 2001): 2189.

31. By early 2006 a new study found a direct relationship between reduction in fine particles and improved human health. For each decrease of 1 microgram of particles per cubic meter of air, death rates from lung cancer, respiratory illness, and cardiovascular disease dropped by 3 percent, extending the lives of 75,000 people per year in the United States. See Nicholas Bakalar, "Cleaner Air Brings Drop in Death Rate," *New York Times*, March 21, 2006, D7.

32. Michael Janofsky, "Tougher Emission Rules Set for Big Diesel Vehicles," *New York Times*, May 11, 2004, A16.

33. For a description of the new public involvement process, see www.epa.gov/stakeholders/policy2003/index.htm.

34. At least some evidence supports the environmentalist position. For instance, a comparative study of enforcement of effluent regulations for the pulp and paper industries in the United States and Canada found that cooperative approaches to regulation may be less effective than traditional "coercive" approaches (Harrison 1995).

35. U.S. Environmental Protection Agency Press Release, January 19, 2000. Announcements like this one may be found at the agency Web site: www.epa.gov/newsroom.

36. Katharine Q. Seelye, "Top E.P.A. Official Quits, Criticizing Bush's Policies," *New York Times*, March 1, 2002, A15; and Seelye, "Enforcement of Environmental Laws Has Slipped, Democrats Say," *New York Times*, October 1, 2002, A20. A Bush EPA spokesperson indicated that the reason for the lower enforcement actions, such as lawsuits, was that the EPA favored negotiated settlements rather than formal legal action.

37. Quoted in the press release cited in note 35. The EPA compliance home page provides multiple links to civil and criminal enforcements actions, environmental justice activities, and compliance assistance: www.epa.gov/compliance/. For a general review of environmental laws, their enforcement, and information sources on environmental crime, see Ronald G. Burns and Michael J. Lynch, *Environmental Crime: A Sourcebook* (New York: LFB Scholarly Publishing, 2004).

38. The organization's Web site is a useful source of information about regulatory oversight issues as well as information disclosure and government accountability issues in general: www.ombwatch.org/. OMB Watch was formed in 1983 during the height of controversy over secrecy in Reagan's OMB.

39. For example, see Rick Weiss, "'Data Quality' Law Is Nemesis of Regulation," *Washington Post*, August 16, 2004, A01. The article is one in a series of three on the law. For a summary of how the Data Quality Act affects environmental policy, see Andrews (2006).

6

Energy and Natural Resource Policies

Much like environmental protection efforts, natural resource policies that stress conservation or preservation command significant public support across the United States. Almost everyone wants to protect treasured national parks, and most people would say we ought to preserve threatened and irreplaceable forests and other lands, wilderness, and endangered species. Yet conflicts arise over the specific means used to achieve such goals and the ways in which competing social values are balanced at any given time and place. For instance, how should we reconcile the desire to maintain or increase short-term economic growth and employment and the longer-term goal of sustainable use of natural resources? Where should such decisions be made—the federal government, state and local governments, or in the private sector—and who should participate in those decision-making processes to ensure accountability to the public?

Such conflicts were common during the 1990s, and they continue to define the politics of natural resources today. They also resemble political battles in other periods in U.S. history. Yet there are important differences. The scale of human intervention is far greater than previously the case, as are the consequences of the policy choices we make. Should the nation protect most of what is left of old-growth forest ecosystems or sacrifice significant portions to protect timber industry jobs? Should dams in the Pacific Northwest be breached to restore free-flowing rivers that are essential to maintain wild salmon populations in the region, or are the benefits of keeping them intact—power generation, irrigation, and shipping—more important? To what extent should the United States try to reduce reliance on fossil fuels as insurance against the possibility of devastating climate change? In such controversies, it may be possible to achieve seemingly conflicting objectives through carefully crafted policies of sustainable development. To do so, however, policymakers and citizens need to devise inventive approaches to decision making that can promote involvement by major stakeholders, foster public dialogue, and build consensus on action.

During the 1990s these issues achieved a new prominence when Secretary of the Interior Bruce Babbitt sought to reverse 12 years of Republican rule that leaned far more toward development interests than the Clinton administration favored. From higher grazing and mining fees for the use of federal lands to a comprehensive survey of the nation's biological capital, Babbitt advocated a natural resources policy agenda that differed dramatically from the goals of the Reagan and George H. W. Bush administrations (Egan 1993a). Often his proposals were more consonant with public sentiment and scientific opinion than the views of his detractors. Yet opposition by the wise use and property rights movements as well as timber, mining, ranching, agricultural, and other development interests added fuel to these policy fires, which burned fiercely around virtually every natural resource issue. On many land use issues, such as protection of critical habitats and coastal land, property rights groups gained political strength after a series of favorable U.S. Supreme Court rulings, most notably in *Lucas v. South Carolina Coastal Council* (1992), a so-called regulatory takings case (O'Leary 2006).

With the election of George W. Bush in 2000, the policy agenda changed again. Under Secretary of the Interior Gail Norton, who served through spring 2006, the administration's actions were reminiscent of the strongly prodevelopment Reagan administration.[1] Although policy changes were often made more quietly than in the Reagan years, the decisions were no less controversial. These ranged from proposed oil and gas drilling in the Arctic National Wildlife Refuge and on other public lands in the West to expansion of logging in national forests and reversal of a scheduled phaseout of recreational snowmobiles in Yellowstone National Park.[2]

These disputes over natural resources underscore the difficulty of making collective choices when conflicting social values are deeply held and winners and losers can plainly see their fates. That is especially so when the political process is open to pressure from powerful interests eager to protect their share of the nation's economic pie and where the decisions may be of little interest to the general public. Scientific studies help resolve questions of fact, but they cannot substitute for political judgments about where the public interest lies. Even the best studies can build only a partial foundation for environmental policy when policymakers struggle to negotiate a middle course broadly acceptable to all sides.

This chapter provides an overview of these issues in two clusters of environmental problems and policies: energy and natural resources. Each could be treated more extensively in separate chapters, but in this combined chapter I emphasize common themes in policy goals and means, and the political conflicts that develop as agencies try to implement the policies. The chapter begins with energy policy because it raises somewhat different kinds of issues. National debate focuses more on what additional policy measures may be needed than on how well current policies are being implemented or the characteristics of the agencies charged with those tasks. Moreover, the states have become active players in energy policy and politics, with some taking aggressive and often innovative approaches to energy conservation, development of renewable energy sources, and reduction in greenhouse gas emissions linked to use of fossil fuels. As was the case with Chapter 5, those who prefer may read the two parts of the chapter independently.

Taken together with the pollution control issues discussed in Chapter 5, the actions covered here complete our initial review of U.S. environmental policies and the politics associated with them. Chapter 7 provides an overview of how both environmental protection and natural resources policies can be evaluated and new directions in policy action considered. Chapter 8 concentrates on sustainable development and international environmental policy.

ENERGY POLICY: GOALS AND MEANS

Energy policy is part environmental protection and part natural resource policy. The United States, however, has no comprehensive energy policy that compares to the extensive bureaucratic and regulatory machinery that governs environmental quality and natural resources. Rather, energy use is determined largely by the marketplace, with each major energy source shaped in part by an assortment of government subsidies and regulations adopted over decades and primarily for reasons that have little to do directly with the goals of energy policy.

Federal and state regulation of coal, natural gas, and oil, for example, has focused historically on prices and competition within each sector. It has served the interests of energy producers by stabilizing markets and ensuring profits at least as much as it has advanced a larger public interest in ensuring reliable energy supplies. Regulation of nuclear power differs because of its historic connection to national security. From the late 1940s on, under the auspices of the Atomic Energy Acts of 1946 and 1954, federal agencies responsible for the civilian nuclear energy program shielded the technology from the marketplace—and from public scrutiny—to ensure rapid growth of its use.

The Atomic Energy Commission (AEC) and its successor agencies, the Nuclear Regulatory Commission (NRC) and the Department of Energy (DOE), vigorously promoted nuclear power as a critical component of the nation's mix of energy resources. Congress contributed by subsidizing nuclear energy through restrictions on liability set by the 1957 Price-Anderson Act (which limits the financial responsibility of plant owners to $10 billion in the event of an accident) and by provision of lavish research and development funds. All this was considered to be essential to create a new civilian nuclear power industry in light of the uncertainties and risks associated with it. In addition, public relations efforts by federal officials over the years have sought to reassure the public on safety and nuclear waste issues. Following the Three Mile Island nuclear accident in Pennsylvania in 1979, however, public opinion turned against building additional nuclear power plants. The Chernobyl nuclear plant disaster in Ukraine in 1986 further eroded public confidence in nuclear power even though that accident involved a faulty plant design not used in the United States.

To the extent that the nation had any discernible energy policy goal before the 1970s, it was to maintain a supply of abundant, cheap, and reliable energy, preferably from domestic sources, to support a growing economy and to ensure a reasonable profit for producers. Policymakers were technological optimists who believed that large centralized energy sources would meet the nation's needs. For years they were convinced that a growing economy demanded ever-increasing energy supplies. Consistent with those beliefs, they championed generous subsidies not only for nuclear energy but also for fossil fuels (Davis 1993).

Increasingly, however, the nation's use of energy has been heavily influenced by environmental policies. It is easy to see why. Exploration for energy sources and their extraction, transportation, refinement, and use can degrade the land, air, and water. The 1989 Exxon *Valdez* accident in Alaska and thousands of lesser oil spills underscore the dangers of moving oil around. Mining coal can ravage the land and poison the waters around mines. Burning oil, coal, and natural gas and their by-products to generate energy and power the nation's cars, trucks, and buses pollutes the air, causes acid rain, and leads to the buildup of damaging greenhouse gases. Use of nuclear power produces high-level waste products that must be isolated from the biosphere for thousands of years. Congress has adopted public policies to deal with all those environmental effects, from clean air and water laws to nuclear waste disposal, surface mining control, and oil spill prevention measures. By doing so, it has profoundly altered the production and use of energy in important, if sometimes unintended, ways.

The debate over energy policy today turns on the combination of energy resources that best promotes the nation's long-term interest and the means that governments might use to encourage or discourage the development of particular energy resources. Governments can try to increase energy supply, decrease demand, or alter the mix of fuels used. In doing so, they may rely on a range of policy approaches. These include regulation, public education or persuasion, taxation, and the use of subsidies such as funding for research and development (R&D) or tax credits and allowances. The choices are never easy, and conflict among diverse parties, particularly regional interests, energy producers and consumers, and environmentalists, is common. Such conflict frequently leads to stalemate and only modest policy advances. Increasingly, however, the states have become adept at finding ways to overcome political conflict and chart new directions in energy policy. In recent years, the United States has spent over $500 billion per year to meet its energy needs in three broad sectors: residential and commercial uses, industrial uses, and transportation. Thus any governmental actions that substantially alter that spending can have major consequences throughout the economy.

Indirect Policy Impacts

Even without a comprehensive energy policy, federal, state, and local governments influence decision making on energy use in myriad ways. They do so through regulation of the by-products (e.g., air pollution), provision of services (e.g., building highways for motor vehicles), tax subsidies, and energy R&D assistance. The effects of those policies are not neutral, and the market is not truly free and competitive. Historically, policies have strongly favored mature and conventional energy sources such as oil, natural gas, coal, and nuclear power. They also have encouraged expansion of energy use rather than decrease in demand through improved energy efficiency and conservation. Studies from the early 1990s indicated that taxpayers spent as much as $36 billion each year on federal energy subsidies, most of which favored fossil fuels and nuclear energy (Koplow 1993; Wald 1992). The DOE asserts that the real subsidy figure is much lower although still large.[3] In 2005 a major assessment of the federal government's energy programs by the U.S. Government Accountability Office (GAO) estimated tax-related subsidies alone at $4.4 billion per year, with most of the benefits (about 88 percent) going to fossil fuel production (U.S. GAO 2005a).

An example of how such indirect forces work can be seen in the cost of gasoline. The *price* paid at the pump, nearly $3.00 a gallon on average for regular gasoline in April 2006, is not the true *cost* of using the fuel. That amount does not reflect the full expense of road construction and maintenance or the environmental damage and other externalities related to transporting the oil around the world in supertankers and ultimately burning its gasoline derivative in our cars, vans, sport utility vehicles (SUVs), and trucks. A comprehensive analysis of the "optimal" gasoline tax based on only some of these repercussions concluded that it should be close to $1.00 a gallon rather than the prevailing rate of 42 cents (Parry 2002). Environmental groups put the full social costs of gasoline much higher, with some of them including the national security costs to maintain access to Middle East oil fields. Whichever method is used to calculate the social cost of gasoline, the market price is all that drivers see. Over the past several decades that price has been insufficient to stimulate demand for fuel-efficient vehicles or to encourage increased public use of mass transit as an alternative to automobiles. However, with gasoline prices rising sharply in 2005 and 2006, the pattern has changed, prompting greater public demand for fuel-efficient cars, trucks, and SUVs. Because the public becomes accustomed to what remains an artificially low price for gasoline, and direct tax increases are so visible and resented, policymakers are loath to raise gasoline taxes. Indeed, when gasoline prices rose in 2002 and again in 2005 and 2006, many legislators were quick to propose *reducing* gasoline taxes to curry favor with their constituents, even though any such reduction would be no more than a few cents per gallon.[4]

Shifting Energy Priorities

These varied and often obscure government subsidies have a perverse effect. They sanction and stimulate the use of environmentally risky energy sources while erecting barriers to sustainable sources. Much has changed since 1990, however. Under both the Bush and Clinton administrations, policies and administrative priorities shifted enough that renewable energy sources, conservation, and improved efficiency began receiving new attention and support in both the public and private sectors. George W. Bush's proposed national energy policy of 2001 (discussed later) also played a role, even though the proposal centered on increased use of fossil fuels. A conversion to sustainable energy sources remains the long-term goal of the environmental community, and increasingly that goal is widely endorsed worldwide, in part because of concern over the impact of fossil fuel use on climate change. The crucial policy questions concern precisely what strategies best promote such a goal and also serve short-term energy and economic needs.

Environmentalists have pressed for an early and rapid shift away from fossil fuels and nuclear power and toward solar power, wind energy, geothermal sources, use of biomass, and other forms of renewable energy. They argue that such a transition is possible with well-designed public policies and the political leadership to get them enacted and implemented (Cooper 1999; Hunt and Sawin 2006; Sawin 2004; U.S. GAO 2005a). Others, particularly utility executives, have disagreed and argued that such hopes for a renewable energy future are unrealistic. They see a smaller potential for solar, wind, and other renewables, and more limitations to energy conservation. Thus they suggest a longer-term reliance on fossil fuels and a continuation or expansion of nuclear power (Marcus 1992).[5] An examination of recent policy history indicates how these two different visions of a U.S. energy future have shaped policy choices.

■ THE ENERGY POLICY CYCLE: 1973–1989

At several times over the past three decades, the United States has struggled with defining national energy policy goals, with only limited success. The early efforts, during the 1970s under Presidents Richard Nixon, Gerald Ford, and Jimmy Carter, were driven largely by concern for the security and stability of the energy supply in the wake of the 1973 oil price shock. In that year, the Organization of Petroleum Exporting Countries (OPEC) imposed an embargo on the sale of their oil, which led to a quadrupling of world oil prices and severe economic repercussions. In previous decades, little thought was given to energy conservation, and demand for energy grew dramatically. After 1973, with the reliability of oil supplies called into question, both the federal and state governments made greater efforts to encourage conservation and efficiency of use through a variety of taxation and regulatory actions. Such efforts included adoption in 1975 of the Energy Policy and Conservation Act. That act established the Corporate Average Fuel Economy (CAFE) standards for motor vehicles, extended domestic oil price controls, and established the Strategic Petroleum Reserve to stockpile oil for future emergencies (Goodwin 1981; Marcus 1992).

Carter's National Energy Plan and Conservation Gains

Under the Carter administration, energy policy goals began shifting to provision of secure and clean energy sources, with reliance on market forces still the preeminent policy approach. President Carter made his National Energy Plan, which he called the "moral equivalent of war," a top policy priority in 1977 and 1978. A small ad hoc energy task force working under the direction of James Schlesinger, Carter's secretary of energy, assembled the plan to meet a presidential deadline of April 1977. The group emphasized a strong governmental role rather than reliance on the private sector, and it looked more to conservation than to increasing domestic supplies for solutions to the energy crisis.

The plan drew little support on Capitol Hill. Congress objected to many of its provisions, and it also was lobbied heavily by oil and natural gas producing industries, utilities, automobile companies, and labor, consumer, and environmental groups, all of whom found something to dislike in the plan. As a result, Congress enacted some of Carter's proposals and rejected others without substituting an equally comprehensive energy policy (Kraft 1981).

In the end, Congress approved five key components, which collectively were called the National Energy Act of 1978. Among them was the Natural Gas Policy Act, which partially deregulated and altered natural gas pricing to make the fuel more competitive with other sources. Also in the package was the Public Utilities Regulatory Policy Act (PURPA), which helped create a market for small energy producers using unconventional sources such as solar and geothermal. Other provisions dealt with energy conservation, power plant and industrial fuel use, and energy taxes. Among other actions, Congress approved tax credits for home insulation, energy efficiency standards for home appliances, and taxes on so-called gas guzzler cars. Environmental quality was a consideration at the time but not the main concern. Indeed, Carter's plan aimed to *expand* use of coal because of its domestic abundance despite the environmental consequences of using such a notoriously dirty fuel. Yet Carter also greatly increased support for renewable energy sources.

In 1977 Congress established the Department of Energy (DOE), which consolidated previously independent energy agencies into a cabinet department, with the Nuclear Regulatory Commission remaining an independent agency charged with overseeing nuclear safety. The DOE's primary mission, however, was not energy but national defense; it was responsible for overseeing nuclear weapons production. Most of the DOE's budget supported defense-related activities, although by the mid-1990s the department's budget included about $5 billion a year for waste management and environmental restoration at contaminated facilities, primarily nuclear weapons production sites.

Despite these policy and institutional limitations, the United States (and other industrialized nations) made great strides in energy conservation in the 1970s and 1980s. Slower economic growth and a decline in older and inefficient heavy industries contributed to the energy savings. Consumer and industry demand for energy-efficient cars, buildings, lighting, motors, and appliances made a difference as well. American industry in the late 1980s used only 70 percent of the energy needed in 1973 to produce the same goods. Appliances in the early 1990s were about 75 percent more efficient than they were in the late 1970s. Passenger automobiles in 1991 averaged about 22 miles per gallon compared with only 14 miles per gallon in 1973 (U.S. DOE 1998).[6]

These gains were impressive, even if a growing population, a stronger economy, and Americans' penchant for larger vehicles, larger homes, and a wider variety of electrical appliances (from air conditioners to computers) translated into increased energy use over time (Myerson 1998; U.S. DOE 1998). From today's perspective, it would be hard to call many of the energy policies of this era a great success because government programs remained complex, contradictory, and inefficient. Moreover, despite these improvements in energy efficiency, energy use per person in the United States has remained more than double that of Japan and most European nations.

Reagan's Nonpolicy on Energy

Many of the most innovative policies of the 1970s, including government support for conservation and development and use of alternative energy sources, did not last long. What remained in the early 1980s was cut back sharply during the Reagan administration. President Ronald Reagan strongly opposed a federal role on energy policy and favored reliance on the "free market." He sought (unsuccessfully) to dismantle the DOE, whose very existence symbolized federal intrusion into the energy marketplace. Some of his positions were broadly endorsed at the time because energy prices were declining. Thus Congress repealed tax breaks for installing energy-saving devices and approved the Reagan budget cuts that effectively ended conservation and renewable energy programs (Axelrod 1984; Rosenbaum 1987). Between 1980 and 1990, solar and renewable energy research funding in the DOE declined by some 93 percent in constant dollars, and the department's energy conservation budget fell by 91 percent between 1981 and 1987.[7] All that was particularly striking because conservation of energy is one of the most effective ways to reduce dependency on imported oil and lower environmental risks at a modest cost. It is a premier example of what analysts mean when they say smart policy involves picking the lowest hanging fruit on the energy tree, that is, getting a great return for a minimal effort.

The Reagan administration's energy budget also concealed inconsistencies in its ostensible reliance on free market forces. For example, support for nuclear programs was increased even while virtually every other program was cut back sharply, usually without much attention paid to evidence of program success or failure. Programs to prepare for oil emergencies suffered because Reagan did as little as possible to meet legislative targets for filling the Strategic Petroleum Reserve, leaving the nation vulnerable to oil price shocks. Reagan also ordered his staff to remove solar panels installed at the White House by President Carter, a symbol in conflict with the administration's energy policy agenda. One journalist described the essence of the Reagan strategy as "duck, defer, and deliberate" (Hogan 1984).

ENERGY POLICY FOR THE TWENTY-FIRST CENTURY

Energy issues reappeared on the political agenda in the late 1980s as the nation's dependence on oil imports rose once again and concern began to mount about global climate change following the hot and dry summer of 1988. In 1970 the United States imported 23 percent of its oil. By 1991 the figure climbed to 45 percent and by 2005, to over 58 percent. The DOE estimates that by 2025 that number will rise to 68 percent. The reasons for increased reliance on imported oil are plain enough: a decline in domestic energy production, complacency among both the public and policymakers, and the increased use of motor vehicles. Although domestic energy production is once again a priority, its decline over the past several decades can be explained in part by the stringent requirements of new environmental laws, including the National Environmental Policy Act (NEPA) and the Clean Air Act. NEPA mandated arduous environmental impact statements that made clear the environmental consequences of energy extraction and use, whether the sources were oil, coal, or nuclear power. These effects prompted a debate that continues to this day over whether environmental goals are compatible with the level of energy production the nation has experienced in recent years.

As discussed in Chapter 2, the United States and other nations rely heavily on fossil fuels: coal, oil, and natural gas. About 86 percent of the energy consumed in the United States and in most other nations in recent years has come from fossil fuels (see Table 2.3). Use of such fuels produces prodigious quantities of carbon dioxide and thus contributes to the risk of global climate change.

Reliance on oil imports to meet U.S. energy needs has proven to be a particularly risky strategy. Some two thirds of the 20 million barrels of oil used in the United States each day goes to transportation: trucks, planes, and automobiles. The oil imports needed to satisfy America's insatiable appetite have widened the U.S. trade deficit, contributed to inflation, and increased dependence on a politically unstable region of the world. According to the DOE, in 2005 about 26 percent of oil imported into the United States came from Persian Gulf nations.

Despite important environmental, economic, and national security impacts of the nation's energy use, policymakers have been reluctant to push the public to change its energy habits through either higher fuel efficiency standards (regulation) or significant increases in the gasoline tax (market incentives). Energy issues have continued to be low in salience for both the public and for policymakers, and the media tend not to cover them to any great extent except during periods of energy crises or rapidly rising prices. These characteristics have greatly constrained formulation of U.S. energy policy since the late 1980s. Actions taken during the presidential administrations of George H. W. Bush, Bill Clinton, and George W. Bush illustrate the prevailing politics of energy policy and the continuing challenges that advocates of stronger policy action are likely to face over the next decade.

The Bush Administration's National Energy Strategy

In 1989 President Bush directed his DOE to develop a National Energy Strategy (NES), which it prepared following extensive analysis within the department as well as nationwide public hearings. Bush defended the NES as an acceptable balance of energy production and conservation, whereas environmentalists argued that the plan tilted too much toward production, risking environmental damage in the process, and that it did not do much for energy conservation or mitigation of climate change. They successfully opposed opening the Arctic National Wildlife Refuge to oil and gas exploration, and they pressed hard, but without success, for big increases in the CAFE standards as an alternative to increasing oil supplies. Eventually, the wildlife refuge and the CAFE provisions were omitted from the final legislation to gain support from each side. Both issues would reappear when Bush's son, George W. Bush, sent his own energy policy proposals to Congress in 2001 (discussed later).

As is usually the case with energy policy bills, in 1991 Congress was besieged by lobbyists, particularly from energy interests and automobile manufacturers, who sought to maintain their advantages under current policies. Auto companies, for example, opposed higher CAFE standards on the grounds that they would compromise safety by shifting production to smaller, more dangerous cars. Independent studies, including one by the congressional Office of Technology Assessment (OTA), effectively undercut that argument. The OTA found that better design and safer technologies could offset the risk of lower vehicle weight or smaller size (U.S. Office of Technology Assessment 1991b). A study by the National Research Council released in 2001 largely confirmed the OTA findings. It concluded that major gains in auto fuel economy were possible without sacrificing safety and with use of existing technologies, providing enough time (10 to 15 years) is allowed for manufacturers to meet higher standards.[8]

The outcome of congressional decision making in the early 1990s was largely political gridlock. There was too little concern and consensus about energy policy among the public and no effective way to restrain the politics of self-interest of energy producers. Thus the final bill displeased environmentalists, and other key players acknowledged that it would be merely a foundation on which to build a more comprehensive energy policy in the future (Idelson 1992a). Nevertheless, the 1992 Energy Policy Act set out some important goals and established unusual incentives for achieving them. The ultimate effects will depend on how well the policy is implemented.

The 1992 act, a massive measure running to some 1,300 pages, called for greater energy conservation and efficiency in electric appliances, buildings, lighting, plumbing, commercial and industrial motors, and heating and cooling systems. It also streamlined licensing requirements for nuclear power plants in the hope of jump-starting an ailing industry. In addition, it provided tax relief to independent oil and gas drillers to try to stimulate increased production.

The energy act also required the use of alternative-fuel fleet vehicles by the federal government, to be phased in slowly. State government and private and municipal fleet vehicles were to follow a somewhat less demanding schedule, although Congress wrote in many exemptions to the requirement. California and several northeastern states went beyond the federal requirement because their clean air rules mandate use of alternative-fuel vehicles by the public as well as state agencies (Idelson 1992b).

These were significant achievements, yet problems remained. The market forces that determine energy prices still did not adequately reflect either the environmental or national security costs of using energy. The 1992 act did not raise the CAFE standards for motor vehicles, which was the top priority of environmental groups, nor did it do much to reduce the use of oil, which accounts for 40 percent of U.S. energy consumption. The provisions for alternative-fuel vehicles, although innovative, have had only a minor effect on the nation's oil use. The act also was unlikely to either cap or reduce dependence on imported oil; indeed, as noted earlier, by 2005 the United States imported over 58 percent of its oil, a figure that continues to rise.

The Clinton Administration Tries Its Hand

These deficiencies of the 1992 act were apparent as President Bill Clinton assumed office in January 1993. Environmental groups, still unhappy with the act, urged the president to create a high-level energy task force to review conflicting studies and build political consensus for a more effective energy policy. Clinton's transition staff promised a series of actions to accelerate energy efficiency in buildings and appliances, government purchase of alternative-fuel vehicles and energy-efficient computers, and research support for conservation technologies and renewable energy sources. The president announced in his Earth Day address in April 1993 that he would issue executive orders promoting such actions where possible. One such order directed all federal agencies to achieve by 2010 a 35 percent improvement in energy efficiency and a 30 percent cut in greenhouse gas emissions.[9] If sustained over time, it could have an appreciable effect on energy use and federal expenditures.

The Btu Tax and Gasoline   President Clinton learned early in his administration that solving the nation's energy problems entailed overcoming serious political obstacles. As part of his deficit-reduction package announced in early 1993, for example, the president had proposed a broad energy tax based on the heat output of fuel, or British thermal units (BTUs). He expected the tax to raise some $72 billion over five years while simultaneously reducing the use of fossil fuels, thus curbing pollution and reducing oil imports. The proposal bore some resemblance to the carbon tax (based on carbon dioxide emissions) that had long been advocated by environmentalists.

Despite these high hopes, however, Clinton's BTU tax was an instant political failure. It was greeted by a tidal wave of opposition on Capitol Hill, reflecting complaints from industry groups and others (farmers, energy-producing states, and states reliant on home heating oil) that the plan would cost them too much money, reduce their competitiveness, and put people out of work. The National Association of Manufacturers, the U.S. Chamber of Commerce, the Chemical Manufacturers Association (later renamed the American Chemistry Council), and the American Petroleum Institute, among others, worked actively to defeat the tax through sophisticated use of satellite feeds, talk radio, opinion polls, a blizzard of newspaper editorials, and mass mailings to citizens urging them to protest the tax (Wines 1993). In the end, Congress agreed only to a 4.3 cent per gallon increase in the federal gas tax, despite the lowest market price for gasoline in a generation (Wald 1993).

Gas taxes in the United States remain well below those of other industrialized nations. In 2005 federal and state taxes (state taxes vary widely) were about 17 percent of the average cost of a gallon of gasoline at the time or, as noted earlier, about 42 cents per gallon; some local governments also tax gasoline. In Europe, however, taxes are up to 80 percent of the cost of gasoline paid at the pump, which explains why the cost of gasoline there (and in Japan and Canada)—$4.00 to $7.00 per gallon—is substantially higher than in the United States. The politics of energy in recent years has dictated that only painless measures would be acceptable in the U.S. Congress and at the state level.

A similar reluctance to constrain the use of gasoline is evident in federal fuel economy standards. For six years beginning in 1995, Congress enacted legislation that blocked the Department of Transportation from reviewing or changing fuel economy standards for vehicles in an effort to prevent President Clinton from raising mileage standards. Congress made that decision even as the average fuel economy of U.S. vehicles dropped to its lowest level since 1980 (Bradsher 1999b). For the 2003 model cars and passenger trucks, the EPA reported an average of 20.8 miles per gallon, some 6 percent *below* the high point of 15 years earlier. Before Americans began buying so many SUVs, the average was 22.1. New tougher air pollution rules for automobiles that the EPA issued in 1999, however, are likely to be met in part through improvements in fuel efficiency. In early 2006 the Bush administration announced a modest increase in fuel economy standards for SUVs, pickup trucks, and vans, an action that environmental groups criticized as insufficient.[10]

The Partnership for a New Generation of Vehicles   The Clinton administration's Clean Car Initiative, later renamed the Partnership for a New Generation of Vehicles (PNGV), was expected to help achieve some of the same objectives as the rejected BTU tax and ultimately assist the nation in raising fuel economy. The PNGV called for the federal government to coordinate its R&D spending with the three largest U.S. automobile makers (Ford, General Motors, and DaimlerChrysler). Announced in 1993, the program was intended to produce a "supercar" that could get 80 miles per gallon with low pollutant emissions and without a loss in performance, passenger capacity, or safety. It enjoyed some success, and it may have moved some automakers, particularly Honda and Toyota, to begin selling fuel-efficient hybrid vehicles in the U.S. market in 2000. Hybrids use a small gasoline engine in combination with electric batteries, and the compact hybrids such as the Honda Civic and Toyota Prius get more than 45 miles per gallon in city driving. All the automakers have since begun marketing or planning for hybrid vehicles. Their interest has been sparked by public enthusiasm for the hybrids, available federal and state tax benefits for purchasers, and substantially higher gasoline prices in 2005 and 2006. The Bush administration decided in 2002 to end the PNGV program and focus instead on federal research and development support for a much longer-term initiative to develop hydrogen-based or fuel cell–powered vehicles. The new program was called FreedomCAR (Freedom Cooperative Automotive Research).

Beyond the PNGV and the other initiatives just described, the Clinton administration took other modest steps toward strengthening U.S. energy policy. It extended by 10 years a moratorium on offshore oil and gas drilling that began in the first Bush administration in 1990. It endorsed the Kyoto Protocol, which calls for reduction of U.S. greenhouse gas emissions, although it did little to push it in the face of strong congressional opposition. The administration also sharply increased spending on energy conservation and renewable energy resources, and in 1998 it consolidated various energy initiatives into a Comprehensive National Energy Strategy prepared by the DOE, which it transmitted to Congress (Cooper 1999). In its fiscal 2001 budget, the administration recommended to Congress sizable increases in funding for global climate change, clean energy, and energy efficiency, and a new series of tax credits for energy-efficient homes and cars.

Energy Policy Under George W. Bush

From the first days of President George W. Bush's administration, it was clear, although hardly unexpected, that new energy policy priorities would prevail. For example, the president decided to keep some Clinton administration energy efficiency rules for appliances but to oppose higher standards for new central air-conditioning systems. The rules were set to go into effect in February 2001 after years of development and negotiations with the affected industries. The air-conditioning rule sought to lower energy use by 30 percent from current minimum standards, but most manufacturers argued that 20 percent was sufficient. Anything higher, they said, would impose too great a cost on consumers, possibly leading them to keep older and less efficient units. The 30 percent standard, however, would have lowered peak demand for electricity on warm days and thus deferred building of additional power plants to meet higher energy needs.[11] Bush's decision to oppose the 30 percent standard was widely condemned in the press, particularly in light of an energy crisis in California at the time. The administration also was sued over the decision by several states and consumer and environmental groups.

Controversies over the administration's energy policies did not let up over the next five years. Most of the attention focused on Bush's national energy plan, which he announced in May 2001. Prepared by a secretive task force chaired by Vice President Dick Cheney, the plan called for significant increases in the use of fossil fuels and nuclear energy as well as easing of environmental regulations that might inhibit new energy production. As discussed in Chapter 3, the Cheney task force consulted closely with major energy producers but not with environmental interests. Its recommendations to the president focused heavily on increasing energy supplies rather than reducing demand through conservation. Because of that strategy, it argued the nation needed to build 1,300 new power plants by 2020. Cheney himself dismissed the idea of conservation as a minor concern. It "may be a sign of personal virtue, but it is not a sufficient basis for a sound, comprehensive energy policy," he said (Kahn 2001, 18).

Cheney's comment was at odds with studies by scientists at five prominent national energy laboratories that were completed before Bush took office. Those studies found that market-based, energy efficiency policies could reduce the nation's energy needs by fully a third through 2010.[12] Similarly, the Natural Resources Defense Council (NRDC) developed its own alternative to the Bush plan, which it termed a "responsible energy policy for the 21st century." The NRDC plan was grounded in increased energy efficiency, use of relatively clean natural gas, and decreased use of oil and coal. In a parallel move, the Union of Concerned Scientists in late 2001 released a Clean Energy Blueprint that contrasted sharply with the Bush administration's energy plan. Consistent with these reports, in 2006 the nonpartisan American Council for an Energy Efficient Economy (ACEEE) concluded that the United States could achieve a 24 percent reduction in its electricity use, saving the nation some $30 billion a year.[13]

The Bush energy proposal initially did not fare well in Congress. The Republican House of Representatives approved it after what the press called "aggressive lobbying by the Bush administration, labor unions and the oil, gas and coal industries."[14] The House bill included generous tax and research benefits for the oil, natural gas, coal, and nuclear power industries, and it permitted oil and gas drilling in the Arctic National Wildlife Refuge (ANWR), a perennially contentious issue. Those same proposals, however, could not pass muster in the Senate, but environmentalists were not successful there either. In a replay of the 1991 energy debate, the Senate defeated efforts by environmentalist groups to increase auto fuel efficiency and also rejected Bush's proposal to drill in ANWR (pronounced "ann waar"). Despite extended negotiations, neither side was prepared to compromise given the intense and conflicting views within the core constituencies of each political party.[15]

It is a telling comment about U.S. energy politics that members of Congress could not muster support for a national energy policy even in the aftermath of California's well-publicized struggle with an energy crisis, new concern over the integrity of the nation's electric power grid, and another war in the oil-rich Middle East (Adams 2002a). In the hope of generating more support for his bill, the president tried to link it with national security concerns following the terrorist attacks of 2001, but he was largely unsuccessful in doing so (Cooper 2002). That relationship was more broadly endorsed by 2006 as a number of conservative organizations began warning about the nation's dependency on imported oil. Competing energy bills were debated repeatedly in Congress for the next four years with similar partisan divisions. Democrats favored increases in auto and truck fuel efficiency standards and they opposed drilling for oil in ANWR. Republicans were equally adamant that ANWR must be opened to energy development, but they opposed any increase in fuel efficiency standards. Intense lobbying by car manufacturers, labor unions, the oil and gas industry, and environmentalists continued. There were also regional divisions over whether Congress should approve a liability waiver for the gasoline additive and groundwater contaminant MTBE; without such a waiver, states where MTBE is produced could be hurt economically.

The political dynamics of the energy debate changed in 2005 as gasoline and other fuel prices, and public discontent over them, rose. The House passed yet another version of the president's energy policy, with Democrats critical of its many tax breaks for energy producers and its modest attention to energy efficiency and renewable fuels. President Bush pressed Congress to pass his energy package even while conceding that it would do nothing in the short term to lower gasoline prices (Bumiller and Hulse 2005). The president also rejected efforts in Congress to add to the energy bill requirements to reduce emissions of greenhouse gases associated with the use of fossil fuels.

By summer 2005 Congress surprised many when it managed to resolve differences between the two political parties and approve the Energy Policy Act of 2005, the first major overhaul of U.S. energy policy since 1992. The bill passed with bipartisan support and President Bush signed the measure on August 8, saying it would spur new domestic production of oil and natural gas and encourage expansion of renewable sources of energy. The emphasis in the 1,700-page law, however, clearly was on expansion of conventional fossil fuel sources and nuclear power. It includes no new requirements for improving fuel efficiency standards for automobiles and SUVs, it does not mandate any reduction in greenhouse gas emissions, and it imposes no new requirements on utilities to rely more on renewable power sources. Indeed, the

ACEEE estimated in 2004 that even if all of the energy-saving provisions of the draft energy bill at that time were approved, the nation would save only 1.5 percent of its energy consumption over the next 16 years (Kady and Poole 2004).

Consistent with the president's initial proposal, the law gives billions of dollars in federal tax credits and other subsidies to energy producers as an incentive to generate more energy. The granting of such benefits meant that the bill's estimated cost of $12.3 billion over 10 years was twice what the president had proposed in 2001. Critics were quick to say that the incentives were excessively generous ("spectacular give-aways" was one newspaper's summary) and unnecessary at a time when energy prices were reaching new highs. They also faulted Congress for including thousands of individual pork-barrel projects in the bill to ensure its passage (E. Andrews 2006; Grunwald and Eilperin 2006). The law calls for expanded energy research and development, and, to the dismay of environmentalists, it includes provisions to streamline the process for building new energy facilities (i.e., to reduce consideration of environmental impacts). In addition, the measure requires utilities to modernize the nation's electricity grid to ensure reliable delivery of electric energy.

Some provisions of the new law are more likely to please environmentalists. There are to be new energy efficiency standards for federal office buildings, programs to encourage the states to foster energy conservation, and requirements for the federal government to purchase an increasing percentage of its electricity from renewable sources. There are new tax deductions or credits for consumers who purchase renewable power systems for their homes or improve energy efficiency in their homes, or who buy hybrid vehicles; however, these are fairly modest and available for only a few years. There are more substantial provisions of this kind for commercial buildings. The law also authorizes billions of dollars for R&D intended to increase energy efficiency, diversify energy supplies, and reduce environmental impacts of energy use. Some of that money will support research on renewable energy sources such as wind, solar, and biomass, and some will fund research into new nuclear energy technologies. Although fuel economy standards were unchanged, the law requires the Department of Transportation to study the feasibility of changing those standards (Evans and Schatz 2005).

In a fitting example of the continuing constraints on federal energy policy, President Bush declared in his State of the Union address in January 2006 that the United States was "addicted to oil, which is often imported from unstable parts of the world." The president announced several initiatives "to change how we power our homes and offices," and to promote new energy technologies, particularly generation of ethanol. Members of Congress and energy analysts showed no enthusiasm for the proposals, and the president himself made clear that he remained opposed to higher vehicle fuel economy standards or any increase in the gasoline tax, the two actions most likely to have a real impact on U.S. oil consumption (Bumiller 2006). Although Americans remain overwhelmingly opposed to higher gasoline taxes, recent surveys show that a majority favors such actions if it would reduce U.S. dependence on foreign oil or help combat global warming (Uchitelle and Thee 2006).

State and Local Energy Initiatives

Some of the most promising energy policy initiatives occur outside Washington, D.C. State and local policymakers can more easily build consensus for innovations than is possible in the contentious arena of national politics (Rabe 2006). A good example is Sacramento, California, where residents voted in 1989 to close their publicly owned but troubled Rancho Seco nuclear power plant that provided half of the local power. The Sacramento Municipal Utility District (SMUD) became a thriving laboratory for energy conservation and use of renewable fuels. Among other actions, in 1997 SMUD announced that it would buy 10 megawatts of solar cells over the next five years, at that time the largest purchase of photovoltaic cells ever by a utility. Some 4,000 of its customers volunteered to pay a few more dollars a month as "PV Pioneers" (Wald 1997). Use of solar panels of this kind has been increasing sharply in recent years, helping bring down the price and make the panels more affordable (Sawin 2004).

Innovations at the state and local levels are not limited to Sacramento. Tight environmental restrictions throughout California have made conservation and efficiency highly attractive to utilities in the state that now find it difficult or impossible to build additional generating plants. Some of the same forces are emerging in states such as Minnesota, Wisconsin, and Colorado. Helping customers buy more efficient appliances and conserve energy (so-called demand-side management, or DSM) is the equivalent of constructing new plants.

Another example of state-level innovation concerns home construction. The 1992 Energy Policy Act requires states to review their residential building codes to determine whether they need revisions to meet or exceed the Model Energy Code (MEC). Newly constructed homes financed with federal mortgages must be built to MEC standards, regardless of the state code. In some states such as Wisconsin, however, the codes were revised to set minimum energy standards for new homes, the first revision since the mid-1970s. In addition, in 1999 the state began an Energy Star home rating system and held a series of technical workshops across the state to acquaint builders and contractors with energy-saving technologies and to encourage their use in new homes. By 2006 the state Energy Star home industry was thriving, with customers eager to minimize home heating and cooling costs. Other examples of state and local policy innovations on energy and climate change abound. Box 6.1 summarizes some of the most notable of them in recent years.

▥ NATURAL RESOURCES AND POLICY CHANGE

Equally significant changes have been taking place in U.S. natural resources policy since the late 1980s. As noted earlier in the chapter, however, the emphasis can shift substantially from one presidential administration to the next. Despite the differing policy agendas of Interior Secretary Bruce Babbitt in the Clinton administration and his counterpart, Gail Norton, in the first six years of the Bush administration, over the past several decades an historic shift has taken place away from resource policies that favor economic development. These changes are also evident at state, local, and regional levels where governments, environmental groups, and the private sector have found common cause in promoting sustainable community initiatives and developing ecosystem management approaches that promise to overcome the often fragmented and ineffective policy actions of the past (Koontz et al. 2004; Lowry 2006; Mazmanian and Kraft 1999; Sabatier et al. 2005; Thomas 2003).

BOX 6.1
State and Local Energy Policy Initiatives

Although the federal government has struggled in recent years to overcome policy gridlock on energy issues, state and local governments have become increasingly active and creative in addressing energy issues, including their link to climate change. For example, over half of the states have adopted some form of climate change legislation or have an executive order that sets out requirements for reducing greenhouse gas emissions (Rabe 2006). By mid-2005, 132 mayors in 35 states pledged to carry out provisions of the Kyoto Protocol on climate change (discussed in Chapter 8). There were many other indicators as well that the political atmosphere on the issue was becoming more conducive to action (Kriz 2005). In a related move, as of early 2005, 21 states had adopted renewable portfolio standards (which specify that state utilities produce a certain percentage of electricity through use of renewable energy sources), and more were considering doing so (Rabe and Mundo 2007). The energy policy examples listed here illustrate the kinds of actions taken by state and local governments:

- In 2002 California approved legislation that for the first time would compel automakers to limit emissions of carbon dioxide by building more fuel-efficient vehicles. In 2004 the California Air Resources Board (ARB) released its draft regulations. They mandate a 1 to 2 percent reduction in emissions beginning with the 2009 model year and rising slowly by 2016 to about 30 percent below the levels projected for 2009. The auto industry was strongly opposed to the requirements but could not halt the measure; it has since challenged it in the courts. The ARB staff believes that lower operating costs will more than offset the higher cost of vehicles under the plan. Cars and light trucks are responsible for fully a third of the nation's greenhouse gas emissions and 40 percent of California's. Polls in California in 2002 indicated that 81 percent of the public favored requiring automakers to further reduce greenhouse gases as mandated by the new legislation.

- In 2000 the Seattle city council pledged to meet the city's future electricity needs through renewable energy and gains in energy efficiency. The city indicated that it would strive to have no net emissions that are linked to global climate change. In 2001 the mayor proposed that Seattle become the nation's largest purchaser of wind power by a public utility. Seattle City Light also initiated a program to allow city residents to volunteer to pay more to purchase power from renewable energy sources. The extra money would go into a fund to buy clean energy sources.

- In 2000 and 2001, electricity prices in California rose dramatically as a consequence of a poorly conceived state energy deregulation plan and a short-term shortage of energy sources that led to frequent power outages. In response, state policymakers adopted the nation's most ambitious and largest energy conservation program, with a strong focus on incentives for individuals to conserve energy. For example, those who cut their previous electricity use by 20 percent or more would earn a special rebate of 20 percent on their 2001 electricity bills, in addition to the direct savings they enjoyed from using less electricity. The state called this a "pay-to-conserve" program. A state Consumer Energy Center Web site (www.consumerenergycenter.

(Continued)

org/) provides details to state residents on demand reduction programs. By 2001 the state had cut its electricity use by 10 percent over the previous year, a dramatic change that prevented further power outages that year. Energy conservation worked (Behr 2001). As a result of this and related energy efficiency programs, by 2006 per capita electricity consumption in California was far below the national average.

Natural resource policy actions invite sharp conflict as different interests clash over how best to use the resources, evident in disputes over drilling for oil in ANWR, increasing logging in national forests, and protecting habitats of threatened and endangered species. Yet they also signal the potential for a new era of cooperation as environmentalist groups and development interests try to find ways to reconcile environmental and economic goals. Even if many of the battles continue and the ultimate outcome remains uncertain, one thing is clear. Some of the most ineffective and inefficient natural resource policies of past decades have come under increasing attack (Lowry 2003, 2006). Slowly, what had been a laissez-faire stance on ecologically damaging activities and generous government subsidies for shortsighted and uneconomic resource extraction have been giving way to a new goal of sustainable development. The short-term conflicts get much attention in the press, but the more important story is the redefined resource agenda and new public values driving natural resource decision making, from the local to the international level.

Environmental Stewardship or Economic Development?

The United States is richly endowed with natural resources. Even though the federal government gave away much of its original land before the early-twentieth-century conservation movement curtailed the practice, the public domain includes over 650 million acres, or a quarter of the nation's total land area. About half of that is in Alaska, and much of the rest is in the spacious western states. These public lands and waters include awe-inspiring mountain ranges, vast stretches of open desert, pristine forests, spectacular rivers and lakes, and the magnificent national parks: Yellowstone, Yosemite, Grand Teton, and Grand Canyon. They also contain valuable timber, minerals, energy resources, and water vital to irrigated crops in the West. Even submerged offshore lands are precious. The federally governed 1 billion acres of land on the outer continental shelf (OCS) contain an estimated 40 to 60 percent of the nation's undiscovered oil and natural gas reserves.

Congress has chosen to set aside some areas—the parks, wild rivers, wilderness areas, and national seashores—to protect them from almost all development. Most public lands are only partially protected. They are subject to long-standing, but intentionally vague, "multiple-use" doctrines that Congress intended to help balance competing national objectives of economic development and environmental preservation. Thus agency administrators are expected to protect and exploit resources simultaneously. They preserve public lands and waters for recreation and aesthetic enjoyment and protect ecologically vital watersheds and fish and wildlife habitat. Yet they also try to ensure commercial development of the commodities on those lands, such as minerals and timber. Agency officials serve as stewards of the public domain, a job that involves refereeing the many disputes that arise among the multitude of interests competing for access to it.

Natural resource policies govern those decisions, most of which fall within the jurisdiction of the Interior Department and Agriculture Department. Each of the major policies, agencies, and public land systems is described later. Conflicts over these policies and the decisions the agencies have made to implement them have escalated dramatically since the late 1960s. Among the primary reasons for the new controversy are the rise of the environmental movement and public support for its goals, rapid population growth in the West where most of the public lands are located, and surging interest in recreation (such as mountain climbing, white-water rafting, and off-road vehicle use). Each of these social changes has created new demands on the public lands and the agencies that govern them. For example, those who want greater access to public lands for recreation may compete with commercial interests that seek to harvest the resources, such as minerals and timber. Ultimately, government agencies have to make choices about who gains access to public lands and who does not.

Added to these developments are what economists call structural economic shifts that have imperiled some commercial activities in the West, including extractive industries such as forestry and mining that have been in decline for some time. They also include traditional activities such as ranching, which depends on low-cost grazing on public lands, and farming; in the arid West, that means dependence on federally subsidized irrigation water. Changes in these economic enterprises can severely threaten thousands of people in the West whose livelihoods depend on continued access to public lands and waters. Even with a robust national economy, such individuals, and the communities in which they live, suffer genuine harm. Deservedly or not, they often blame environmental policies and actions of the federal government for their dire situation (Brick and Cawley 1996; Switzer 1997; Tierney and Frasure 1998).

As the wise use movement of the 1990s vividly demonstrated, crafting solutions that satisfy all these parties is always difficult. The extent to which consensus can be built will test the nation's capacity to put the concepts of sustainable development and ecosystem management into practice. Success is likely to depend on generating credible and compelling scientific analyses of the environmental effects of resource use and also on designing policies to mitigate unavoidable and adverse economic and social repercussions. Few people advocate having such crucial value choices made by a centralized and distant bureaucracy. Thus equally important to the goal of sustainable development is the creation of decision-making processes capable of fostering constructive policy dialogue and consensus building among stakeholders at all levels of government, and especially in affected communities (Mazmanian and Kraft 1999; Weber 2003; Wondolleck and Yaffee 2000).

The Environmentalist Challenge to Resource Development

Natural resources policy has a much longer history in the United States than either environmental protection or energy policy. As discussed in Chapter 4, policies designed to encourage settlement of the West transferred over 1 billion acres of federal domain land to the states and private parties before ended officially in 1976. Well before the environmental decade of the 1970s, the conservation movement instituted the first of a series of protectionist policies with the creation of national parks and monuments and the establishment of the National Park Service, Forest Service, Bureau of Reclamation, and other federal resource agencies. For most of the twentieth century, conflicts over protection and development of federal lands had been relatively muted and politically contained, in part because natural resource subgovernments, also discussed in Chapter 4, dominated the issues and promoted consensus on policy goals and means (Clarke and McCool 1996; Culhane 1981; McCool 1990). Scholars disagree about the extent of agency "capture" by the regulated interests (such as the influence of logging and mining companies in Interior Department agencies). Yet it would be fair to say that long-settled policies that governed mining, logging, grazing, agriculture, and other uses of public lands and waters have rarely emerged as major political issues with the larger public. All that changed as the environmental movement gathered steam in the 1960s when it scored its first policy successes in resource conservation.

Gains in Resource Protection and Political Access   The Wilderness Act of 1964 created the National Wilderness Preservation System to set aside undeveloped areas of federal land where "the earth and its community of life are untrammeled by man." The Land and Water Conservation Fund Act of 1964 provided federal grants to the states for planning for, acquiring, and developing land and water areas for recreation. The fund also provides money to buy property for national parks, forests, and refuges managed by the federal government. In 1968 Congress established the National Wild and Scenic Rivers System to protect free-flowing rivers in their natural state.

In a fitting symbol of the dozens of environmental measures to follow, on its last day in session in December 1969, Congress enacted the National Environmental Policy Act (NEPA), and President Richard Nixon signed it into law on January 1, 1970. NEPA (pronounced "knee pah") requires the preparation of environmental impact statements (EISs) for all "major Federal actions significantly affecting the quality of the human environment" (Caldwell 1998). Of equal importance was the creation by NEPA and other statutes and judicial rulings of the 1970s of a major role for the public in environmental decision making, altering forever the political dynamics of natural resources policy (Dana and Fairfax 1980).

These new policies, and the political movements that inspired them, brought to the fore the previously latent conflicts in natural resources that are now so common. During the 1970s environmentalists gained access to the natural resource subgovernments, from the national to the local level. They became regular participants in agency decision making, and they gained powerful allies on Capitol Hill as natural resources committees and subcommittees began to reflect the public's strong support for resource preservation efforts. They also played an active role in the courts, using NEPA's environmental impact statement process to oppose many development projects that they viewed as environmentally damaging (Caldwell 1998; Wenner 1982).

Reaction in the West   None of this change was good news for traditional resource constituencies, especially in the western states. They saw their historic access to public lands and waters jeopardized by the new demands for preservation and recreation and by a different set of policy actors who were unlikely to acquiesce to the old distributive formulas. In the early 1980s, and more recently under wise use and property rights banners, the user groups fought back using rhetoric and political symbols equally as powerful as those offered by the environmental community (Brick and Cawley 1996; Cawley 1993; Davis 2001).

Environmentalists speak passionately about preserving nature, particularly wilderness areas, and they often base their arguments in environmental science and ecology. Ecosystem management, for example, has emerged as a powerful concept that derives in large part from recent advances in ecology (Cortner and Moote 1999). Ecologists also are likely to identify the varied and essential "services" that nature provides to humans, such as purification of air and water, prevention of flooding, and provision of food (Daily 1997). Yet equally important to many environmental groups and individuals are the strong aesthetic and moral values they hold about conservation of natural systems (Kellert 1996).

In contrast, user groups are much more likely to adopt a utilitarian or instrumental view of natural resources. They talk about both economic and commercial values and the preservation of local communities long dependent on public lands and waters. They refer as well to threats posed to the western "way of life" and culture, and they remain skeptical about the science behind environmentalist assertions (Egan 1993b; Kriz 1993). Some have been particularly critical of the ecosystem management approaches to which federal agencies have turned. For all these reasons, user groups evince a distinct preference for state and local control of public lands over federal dominance and for private property rights over governmental regulation. They are convinced that decisions on natural resources will be more rational if they are made locally and if property owners are more fully in control of their own land (Tierney and Frasure 1998).

It comes as no surprise that debate between the two sides in these land use battles often has led to increased acrimony, polarization, and political stalemate. The issues have been difficult to resolve through conventional political processes, particularly when the federal government battles with local property owners and commercial users of public lands and one or both parties try to litigate the dispute. Fortunately, some signs indicate that collaborative planning and decision making at the community and regional levels can help resolve such disputes (discussed later).

Although such new forms of collaboration and dispute resolution are promising, it is important to understand as well that conflicts over natural resource policies since the 1960s have reflected the real disaffection of traditional beneficiaries of federal largesse. Their resentment over new federal policies that were likely to curtail their benefits grew throughout the 1970s. They also took exception to an intrusive federal government that dominated state and local land use decisions. In many ways, the Sagebrush Rebellion greatly influenced Ronald Reagan's environmental agenda. It set in motion the determined and controversial efforts by James Watt, Reagan's first secretary of the interior, to reverse two decades of progressive natural resource policies (Culhane 1984; Kraft 1984; Leshy 1984).

Ultimately, Watt and his successors at Interior through George Bush's presidency—William P. Clark, Donald P. Hodel, and Manuel Lujan Jr.—changed few formal resource policies that could not be undone by Bruce Babbitt in the Clinton administration or by future secretaries of the interior.[16] The major policies and programs continue to reflect the ambivalence the nation displays toward the use of natural resources. Strong public support exists for resource conservation and environmental preservation, but these issues typically fail to command the visibility needed to mobilize the public. The result is that consensus in Congress on these statutes is less than robust. Members of Congress also tend to be highly sensitive to the pleas of politically significant constituencies. Mining, logging, forestry, and agricultural interests lobby intensely to protect their benefits, and they are well represented on Capitol Hill. That is particularly so in the Senate, where sparsely settled western states enjoy the same representation as the most populous states.

These institutional and political characteristics help explain a good deal of the congressional opposition to the Clinton administration's proposals for reform of natural resource policies. Just as important, however, is the absence of public concern over issues such as mining, logging, and grazing on public lands. Few people not directly affected by the policies are likely to think much about proposals for reform of the Mining Law of 1872 or appropriate fee structures for grazing cattle on federal land. The low salience of the issues weakens the reformers' ability to push their agenda, and it contributes to the legislative gridlock that has characterized these policy conflicts in recent years.

Ironically, the West is being transformed politically by an enormous influx of so-called lifestyle refugees into Arizona, Colorado, Idaho, Montana, Oregon, Nevada, New Mexico, Utah, and Washington. The New West is overwhelmingly urban and suburban, and it has many of the fastest growing states in the country. It is being built not on the extractive industries such as mining and forestry that dominated the West in decades past, but on communications, electronics and computer manufacturing, tourism, and retirees (Egan 1998). As one sign of the transformation, the number of metal miners in the United States fell by half between the early 1980s and late 1990s as more of the business shifted to other nations (Brooke 1998). These demographic and economic changes already have affected Congress as noted earlier, and they are likely to have a more significant effect on both local and national environmental politics and policies over time.

Natural Resource Policies and Agencies

Much like federal energy policy, natural resource policies are both simple and complex. They are simplest at the level of basic choices made about preservation or development of public resources or equity in the payment of user fees. They are most convoluted in the detailed and arcane rules and procedures governing program implementation. Debates over policy proposals similarly can be fairly straightforward or all but indecipherable to those outside the resource policy communities.

Table 6.1 offers a brief description of the major federal natural resource policies and lists their implementing agencies.[17] To understand the politics of natural resources policy requires us to pay at least some attention to the agencies themselves. Congress has granted the agencies great discretion to interpret and implement the statutes, which puts them at the center of political battles over protection versus economic exploitation of the public domain at a time of fundamental policy and administrative changes. The conflicts can be illustrated with a selective review of how the agencies are implementing the new resource policies.

Administration of public lands is assigned chiefly to four federal agencies. The Bureau of Land Management, the Fish and Wildlife Service, and the National Park Service are housed in the Interior Department. The Forest Service, often at odds with the Interior Department, has been in the Department of Agriculture since Gifford Pinchot had the nation's newly created forest reserves transferred there in 1905. Together, the four agencies control more than 625 million acres (about 1 million square miles), or over 96 percent of the total public domain lands. The remaining lands fall under the jurisdiction of the Department of Defense, other Interior and Agriculture departmental agencies such as the Bureau of Reclamation, the Department of Energy, and the Tennessee Valley Authority. Other agencies are involved in scientific studies and monitoring of public lands that contribute to policymaking, such as

TABLE 6.1

Major Federal Natural Resource Policies

Statute	Implementing Agency	Key Provisions and Features
Multiple Use–Sustained Yield Act of 1960, PL 86-517	Interior Department: Forest Service	Defined multiple-use and sustained yield concepts for the Forest Service. Required that officials consider diverse values in managing forestlands, including protection of fish and wildlife. Made clear that the forests should be managed to "best meet the needs of the American people" and not necessarily to yield the highest dollar return.
Wilderness Act of 1964, PL 88-577	Agriculture Department; Interior Department	Established the National Wilderness Preservation System comprised of federal lands designated as "wilderness areas," to remain "unimpaired for future use and enjoyment as wilderness." Authorized review of public lands for possible inclusion in the system.
Land and Water Conservation Fund Act of 1964, PL 88-578	Interior Department	Created the Land and Water Conservation Fund, which receives money from the sale of offshore oil and gas leases in the outer continental shelf. Authorized appropriations from the fund for matching grants for state and local planning, acquisition, and development of land for recreation purposes and for acquisition of lands and waters for federal recreation areas.
Wild and Scenic Rivers Act of 1968, PL 90-542	Interior Department	Authorized protection of selected rivers with "outstandingly remarkable features," including scenic, biological, archaeological, or cultural value. Rivers may be designated as wild, scenic, or recreational.
National Environmental Policy Act of 1969, PL 91-190	All agencies; coordinated by the Council on Environmental Quality	Declared a national policy to "encourage productive and enjoyable harmony between man and his environment"; required environmental impact statements; created the Council on Environmental Quality.
Marine Protection Research, and Sanctuaries Act of 1972 (Ocean Dumping Act), PL 92-532	U.S. Environmental Protection Agency	Authorized research and monitoring of long-range effects of pollution, overfishing, and other acts on ocean ecosystems. Regulated ocean dumping through an EPA permit system that allows disposal of waste materials only in designated areas.
Coastal Zone Management Act of 1972, PL 92-583	Office of Ocean and Coastal Resource Management	Authorized federal grants to states to develop coastal zone management plans under federal guidelines and to acquire and operate estuarine sanctuaries.

Statute	Implementing Agency	Key Provisions and Features
Marine Mammal Protection Act of 1972, PL 92-522	National Marine Fisheries Service	Established a moratorium on the taking of marine mammals and a ban on importation of marine mammals and products made from them, with certain exceptions. Created a federal responsibility for conservation of marine mammals.
Endangered Species Act of 1973, PL 93-205	Fish and Wildlife Service, National Marine Fisheries Service	Broadened federal authority to protect all "threatened" as well as "endangered" species; authorized grant program to assist the states; required coordination among all federal agencies.
Federal Land Policy and Management Act of 1976, PL 94-579	Bureau of Land Management	Gave Bureau of Land Management authority to manage public lands for long-term benefits; officially ended policy of disposing of public lands through privatization. Provided for use of national forests and grasslands for livestock grazing under a permit system.
National Forest Management Act of 1976, PL 94-588	Forest Service	Extended and elaborated processes set out in the 1974 Forest and Rangeland Renewable Resources Planning Act. Gave statutory permanence to national forestlands and set new standards for their planning and management, including full public participation; provided new authority for management, harvesting, and selling of timber, and restricted timber use to protect soil and watersheds; limited clear-cutting.
Surface Mining Control and Reclamation Act of 1977, PL 95-87	Interior Department, Office of Surface Mining	Established environmental controls over surface mining of coal; limited mining on farmland, alluvial valleys, and slopes; required restoration of land to original contours.
Alaska National Interest Lands of 1980, PL 96-487	Interior Department; Agriculture Department	Protected 103 million acres of Alaskan land as national wilderness, forest, wildlife refuges, and parks, and other areas of special management and study.

the U.S. Geological Survey in the Interior Department and the Natural Resources Conservation Service, located in the Agriculture Department (U.S. GAO 1997b).[18]

As Clarke and McCool (1996) demonstrate, each agency has its distinctive origins, constituencies, characteristics, and decision-making style. Fish and Wildlife Service and National Park Service lands are governed by specialized missions and for the most part are well protected from development. In contrast, Forest Service and Bureau of Land Management lands are subject to multiple-use doctrines that pose a greater risk of environmental degradation. These doctrines also require agency administrators to juggle competing interests and reconcile conflicting interpretations of the law, always under the watchful eye of Congress and the interest groups and industries that are affected. The two agencies, however, have markedly different histories and orientations (Dana and Fairfax 1980).

Managing the Nation's Forests

Forests occupy about a third of the U.S. land area, with the majority owned privately or by the states. The nation had been losing half a million acres of private forestland a year to urban expansion and agriculture, which contributed to ardent interest in those forest lands under federal control. According to more recent figures, however, that trend of forest loss has been reversed (CEQ 1998). Moreover, the Department of Agriculture natural resources inventory, which is compiled every five years by the department's Natural Resources Conservation Service, found that total nonfederal forestland in the nation has increased since 1982. Most of the increase appears to be in private timberland. The inventory also found, however, an accelerating rate of loss of forestland because of urban and suburban development. Particularly noticeable was the loss of trees in urban areas as cities expand outward (Pope 1999b; Seelye 2001).[19] Even if the overall trend of lost forestland has changed, concern continues over the quality of the remaining land as well as fragmentation and other alterations of land that provides critical habitat to species.

The responsibility for managing the federal lands and the Forest Service itself reflect the era when both were born: Pinchot's progressive conservation movement in the early twentieth century. Its awkward blend of resource protection and use continues to this day. The Forest Service has a long tradition of professional forest management, although environmentalists often have faulted it for excessive devotion to the interests of the timber industry. They have been particularly critical of the service's approval of clear-cutting of forests and its insufficient protection of habitat and biological diversity (Culhane 1981; Lowry 2006).

At the instigation of the Forest Service and to respond to an increasing number of people seeking to enjoy the trails and streams of the national forests, Congress enacted a milestone statute in 1960, the Multiple Use–Sustained Yield Act. It defined multiple use as including outdoor recreation, fish and wildlife, and ranging as well as timber production, and the act made clear that the forests should be managed to "best meet the needs of the American people" and "not necessarily [through] uses that will give the greatest dollar return." The act set no priorities, and thus it gave the Forest Service discretion to expand its preservation of forest resources.

The National Forest Management Act   Environmentalist concern rose significantly as the Forest Service began implementing the National Forest Management Act (NFMA) of 1976 early in the Reagan administration. The NFMA amended the 1974 Forest and Rangeland Renewable Resources Planning Act, which had set timber production as a primary goal. The 1974 act, however, also had established a general planning process that helped shift the Forest Service (and the Bureau of Land Management) away from what had been an overwhelming emphasis on timber production.

The 1976 act extended this process and added further specifications. It required the Forest Service to prepare long-term comprehensive plans for the lands under its jurisdiction and to involve the public in its decision making through meetings and hearings. Thus the process made explicit the trade-offs between protecting the forest environment and allowing commercial development of it under the legal doctrines of sustained yield and multiple use.

Conflicts between forest preservation and development became especially acute as the Forest Service came under growing pressure in the mid-1980s to increase allowable timber harvest. It tried to resist such demands from political appointees in the Reagan administration out of concern that even the level of timber harvesting at that time was not sustainable. Such pressures on the Forest Service continued through the 1980s (Clarke and McCool 1996). Environmentalists and industry, or both, regularly contested the forest plans and the environmental impact statements that accompanied them. Environmentalists argued that the agency was deviating too much from its multiple-use mission and fostering instead "tree farming" in large areas of national forests. These challenges reached a peak in the George H. W. Bush administration when environmentalists frequently filed administrative appeals to delay or block Forest Service timber sales (Schneider 1992). Controversies continued throughout the 1990s over the extent of logging operations in the national forests and the sufficiency of the Forest Service's environmental assessments to document the consequences of timber sales (Cushman 1999). Such disputes over forest plans notwithstanding, the new planning process under the 1976 law has been widely considered a model for natural resource management.

Changes in the U.S. Forest Service   The Forest Service is a large agency, with more than 37,000 employees, a budget of about $5 billion, and responsibility for over 190 million acres of public lands. In recent years, it has cut back sharply on sales of timber and on the revenues it has brought to the federal treasury. Critics have long asserted, however, that the revenue from timber sales is deceptive because the costs incurred by the government in providing access for timber harvesting (e.g., building and maintaining logging roads) has often exceeded the revenue. Hence concern is expressed over below-cost timber sales; even the Forest Service concedes that sales of timber lose money. For these and other reasons, particularly preservation of habitat, some environmental organizations (most notably the Sierra Club) have called for an end to all logging in national forests. Environmentalists say that the nation could save more than $1 billion per year by eliminating the subsidies for logging in the nation's forests.

The Forest Service also supervises grazing, use of water resources, and recreation on its lands, and it does so with a strong sense of mission and high professional standards. In their assessment of federal resource agencies, Clarke and McCool (1996) award the Forest Service one of two "bureaucratic superstar" ratings (the other goes to the U.S. Army Corps of Engineers) based on a reputation for bureaucratic power, professionalism, and political acumen.

Such accolades notwithstanding, like all natural resource agencies, the Forest Service in recent years has been undergoing major changes as it adjusts to new expectations for sustainable resource management and ecosystem protection. Studies by the National Research Council (1990), among others, have encouraged the service to incorporate elements of ecosystem management, for example, by placing greater emphasis on the ecological role of forests and their effects on climate change, educating the public on such issues, and financing Forest Service activities with greater reliance on fees from all users, from loggers and miners to campers and hikers. Such fees would reduce pressures to favor logging (Giltmier 1998; Lowry 2006; O'Toole 1988).

The Clinton administration moved strongly in that direction under several chiefs of the service, including Jack Ward Thomas and Michael Dombeck (Egan 1998; Lewis 1999). Following through on an initiative by Dombeck to place a moratorium on construction of new logging roads in remote areas of national forests, President Clinton announced in October 1999 that he would use his executive authority to speed through permanent protection of some 40 million acres of federal forestland in six states. The proposal, termed "positively breathtaking" by a *New York Times* editorial, sought to create near-wilderness status for the land, prohibiting road building, logging, and mining. It was to add to the 34 million acres of the national forests already classified as wilderness areas. Conservationists applauded the move as a "grand slam," but the timber industry termed it an "extreme form of preservation." Western Republicans in Congress predictably were unhappy with the administration's proposal (Sanger and Verhovek 1999).

Critics might be tempted to view these changes in the Forest Service and the legal protections for forestland as merely the policy preferences of the Clinton administration, but they also reflect recent developments in ecology and an improved understanding of ecosystem functioning. At about the same time the administration was proposing its new approaches to forestland (and other land), an independent 13-member scientific committee recommended that "ecological sustainability" become the principal goal in managing the national forests and grasslands, a position that Clinton's Secretary of Agriculture Dan Glickman endorsed as "a new planning framework for the management of our forests for the 21st century."[20]

In some respects, the directions taken by the Forest Service in the 1990s also were a response to changing demographics and economics, especially in the West. Although timber cutting has declined by about two thirds over the past decade, the number of recreational visitors has leaped by over 40 percent. As one journalist put it in 1999, "hikers, hunters, bikers, campers, and skiers increasingly dominate forest policy" (Brooke 1999). The Forest Service predicted that it would record 1 billion recreational visits a year by 2010.

The administration of George W. Bush was much less supportive of these new perspectives on how to use the national forests. The administration made clear that it favored substantial increases in logging more in line with the preferences of the timber industry. From 2001 through 2005, it approved a series of measures intended to favor logging over preservation. For example, in 2004, after two years of dispute, the administration gave managers of the 155 national forests more discretion in approving commercial activities such as logging, oil and gas drilling, and off-road vehicle use and demanded less assessment of the environmental impacts when revising forest plans. The rules cut back as well on public participation in development of forest plans.[21] The administration also proposed that NEPA reviews be sharply limited to permit the "thinning" of trees and brush in national forests, chiefly in mountain and western states, in light of the threat of wildfires (Allen and Pianin 2002). In addition, Bush succeeded in gaining congressional approval of the Healthy Forests Restoration Act of 2003, a law that will permit increased logging in federal forests (defined as fuel reduction) as one way to limit the risk of wildfires (Jalonick 2004). The combination of the new forest rules and the new law will reduce the ability of environmental groups and others to challenge such actions even though independent studies show that such challenges pose no barrier to fire prevention (U.S. GAO 2003).

The change demonstrated how effective the Bush administration was in portraying or framing a shift in forest policy as protection against wildfires and promotion of forest health; doing so makes it more politically attractive (Vaughn and Cortner 2004). Yet one real concern was the considerable cost to the Forest Service of fighting fires each year. The service spent $1.4 billion in 2002 battling wildfires, triple the cost in 1996. Although timber cutting has declined by 80 percent over the past decade, the agency's budget has grown to cover the rising costs of firefighting. The agency historically has discounted the ecological value of allowing forest fires to burn, and it has tried to put the fires out (Robbins 2004).

The Bush administration did not always disappoint the environmental community. In late 2001 the Bush administration approved a Clinton-era plan to protect old-growth woodlands in 11.5 million acres in the Sierra Nevada mountain range. The administration upheld a Forest Service decision that rejected appeals by loggers, ski resort owners, and off-road vehicle groups. As is often the case, the Forest Service plan took nine years and millions of dollars to create. It was part of the service's efforts to protect the endangered northern spotted owl. Environmentalists cheered the decision; logging interests expressed disappointment.[22]

Battles over Wilderness

The history of wilderness designation demonstrates many of the same conflicts of values over whether public lands should be set aside in a protected status or commercial development permitted. For many, they are economic decisions, incorporating a view of natural resources as commodities to be exploited. Others see the decisions primarily as involving moral choices in which they demand the greatest form of protection possible for the few wild places remaining in the nation. Government policymakers are obliged to follow legal dictates in their decision making, but they are regularly pulled in one of these two directions as they exercise the discretion given to them under the law.

As part of its review of land use in the 1970s, the Forest Service embarked on an ambitious effort to inventory roadless land within the national forest system for possible inclusion in the protected wilderness system. The first Roadless Area Review and Evaluation survey (RARE I) was completed in 1976. It elicited strong disapproval by environmental groups over inadequate environmental impact statements and insufficient public involvement in the process. The Carter administration completed a second survey, RARE II, in 1979. It recommended more wilderness areas but also sought to meet public demand for timber. More litigation by environmentalists and the states followed, again based on insufficient adherence to NEPA procedures.

The Reagan administration was far more skeptical about the value of wilderness preservation, and its actions reflected those beliefs. Interior Secretary Watt provoked enormous controversy over proposals to open wilderness areas to mineral development, which the Wilderness Act allowed under some restrictions. After a 1982 court ruling that questioned RARE II's consistency with NEPA's environmental impact statement requirements, Reagan ordered a broad RARE III on *all* lands on which Congress had not yet acted. His administration strongly favored development over wilderness protection, and Watt went on to withdraw 1 million acres of potential wilderness from additional study and possible protection. Congress and wilderness advocates bitterly opposed those actions, and they cost the administration support for its other policy initiatives on natural resources (Leshy 1984).

The biggest congressional designation of wilderness areas had came just before the Reagan era, in 1980, with the creation of 50 million acres of wilderness in Alaska, much of it on Bureau of Land Management land. In 1990, after years of environmentalist pressure and resistance by Alaska, Congress withheld from logging more than 1 million acres of the Tongass National Forest in southeast Alaska. Nearly 300,000 acres were set aside as wilderness in this last major expanse of temperate rain forest in North America, and limited mining and road building is to be allowed on over 700,000 acres.

As noted earlier, the Clinton administration and environmentalists mounted a major campaign to put even more land into various states of protection, including wilderness designation. Clinton pressed hard for his Lands Legacy initiative, of which additional wilderness preservation was a part (Egan 1999).[23] The administration also provided over $1 billion per year for local, state, and federal agencies to preserve more open lands. Among other decisions, Clinton used the 1906 Antiquities Act to create a number of new national monuments, including the 1.9-million-acre Grand Staircase—Escalante National Monument in Utah's red-rock country (Egan 2000; Kriz 1999).[24]

In the final days of his administration, Clinton issued a sweeping rule to protect roadless areas in the national forests from future road construction, intended to prevent development in nearly 60 million acres of forests and open the way for wilderness designation. Legal challenges by industry and some states followed. By 2005 the Bush administration announced a new and complex procedure to replace the Clinton rules. The State Petitioning Rule would give the governors of each state a choice about which national forest areas located within their states should remain roadless. The new policy reflects the Bush administration's belief that such decisions should be made within each state to reflect local conditions and public preferences and to limit future litigation. Environmentalists said the Bush rule effectively would repeal the Clinton-era wilderness protection plan and hand over the forests to the timber industry and other development interests; they announced that they would fight it in court.[25] In the case of the much disputed Tongass National Forest in Alaska, the Bush administration removed roadless area protection to open up some 9 million acres to mining, road building, and logging, a move favored by Alaska's lawmakers and the timber industry. Yet, reflecting current market conditions for lumber, few timber companies rushed in to bid on the newly opened areas.

Governing the Range

The Bureau of Land Management (BLM) has leaned even more heavily than the Forest Service toward the resource use end of the spectrum. The BLM governs more federal land (about 270 million acres) than any other agency, but it has suffered from a historic indifference to environmental values compared with the Forest Service. The BLM has a budget that is only about 40 percent that of the Forest Service (at $1.9 billion in fiscal 2004) and a staff of about 11,000, far fewer than the number needed to implement its programs. As a result of the Alaska Lands Act in 1980, the bureau was given new responsibility for vast acreage in Alaska, including large areas of wilderness, which now constitutes half of BLM land. The bureau is also in charge of federal mineral leases on all public domain and outer continental shelf lands.

BLM Deficiencies and Needs   Clarke and McCool classify the BLM as a "shooting star" agency that burned brightly for a short time but now faces a precarious future.

It is a relatively new federal agency, formed in 1946 by executive actions merging Interior's General Land Office and the U.S. Grazing Service, two agencies with a reputation for inept land management. The BLM is widely viewed as weak politically and historically highly permissive toward its chief constituency groups, the mining industry and ranchers. Those characteristics have led scholars to term it a "captured" agency (Foss 1960; McConnell 1966).

As Paul Culhane (1981) observed, however, in more recent years the BLM has recruited professional staff with credentials in scientific land management and a commitment to progressive conservation comparable to those in the Forest Service. The difference between the two agencies lies in the political milieu in which they function. To meet new expectations for sustainable resource management on public lands, the BLM will need to gain more political independence from its traditional constituencies and build a broader base of public support.

The Federal Land Policy and Management Act   Congress tried to stimulate such an organizational shift with passage of the Federal Land Policy and Management Act of 1976 (FLPMA), also known as the BLM organic act. FLPMA formally ended the 200-year-old policy of disposing of the public domain, repealed more than 2,000 antiquated public land laws, amended the 1934 Taylor Grazing Act, and mandated wilderness reviews for all roadless BLM lands with wilderness characteristics. More important, the act established the bureau legislatively as an agency and gave it the authority to inventory and manage the public lands under its jurisdiction. Agency officials had sought the authorizing legislation to clarify its responsibilities and to give it the legal authority to apply tools of modern land management. The new legislation helped the BLM establish greater authority over the public lands under a broad multiple-use mandate that leaned toward environmental values and away from a position of grazing as dominant use.

FLPMA gave the BLM full multiple-use powers that matched those of the Forest Service. It defined multiple use in a way that should encourage environmental sustainability:

> Management of the public lands and their various resource values so that they are utilized in the combination that will best meet the present and future needs of the American people . . . a combination of balanced and diverse resource use that takes into account the long-term needs of future generations for renewable and nonrenewable resources, including, but not limited to, recreation, range, timber, minerals, watershed, wildlife and fish, and natural scenic, scientific and historical values.

Like most legislation, FLPMA represented a compromise needed to secure the approval of key interests (Dana and Fairfax 1980).

Much like its counterpart governing the nation's forests, FLPMA established a land use planning process for BLM lands that required extensive public participation and coordination with state and local governments as well as with Indian tribes. Here, too, Congress specifically chose to delegate authority for land use decisions to the agencies. The act increased the authority of the BLM to regulate grazing, allowing the secretary of interior to specify the terms and conditions of leases and permits, including reduction in the number of livestock on the lands. However, it maintained the grazing permit system, the local boards that supervise it, and the existing fee structure. All have been sharply criticized by study commissions and environmentalists for contributing to the degradation of public rangelands (Mangun and Henning 1999).

BLM Lands and the Sagebrush Rebellion

Since the passage of FLPMA, the BLM has been moving slowly toward the new goal of sustainable resource management. Indeed, the Sagebrush Rebellion of the late 1970s largely grew out of the frustration of western ranchers, who were angry over the BLM's implementation of that law. Their reaction was stimulated by decisions concerning grazing fees and protection of wildlife, native plants, and predators (Cawley 1993; Clarke and McCool 1996). The ranchers tried to force the transfer of federal lands to state or private ownership, where they believed they could exert more control. In 1979 the Nevada legislature approved a bill demanding that the federal government turn over all BLM land in Nevada to the state, an action usually credited as the first shot fired in the rebellion. Eighty-two percent of Nevada is federally owned, with smaller, but still large, percentages common in the western states (running from 28 to 68 percent).

The Reagan administration, and particularly James Watt's Interior Department, shared the rebels' political ideology and accommodated their demands to some extent (Culhane 1984). With the election of Bill Clinton, the same battles were joined once more under the new wise use label. BLM lands were at the center of two of the most controversial proposals on Interior Secretary Bruce Babbitt's resource agenda: raising grazing fees and reforming the long outmoded 1872 Mining Law. The law has allowed hard rock mining on public lands without any royalty payments, and it has had few requirements for restoration of lands damaged by mining (Egan 1993a; Kriz 1993; Riebsame 1996).

Babbitt's efforts built on a trend plainly evident in Congress before the 1992 election. For years, members had been seeking revisions in public lands and water policy to respond to increasing demands for preservation and recreation. The shift toward preservation and away from unrestrained resource use could be seen in a diversity of measures in the early to mid-1990s, such as the Omnibus Water Act of 1992 and the California Desert Protection Act of 1994. The former revised western water projects by instituting new pricing systems to encourage conservation and authorizing extensive wildlife and environmental protection, mitigation, and restoration programs; the latter designated some 7.5 million acres of wilderness on federal land within California. As discussed earlier, however, the Bush administration reversed some of these trends. It reflected a more traditional view of natural resource policy priorities that favored industry and economic development (Lowry 2006; Warrick and Eilperin 2004).

Other Protected Lands and Agencies

Some of the public domain is spared the intensity of disputes that characterizes decisions over use of Forest Service and BLM lands. In these cases, Congress has specified by statute that they be secure from much or all development after a decision has been made to place the lands within a protected class. These lands are those governed largely by the National Park Service and the U.S. Fish and Wildlife Service (FWS). Box 6.2 lists the five major divisions of federal lands, one incorporating marine sanctuaries and estuaries, and one incorporating rangelands.

The National Park Service   The National Park System is the most visible of the nation's public lands. The number of visitors grows every year and in recent years

BOX 6.2
Primary Federal Land Systems

NATIONAL PARK SYSTEM

Created in 1872, the National Park System had grown by the early twenty-first century to contain 387 units, of which 54 were national parks, the crown jewels of the system. Most of those are in Alaska and the West. The National Park System also includes over 300 national monuments, battlefields, memorials, historic sites, recreational areas, scenic parkways and trails, near-wilderness areas, seashores, and lakeshores. Most lands are closed to mining, timber harvesting, grazing, and other economic uses. Congress grants exemptions on a case-by-case basis when it approves the parks. For more information, see www.nps.gov/.

NATIONAL WILDLIFE REFUGE SYSTEM

Created in 1903, the National Wildlife Refuge System (NWRS) today is a sprawling and diverse system containing about 93 million acres scattered over all 50 states. The vast majority, 85 percent, are in Alaska. The system has the only federal lands specifically dedicated to wildlife preservation. Refuges are open to some commercial activities, including grazing, mining, and oil drilling. For more information, see www.fws.gov/.

NATIONAL FOREST SYSTEM

Created in 1905, the National Forest System (NFS) includes more than 187 million acres of land in 155 forests, largely in the West, Southeast, and Alaska. There are 50 national forests in 23 eastern states as well. The NFS is managed chiefly by the Forest Service, although some BLM lands are included in the system. For more information, see the Forest Service Web page at www.fs.fed.us/.

NATIONAL WILDERNESS PRESERVATION SYSTEM

Created in 1964, the National Wilderness Preservation System (NWPS) consists of over 106 million acres of land, 56 million of which are in Alaska and most of the rest in the 11 western states. The NWPS contains over 662 wilderness areas of widely varying size. NWPS lands are set aside forever as undeveloped, roadless areas, without permanent improvements or human habitation. Only officially designated wilderness areas are protected from commercial development. Wilderness areas are not entirely separate from the other systems. National and state maps of wilderness areas, and detailed information about each, can be found at www.wilderness.net/nwps/default.cfm.

NATIONAL WILD AND SCENIC RIVER SYSTEM

The river system contains nearly 11,000 total miles in 151 rivers in one of three designations: wild, scenic, or recreational. Rivers are to be in free-flowing condition— that is, unblocked by a dam—and to possess remarkable scenic, recreational, ecological, and other values. The shorelines of designated rivers are protected from federally permitted development. A comprehensive list of protected rivers by state can be found at www.nps.gov/rivers/.

(Continued)

NATIONAL MARINE SANCTUARIES AND NATIONAL ESTUARINE RESEARCH RESERVES

The marine sanctuaries contain 13 sites and 9,000 square nautical miles of unique marine recreational, ecological, historical, research, educational, and aesthetic resources, managed by the National Oceanic and Atmospheric Administration (NOAA). They are, in effect, equivalent to national parks in a marine environment. For more information on the sanctuaries, see www.sanctuaries.nos.noaa.gov/. For information on the estuarine reserves, see www.ocrm.nos.noaa.gov/nerr/.

NATIONAL RANGELANDS

Located chiefly in the 11 western states and Alaska, rangelands consist of grasslands, prairie, deserts, and scrub forests. Much of the land is suitable for grazing of cattle, sheep, and other livestock. Over 400 million acres of rangeland falls under federal control, most of it managed by the BLM and the rest by the Forest Service. Rangelands are the largest category of public domain lands. For more information, see the BLM Web page at www.blm.gov/nhp/index.htm.

Sources: Compiled from government agency and nonprofit organization Web pages as well as the Council on Environmental Quality, *Environmental Quality: The 1997 Report of the Council on Environmental Quality* (Washington, DC: CEQ, 1999). A useful guide to these lands and their facilities can be found at the Web site for the National Parks Conservation Association: www.npca.org.

has been about 300 million. For the most popular national parks, such as Great Smoky Mountains, Grand Canyon, Olympic, Yosemite, Rocky Mountain, Yellowstone, and Grand Teton National Parks, the hordes of tourists are overwhelming the capacity of the parks to accommodate them properly. Demands have been increasing on the parks' water, roadways, and personnel, and maintenance has been deferred at many of the national park units because of chronically deficient budgets for the agency. The National Park Service (NPS) estimated in 1998 that it would cost over $5 billion to deal with the accumulated maintenance needs at national parks, monuments, and wilderness areas (Pope 1998). In more recent years the amount necessary to catch up has been estimated to be between $4.1 and $6.8 billion. Budgets in the Bush administration have fallen well short of what is needed to make a dent in that backlog.

National Park System lands are closed to most economic uses, including mining, grazing, energy development, and timber harvesting, although such activities on adjacent land can seriously affect environmental quality within the parks (Freemuth 1991). These areas are managed by the NPS, an agency with about 19,000 employees (only a small number of them scientists) and a budget of about $2.2 billion. That budget has doubled since 1985, yet it remains insufficient.

Several studies, including one from the National Academy of Sciences and another sponsored by the National Parks Conservation Association, have been highly critical of the Park Service. The reports have emphasized poor training of employees, eroding professionalism within the ranks, and a failure to educate the public on issues related to parklands. Criticism has been especially directed at the service's inadequate capabilities for scientific research that can be used in support of its resource protection policies (Cahn 1993; Freedman 1996; Kenworthy 1992b). William Lowry's (1994) analysis of the Park Service suggests that many of its problems can be traced to weakened political consensus and support for policy goals (especially long-term preservation of parklands). This has led to increased intervention by Congress and the White House to promote short-term and politically popular objectives. Congress approved some action in 1998 in a National Parks Omnibus Management Act, which dealt primarily with the operation of concessions within the parks, development of a training program for Park Service employees, and creation of a new process for the service to recommend areas to be studied for possible inclusion in the park system. In early 2006 the Bush administration announced plans to rewrite the management policies for national parks to emphasize commercial and recreational use of the parks rather than preservation of their natural resources.

Sharp conflict over the use of snowmobiles in Yellowstone and other national parks illustrates the ongoing challenge the Park Service faces today. This is particularly so with efforts to base management decisions more on environmental science than on service to constituency groups. After 10 years of studies and extensive public review, the Clinton administration proposed to exclude snowmobiles from nearly all national parks, monuments, and recreational areas because of the noise and pollution they generate and because of the effects on wildlife. The Park Service wanted to phase in the change over three years to ease the transition. The snowmobile industry and local outfitters, however, remained unhappy, and they persuaded the Bush administration to alter course. Despite continuing public support for the snowmobile ban, the administration sought to allow the vehicles to continue to be used, and environmentalists and others challenged that decision in federal court.

By early 2006 the future of snowmobiles in Yellowstone was becoming somewhat clearer. The old dirty and noisy two-stoke engines are effectively banned from the park. They can only be used with a park guide and are limited to a total of 720 per day at the four park entrances. Additional environmental impact studies are still being conducted to determine the effects of the vehicles on wildlife. In the meantime, visitors rely on newer and quieter four-stroke engines or ride in groups on snow coaches. The use of snowmobiles in Yellowstone in the winter of 2005–2006 dropped well below the 720 vehicles that were allowed.[26] In contrast to the bitter conflict over the snowmobile case, the Bush administration decided to back a National Park Service plan by banning swamp buggies and other off-road vehicles in the Big Cypress preserve in Everglades National Park. Analysts argued that the difference lay in the stronger preference of the local community in Florida for the ban and the power of the state's green voters.[27]

Wilderness Areas and Wildlife Refuges   Like the National Park System lands, wilderness areas (primarily within the National Forest System but including some BLM lands) are given permanent protection against development, as discussed earlier. That is less true, however, for wildlife refuges (governed by the Fish and Wildlife Service). In addition to preserving habitats for a diversity of wildlife, these refuge lands are open to hunting, boating, grazing, mining, and oil and gas drilling, among other private uses. In the early 2000s, for instance, the service allowed oil and gas exploration or production at about 30 of its 530 refuges, although the primary purpose of the refuges is to be habitat conservation. By law, the refuges enjoy a degree of protection second only to that accorded to wilderness areas.

Environmentalists continue to argue for reducing those uses of wildlife refuges that are incompatible with the protection of wetlands, woodlands, deserts, and other fragile habitats. Supportive legislators have introduced such proposals in Congress. Under President George H. W. Bush's director of the FWS, John Turner, the agency began curtailing some incompatible uses of wildlife refuges. It also embarked on a comprehensive inventory of refuges to identify those uses that could pose a threat to wildlife.

In 1997 President Clinton signed the National Wildlife Refuge System Improvement Act (PL 105-57), which was intended to strengthen and improve the refuge system. The act defines the dominant refuge goal as wildlife conservation and provides for compatible wildlife-dependent recreation. It also establishes management guidelines for the FWS to make such compatibility determinations. Priority public uses of refuges include hunting, fishing, wildlife observation and photography, and environmental education and interpretation.

The George W. Bush administration was more favorably inclined toward oil and gas production in the refuges. Most notably, as discussed earlier, it proposed to allow such drilling in ANWR in Alaska, and it has indicated a priority for energy production on other public lands, including within some national parks. The Fish and Wildlife Service argues that such energy production has not been harmful to wildlife in the nation's refuges where it is now allowed. Officials also admit, however, that they do not have enough information to judge such effects across the whole system. The impacts have not been studied sufficiently to draw any firm conclusions.[28]

ENVIRONMENTAL IMPACTS AND NATURAL RESOURCES DECISION MAKING

Two of the most important environmental policies since the late 1960s merit special attention because of their wide application to public (and sometimes private) lands and their attempt to improve the way environmental science is used in natural resources decision making. They are the Endangered Species Act and the National Environmental Policy Act.

The Endangered Species Act

No other natural resource policy better captures the new environmental spirit since the late 1960s than the Endangered Species Act (ESA). It is one of the strongest federal environmental laws, and it symbolizes the nation's commitment to resource conservation goals. For that reason, the ESA has become a lightning rod for antienvironmental rhetoric and protest. The FWS, which implements the act for land-based species (the National Marine Fisheries Service handles water-based species), has been a target of frequent congressional attention and intervention in recent years.

The goal of the 1973 act, according to one leading study, was "clear and unambiguous—the recovery of all species threatened with extinction" (Tobin 1990, 27). A species could be classified as endangered if it was "in danger of extinction throughout all or a significant portion of its range" or threatened if "likely to become an endangered species within the foreseeable future." Congress made the protective actions unqualified. All takings of such a species would be prohibited, whether on state, federal, or private land. Restrictions are less stringent, however, for plants than for animals; plants are not fully protected when they are on private land. In *TVA v. Hill* (1978), involving a tiny fish, the snail darter, the U.S. Supreme Court upheld the act's constitutionality and made clear that under the ESA, no federal action could jeopardize a species' existence, regardless of cost or consequences.

Congress modified the ESA several times after its initial enactment in attempts to mollify the critics. For example, in 1982 it authorized habitat conservation plans. It even created a cabinet-level Endangered Species Committee, dubbed the God Squad, with authority to grant exemptions to the law, which have been rare. As is often the case with environmental policies, the result is a set of complex and cumbersome procedures and decision rules: (1) determining whether a given species is either threatened or endangered and should be listed, (2) designating critical habitats to be protected, (3) enforcing regulations that govern activities directly affecting the species and their habitats, and (4) implementing "recovery plans" for the species.

To complicate matters, Congress has never provided sufficient funds for the FWS to implement the act, and the agency has lacked the bureaucratic strength and resources necessary to fend off constituencies adversely affected by the ESA (Tobin 1990). The FWS has operated in recent years with about 7,800 employees and a budget of $1.3 billion a year.

Implementing the ESA: Achievements and Needs   As stated in Chapter 2, in early 2006 the Fish and Wildlife Service reported that 1,272 U.S. species of plants and animals were listed as threatened or endangered. The agency had designated over 470 critical habitats and developed more than 500 habitat conservation plans and about 1,000 approved recovery plans.[29]

Until very recently, the FWS made relatively slow progress in designating critical habitats even for endangered species, and recovery of species on the list had been quite limited. Indeed, many species became extinct while these bureaucratic processes dragged on. One government study in the mid-1990s estimated that the nation would have to spend $460 million per year over 10 years to develop recovery plans for all species that are candidates for listing, an amount far in excess of the annual FWS budget for the program. In late 2000 the FWS suspended the listing of species because of insufficient funds, and in 2001 the Bush administration proposed a one-year moratorium on a provision in the act that allowed citizens' groups to use the courts to force the FWS to list a species. Officials at the agency again cited its insufficient budget as well as the tendency of the courts to distort the listing process by forcing the agency to spend its limited resources on the species over which it is sued. Environmentalists, who frequently use that provision to sue the agency, denounced the proposal.

To judge from its own data, the agency appears to have made progress in recent years. It has also been particularly eager to publicize its success in protecting the "charismatic megafauna" that attract so much public attention and consume so much of the agency's budget. These species include the American bald eagle, the peregrine falcon, and the California gray whale. Yet relatively few species have been delisted since the passage of the act in 1973.

One of the most important changes in recent years is in the way the act is implemented. Despite the intense publicity given to some conflicts over a particular species, and resulting lawsuits, the federal government, landowners, and other stakeholders increasingly have sought to promote a more cooperative approach to conserving habitat and the species that rely on it. The hope is that land conservation need not unduly prevent economic development. The Bush administration has called this approach "cooperative conservation," and others have termed it collaborative decision making or sustainable development (Singer 2005). One prominent example is a widely praised plan to conserve a large tract of biologically rich land near San Diego, California (Ayres 1997; Lowry 2006). Similar efforts helped build a broad coalition of supporters for a massive federal–state project to restore the Florida Everglades (Stevens 1999).

Even before the more cooperative approaches of the late 1990s and early 2000s, however, studies of the ESA found that it prevented relatively few development projects from going forward. That was because most developers agreed to make adjustments in their plans to avoid disrupting critical habitats (Kenworthy 1992a; Tobin 1990; World Wildlife Fund 1994).

A greater problem with the ESA is that it was designed to focus on individual species rather than the ecosystems of which they are a part. That focus reflects the origin of the law in the early 1970s, which preceded contemporary perspectives on biodiversity conservation and ecosystem management. The need for a broader conception of species conservation is clear today. The northern spotted owl, for example, the object of ferocious battles over timber harvesting during the early 1990s, shares its habitat with over 1,400 other species dependent on old-growth forests; of those species, 40 are listed as threatened or endangered. Yet, predictably, media coverage and political controversy have focused on the owl, distorting public understanding of the real issues.[30]

Slowly both the public and policymakers are coming to understand the larger purpose of biodiversity conservation, both within the United States and internationally. One of the best illustrations of this important change comes from a series of efforts being made in the Pacific Northwest to save wild species of salmon. In one case, under federal court orders to devise recovery plans for the salmon under the ESA, the National Marine Fisheries Service and the U.S. Army Corps of Engineers considered whether to breach four large hydroelectric dams on the lower Snake River in eastern Washington State. By restoring a free-flowing river, the chances for the salmon's survival would be greatly enhanced. Other efforts to restore the salmon, such as use of fish ladders, hatcheries, and transporting young fish downstream, have failed.

Removal of the Snake River dams clearly imposes a short-term cost, especially on local farmers. Yet even some elected officials in the Northwest recognized both the economic and symbolic value of the salmon. John Kitzhaber, then Oregon's governor, captured the new spirit well: "If our salmon runs are not healthy, then our watersheds are not healthy. A highly degraded ecosystem—which is where we are headed today—represents a decision to mortgage the legacy with which we have been blessed for our own short-term benefit. I believe we are better than that."[31]

Similarly, in March 1999 the federal government announced that it would list nine other types of salmon under the ESA, forcing new building restrictions and raising taxes across the Seattle area. Yet polls indicated overwhelming public support in the region for taking whatever action was necessary to restore the salmon runs in the area, which had declined to a fraction of their historical levels (Verhovek 1999).

Assessing Biological Resources   Actions like these listings cannot be taken without a great deal of scientific knowledge to identify species and ecosystem functions that are at risk. The ecosystem management approach now favored by biologists and ecologists thus suggests the need for a significantly improved database of knowledge not only for actions under the ESA but for more effective natural resources management in general. That goal was a major reason for creating a new National Biological Service in the Department of Interior, which was folded into the department's U.S. Geological Survey (USGS) in 1996.

Initially renamed the Natural Resources Science Agency, the program was consolidated into a new Biological Resources division of the USGS. The USGS itself was established in 1879 and is now the nation's largest earth science research agency. The new agency was to consolidate scientific research in an effort to inventory and monitor all plant and animal species in the nation and their habitats. As part of that effort, the Biological Resources division established a National Biological Information Infrastructure, an electronic gateway to biological data and information maintained by federal, state, and local government agencies, private sector organizations, and other partners around the United States and the world.[32] A somewhat comparable private attempt to survey the nation's biological diversity found that the United States is home to more than twice as many native species (more than 200,000) than had been thought previously. The nation was also found to have a more diverse array of ecosystems than any other large country. This inventory of species was conducted over the past 25 years by survey centers in all 50 states, most of them part of state governments and universities. The centers were part of the Natural Heritage Network of the Nature Conservancy, the nation's largest private conservation group. The study also found that as many as a third of the nation's native species are imperiled to some extent and about 7 percent critically. One of the conservancy's scientists summed up the results this way: "We have an amazing amount of stuff. The bad news is that a lot of it is not in very good shape. But there is time to protect it" (Stevens 2000b).

In fall 2002 another private organization, the H. John Heinz III Center for Science, Economics and the Environment, released a new study on the state of the nation's ecosystems, with particular attention paid to gaps in knowledge about the country's lands, waters, and living resources (H. John Heinz III Center 2002). It proposed periodic measures of key ecological indicators in the hope that the information could inform the public and influence public policy decisions. The study reflected an unprecedented collaboration among 150 researchers from government, business, environmental groups, and universities, and it brings together in one place monitoring data from many independent sources. The online version provides access to the full report and offers an extraordinary diversity of information in easily readable form.[33]

Renewing the ESA and Resolving Conflicts   In an effort to appease opponents who repeatedly blocked renewal of the Endangered Species Act during the 1990s, the Clinton White House proposed a diversity of administrative changes intended to ensure that species recovery plans are "scientifically sound and sensitive to human needs." New scientific peer review processes were to be used, representation on planning bodies would be broadened, private landowners would be apprised early in the process about allowable actions, and multispecies listings and recovery plans would receive emphasis (New York Times 1994). In later attempts to accommodate private landowners, the administration strongly encouraged the use of habitat conservation plans on private lands, which hold an estimated 80 percent of all protected species. Such plans are voluntary yet binding agreements in which a landowner adopts conservation measures in exchange for the right to develop the property and a guarantee of "no surprises" with respect to future governmental restrictions on the land's use (Cushman 1998a).

None of this satisfied the ESA's critics in Congress. Over the years they have proposed a series of legislative changes that would give greater weight to the rights of property owners, provide additional incentives for their cooperation, and call for a higher standard of scientific evidence for demonstrating the status of species. As of early 2006, no proposals had attracted sufficient support to win congressional approval. Government scientists have been skeptical of the calls for relying on "sound science," saying such data often do not exist and the requirements would merely benefit those who lose when a species is protected. Environmentalists also complained that the argument is merely a smoke screen for efforts to weaken the ESA. In 2001 the chair of the House Resources Committee captured well the general dilemma of trying to amend the ESA when such diverse expectations and interests collide: "We have not reauthorized it because no one could agree on how to reform and modernize the law. Everyone agrees there are problems with the Act, but no one can agree on how to fix them."[34]

International Efforts to Protect Species   International agreements, especially the Convention on International Trade in Endangered Species (CITES), also play a role in protection of species. U.S. leadership led to approval of CITES (pronounced "cite teas"), which became effective in 1975. The agreement is overseen by the UN Environment Programme in cooperation with the nongovernmental International Union for the Conservation of Nature (IUCN) and the World Wildlife Fund (Caldwell 1996). Other private groups, such as the Nature Conservancy, contribute through negotiating land donations or outright purchase of habitats.

CITES is supposed to operate through a system of certificates and permits that restrict or prohibit international trade of species in different categories of protection (i.e., those threatened with extinction, those that may be threatened, or those whose exploitation should be prevented). Some 30,000 different species of plants and animals are regulated in this manner. As might be expected, it is has been difficult to meet the treaty's ambitious objectives. In particular, it has not succeeded in ending a continuing international market in animal smuggling, especially in Southeast Asia. Japan has been a particular target of environmentalist protest, and African nations have regularly argued with decisions related to protection of the elephant (Vaughn 2004).

The National Environmental Policy Act

Few people in 1969 anticipated the effects that the National Environmental Policy Act would have on decision making across the entire federal government. Yet since its adoption, this procedural policy has transformed expectations for the way government agencies should consider the effects of their actions on the environment. Its influence on land use decisions affecting natural resources has been particularly striking. NEPA's success owes much to the entrepreneurial use of the environmental impact statement process by environmentalists and administrative leaders to advance environmental values, both at the federal level and in parallel cases at state and local levels where similar impact assessments under "little NEPAs" are required (Bartlett 1989; Caldwell 1982, 1998). Some states, such as California and Washington, have been especially demanding in their requirements for impact statements for both state and private projects. Beyond its success in the United States, nearly 100 countries have adopted the environmental impact assessment provisions of NEPA, making it the most frequently copied U.S. statute.

NEPA's Goals and the EIS Process   Even with later amendments, NEPA remains a brief statute at about six pages. Section 101(a) of the act acknowledges the "profound impact of man's activity on the interrelations of all components of the natural environment" and the "critical importance of restoring and maintaining environmental quality to the overall welfare and development of man." The instrument for achieving those goals is the EIS process, which was to use "a systematic, interdisciplinary approach" to ensure the "integrated use of the natural and social sciences" in planning and decision making. As stated in section 102(2)(c), EISs are to offer a detailed statement on the environmental impact of the proposed action, any adverse environmental effects that cannot be avoided, alternatives to the action contemplated, the relationship between "local short-term uses" of the environment and the "maintenance and enhancement of long-term productivity," and any "irreversible and irretrievable commitments of resources" that the proposed action would require.

In addition, the statute calls for wide consultation with federal agencies and publication of the EIS for public review. The intent was not to block development projects, but to open and broaden the decision-making process. As was the case with protection of species under the ESA, few actions have been halted entirely. Instead, agencies follow one of two courses of action. The first is that they no longer even propose projects and programs that may have unacceptable impacts on the environment. The second is that when they do both propose and move ahead with projects and programs, they employ mitigation measures to eliminate or greatly reduce the environmental impacts.

Compliance and Policy Learning in the Bureaucracy   During the 1970s and 1980s, federal agencies grew accustomed to NEPA requirements and to public involvement in their decision making. Some, like the much-criticized U.S. Army Corps of Engineers, dramatically altered their behavior in the process (Mazmanian and Nienaber 1979). Others, such as the Department of Energy, made far less progress in adapting to the new norms of open and environmentally sensitive decision making. They serve as a reminder that statutes alone cannot bring about organizational change (Clary and Kraft 1989).

The Council on Environmental Quality (CEQ) has tried to help with the process of organizational adaptation. It is responsible under NEPA for supervising the EIS process, and it has worked closely with federal agencies through workshops and consultations to define their NEPA responsibilities. With a series of court rulings, CEQ regulations have also clarified the extent of the mandated EISs and the format to be used to enhance their utility. CEQ regulations distinguish environmental assessments (EAs) from EISs. The EAs are more limited in scope and more concise, and they are used when a project and its impacts do not require a full EIS under NEPA. Agencies also keep a Record of Decision (ROD), a public document that reflects the final decision, the rationale behind it, and commitments to monitoring and mitigation (Eccleston 1999).[35]

Administrative Challenges under NEPA   As noted, the EIS process has been used frequently by environmental groups to contest actions of natural resource agencies, such as the Forest Service and the Bureau of Land Management. That pattern continued throughout the 1990s and early 2000s. About 500 to 600 draft, final, and supplemental EISs were filed by all federal agencies each year, most prepared by the Department of Agriculture (forestry and range management), the Department of Transportation (highway construction), the Interior Department (parks, forests and range management, mining), and the U.S. Army Corps of Engineers. There are many more EAs than EISs prepared each year.

Unfortunately, many impact statements still fall short of the expectations for comprehensive and interdisciplinary assessments of likely environmental effects. Thus they disappoint those who have hoped the mandated administrative process would "make bureaucracies think" about the consequences of their actions. Some impacts have been ignored as unimportant, and others have proved hard to forecast accurately. Obviously, limited knowledge of biological, geological, and other natural systems constrains anyone's ability to forecast all significant impacts on the environment of development projects. Thus improvement of EISs will require expanded knowledge of ecosystem functioning as well as of related natural and social systems. For many projects, policymakers of necessity have to make decisions under conditions of some uncertainty.[36]

Partly because of these deficiencies, court cases under NEPA continue. According to the CEQ, in 2004, 150 cases were filed in which there was a NEPA claim against the federal government. The Agriculture Department was the most frequent defendant, followed by the Interior Department. The most common complaint over the years has been that no EIS was prepared when one should have been or that the EIS or EA was inadequate. The most frequent plaintiffs by far in these cases have been environmental groups and individual or citizen groups, as has been the case since 1970.

In a novel NEPA suit filed in late 2002, the city councils of Oakland, California, and Boulder, Colorado, joined Friends of the Earth and Greenpeace in challenging two federal agencies over their failure to conduct environmental reviews prior to funding projects that contribute to global climate change. The two agencies, the Export-Import Bank and the Overseas Private Investment Corporation, provided some $32 billion over the past decade for fossil-fuel extraction projects overseas (such as oil pipelines and coal-fired power plants) but did not assess the impact on climate change. The agencies said there was no impact, but they did not conduct any assessments to reach that conclusion. The suit sought to force the agencies to conduct such assessments in the future.[37]

Because NEPA has been used so effectively by environmentalists to challenge development projects, it has its share of critics. Responding to their concerns about delays in developments such as building a new dam or logging in federal forests, the Bush administration targeted NEPA for reform in ways that caused alarm among environmental groups. The administration asserted that environmentalists had abused NEPA by filing thousands of nuisance lawsuits that were intended to halt development. Therefore, as noted earlier in the discussion of U.S. forestland, it sought to streamline and speed up the NEPA process as it applied to highway and airport construction and logging of national forests, among other activities. It also sought a congressional exemption for certain agencies (particularly the Defense Department) from its requirements.[38] In addition, the administration tried to exempt most U.S.-controlled ocean waters from NEPA but lost that battle in federal court. In 2002 the CEQ established an interagency NEPA Task Force to review the law's effects and recommend changes in its implementation. That action created further suspicion among environmental groups while receiving strong endorsements from conservatives and development interests. Bush's CEQ chair, James Connaughton, argued that the task force sought to make NEPA more effective by increasing coordination and integration among government agencies, using better information technology to create and distribute documents, and creating more interaction with local interested parties.[39]

■ CONCLUSIONS

Much like environmental protection policy, criticisms of energy and natural resources policy are plentiful. They come in a variety of forms, as do the proposals for reform, and many of them were reviewed throughout the chapter. Some of the proposals are similar to those associated with environmental protection policy: for example, regulations should be more flexible to take into account local conditions and stakeholders should be given sufficient opportunity to voice their concerns. Also similar, but with environmentalists making the case this time, is that market incentives be used to improve environmental protection, particularly that user fees be set at a level that discourages environmental degradation and fosters sustainability. Improved scientific knowledge and better integration of decision making across programs and agencies are common suggestions here as well, and they are crucial to developing sufficient institutional capacity for ecosystem management and sustainable development. Some of these issues are discussed in Chapter 7.

As repeated efforts to devise acceptable and legal solutions to the protection of old-growth forest ecosystems in the Pacific Northwest attest, natural resource policies also require the development of creative ways to involve the American public in policy decisions that affect their communities and livelihoods while maintaining adherence to professional norms of natural resource management. Some would dismiss such hopes as unrealistic. Yet experience in the Pacific Northwest and elsewhere suggests the economic livelihood of rural communities can indeed be reconciled with resource conservation. It has been achieved through small-scale efforts to develop environmentally sound businesses and through the realization that the future economy of many communities depends more on maintenance of recreation and tourism opportunities than on traditional extractive industries. At this level, removed from the often bitter and ideological national debates over balancing the economy and the environment, new approaches seem to work (Mazmanian and Kraft 1999; Weber 2003).

No shortage of examples illustrates that development interests, environmentalists, and state and local officials can work together and resolve their differences (Johnson 1993; Koontz 2005; Wondolleck and Yaffee 2000). Local and regional ecological restoration efforts suggest similar possibilities. Examining the Chesapeake Bay Program, for instance, Knopman, Susman, and Landy (1999, 26) say that it "stands as a model of public–private partnerships, regional cooperation, and citizen engagement" and illustrates well the potential of such "civic environmentalism," although others disagree with that assessment (Ernst 2003). The authors point as well to the establishment of public land trusts across the nation, collaborative watershed councils in the Pacific Northwest, and similar local and regional environmental success stories involving collaboration among citizens, property owners, environmental action groups, and local, state, and federal agencies (see also Fairfax and Guenzler 2001; Sabatier et al. 2005). Other studies find comparable achievements through ad hoc and voluntary processes that have helped foster consensus in the creation of habitat conservation plans under the federal Endangered Species Act as well as build public support for restoration of degraded ecosystems, reclamation of contaminated mining sites in the West, smart-growth strategies in urban and suburban areas, and the redevelopment of contaminated urban land (Gottlieb 2001; Johnson 2006; Lowry 2006; Paehlke 2006; Portney 2003; Shutkin 2000).

These experiments in environmental mediation and collaborative decision making clearly are promising, even if obstacles remain in applying them on a larger scale. Such approaches may be particularly difficult to use when participants hold passionate and conflicting views about the values at stake, such as with protection of ecologically critical and aesthetically treasured wilderness areas; access to valuable timber, energy, water, and mineral sources; and protection of property rights and jobs in economic hard times. Many people will see little reason to compromise on what they consider to be fundamental principles. One conclusion is that to make sustainable development a reality over the next several decades requires a search for new ways to make these critical choices about our collective environmental future. This need is as vital in the many arenas outside government that shape energy and natural resources as it is within government itself.

DISCUSSION QUESTIONS

1. Why has it been so difficult for the federal government to adopt a comprehensive national energy policy? What might be done to increase public concern about energy issues and build support for energy policy?

2. The United States has long had substantial subsidies for the development and use of fossil fuels and nuclear power, but not to the same extent for renewable energy sources, energy efficiency, and conservation. What explains the different treatment of these energy sources? Should the federal and state governments provide comparable subsidies to spur development of alternative sources of energy such as wind power and solar power?

3. Most natural resource policies establish procedures for resolving conflicts between the objectives of economic development and conservation. What are the most promising ways to try to integrate these concerns and promote a transition to sustainable use of resources? For example, what kinds of decision-making

processes could help resolve conflicts over issues such as the use of snowmobiles in national parks, restrictions on timber harvesting or mining operations, or oil drilling in wildlife refuges?

4. Are the procedures established by the National Environmental Policy Act for conduct of environmental assessments and impact statements working well or not? Should those procedures be continued, or, as the Bush administration has proposed, should they be streamlined to permit faster action on economic development projects such as highway construction and logging operations?

5. The Endangered Species Act (ESA) has been faulted for giving too much weight to protection of threatened or endangered species and too little to the rights of property owners and others affected by decisions under the act. Should the ESA be changed to respond to these criticisms? Is there a way to alter it to make it both more effective in protecting species and biological diversity and also more acceptable to the public and the constituencies affected by it?

SUGGESTED READINGS

Brick, Philip D., and R. McGreggor Cawley, eds. *A Wolf in the Garden: The Land Rights Movement and the New Environmental Debate.* Lanham, MD: Rowman and Littlefield, 1996.

Davis, Charles, ed. *Western Public Lands and Environmental Politics,* 2nd ed. Boulder, CO: Westview Press, 2001.

Davis, David Howard. *Energy Politics,* 4th ed. New York: St. Martin's, 1993.

Lowry, William R. *The Capacity for Wonder: Preserving National Parks.* Washington, DC: Brookings Institution, 1994.

Sabatier, Paul, Will Focht, Mark Lubell, et al., eds. *Swimming Upstream: Collaborative Approaches to Watershed Management.* Cambridge, MA: MIT Press, 2005.

Wondolleck, Julia M., and Steven L. Yaffee. *Making Collaboration Work: Lessons from Innovation in Natural Resource Management.* Washington, DC: Island Press, 2000.

ENDNOTES

1. Norton announced her resignation in March 2006, saying she had accomplished much of what she sought to do as interior secretary. The press speculated that the many conflicts over natural resource policy had taken their toll on her. See Matthew L. Wald, "Key Player for President Is Resigning at Interior," *New York Times,* March 11, 2006, A11. President Bush named Idaho governor Dick Kempthorne as Norton's replacement.

2. For a review of the Bush administration record on natural resource policy, particularly the effort quietly to rewrite critical rules, see Felicity Barringer, "Bush Record: New Priorities in Environment," *New York Times,* September 14, 2004, 1, A18; and Joel Brinkley, "Out of Spotlight, Bush Overhauls U.S. Regulations," *New York Times,* August 14, 2004, 1, A10.

3. The DOE calculates only direct subsidies such as tax expenditures and research and development, not indirect subsidies such as highway construction. Still it found the annual subsidies to total about $5 billion in the early 1990s (Wald 1992) and about $4 billion in 1999. The studies are available at www.eia.doe.gov.

4. The target in 2002 was the small gas tax increase added in 1993 after the failure of President Clinton's proposed BTU tax (discussed later in the chapter). In late April 2006, Democrats called for a 60-day moratorium on collecting federal gasoline taxes, and Republicans favored reducing some of the tax breaks given to oil companies in the 2005 energy bill, discussed later. See Edmund L. Andrews and Michael Janofsky, "Second Thoughts in Congress on Oil Tax Breaks," *New York Times*, April 27, 2006, 1, C9.

5. For energy industry views, see the Web site for the Edison Electric Institute: www.eei.org. Issues ranging from clean air rules to climate change are covered at the site. See also the American Petroleum Institute at www.api.org and the American Coal Council at www.americancoalcouncil.org.

6. As noted in Chapter 2, one of the best sources for up-to-date statistics on energy use is DOE's Energy Information Administration: www.eia.doe.gov/. The site includes data on U.S. energy sources, historical patterns, and forecasts for future demand.

7. These figures reflect my own calculations of budgetary change in these periods, drawn from the annual federal budgets and adjusted for inflation.

8. National Research Council, *Effectiveness and Impact of Corporate Average Fuel Economy (CAFE) Standards*. Washington, DC: National Academy Press, 2001. Available online at www.nap.edu/catalog/10172.html.

9. White House press release, "The Greening of the White House: Saving Energy, Saving Money and Protecting Our Environment," December 2, 1999. On the same day, the White House announced new consumer incentives by major American corporations to help promote energy-efficient products. Among the companies were Best Buy, Home Depot, Maytag, Phillips Lighting, and Whirlpool.

10. See Matthew L. Wald, "U.S. Raises Standards on Mileage," *New York Times*, March 30, 2006, C1, 4. When the standards are fully phased in, they should produce a fuel savings of about 8 percent. For the first time, large SUVs weighing more than 8,500 pounds will be covered by mileage standards.

11. See Matthew L. Wald, "Clinton Energy-Saving Rules Are Getting a Second Look," *New York Times*, March 31, 2001, A9. By November 2005 the DOE was also widely criticized for its failure to issue any new energy efficiency standards for household appliances. It has repeatedly missed congressionally set deadlines for water heaters, dryers, furnaces, and many other products. In the absence of DOE action, the states have become the real force behind improved appliance efficiency. See Ben Evans, "Calls for Conservation Are, So Far, Just Calls," *CQ Weekly*, November 7, 2005, 2968–69.

12. Joseph Kahn, "U.S. Scientists See Big Power Savings from Conservation," *New York Times*, May 6, 2001, online edition.

13. The NRDC plan is posted on its Web site: www.nrdc.org. The Union of Concerned Scientists study can be found at its site: www.ucsusa.org. The ACEEE report can be found at www.aceee.org

14. Chuck McCutcheon, "House Passage of Bush Energy Plan Sets Up Clash with Senate," *CQ Weekly*, August 4, 2001, 1915–17.

15. See David E. Rosenbaum, "Senate Passes an Energy Bill Called Flawed by Both Sides," *New York Times*, April 26, 2002, A16.

16. Bush differed less from Reagan on natural resources issues than he did on environmental protection. His appointees to natural resources agencies were similar to Reagan's.

17. For a fuller description of natural resources policy, see Mangun and Henning (1999) and Davis (2001); for a more historical assessment, see Andrews (1999) and Klyza (1996).

18. Federal authority to regulate land use comes from the Constitution, Article 4, Section 3, which gives Congress the "power to dispose of and make all needful rules and regulations respecting the territory or other property belonging to the United States."

19. For a news summary of the report, see William K. Stevens, "Sprawl Quickens Its Attack on Forests," *New York Times*, December 7, 1999, D6. The National Resources Inventory report, released in 1999 and revised in late 2000, is available at www.nrcs.usda.gov/technical/NRI/. Specific inventories for land use, wetlands, soil erosion, urbanization, and the like, are available in separate documents, some of which are newer.

20. The committee's report was not without controversy. Some ecologists and foresters questioned whether sustainability is a clear enough concept to serve such a purpose, and others saw such a priority-setting exercise as an inherently political choice that ultimately must be made by Congress. See Charles C. Mann and Mark L. Plummer, "Calls for 'Sustainability' in Forests Sparks a Fire," *Science* 283 (March 26, 1999): 1996–98.

21. Felicity Barringer, "Administration Overhauls Rules for U.S. Forests," *New York Times*, December 23, 1, A18. For the earlier history of the rules, see Robert Pear, "Bush Plan Given More Discretion to Forest Managers on Logging," New York Times, November 28, 2002, 1, A27.

22. See Barringer, "Bush Record," and Brinkley, "Out of the Spotlight."

23. President Clinton proposed the $1 billion Lands Legacy initiative in his fiscal 2000 budget, and he increased the requested funds to $1.4 billion for fiscal 2001. More than half of the funding was to go to state and local conservation efforts. For news coverage, see Kriz (1999b) and Pope (1999b). The details are in a White House press release, "Lands Legacy: Lasting Protection for America's Natural Treasures," February 7, 2000.

24. One of the best Web sites for keeping up with activities affecting wilderness areas is www.wilderness.net/. The National Wilderness Preservation System is covered in some detail at the site.

25. Felicity Barringer, "Bush Administration Rolls Back Rule on Building Forest Roads," New York Times, May 6, 2005, A14. For a broader assessment of differences in forest decision making at the state and federal level, see Koontz (2002).

26. Jim Robbins, "Gone! Snowmobile Herds and Tourists," *New York Times*, February 28, 2006, A12.

27. Blaine Harden, "National and State Politics Help Safeguard a Swamp," *New York Times*, April 3, 2002, 1, A14.

28. Douglas Jehl, "Wildlife and Derricks Coexist, But the Question Is the Cost," *New York Times*, February 20, 2001, 1, A14. For a discussion of natural gas drilling proposed for Padre Island National Seashore in Texas, see Blaine Harden, "Approval of Park Drilling Angers Environmentalists," *New York Times*, November 22, 2002, A16.

29. A summary and more detailed accounts can be found at the Web site for the Fish and Wildlife Service: www.fws.gov/. The site also includes U.S. regulations pertaining to endangered species, habitat conservation plans, and similar information.

30. For an extended treatment of the prominent northern spotted owl case, see Yaffee (1994). Several of the key court cases over the owl are highlighted in O'Leary

(2006). For an update on the effects of the Northern Forest Plan that was to protect 9.8 million hectares of federal land in California, Oregon, and Washington while also providing for timber harvests, see Erik Stokstad, "Learning to Adapt," *Science* 309 (July 29, 2005): 688–90. The plan seems to be working. Timber harvests did decline, as did jobs in the industry. But the region gained many more jobs than were lost, and except for some rural communities, the area did not suffer economically.

31. For the Snake River story, see Kriz (2000a). The governor was quoted in "Saving the Snake River Salmon," *New York Times,* April 2, 2000, Week in Review, 14. For a broader review of controversies over removal of dams across the nation, see Pope (1999a), Baish, David, and Graf (2002), and Lowry (2003).

32. The Web site for the new program is www.nbii.gov/.

33. The report is available at www.heinzctr.org/ecosystems. The report also lists selected ecological indicators and Web sites for the nation as a whole and for selected ecosystems, watersheds, states, and communities.

34. Cited in *Science and Environmental Policy Update,* the Ecological Society of America online newsletter, April 20, 2001. For an update on conflicts over the act in Congress, see Felicity Barringer, "Endangered Species Act Faces Broad New Challenges," *New York Times,* June 26, 2005, A18.

35. The Council on Environmental Quality maintains a NEPA Net, with the full text of the statute, current regulations and guidance documents, statistics regarding NEPA and its impacts, an overall evaluation of NEPA, and links to other Web sites: http://ceq.eh.doe.gov/nepa/nepanet.htm. See also the EPA Web site for NEPA implementation: www.epa.gov/compliance/nepa/index.html.

36. For a review of NEPA's application and assessments of its effects on environmental decision making, see a symposium edited by Bartlett and Malone (1993), and a special issue of the journal *Environmental Practice* on NEPA (December 2003). See also Caldwell (1998). All EISs prepared by federal agencies are filed with the EPA and available through the agency's Web site.

37. Katharine Q. Seelye, "Western Cities Join Suit to Fight Global Warming," *New York Times,* December 24, 2002, A16. Oakland officials have concerns about rising sea levels and Boulder officials are worried about a diminishing snowpack that could affect the city's water supply.

38. See Michael Janofsky, "Pentagon Is Asking Congress to Loosen Environmental Laws," *New York Times,* May 11, 2005, A14. For the military, the administration argued that NEPA and other environmental laws seriously interfere with military readiness and training. The military spends about $4 billion a year to comply with various environmental laws. The Pentagon argued that the money could be better spent for direct military preparedness.

39. The task force has its own Web page at http://ceq.eh.doe.gov/ntf/. For a discussion of the controversies raised by the Bush initiatives on NEPA, see an extensive article by Margaret Kriz: "Bush's Quiet Plan," *National Journal,* November 23, 2002, 3472–79.

Evaluating Environmental Policy

By any measure, the next several decades present significant challenges for environmental and natural resource policies, both within the United States and worldwide. The previous chapters examined many of these challenges, from public exposure to toxic chemicals to loss of biological diversity and the threat of devastating global climate change. They also surveyed the policy actions taken by different levels of government in response to these problems and described some of the policy achievements and deficiencies. As we saw, disagreements often arise over whether to continue present policies, such as the Clean Air Act or the Endangered Species Act, or change them in some way. If policy change is the likely course of action, many possible directions are available. The promise of such change can be seen in the success of many different kinds of policy innovations at the state and local level discussed in previous chapters. But changing a policy does not guarantee improved performance. Much depends on how carefully the new policy is designed and carried out.

This chapter builds on the previous discussions to make a case for evaluation of current environmental policies as well as assessment of the policy alternatives that are commonly suggested to complement or replace them. Chapter 8 continues this focus by examining the third generation of environmental policy and the long-term goal of sustainable development, particularly at the international level.

■ CRITIQUES OF ENVIRONMENTAL POLICY

Concern over the effectiveness, efficiency, or equity of modern environmental policy is not new. It dates back at least to the late 1970s during the Carter administration, and it was a prominent feature of Ronald Reagan's presidency during the 1980s (Vig and Kraft 2006). The distinction today is that dissatisfaction with environmental and natural resource policies is far more widespread and persistent than it was in the past.

As we saw in Chapters 5 and 6, business and industry groups have long complained that the nation imposes excessive costs and other burdens on society. A common argument is that government may overregulate in an effort to deal with relatively minor risks to public health and the environment. In doing so, it may place unnecessary costs on individual firms and the economy as a whole. State and local governments struggling to meet federal environmental mandates have demanded greater flexibility and increased federal funds to cope with their manifold responsibilities. Natural resource users such as ranchers, loggers, miners, and farmers fight to prevent what they view as precipitous and unwarranted loss of federal subsidies that have helped assure them of financial success. Workers in those industries and the communities in which they live often blame environmental policies (and environmentalists) for threatening their economic livelihood.

Analysts at conservative and libertarian think tanks such as the Heritage Foundation, the Competitive Enterprise Institute, and the Cato Institute tend to object in principle to regulation and natural resources decision making dominated by the federal government. As an alternative, they favor shifting environmental responsibilities to state and local levels and reliance on private markets (Anderson and Leal 1997, 2001; Greve and Smith 1992; Higgs and Close 2005). They are joined in many of these positions by supporters of the property rights and wise use movements, and they have enjoyed strong support for their positions in the administration of George W. Bush.[1]

Environmentalists are unhappy as well, but for different reasons. They applaud the strong policies adopted since the 1960s, but they argue that too frequently environmental protection measures are compromised and weakly enforced by public officials insufficiently committed to their goals. They also believe that providing too much regulatory flexibility can encourage industry to evade the law and thus slow achievement of environmental goals (Schoenbrod 2005). They fear as well that some of the new approaches used in natural resources management, such as collaborative decision making, may tilt excessively toward development at the expense of ecosystem health.

Some of these criticisms have more merit than others, but all should be taken seriously. Since 1970 both government and industry have invested large sums of money in scientific research, technological development, and pollution control and abatement. Total federal spending on environmental and natural resource policies in the past several years has been about $30 billion a year (Vig and Kraft 2006). As noted earlier, however, the private sector and state and local governments pay most of the costs of complying with federal environmental protection policies. That cost doubled between 1970 and 1995 (CEQ 1999), and is now about $200 billion per year; it is likely to continue to increase. Comparable costs and burdens are associated with natural resource policies. It is reasonable to ask, therefore, as many critics do, what such expenditures bring the public in return. Are the costs justifiable in light of the goals of environmental policies and their achievements? Will they continue to be in the future?

Economic efficiency is not the only standard by which to judge environmental policies, although it is an important one. Using other criteria, such as equity or environmental justice or the extent of public participation, analysts, policymakers, and citizens often ask which policies and programs have proven to be the most successful and which the least (Beardsley, Davies, and Hersh 1997; Bennear and Coglianese 2005; Knaap and Kim 1998). What effects have they had, and what are the implications for redesigning environmental policies for the twenty-first century? These kinds of questions were highlighted in the framework introduced in Chapter 1.

Much of the debate today centers on whether the command-and-control regulation adopted during the first era of environmental policies should be reformed. Should the nation rely more on market incentives, provision of greater flexibility in implementation and enforcement, and devolution of responsibility to the states? Would doing so make environmental policy less costly, more acceptable to society, and more effective in achieving policy objectives? Equally significant is the broader task of formulating new environmental and resource policies that can steer the nation and world toward the long-term goal of sustainable development (Mazmanian and Kraft 1999). The complex and formidable third generation of environmental problems, such as climate change and loss of biodiversity, will thoroughly test our capacity to design, adopt, and implement such policies (see Chapter 8).

■ ENVIRONMENTAL POLICY EVALUATION

There is not much debate over the need to evaluate how well environmental policies are working, or how efficient they are, or how equitable they are. Environmentalists, policymakers, public health experts, business leaders, and academic students of environmental policy all agree on this score. They also advance many different arguments for conducting and using such evaluations to improve environmental policies. One is that environmental policies can be costly, as we have seen, not only for government but also for industry and others who must comply with resulting regulations. Thus it is reasonable to ask if the policies are achieving their goals, and at a reasonable cost to society. A second is that because of high and continuing federal deficits, government budgetary resources are likely to remain scarce in the future. With limited money available, evaluations can help in making decisions about where best to invest those funds, that is, on how to set priorities. A third is that many environmental and natural resource policies and programs are technically complex, making it difficult to determine how well they are working, particularly in the short term. In such cases, formal or systematic evaluations can provide better answers than available otherwise. Such information might also provide some assurance to the public that the policies or programs are on the right track.

Even if nearly everyone thinks that such evaluations are a good idea, the reality is they come in many different forms. Some are more reliable and useful than others. For example, the U.S. Government Accountability Office (GAO) is noted for its rigorous assessment of environmental and energy programs, as are panels of the National Academy of Sciences. Similarly, some prominent think tanks, such as Resources for the Future, the Brookings Institution, and the National Academy of Public Administration (NAPA), provide comprehensive and sound evaluations of government programs; many also propose innovative ideas for policy reforms (Harrington, Morgenstern, and Sterner 2004; Kettl 2002; Morgenstern and Portney 2004; NAPA 1995, 2000).

Other evaluations, however, may not live up to the high standards set by these kind of organizations. Congressional committees may conduct oversight hearings or initiate limited investigations of the EPA or other government agencies and issue reports and recommendations of varying quality. Environmental groups such as the Sierra Club or the Natural Resources Defense Council issue their own critiques of government programs and offer alternatives, and business organizations do the same.

Many of these were discussed in previous chapters. The best of these kinds of studies gather extensive scientific data and analyze the results objectively. Others, however, may more closely resemble partisan or ideological posturing on programs and agencies. Given the variable standards that are applied in such evaluations, policies and programs that some (e.g., conservative groups) judge to be failures are likely to be considered ringing successes by others (e.g., environmental groups). Because of these differences, evaluations and studies that recommend new directions in environmental policy need to be read critically and not simply accepted at face value.

What is the best way to determine whether environmental policies are working well and to consider whether policy alternatives would work better? In theory, evaluation of policies and programs is straightforward. One would specify a policy or program's goals and objectives. Appropriate measures of those goals and objectives would be developed, and pertinent data would be collected and analyzed. The resulting information would be carefully considered by policymakers and others interested in the policies and programs. Those deemed to be successful would be kept and those that are failures would be reformed or eliminated.

In reality, assessing environmental policy is more complex. It can also be a deeply political process. There are winners and losers in policy choices, and each side is likely to take an active interest in any efforts to evaluate policies and programs that affect them. Think about federal subsidies to agricultural, mining, and timber industries and how important they are to the beneficiaries. Or consider how the trucking industry or coal-fired power plants would be affected by changes in the Clean Air Act, or how environmental groups would respond to proposals to reduce federal support for energy conservation and renewable energy research. Supporters may shield some programs from critical assessment, whereas those that are politically vulnerable may have repeated evaluations thrust upon them by well-placed critics in Congress or the executive branch, or their equivalents at state and local levels.

None of these constraints diminishes the genuine need for serious environmental policy and program evaluations (Knaap and Kim 1998). Their value lies in contributing to systematic, critical, and independent thinking in the policy-making process. In addition, the Government Performance and Results Act (GPRA) of 1993 requires that all existing programs be evaluated regularly and their performance or achievements be demonstrated. The act encourages agencies to focus on results, service quality, and public satisfaction, and it requires both annual performance plans and annual performance reports.

Evaluation generally means appraising the merit of governmental processes and programs. The term *policy evaluation* usually refers to judging the worth or effects of public policies. It may include an assessment of policy goals or the means used to achieve them (such as regulation versus market incentives), an analysis of the process of implementation (such as federal–state relations in enforcement actions), or an appraisal of their effects (e.g., how much they cost and the value of the benefits they provide).

Program evaluation is a more specialized term. It means judging the success of programs that have already been approved and have been implemented and, especially, determining whether and how they affect the problems to which they are directed. Among other effects, analysts seek to learn how programs alter individual and corporate behavior (e.g., actions to comply with environmental laws), how they change the way decisions are made (such as encouraging public involvement or collaboration at the local level), and especially whether over time they improve environmental quality itself.

Most environmental evaluations understandably focus on what analysts call program *outcomes*, the actual effects of public policies on environmental conditions. These outcomes are distinguished from program *outputs*, which are agency decisions made under the law, such as the number of inspections made, administrative orders issued, or other enforcement actions taken. Even when done properly, however, looking at environmental outcomes such as air and water quality or improvements in ecosystem health is not sufficient. To get a fuller picture of how environmental programs are working and what might be changed to improve them requires an examination of how decisions are made and how well institutions perform (Bartlett 1994; Knaap and Kim 1998).

Program Outcomes

In outcomes evaluation, analysts compare measures of environmental quality outcomes with policy objectives. In effect, they are asking whether the air and water are cleaner, the drinking water safer, the hazardous waste sites cleaned up, and endangered species protected. Chapter 2 reviewed these kinds of data, and references throughout the text (particularly in the endnotes, tables, and boxes) indicate where you may obtain current data on agency and other organization Web sites. However, evaluating environmental policies by using such indicators of public or ecological health is almost never as simple as imagined. Experts may disagree about which environmental indicators are most appropriate, the necessary data may not be available or sufficient, and there may be questions of how to interpret the data (Ringquist 1995).

Many questions arise about how to conduct such evaluations, and thus both proponents and critics of environmental programs can use outcome measures to demonstrate either impressive policy achievements or serious shortcomings. As Chapter 2 indicated, much depends on the indicators that are chosen, the time period for which data are collected, and how the evidence is assessed. The conclusions that are reached may have profound implications for agency management and program implementation, redirection of program priorities and spending, or decisions to change the policy itself. Thus it is important to get the evaluations right.

Examining Decision Making and Institutions

As important as policy outcomes are, they are not everything. Many analysts also ask about whether there has been sufficient public participation, whether decisions are well grounded in science and economic analysis, whether a program (such as federal wilderness protection) is being implemented at the right level of government, or whether an agency has sufficient resources to implement the policy successfully. All of these questions suggest the need for a different kind of evaluation that focuses not on environmental outcomes but on decision-making processes and on the characteristics of government institutions. Analysts sometimes refer to these as *process evaluations* and *institutional evaluations*. The first attempts to evaluate the merit of decision-making processes themselves, such as opportunities that are provided for public involvement (Bartlett 1990; Beierle and Cayford 2002; Dryzek 1987). Advocates of environmental justice, for instance, argue strongly for community participation in evaluation of hazardous or nuclear waste threats (Bullard 1994; Kraft 1996, 2000; Ringquist 2006). The second asks about the strengths and weaknesses of the institutions charged with implementing environmental policies. For example, does an agency have sufficient capacity to handle its policy responsibilities, or are the states able to take on additional duties if current federal powers are further devolved to them? How strongly does the agency enforce current law? Is the agency well managed, and does it develop good working relationships with key stakeholders so that it can be more successful (Durant, Fiorino, and O'Leary 2004; Scheberle 2004)?

▥ SIGNS OF PROGRESS

Using all three forms of evaluation gives a more complete and realistic picture than is possible by examining outcomes alone. In this section, we consider selective evidence on outcomes, decision making, and institutions. The discussion draws especially from the outcome measures presented in Chapter 2, and to a lesser extent in Chapters 5 and 6. That evidence suggests progress has been made in meeting environmental quality goals in some areas while falling short in others. As the earlier reviews indicated, no simple generalization can capture the full story across all environmental protection and natural resource policies. Yet a strong case can be made that conditions would likely be substantially worse today if the major environmental policies had not been in place.

Environmental Protection Policies

Such a conclusion is particularly valid for air and water pollution control, where enormous gains have been recorded since the early 1970s. Even better results might have been obtained in these and other areas had sufficient resources been provided to the EPA and state agencies, had the programs been better managed, had the federal government established better working relations with the states, and had less time been spent by all parties in lengthy and contentious administrative and legal proceedings.

Where additional improvement must be made, for example, in controlling toxic chemicals, cleaning up abandoned waste sites, and reducing hazardous air pollutants, these conclusions should inspire at least some confidence in the regulatory approaches that have been so widely disparaged since the early 1980s. They should also help suggest the kinds of policy and administrative changes that might improve the effectiveness and efficiency of environmental policies and yield better results in the future. Economists in particular have argued that many provisions of environmental policies would be difficult to defend in terms of economic efficiency, whereas others could easily pass muster on that standard (Fischbeck and Farrow 2001; Portney and Stavins 2000).

For example, hazardous waste remediation at both private sites and government facilities, such as former nuclear weapons plants and military installations, will tax the resolve and resources of government and industry for decades to come. For the very large number of sites needing cleanup, as noted earlier in the text, the nation will spend hundreds of billions of dollars over the next 30 to 50 years in pursuit of that goal (Probst and Konisky 2001; Probst and Lowe 2000). The scope of these activities demands that programs be well designed and managed and the funds be used efficiently. Yet evaluations by the GAO, the Office of Technology Assessment, and independent analysts have long criticized remediation efforts on nearly all counts, from ineffective use of contractors to handle the cleanup tasks to insufficient provision for public involvement in decision making. Clearly, the nation needs to do a better job (Kraft 1994b).

Perhaps the greatest environmental policy success has been recorded in air pollution control. As discussed in Chapter 2, most of the key indicators show that emissions and concentrations of pollutants have declined impressively and that air quality has been improving nationwide. The latest reports on air quality from the EPA confirm the long-term trend despite continued population and economic growth and increased reliance on the automobile (U.S. EPA 2003, 2005). At least some of the improvement is clearly attributable to enforcement of the Clean Air Act.

State-level studies support this argument. Ringquist's comparison of the 50 states concluded that "strong air quality programs result in decreased levels of pollutant emissions" even when controlling for other variables such as the states' economy and politics. The stronger programs produce greater reductions in ambient air pollutants. Enforcement is a key factor. States that vigorously enforce controls on stationary sources have lower emissions. The most important variables are consistency in enforcement and well-focused and well-supported administrative efforts (Ringquist 1993, 150–51). The states would be less effective in producing such outcomes without a powerful federal EPA to back them up as a so-called gorilla in the closet and thus spur enforcement actions that regulated parties will take seriously.

Some of these same conclusions apply to water pollution control. The nation's water quality has improved significantly since the 1960s thanks to the Clean Water Act and the Safe Drinking Water Act. Progress here, however, has been much more uneven and slower in coming than in air quality. As highlighted in Chapter 2, there have been substantial reductions in discharge of pollutants from point sources and advances in drinking water quality, particularly in cities. In contrast, controlling nonpoint sources has enjoyed only minimal success and remains a major focus of current water quality program efforts. Groundwater quality in many areas continues to deteriorate as well (U.S. EPA 2002b). These conditions help explain Ringquist's (1993) findings that states with stronger and more comprehensive water quality programs experienced no greater improvement in stream quality over the time period he studied.

The picture is similarly mixed on toxic chemicals and cleanup of hazardous waste sites. The EPA's annual Toxics Release Inventory shows important reductions in releases of toxic chemicals by major industrial sources (thanks to mandatory public disclosure of emissions data). Other pollution prevention programs, from the EPA's 33/50 effort to reduce releases of the most dangerous chemicals to the agency's Energy Star energy efficiency program, have had significant success (Press and Mazmanian 2006). Even cleanup actions under Superfund arguably have accomplished far more than usually acknowledged.

In these and other programs, deficiencies in the major environmental protection policies have hardly gone unnoticed. Dozens of studies by academics, research institutes, environmental groups, and business organizations have provided detailed criticism and recommendations for policy change. Many of these studies have been harshly critical of the command-and-control policies adopted in the 1970s as ineffective, inefficient, and overly intrusive, and they have recommended greater use of a diversity of new approaches. Such approaches range from public education and market incentives to greater decentralization of environmental responsibilities to states and communities (e.g., Davies and Mazurek 1998; Fiorino 2006; National Academy of Public Administration 1995, 2000; Portney and Stavins 2000; Sexton et al. 1999).

Particularly at the national level, policymakers have had at their disposal abundant critical analyses and proposals for policy change. Nonetheless, as indicated in Chapter 5, members of Congress have been unable to agree on how to rewrite most of the key statutes to address the concerns and recommendations from these studies. Hence the deficiencies in these programs remain, and both the EPA and the states have struggled to adopt at least some of the new policy recommendations through administrative means (Durant, Fiorino, and O'Leary 2004; Vig and Kraft 2006).

Natural Resource Policies

Judging the success of natural resource policies is no easier than determining whether clean air and clean water policies are working. The kinds of measures often used here—acres of "protected lands" set aside in national parks and wilderness areas, the number of annual visitors to national parks, and the like—are useful but highly imperfect indicators of the policy goals of providing recreational opportunities, preserving aesthetic values, and especially protecting ecological systems. Other yardsticks can be used for the economic functions of natural resource policies such as ensuring the availability of sufficient rangeland, timber, minerals, water, and energy resources. As discussed in Chapter 6, natural resource agencies such as the National Park Service, the Forest Service, and the Fish and Wildlife Service (FWS) report regularly on these activities. Such reports permit some modest assessment of important qualities of U.S. natural resources policy, its achievements and its shortcomings.

For example, since 1964 Congress has set aside 106 million acres in the National Wilderness Preservation System, and since 1968 it has designated over 10,800 protected miles in the Wild and Scenic Rivers System. The FWS manages about 93 million acres in the National Wildlife Refuge System, which is *triple* the land area of 1970. The National Park System grew from about 25 million acres in 1960 to over 83 million acres by the early 2000s, and it *doubled* the number of units in the system.

If such results suggest impressive dedication to setting aside land in a protected status and meeting the recreational needs of the American public, there are some equally troublesome statistics in the government's reports. The nation continues to lose ecologically critical wetlands to development. Despite the encouraging signs of growth in acreage and visits to national parks, plenty of problems remain, from congestion and crime to air pollution from nearby power plants and threats from other developments.

In some respects, the Endangered Species Act (ESA) is typical of the halting progress and widely disparate assessments of resource policies. Although there have been impressive achievements in listing species and establishment of habitat conservation plans, the act has saved few species, and it is not preventing the loss of habitats and continued degradation of ecosystems. Moreover, in a 2006 report, the GAO concluded that the success of the act "is difficult to measure" because recovery plans indicate that species might not be recovered for up to 50 years. Hence the GAO concluded that "simply counting the number of extinct and recovered species periodically or over time" may not tell us much about the overall success of the recovery programs (U.S. GAO 2006). Part of the explanation for the act's limited success to date lies in a chronic and severe shortfall in budgets and staff for doing the work mandated under the act. The design of the ESA itself is also to blame, as is the tendency of the FWS to concentrate its limited resources on charismatic species that attract public support. Moreover, the ESA has run into furious political opposition because it exemplifies for many the threat that government regulation can pose to property rights and development projects. Such conflicts have impeded its success.

Data Assessment and Public Dialogue

Aside from such compilations of annual losses and gains in resource use, as the ESA example illustrates, policy conflicts continue over the core question of how to balance economic development and environmental preservation. These controversies exist despite much more frequent use by both government and the business community of the concept of sustainable development. Whether the issue is offshore oil and gas drilling, hard rock mining on public lands, grazing rights and fees, agriculture and water use, or preservation of old-growth forests, the choices often pit environmentalists against resource industries and local communities. Disputes over old-growth forest ecosystems and how best to protect them were particularly acute during the 1990s, with the northern spotted owl playing a highly visible, if largely symbolic, role.

As discussed in Chapter 6, however, many communities and regions have developed new approaches to resource management that bring together environmentalists, citizens, development interests, and public officials in ways that often promote consensus over local development and environmental issues (Lubell 2004; Sabatier et al. 2005; Weber 2003; Wondolleck and Yaffee 2000). These success stories speak to the potential for more widespread public dialogue over natural resources and environmental protection. Yet for such public involvement to succeed, better indicators of ecosystem functioning and health are needed.

In that regard, among the most striking omissions in efforts to evaluate environmental protection and natural resource programs are reliable measures of ecosystem health. Ecologists are not entirely in agreement on what it means to call an ecosystem healthy or sustainable, and controversy exists as well over the most appropriate ecological indicators to use (Harris and Scheberle 1998). Yet there is little question that such measures of ecosystem functioning and health are essential if changes over time in national forests, rangelands, parks, wilderness areas, and other public and private lands are to be tracked (Heinz Center 2002; O'Malley and Wing 2000). How do we know, for example, if local land use controls promote healthy rivers, lakes, and bays if we have no way to measure the health of water bodies and the organisms they contain? At a minimum there needs to be more regular monitoring of critical ecosystem functions and assessment of what the data mean. Unfortunately, that may be difficult to do as recent budget cuts hinder the collection of such data (Schwartz 2006).

The very idea of ecosystem management is based on the assumption that we can learn how ecosystems function and how they respond to changing stressors in the environment (Cortner and Moote 1999). Similarly, the movement toward sustainable communities and regions is predicated on the belief that we can develop meaningful indicators of ecosystem functioning, say within watersheds. The pursuit of sustainable communities depends as well on the selection of appropriate and publicly acceptable measures of the communities' social and economic health, which in some ways is equally challenging (Mazmanian and Kraft 1999; Portney 2003; Wackernagel and Rees 1996).

Agencies, environmental groups, and scientists can help promote citizen involvement and collaborative decision making by assisting the public in understanding the data being produced and by facilitating discussion of what the information means. Such assistance and community dialogue are particularly crucial at local and regional levels, where citizens may be poorly equipped to assess environmental and other community problems and decide how best to deal with them. Scientists are often reluctant to play such an active role in public affairs, yet forecasts of dire environmental trends have prompted numerous pleas from prominent scientists for the scientific community to become far more engaged in precisely these kinds of activities (Lubchenco 1998; Rowland 1993).

▓ COSTS, BENEFITS, AND RISKS

The improvements in air and water quality since 1970, and other signs of progress in environmental and natural resources policy, are welcome news. Yet such findings do not address some of the major criticisms directed at those policies. One of the most important is that environmental gains come at too high a cost—in money, jobs, property rights, freedom to choose—and that alternative approaches such as market incentives or providing greater flexibility to industry and state and local governments would allow for achievement of the same environmental quality at a lower cost to society (Freeman 1990, 2006; Portney and Stavins 2000). Portney has expressed the argument succinctly:

> How then do we distinguish wise from unwise policy proposals? The answer is at once very simple and very complicated. In my view, desirable regulations are those that promise to produce positive effects (improved human health, ecosystem protection, aesthetic amenities) that, when considered qualitatively yet carefully by our elected and appointed officials, more than offset the negative consequences that will result (higher prices to consumers, possible plant closures, reduced productivity). In other words, wise regulations are those that pass a kind of common-sense benefit–cost test. (1994, 22–23)

According to Portney, economic research demonstrates that the nation can meet present environmental goals for perhaps as little as 50 percent of the annual cost of complying with federal environmental regulations. Even if the amount saved is well less than 50 percent, it could nevertheless be substantial. Such reductions can be achieved, Portney says, through an explicit, although *qualitative* and open, weighing of costs and benefits in the policy process (a process that compensates for the limitations of quantitative cost–benefit analysis). Some stringent environmental regulations could easily survive such a test (e.g., removal of lead from gasoline and the phaseout of CFCs are two historical examples), whereas others might not.

These kinds of arguments for considering economic costs are hard to dismiss. Objections can certainly be raised to relying uncritically on formal cost–benefit analysis or risk assessment, and environmentalists and many others have done so (O'Brien 2000; Swartzman, Liroff, and Croke 1982; Tong 1986). In 2005, for example, the GAO identified four significant shortcomings in the EPA's economic analysis of its proposed options for controlling release of mercury, including a failure to estimate "the value of the health benefits directly related to decreased mercury emissions." The agency concluded that those weaknesses limited the usefulness of the analysis for policymakers (U.S. GAO 2005c). Despite such examples of poor analysis, it is difficult to argue that costs and benefits of environmental policies should not be considered at all or should be given little weight. As Portney and many other critics have suggested, at a minimum society has to confront some inescapable trade-offs between environmental regulation and other forms of economic investment. Money spent on the environment is not available in the short run for other social purposes such as education or health care. Even the promise of sustainable development cannot entirely eliminate such choices, however much it might point to myriad ways to better reconcile environmental protection and economic growth and to the prospect of full compatibility of economic and ecological goals in the long run.

The trade-offs become starker as environmental management deals with marginal gains in environmental quality. That is, as we reduce pollutants to small residual amounts, the marginal dollar cost of each additional unit of improvement can rise sharply (Freeman 2006; Tietenberg 2006a). The tendency of legislators to draft what economists call "absolutist" and unrealistic goals such as "zero discharge" or "lowest achievable emissions" does not take into account such marginal costs. Nor is public support for environmental protection informed by such economic thinking. With costs of environmental protection continuing to rise, the case for reconsidering such goals is compelling.

Comparing Risks and Setting Priorities

A variant of the argument for making greater use of cost–benefit analysis or its close cousin, cost-effectiveness analysis, as we saw earlier, is to use comparative risk assessment in which health and environmental risks are ranked to allow for the setting of policy priorities. The EPA has argued repeatedly since its initial report in 1987, *Unfinished Business*, for risk-based priority setting. Its 1990 study, *Reducing Risk*, made the case convincingly and reached a large audience of influential policymakers (U.S. EPA 1990b).

The agency's Science Advisory Board, which wrote the 1990 study, concluded that the EPA should target its environmental protection efforts, or set priorities, on the basis of opportunities for the greatest risk reduction, using "all the tools available to reduce risk" (such as public education and market incentives as well as regulation). Too often, the report noted, environmental statutes and agency decisions emphasize some risks of relatively little import while neglecting others of much greater magnitude. The report urged that more attention be given to ecological as well as to public health risks, improving the data and methodologies for risk assessment, emphasizing pollution prevention, and improving public understanding of environmental risks to assist in the national effort to redirect priorities.

Subsequent analyses of environmental protection policies have emphasized the same line of argument (Andrews 2006; Davies 1996; National Academy of Public

Administration 1995, 2000; Sexton et al. 1999). This is the core question: If available resources are limited, how can they best be used to minimize public health risks and promote environmental quality? The premise here is that although environmental policies may reduce risks, some are far more efficient at doing so than others. Thus, depending on which programs are well funded and which regulations are aggressively enforced, governments and private parties can spend a great deal of money without a concomitant return in risk reduction. That is, the public's health and the quality of the environment may not be improved enough to justify the actions taken.

Some environmental protection efforts could easily withstand such a comparative risk test. Examples include regulating urban smog, fine particulates, and lead; instituting new efforts to deal with indoor air quality; and (up to a point) limiting the buildup of greenhouse gases through reduction in use of fossil fuels. Other programs, such as cleanup of hazardous waste sites, would probably fail to measure up quite as well. Public acceptance of this approach is by no means guaranteed given often sharp differences between public views of the risks posed and those of technical experts. A further impediment is the substantial decline of public confidence in both scientific experts and government. As argued in Chapter 5, credible risk rankings of this kind also depend on improved databases and use of better analytic methodologies for health and ecological risk assessments (Davies 1996).

Some efforts have been made to try this kind of comparative risk study at the state level, at the encouragement of the federal EPA. For example, in 1994 a new report prepared for the California EPA was praised by scientists for its careful review of evidence on dozens of environmental hazards and the risks posed by each. The two-year study by 100 scientists was hailed especially for its careful explanation of methodologies, data sources, and assumptions behind the risk assessments. The report may serve as a model for other states as the federal EPA presses them to identify and act on their most serious environmental risks (Stone 1994).

Controversies over Cost–Benefit Analysis and Risk Assessment

These thoughtful and constructive efforts to use more economic analysis and risk assessments should be clearly distinguished from proposals debated in Congress during the late 1990s and early 2000s that would have imposed far more demanding requirements on the EPA and other agencies, even for fairly minor regulatory actions. Most of these measures were intended to slow the regulatory process and avert costs rather than to facilitate better understanding of the costs and risks (Andrews 2006). By one count, proposals of this kind could have increased the number of regulatory analyses conducted each year by 30-fold while providing little useful information to policymakers and the public (Portney 1995). The result might well have been "paralysis by analysis" as agencies struggled to meet highly prescriptive congressional demands for cost assessments and other activities that offered little hope of improving environmental policy. Although the House voted several times for such regulatory reform measures, they failed to gain Senate approval (Kraft 2006).[2]

Many environmentalists object on even more fundamental grounds to putting policy choices in economic terms. In some cases, they prefer that policy debate take place in moral rather than economic terms. Protection of biodiversity or promotion of ecosystem health, for example, might be grounded in environmental ethics that recognize the rights of other species and future generations (Paehlke 2000). As Sagoff (1988) put it, such a moral attitude "regards hazardous pollution and environmental degradation as evils society must eliminate if it is to live up to its ideals and aspirations" (195–96). Economic analysis, in contrast, tends to value the environment primarily in terms of its instrumental value to humans. From this perspective, balancing the benefits of social regulation against the costs seems to be merely a matter of "organized common sense" (Freeman 2006).

In considering the use of risk assessment and cost–benefit analysis, environmentalists question how objective the exercise will be. In particular, they tend to be skeptical that in this kind of economic calculus all the relevant costs and benefits can or will be measured and weighed fairly. This skepticism is a legitimate concern shared by many policy analysts (Anderson 2006; Kraft and Furlong 2007; Tong 1986). For environmental policy, benefits typically are harder to estimate than costs. Benefits such as improved public health from reduced exposure to toxic air pollutants are difficult to document and their value subject to considerable debate. In contrast, the costs imposed on industry may be easy to identify and easily measurable. In addition, analysts may heavily discount long-term benefits to public health and the environment because those benefits could come far in the future, and their future value has to be compared to the present value of the dollar (which is usually much lower).[3] These objections are less an indictment of the principle or professional practice of cost–benefit analysis than they are an expression of distrust in the way such analysis may be used by partisan advocates. They also reflect doubt that the political process will afford an open dialogue on the critical policy choices at stake—such as restrictions on mining operations, logging of forests, or removal of dams—to protect species and ecosystems.

Even the strongest advocates of cost–benefit analysis concede that the method is most appropriate when the requisite data are available and when its limitations are recognized both by those doing the analysis and those who use it in making decisions. As is the case with risk assessment, invariably critical choices must be made in specifying the most important costs and benefits to be considered, which can be measured and which cannot, the way in which intangible values such as human health are weighed, and how long-term benefits and costs are dealt with to make them comparable to present dollar values (Harrington, Morgenstern, and Nelson 1999; Tong 1986). Above all else, cost–benefit analysis and risk assessment must be recognized as providing only one kind of information to consider in making environmental policy decisions. Such analysis should not necessarily determine the outcome when other important values are at stake.

The EPA itself, as discussed in Chapter 5, is required to justify its regulatory proposals with this kind of economic analysis, which is subject to review by the White House's Office of Management and Budget (OMB). Thus the agency engages in extensive analysis of its regulations, which are usually a contentious part of the political debate over new rules, such as those put into effect for ozone and fine particulates in 1997. Occasionally, the agency engages in an even more comprehensive analysis of the costs of its regulatory activities.[4] One example dealing with the costs and benefits of the Clean Air Act is given in Box 7.1. The OMB itself periodically publishes its estimates of the costs and benefits of federal regulatory programs, including those managed by the EPA (U.S. OMB 2003).

BOX 7.1
The Costs and Benefits of the Clean Air Act

The Clean Air Act Amendments of 1990 require the EPA to conduct periodic studies (subject to external review) to assess the costs and benefits of the act's overall effects. The agency concluded in a 1997 study that the total monetized benefits realized between 1970 and 1990 were between $5.6 trillion and $49.4 trillion, with a mean estimate of $22 trillion. The direct compliance expenditures were estimated to be $0.5 trillion ($523 billion). A large part of the benefits came from reducing two pollutants, lead and particulate matter. The study used an array of computer models to compare two scenarios. One was the actual environmental and economic conditions that have been observed. The second was built from a projection of conditions that would have prevailed without the federal, state, and local programs developed pursuant to the goals of Clean Air Acts of 1970 and 1977. In a follow-up study released in late 1999, the EPA forecast that in the year 2010, the benefits of the act would exceed its costs by four to one: that is, an estimated $110 billion for the benefits expected and $27 billion for the anticipated costs. Does this kind of comparison of costs and benefits of the Clean Air Act seem valid? What objections might be raised? Both studies are available at the EPA's Web site: www.epa.gov/oar/sect812. For a critique of the study and its conclusions, see Krupnick (2002).

Environmentalists' Use of Economic Analysis

Despite a continuing discomfort with economic analysis, environmental groups increasingly conduct their own studies as a counterpoint to government and industry arguments about the high cost of environmental actions. The Wilderness Society released a report in 1994, for example, contending that recreation and tourism in national forests bring in more money than timber harvests. For the area studied (five states in the Southeast), the society put the value of harvested timber at $32 million a year and the economic benefits each year of recreation and tourism at $379 million. The report concluded that present policies emphasizing timber production were "out of step with economic realities" (Smothers 1994). Environmentalists have used similar studies to support arguments for protecting old-growth forests in the Pacific Northwest, where the region's economy depends heavily on tourism.

In a related study, the World Wildlife Fund and the Oregon Natural Resources Council found that counties in the West with the highest proportion of protected federal lands (such as wilderness areas, national monuments, and national parks) also have benefited from the highest income rates and job growth in recent years. The groups reviewed data for 410 counties in 11 states in the region for the period 1969 to 1997 and examined nine counties in Oregon in greater detail. Although logging, mining, ranching, and farming have been in decline, they have been replaced by a growing service economy stimulated by tourism and the attraction of retirees who value the area's scenery and clean air.[5]

Examples of such economic analysis commissioned by environmental groups, sometimes working with government agencies and the private sector, are increasingly common. In an unusual three-year study focusing on the Chicago metropolitan area, the Forest Service found that planting thousands of trees would bring a net benefit of $38 million over 30 years by reducing costs of heating and cooling buildings and by absorbing air pollution. Just three strategically placed trees could save a Chicago homeowner $50 to $90 a year (Stevens 1994). Studies of this kind led Chicago to initiate extensive rooftop gardens as part of a five-city pilot project assisted by the U.S. EPA's Urban Heat Island Project and the DOE. The DOE itself, working with the nonprofit American Forest group, directed a Cool Communities Program that focused on planting trees (Claiborne 1999). In a related move, the Los Angeles Department of Water and Power began a program in 2002 to give away 100,000 shade trees to its customers to help cool homes and reduce demand for electricity for air conditioners as well as to remove air pollutants.

Environmental groups in the Great Lakes area made much of recent studies on the deceptively low price of the road salt used to melt snow and ice in winter. The EPA has put the damage to vehicles, highways, bridges, and related infrastructures at $5 billion a year. Hence local governments might find that buying "more expensive" substitutes for salt is actually cheaper when environmental impacts and other damages from salt are factored into the equation. In the early 1990s, one New York state agency estimated that winter road salt carried a *true* cost of $800 to $2,000 per ton (far higher than the alternatives) when one considers the effect on wetlands, freshwater supplies, and vegetation, among other environmental damage.[6]

▓ JOBS, THE ECONOMY, AND THE ENVIRONMENT

Aside from objections to the inefficiency of some environmental regulations, a broader indictment has been made against environmental policy. Some scholars, public officials, and advocacy groups have implied that the nation must choose between two paths in fundamental conflict, suggested in the "economy versus the environment" debate of the 1990s. Conservative critics of environmental policy, for example, have argued that environmental regulation slows the rate of economic growth and thereby unintentionally makes the population worse off.

Wildavsky (1988), for instance, asserted that by "searching for safety" and favoring governmental regulations that constrain economic investment and growth, environmentalists actually cause the population to be less safe. That is because fewer people can afford a lifestyle (e.g., diet, physical security, and access to health services) that historically has been associated with improved health and well-being. His argument hinges on the questionable assumptions that regulations deal with trivial risks to public and ecosystem health and that investment in environmental protection weakens the economy and individual prosperity enough to more than offset whatever additional safety environmental policies produce (see also Douglas and Wildavsky 1982; Wildavsky 1995).

A special version of this argument is the "jobs versus the environment" conflict that became a significant issue in the 1992 presidential election campaign. President George H. W. Bush spoke out against "environmental extremists" and pledged to save the jobs of lumber workers in the Pacific Northwest. "It's time to put people ahead of owls," the president said, even if that meant sacrificing the nation's ancient and irreplaceable forests in Northern California, Oregon, and Washington. Candidate Bill Clinton promised that, if elected, he would tackle the stalemate between lumber workers and environmentalists.

During the debate in Congress in 2002 over George W. Bush's proposal to drill for oil and gas in ANWR (described in Chapter 6), proponents of drilling repeatedly cited a 1990 economic study suggesting that opening the refuge for commercial oil production would create some 735,000 jobs. Independent economists said the figure was suspect, however, because the assumptions on which it was based were probably no longer valid. A separate study prepared for the DOE in 1992 indicated that the number was only a third of this amount, about 222,000 jobs, and only when ANWR drilling reached peak production. Environmentalists argued that the real number was much lower yet. They suggested that perhaps 50,000 jobs were at stake. Despite questions raised about the initial study, labor unions lobbied hard for opening ANWR to drilling because of the jobs they expected to be made available.

Employment, Business Costs, and Environmental Policy

As the ANWR example illustrates, anecdotal evidence related to the economic impact of environmental policies is easy to come by, but not very helpful. Protection of the northern spotted owl was said to cost from 20,000 to 140,000 jobs. The American Petroleum Institute put the blame on environmental restrictions for the loss of 400,000 jobs in the 1980s (Bezdek 1993). Mining companies have claimed that legislation to reform the 1872 Mining Law could cost 47,000 jobs in an industry that has already suffered a substantial loss of its jobs; the Bureau of Mines had a far lower estimate of only 1,110 lost jobs (Camia 1994).

Job losses clearly have occurred in specific industries, communities, and regions as a result of environmental mandates. There may be fewer losses than initial estimates often suggest, although that is of little comfort to those who lose their jobs or to the businesses forced to close their doors. Fortunately, there is much that government can do to minimize adverse effects through job retraining programs, subsidized loan programs, and other policy interventions, similar to what is done in communities affected by natural disasters such as floods and storms. Successful implementation of environmental policies requires that policymakers think more seriously about using such approaches to avoid needless conflict over otherwise broadly endorsed environmental goals.

At the national or macroeconomic level, environmental policies have only a small effect on the economy no matter what measure is used: inflation, productivity, or jobs (Portney 2000). At this level, economic analyses have found that environmental policies increase inflation and decrease productivity *only very slightly*. Those policies have also led to a net increase in employment (Peskin, Portney, and Kneese 1981; Tietenberg 2006a).[7] To explore that relationship, a team of economists from Resources for the Future recently studied four heavily polluting industries: pulp and paper, plastics, petroleum refining, and iron and steel. They found that increased environmental spending in these industries *did not* cause a significant reduction in industry-level employment (Morgenstern, Pizer, and Shih 1999).

It is apparent that the costs of complying with environmental regulations, even when substantial, are far lower than many other costs of doing business, such as providing for employee health care insurance and maintaining competitive salaries. One study, for instance, put pollution control costs at only 1 percent of total company costs on average for manufacturing industries; the highest costs were found for basic chemical industries, where it was 3 percent (Eskeland and Harrison 2003). Yet too often the environmental expenditures are singled out for criticism. Of course, as noted earlier, when compliance costs are higher than they need be because of inefficient rules and regulations, those requirements could be changed and greater flexibility provided to the business community. Much recent action by both the EPA and the states to reform environmental policies has been directed at precisely these ways of reducing costs.

Even when employment and other economic effects are larger than these numbers indicate, economist Paul Portney offers an important observation: "Counting jobs created or destroyed is simply a poor way to evaluate environmental policies" (1994, 22). A policy, and the regulations it generates, may cost jobs and still be judged desirable because it eliminates harmful pollution or protects valued resources. This does not make the loss of jobs any more acceptable, either to the communities in which they occur or to elected officials who represent those communities. Conversely, policies that generate jobs may be bad for the environment and public health. Policymakers should be able to design employment policies that do not produce such negative effects.

These dilemmas speak to the need for sustainable development. Sustainability requires attention to what is environmentally sound and economically efficient, but also to what is socially and politically acceptable and just. The trick for policymakers is how to develop policies that can meet all of these expectations. Effective political leadership is one way to do that. Increasingly, labor unions also recognize that the old debate about jobs and the environment is unproductive. Some, for example, the Alliance for Sustainable Jobs and the Environment (www.asje.org), are beginning to stress the need for sustainable jobs and environmental policies that protect the health of workers, their families, and the communities in which they live.

One area that does hold much promise for job creation while simultaneously promoting sound environmental policy is development of new environmental technologies. Ten years ago, the Organization for Economic Cooperation and Development (OECD) estimated the world market for environmental technologies at $200 to $300 billion a year; it anticipated sustained growth in that market over the next few decades (Gardiner 1994). One reason for that optimistic forecast was the agreements reached at the 1992 UN Conference on Environment and Development. Developed nations pledged to provide a major infusion of Western technology and funds to assist developing nations in designing environmentally sustainable economies. Although the United States and other developed nations have fallen short of that commitment, nonetheless a great deal of both public and private capital is being invested in environmental technologies in developing nations (French 2002). Depending on the level of future financial assistance and the success of this technology transfer, the global market for environmental technologies could soar in the decades ahead.

Much the same kind of growth rate is projected for the U.S. environmental technology industry, which consists of more than 50,000 businesses employing over 1.3 million people. Together they generated about $180 billion in revenues a year in the mid-1990s, triple the 1980 amount (CEQ 1999). In a striking illustration of this potential, a study by economists at the University of California, Berkeley in 2006 found that California's plan to reduce sharply its greenhouse gas emissions will create tens of thousands of jobs in the state and boost its economic output by some $60 billion by 2020. The state's gains come in part from its anticipated sales of greenhouse gas–reducing technologies.[8] As the California example suggests, the general estimates for the environmental technology sector may be too low. The National Recycling Coalition, for example, said that in 2002 the U.S. recycling industry alone employed about 1.1 million people and generated an annual payroll of about $37 billion. The recycling industry is larger than either the mining or the waste management and disposal industries. Such developments are consistent with a long-standing argument advanced by environmentalists: adoption of environmentally benign technologies and encouragement of energy efficiency, source reduction, waste recycling, and similar efforts will improve employment because these tend to be more labor intensive than the polluting technologies and practices they replace (Paehlke 2006; Renner 2000).

Seeking Common Ground: Toward Environmental Sustainability

Although some of these arguments about the positive economic effects of environmental policies are long on hope and short on empirical evidence, recent studies lend support. Lax environmental standards seem to insulate inefficient and outmoded firms from the need to innovate and invest in new equipment. Such investments are likely to be essential to compete successfully in a twenty-first-century global economy (Bezdek 1993; Porter and van der Linde 1995). There may be some short-term economic advantages to weak environmental laws, as debates over the North American Free Trade Agreement (NAFTA) and other international trade issues have highlighted (Vogel 2006). Over the long run, however, policies that promote environmentally sound and efficient technologies and processes, not those that are environmentally degrading and wasteful, seem to offer the best hope, particularly if full cost accounting is used to assess environmental damages fairly (discussed later).

Some of the most compelling evidence of the relationship between the economy and environmental policy comes from analysis of state policy efforts. Meyer sought to test the widely accepted proposition that environmental programs adversely affect economic growth. He examined the 50 states, comparing those with strong, moderate, and weak environmental policy records in terms of employment, economic output, and productivity over a 20-year period through the early 1990s. He found that states with stronger environmental policies did not fare less well economically than those with weaker programs. In fact, he reported a "consistent and systematic *positive* correlation between stronger state environmentalism and stronger state economic performance across four of the five indicators. States with stronger environmental standards tended to have higher growth in their gross state products, total employment, construction employment, and labor productivity than states that ranked lower environmentally" (Meyer 1993, 1–2).[9]

Bowman and Tompkins (1993) used different measures of state environmental policy commitment, considered different time periods, and employed a multivariate model to explain economic growth and development. They acknowledged that such analysis is difficult because of the interrelationship of the variables, and their results differ in important ways from Meyer's. Yet they too concluded that "environmentalism is not invariably associated with restricted economic growth—indeed, if anything, most of the evidence . . . favors the suggestion that it is at least *associated* with higher levels of economic growth."[10]

In yet another analysis of these relationships, Feiock and Stream (2001) examined change in economic performance of the 50 states between 1973 and 1991. They argue that the growth versus environment debate presents a false trade-off because of the complex relationships involved. Some elements of state environmental policy "may provide disincentives for economic growth," whereas others "may encourage investment" and thus promote growth. Many benefits of regulation, they found, may be obtained with "little or no economic loss." In the end, their analysis confirms that "certain environmental policy designs may enhance, rather than impede, economic development" (314).

Environmental Justice

Another critical aspect of pursuing sustainability, especially at the local level, is the need to consider environmental justice. Critics argue that social or community well-being must take into account inequalities among groups in the population, particularly the poor and minorities. The environmental justice movement has focused on the inequitable burden that is often placed on poor and minority communities that have rates of exposure to toxic chemicals and other pollutants that are higher than usual (Bryant and Mohai 1992).

A study by the EPA in 1992 confirmed a disproportionate impact on poor and minority groups (U.S. EPA 1992a), and many other studies since that time have reached similar conclusions (Ringquist 2006). The EPA urged an increased priority within the agency be given to equity issues and to targeting of high concentrations of risk in specific population subgroups, and the Clinton administration took actions to address those concerns. The agency established an Office of Environmental Justice (OEJ) to deal with environmental impacts on minority and low-income populations. The OEJ defines environmental justice as "the fair treatment and meaningful involvement of all people regardless of race, color, national origin, or income with respect to the development, implementation, and enforcement of environmental laws, regulations, and policies."[11]

On February 11, 1994, President Clinton issued Executive Order 12898, which called for all federal agencies to develop strategies for achieving environmental justice. The order also reinforced existing law by forbidding discrimination in all agency policies, programs, and activities on the basis of race, color, or national origin. This executive order is overseen by the OEJ, which has developed elaborate guidelines for its implementation and compliance. Each of the 10 EPA regional offices around the country has an environmental justice coordinator who is to facilitate this process.[12]

Since that time, interest in questions of environmental equity has grown both within and outside of government, even if further policy actions have been modest (Foreman 1998; Ringquist 2006). In part, the new visibility of these issues reflects successful grassroots organizing in poor and minority communities. It also signals a new willingness in established civil rights organizations to devote more attention to environmental health issues and a determination in the national environmental organizations to incorporate environmental justice concerns (Bryant 1995). As more and better data are collected on exposure to hazardous and toxic chemicals and their health effects, the issues may gain more public attention.

The trend is important for another reason. More than any other recent development, concern over environmental equity forces policymakers to confront the ethical issues inherent in choosing environmental policy strategies. Whether the focus is on inequitable exposure to environmental pollution across population subgroups within the United States or other nations, or on the enormous economic and environmental inequities between poor and rich nations, the contrasts are remarkable. They make clear that policy decisions involve more than questions of environmental science and technology. They also go beyond consideration of aggregate national costs and benefits, which is the most common way to view the economic effects of environmental policies. The distribution of risks, costs, and benefits across the population, and across generations, merits greater attention in evaluating environmental policy.

REFORMING ENVIRONMENTAL REGULATION

As noted throughout this book, a persistent criticism of environmental policy is that it relies too heavily on centralized, technically driven, command-and-control regulation in which government sets environmental quality goals, methods to achieve them, and deadlines, with penalties for noncompliance. Aside from the issue of costly inefficiencies addressed earlier, such regulation is often said to be poorly conceived, cumbersome, time consuming, arbitrary, and vulnerable to political interference (Davies and Mazurek 1998; Sexton et al. 1999). Some add to the litany of complaints that Congress cannot seem to resist the temptation to add pork-barrel ingredients to the regulatory recipe. Examples are easy to find, from funding during the 1970s and 1980s of municipal sewage treatments plants that were overbuilt for the populations they served to contemporary subsidies for highway construction and maintenance, farming, mining, and ranching. Hence, in recent years, economists and policy analysis have suggested a range of alternatives that may either substitute for direct regulation or supplement it (Freeman 2006; Portney and Stavins 2000; Stavins 1991).

The Case for Policy Alternatives

There is little real argument today over the wisdom of using such alternatives to regulation as market-based incentives, provision of information, public education, negotiation, voluntarism, stakeholder collaboration, and public–private partnerships. They are among the policy approaches that governments at all levels consider, and they have enjoyed wide use in recent years (Durant, Fiorino, and O'Leary 2004; Mazmanian and Kraft 1999). Many environmental problems simply cannot be addressed effectively with traditional regulatory tools alone, but incentives and educational efforts may be useful supplements. One example is nonpoint water pollution control that must deal with thousands of dispersed sources such as small farms. Another is indoor air quality, which affects people in millions of individual homes and commercial buildings. A third is individual consumer purchases for which energy efficiency, recycling, or other environmental goals might be sought. The use of product labels and other forms of communication to inform consumers about their choices is common. "Green labeling" has been widely used in Europe and may soon become more visible in the United States (Mastny 2004). Table 7.1 lists some of the most commonly considered policy approaches to deal with environmental and resource problems.

As appealing as some of the alternative approaches are, most come with limitations or disadvantages as well as advantages. Many questions come to mind. Are these alternatives, such as market incentives, likely to be as effective as regulation? Will they be cheaper or more easily implemented? Will they be more efficient in the use of society's fiscal resources? Will citizens be capable of using the information they are given to better achieve their goals, such as minimizing contact with toxic chemicals,

TABLE 7.1

Policy Alternatives for Environmental Protection

Government Action	Description and Illustrations
Regulation	Establishment and enforcement of standards, with sanctions for noncompliance (environmental regulation under the Clean Air Act, Clean Water Act, and Superfund; energy efficiency requirements)
Using market incentives	Imposition of taxes or charges or development of tradable permits that create incentives and disincentives for action (raising gasoline taxes to encourage fuel conservation; creating tradable permits for sulfur dioxide emissions)
Education	Provision of information to the public through formal programs or other actions (Toxics Release Inventory disclosure, automobile fuel efficiency labels, appliance efficiency labels, environmental education programs)
Taxing and spending	Taxation of an activity at a level that encourages or discourages it (tax credits to encourage purchase of fuel-efficient vehicles, green taxes to discourage corporate pollution) or spending money on preferred programs (energy R&D support)
Purchasing goods and services	Purchase of products and services for government agencies (fuel-efficient fleet vehicles or recycled paper products for federal or state governments)
Rationing	Limitation of access to scarce resources (permits for backpacking and limited campsites in national parks, restrictions on energy or water use during periods of scarcity, limits on fishing and hunting)
Privatization and contracting out	Transfer of public services or property from government to the private sector (concessions at national parks, sale of federal property) or contracting out for services (DOE contracts for cleanup of former nuclear weapons production facilities)
Charging fees	Imposition of fees for government services (use of national, state, or county parks; fees charged for use of public lands for grazing, mining, timber harvesting; variable pricing for household waste)
Use of subsidies	Provision of loans, direct payments, tax credits, and price supports (low fees for mineral and water rights, agricultural and irrigation subsidies, financial incentives to protect wetlands under the federal Wetlands Reserve Program)
Creation of public trusts	Placement of property in public trusts (local land conservation trusts, some components of the federal Wetlands Reserve Program)
Support of research and development	Conduct or support of research and development (support for environmental research at the EPA, NOAA, and NSF; energy research sponsored by the DOE)
Assessment for damages	Use of tort law to award damages to plaintiffs for harm suffered, or government imposition of damage assessments (private suits against corporations for damages; natural resource damage assessments under Superfund)
Self-regulation	Voluntary adoption of performance standards by industry or others (ISO 14000 environmental management system standards, chemical industry's Responsible Care program; state programs for environmental self-regulation)

reducing pesticide exposure through the food supply, or improving the quality of drinking water (Hamilton 2005; Stephan 2002)?[13]

Unfortunately, there is little empirical evidence that answers such questions definitively. Few rigorous evaluations have been done for the conventional regulatory programs and even fewer are available for the kinds of policy innovation under discussion (Davies and Mazurek 1998; Knaap and Kim 1998). What we do have is a plethora of innovative state and local actions that appear to have worked well (e.g., John and Mlay 1999; Knopman, Susman, and Landy 1999; Rabe 2004, 2006; Weber 2003). There have also been some experiments in regulatory flexibility and collaborative decision making at the federal level that offer a mixed picture (Coglianese 1997; Coglianese and Allen 2004; Koontz et al. 2004; Kraft and Scheberle 1998; Marcus, Geffen, and Sexton 2002). Similarly, elaborate case studies of collaborative decision making in water quality (Kraft and Johnson 1999), use of market-based approaches in air quality (Mazmanian 1999), and use of ecosystem management in the Great Lakes region (Rabe 1999) indicate substantial potential for alternatives to command-and-control regulation. Yet they all suggest some major limitations to these new approaches as well. Examination of several of these approaches illuminates both their potential and their pitfalls.

The Promise of Market Incentives   The basic logic of market alternatives is clear enough. If, for example, motorists drive a great deal and are thought to be wasting fuel, contributing to traffic congestion and pollution, and also to the buildup of carbon dioxide in the atmosphere, how might such behavior be discouraged? Various regulatory schemes might work, from setting high fuel economy standards for automobiles, vans, and SUVs to restricting use of private vehicles through carpooling and other means. Yet such actions would involve a level of bureaucratic intrusion that may be socially unacceptable and politically infeasible. Such standards also have not worked very well over the past two decades in reducing the use of motor vehicles and gasoline (Portney 2002). Although the average automobile is far more efficient today than 20 years ago, public preferences have decidedly come to favor inefficient vans, light trucks, and SUVs.

A market alternative would be to raise gasoline taxes sufficiently to achieve the same goals (Parry 2002). Higher prices for gasoline would create incentives for motorists to drive less, seek more fuel-efficient vehicles, and rely more on mass transit. Over time, changing consumer preferences could build a market for efficient vehicles to which automobile manufacturers could respond. In theory, a market incentive such as this one can reduce the bureaucratic intrusiveness and costs associated with direct regulation. Regrettably, as noted earlier in the text, public resistance to higher fuel costs and timidity on the part of public officials makes imposition of such a gas tax (or a broader carbon tax) politically infeasible at this time. In principle, however, this kind of policy approach offers an alternative to regulation that is appealing on many grounds (Freeman 2006; Tietenberg 2006a).

Similar cases have been made for imposition of so-called green taxes to discourage pollution. One OECD study in 2001 found that even though the large U.S. economy leads the world in pollution, it imposes the lowest green taxes as a percentage of GDP of any industrial nation. Thus there would seem to be plenty of opportunity to consider expanded use of green taxes in the United States, particularly when the economy is doing well and such taxes might be viewed less negatively.

Both the EPA and the states have experimented since the 1970s with market incentives and other alternatives to regulation.[14] These innovations are encouraging, if still controversial and limited in actual use. Some of the earliest applications of the approach were in air pollution control where offsets and so-called bubbles were created to introduce greater flexibility and promote economically efficient solutions. Offsets allow new sources to locate in nonattainment areas if other sources in the area can reduce their emissions. The bubble concept treats a facility as if its various emissions were under a single umbrella, or bubble. Firms may establish a new pollution source by reducing emissions elsewhere in their facility. Congress went further in the 1990 Clean Air Act when it authorized emissions trading to reduce precursors of acid rain. The idea is that some firms will find it relatively inexpensive to reduce emissions; for others, it will be costly. The latter can purchase permits or allowances from the former to release those emissions, creating an identical overall reduction in emissions but at a lower cost to the affected firms. Thus the market in sulfur dioxide permits has allowed more efficient (less costly) reduction in emissions while meeting the act's acid rain goals (Kerr 1998).[15] Others see considerable potential for use of market incentives, from encouraging smarter use of flood plains (Sheaffer, Mullan, and Hinch 2002) and protecting endangered species on private lands to energy conservation by citizens and corporations, control of greenhouse gas emissions in Europe, and control of sulfur dioxide emissions in countries such as China (Kruger and Pizer 2004; Shogren 2004; Tietenberg 2006b; Wang et al. 2004).

Even those analysts who have been among the strongest supporters of market-based environmental tools, however, recognize their limited achievements to date. For example, Hockenstein, Stavins, and Whitehead (1997) concluded in one review of the experience that "market-based instruments have generally failed to meet the great expectations that we had had for them. As a result, they now lie only on the periphery of environmental policy" (13). Other analysts have expressed concern that such market trading schemes, even if effective, may result in local toxic "hot spots" that could exacerbate problems of environmental injustice; poor and minority populations living close to the source of emissions could see their exposures increase (Solomon and Lee 2000). Supporters of market incentives have by no means given up. Rather, they argue that the next generation of these instruments must be better designed to become a more central element in environmental policy.

Innovation by State and Local Governments   John (1994) examined similar innovations at the state level. He showed how, through the use of nonregulatory tools and cooperative approaches, state governments reduced the use of agricultural chemicals in Iowa, helped devise a plan for restoring the Florida Everglades, and used demand-side management to conserve electricity in Colorado. Sometimes such programs work well and sometimes not. But proponents of them express great faith that they can be, as one set of authors put it, "at once more effective and flexible than current arrangements yet also more democratic." They based their assessment on cases as diverse as state use of Toxics Release Inventory data, restoration of the Chesapeake Bay in Maryland, and the development of habitat conservation plans in California (Karkkainen, Fung, and Sabel 2000, 690).

A case that illustrates both the potential and limitations of such innovation is the use of market incentives to control air pollution in Southern California. In 1993 the South Coast Air Quality Management District sought to minimize adverse economic effects of its clean air program in the Los Angeles metropolitan area. It adopted market incentives as a less costly way to achieve clean air goals. A local market in pollution credits (the Regional Clean Air Incentives Market, or RECLAIM) replaced dozens of rules. Overall industrial emissions were to be reduced each year and achieve a total cut in nitrogen oxide emissions of 75 percent by 2003 and 60 percent in sulfur dioxide emissions from previous levels. Nearly 400 large companies were given flexibility to find the cheapest way to achieve those reductions. They could trade pollution rights within a declining cap on total emissions (Kamieniecki, Shafie, and Silvers 1999; Mazmanian 1999). The program worked well for the first six years it was in place but faltered when the price of permits rose sharply in 2000 and 2001, a consequence of the electricity crisis in California (Freeman 2006). An official at the state Air Resource Board even argued that RECLAIM "hasn't done as well as the regulations it replaced."[16]

Other examples suggest the diverse uses of market incentives and similar alternatives at state and local levels. For reasons discussed in Chapter 5, local governments are hard-pressed to treat growing quantities of wastewater and to meet rising quality standards for wastewater that flows into streams, rivers, and bays. Cities across the nation have concluded that they are better off extending rebates to residents willing to install new toilets than treating the extra wastewater that would otherwise be generated. New models being marketed under EPA rules that took effect in January 1994 use only 1.6 gallons of water per flush in comparison to over 3 gallons for the older ones.

Parallel innovations in energy conservation have occurred, as discussed in Chapter 6. Utilities in the early 1990s offered discounts of 80 percent or more to customers buying energy-efficient lightbulbs. It was cheaper for the companies virtually to give away the new bulbs than to build the extra generating capacity they would need to meet consumer demand. The regulatory and financial hurdles of designing, getting approval for, and building additional plants made the lightbulb offers attractive in comparison. Much the same is true of rebates offered by utilities to buyers of energy-efficient appliances such as refrigerators, washers, dryers, and central air-conditioning systems.

Even with market incentive systems, much of the activity now required under regulatory policies is still needed. Environmental quality criteria and standards must be set, and monitoring and compliance actions continued. The most important difference lies in giving state and local governments and industry greater flexibility in the means they use to achieve the goals. In some cases, market incentives may not work as well as regulation, and they may not achieve environmental goals as quickly. As noted earlier, much depends on how such innovations are designed, the extent of public and policymaker commitment to them, and the skill with which programs are implemented. When such incentives fail to do the job, governments always have the option of returning to mandatory standards and regulation.

Assessing New Policy Approaches

As discussed earlier, some skepticism is warranted in appraising these new policy instruments, particularly when experience with them is limited. Just as environmentalists and policymakers favored regulatory policies in the 1970s and 1980s, the language of business schools has dominated policy debate in the 1990s and early 2000s.

Policy analysts have urged that programs be more customer driven, decentralized, and competitive, and that citizens, communities, and bureaucrats be empowered to take action in an entrepreneurial spirit. Mission-oriented problem solving and flexibility were to replace fixed rules and procedures, and design and market incentives often have been favored over planning and regulation. Privatization and contracting out also have been touted as more effective than relying on government employees (Durant, Fiorino, and O'Leary 2004; Sexton et al. 1999). Self-regulation by industry through adoption of environmental management systems is cited as a tool that can improve environmental performance more effectively and efficiently than government regulation (Coglianese and Nash 2001, 2002; Potoski and Prakash 2005).

Governments are often urged to support such actions, sometimes as an alternative to regulation. For instance, the EPA recently introduced an Environmental Performance Track program, a voluntary public–private partnership that recognizes and rewards businesses and public facilities for exceptional environmental performance that exceeds regulatory requirements. Initiated by the Clinton administration, the program has been strongly embraced by the Bush administration as a way to make environmental protection efforts less burdensome to the business community. It enrolls some of the most environmentally responsible companies in the nation and promises them fewer routine inspections; it also frees them from some regulatory rules. Critics, however, fault the program for being too soft on industries that continue to miss federal pollution standards (Adams 2006; see also Fiorino 2006).

Many of these proposals are problematic, whereas others may be reasonable supplements or alternatives to current practice. Few, however, have been studied carefully. Policy analysis and program evaluation could help separate the promising approaches from the unworkable and give policymakers some guidance as to which actions are most likely to pan out (Eisner 2004; Press and Mazmanian 2006). For which environmental programs does decentralization make sense, and for which does a centralized, uniform national policy work best? To what extent can reliance on private lawsuits reduce the need for government regulation in, for example, oil spill prevention? A brief review of several alternatives to regulation hints at the mixed picture they present.

Tort Law and Natural Resource Damage Assessments   Before the expansion of environmental laws in the 1970s, legal recourse for environmental harm rested largely on common-law concepts such as personal injury and liability for damages. Those injured could ask the courts for compensation for the harm suffered (McSpadden 2000). Even though environmental policy now provides many other ways both to prevent such harm and to compensate those injured, tort law can supplement other measures. Torts refer to injuries to a person's body, financial situation, or other interest that are caused by another person's negligence or carelessness. Environmental lawyers have tried to use tort law to deal with exposure to toxic chemicals, lead paint, and a variety of other environmental harms.[17]

One illustration of the potential of using tort law comes from the 1989 Exxon *Valdez* oil spill cleanup and settlement. Exxon spent over $2 billion cleaning up Prince William Sound in Alaska and $1.3 billion in civil and criminal penalties and settlements of claims filed by some 11,000 residents and businesses in the area. In August 1994 a federal jury ordered Exxon to pay $289 million in compensatory damages to over 10,000 Alaskan fishers who had filed a class action lawsuit. The biggest judgment by far was another jury decision in September 1994 ordering the oil company to pay $5 billion in punitive damages to approximately 34,000 fishers, landowners, and other Alaskans. The huge award, which Exxon appealed, was by far the largest civil judgment ever in a pollution case. It nearly equaled Exxon's net earnings of $5.3 billion in 1993 (Schneider 1994b). In late 2001 the Ninth Circuit Court of Appeals ruled that the award was excessive and ordered the judge in the case to set a lesser amount, probably no more than $1.6 billion.[18] As of early 2006, the same court was hearing Exxon's appeal in the case.

Perhaps the greatest limitation to using tort law to compensate for environmental damage is that it does nothing to prevent the injury or loss. Even the extensive cleanup effort after the *Valdez* accident captured only 3 to 4 percent of the oil that was spilled, and the effects on marine life were profound. It is also difficult to prove the existence of some kinds of environmental harm (e.g., health effects) and to show convincingly under rules of law that the harm is directly related to a specific company or practice. Those limitations were demonstrated well in Jonathan Harr's book *A Civil Action*, which was turned into a 1999 film starring John Travolta. The story focused on a case involving eight families in Woburn, Massachusetts, who had children who died from leukemia. Their lawyers found it difficult and costly to show that illegally dumped toxic chemicals entered the community's water supply and were directly responsible for the children's deaths.

Perhaps more practically, as a result of recent court decisions, the Interior Department and other agencies are making more use of natural resource damage assessments. Such assessments are mandated by the Superfund amendments of 1986 for natural resource trustees. Some of those assessments will include measurement of the loss of so-called passive uses of the environment by citizens not directly affected, a move that environmentalists applaud. Economists use contingent valuation methods (i.e., indirect measures of valuation) that rely on public opinion surveys to estimate those values, for which there is no market equivalent. One such assessment in northeastern Wisconsin put the cost of damage to local water bodies and habitat from PCB contamination at nearly $300 million; area pulp and paper companies were expected to compensate in part through habitat restoration and creation of public parks. If widely used to assess damages under federal environmental laws, such methods could dramatically alter the willingness of corporations to engage in high-risk endeavors for which they could be held financially liable.

Contracting Out and Privatization   The use of market incentives and tort law is still limited. These approaches may turn out to work far better in some instances than in others, but it is difficult to generalize about their promise. A few examples of contracting out and privatization suggest what needs to be examined.

Consider the tendency of some government agencies to rely heavily on outside contractors, which can be viewed as a form of privatization. The Bush administration announced in November 2002 that it was giving serious consideration to privatizing as many as half of the civilian jobs in the federal workforce. It defended the action as likely to save taxpayers money by ensuring the lowest cost for many routine government duties.[19] Yet many analysts are skeptical about how well privatization and contracting out can meet such expectations (Savas 2000).

Some of the evidence to date gives cause for concern. Kettl, for example, reports that the EPA depended so much on contractors for its Superfund program that it turned to them for help in responding to congressional inquiries, analyzing legislation, and drafting regulations and standards. Contractors "drafted memos, international agreements, and congressional testimony for top EPA officials. . . . They even wrote the Superfund program's annual report to Congress" (Kettl 1993, 112). Cases such as this one led the GAO to be sharply critical of the EPA's lax supervision of contractors, which the GAO argued made the agency vulnerable to contractor waste, fraud, and abuse (U.S. GAO 1992). Much the same could be said for many DOE programs. The DOE is the world's largest civilian contracting agency, and in 1997 it earmarked more than 90 percent of its $17.5 billion budget for contracts. In 2002 the GAO estimated that about three-quarters of the DOE's budget was spent at some 30 major research, development, production, and environmental cleanup sites around the country, with most of the work being done by contractors. For years, however, government auditors pointed to severe weaknesses in the DOE's contracting practices, many of which continue today (U.S. GAO 1997a, 2002).[20]

Each case for privatization or greater reliance on competitive markets must be assessed on its own terms. Markets and incentives may work well in some instances and not in others. There is no persuasive case for across-the-board reductions in government budgets and staff (as emphasized in the 1980s) and a switch to market mechanisms on the grounds that markets are inherently superior for allocation of public goods. One must also remember that markets must be structured in some fashion and also policed, and consumers must have access to the necessary information to make rational choices. These requirements imply a continued need for government bureaucracies and the courts to ensure sufficient consideration of the public interest in environmental protection.

■ NEW DIRECTIONS IN ENERGY AND NATURAL RESOURCES POLICY

As several of these examples and the discussion in Chapter 6 illustrate, many of the same ideas prominent in discussions of environmental protection policy are proposed for reform of natural resources and energy policies. Critics of all stripes have long found fault with policies they consider outmoded, costly to the government, and environmentally destructive. These distributive or subsidy policies include extensive federal support of commercial nuclear energy from its inception in the 1950s, below-cost sales of timber by the Forest Service, and the U.S. Army Corps of Engineers' long-standing preference for building dams and levees as the chief way to control flooding. Other prominent examples are minimal grazing and mining fees for use of federal land in the West that have led to degradation of land and water supplies and lost revenue to government, and subsidies that encourage farming on flood-prone land by reimbursing crop losses when rivers overflow.[21] Most of these policies have had strong support in Congress and powerful constituencies prepared to defend them, making their elimination politically difficult in any administration.

The contemporary political climate, however, suggests that such inefficient and ineffective policies will continue to be examined critically and possibly eliminated (Clarke and McCool 1996; Davis 2001; Lowry 2006). For example, members of both major political parties have evinced greater interest in reducing the scope of government and curtailing outmoded and costly public policies. Moreover, environmentalists have increasingly been joined by advocates of free market economics and conservative taxpayer organizations in protesting against federal programs that harm the environment and may cost the nation billions of dollars. In recent years, such coalitions have named federal subsidies for timber, mining, energy, and waste disposal, and subsidized irrigation for farmers, among others, as areas of concern and have urged Congress to eliminate such programs.[22]

The Appeal of User Fees

Among the most important natural resources policy reforms is the imposition of higher fees for those using public lands. Additional fees bring more money to the federal treasury, although that is not the main reason for instituting the changes. The purposes are to eliminate inequitable subsidies to user groups, especially for programs that degrade the environment and deplete or waste natural resources, and to increase market efficiencies (Lowry 2006; Myers and Kent 2001; Roodman 1997).[23] By one estimate, the federal government spends approximately $17 billion a year to manage resources that produce less than $7 billion a year in revenues, and it also must cover the cost of repairing environmental damage. Those costs may be quite high. For example, analysts estimate more than 200,000 abandoned mines exist in the United States, and the cost of cleanup could be more than $72 billion (McClure and Schneider 2002; Pope 1999b). Not all are as severely contaminated as the infamous Summitville mine in Colorado, but many threaten both surface water and groundwater (Perlez and Johnson 2005).

In perhaps the most egregious case under the 1872 Mining Law, Secretary of the Interior Bruce Babbitt was forced by a federal court ruling in May 1994 to sign a contract with a Canadian-based mining company, American Barrick Resources, for a mere $9,565. That contract gave the company the right to mine an estimated $10 billion worth of gold on public land without paying any royalties (Cushman 1994e). There is no shortage of examples of comparable inequities in other areas of natural resource policies.

At a different level of government, user fees and similar incentive programs have been widely adopted. Thousands of communities across the nation, for example, have instituted variable pricing programs for household waste. In most cases, prepaid garbage bags or stickers to attach to the bags are required for collection of household garbage. The most successful programs of this kind institute a public education and recycling program that can help alert citizens to the value of minimizing household waste that heads to municipal landfills.

Privatization of Public Land

Despite its poor reputation during the Reagan administration's efforts at environmental deregulation (Vig and Kraft 1984), proponents of the privatization of public lands continue to argue forcefully that private ownership of what are now public lands would likely increase efficiency in management and yield an optimal mix of goods and services for society. Advocates take this position in part because they believe that public bureaucracies have failed to manage natural resources efficiently and that agency employees have few direct incentives to do so. They believe that even noncommodity values such as wilderness and recreation can be better served in private markets (Anderson and Leal 1997, 2001; Higgs and Close 2005; Stroup and Baden 1983; Yandle 1999).

Such a position may be compelling on the grounds that federal agencies have indeed not managed the public domain very well. Yet critics of privatization assert that although markets may be more efficient than public bureaucracies in managing commodities such as energy resources, minerals, and timber, they are not reliable mechanisms for determining collective values for parks, preservation of wildlife, and maintenance of critical ecosystem functions. Moreover, emphasis on efficiency alone tends to neglect other public values such as equity in access and assurance that land and other resources will be preserved for future generations (Lowry 2006).

Representing a different kind of private action that is gaining favor in environmental circles, since 1951 the Nature Conservancy has purchased ecologically sensitive land to preserve habitats and species. With the assistance of its more than 1 million members, the conservancy has helped protect more than 15 million acres of habitat in the United States and more than 102 million acres worldwide. The conservancy has some 400 offices in 28 countries, and it manages more than 1,340 preserves, which constitutes the largest system of private nature sanctuaries in the world.[24] It also works with developers, industry, farmers, and local governments to encourage new approaches to resource management. Other environmental groups have pursued similar strategies. Nonprofit land trusts, for example, have been established around the nation to work toward conservation of ecologically sensitive land (Fairfax and Guenzler 2001). The lands that are acquired in this way often are turned over to government agencies to manage.

Even more striking is the effort by some wealthy individuals to buy tracts of land to set aside for conservation purposes, a pattern set years ago by the Rockefeller family, among others (Fairfax et al. 2005). No one seems to have done more in this regard recently than Cable News Network founder Ted Turner. In the late 1990s, Turner established a billion-dollar trust fund through the UN Foundation that focuses on programs dealing with children's health, environmental conservation, climate change, women's issues, and population growth. In addition, Turner acquired substantial land in South America and several large ranches in Montana, New Mexico, and Nebraska that are devoted to wildlife conservation. A rich American couple, Douglas Tompkins and his wife, Kristine McDivitt, own more than 2,000 square miles of wilderness in southern Chile, an area larger than Rhode Island. They hope to conserve most of the land and eventually donate it to the people of Chile.[25]

A variation on the use of privatization to conserve public land is the very successful Wetlands Reserve Program (WRP) established under the federal Farm Bill and administered by the Agriculture Department's Natural Resources Conservation Service. This voluntary program provides significant financial incentives for farmers to retire marginal lands for use in wetland restoration or conservation. It is a kind of contractual conservation trust or easement of varying time duration; some are for 30 years and others are set up permanently. There is also a wetland restoration cost-sharing agreement available for a minimum of 10 years to reestablish degraded or lost wetland habitat. The most recent Farm Bill authorizes up to 2.2 million areas for inclusion under the WRP, double the previous amount. In addition to the WRP is a related Conservation Reserve Program that offers annual payments and cost sharing to establish long-term resource-conserving cover on environmentally sensitive land.[26]

Social Cost Accounting

An even more important step to take advantage of market forces is the adoption of economic accounting measures that reflect the depletion or degradation of natural resources and thus more accurately depict the country's standard of living and the sustainability of its consumption of resources. For instance, the CEQ reported during the early 1990s that agriculture, forestry, fisheries, and mining combined contributed more than $130 billion to the nation's economy. Yet such national income accounts almost never reflect the obvious loss that occurs when natural resources are exhausted or damaged.

Ecologists have broadened the dialogue over social cost accounting by highlighting the many free ecosystem services that nature provides to human society, which are rarely reflected in national accounting mechanisms (Costanza et al. 1997; Daily and Ellison 2002; National Research Council 2004). A study published in *Science* in 2002, for instance, examined five stringently selected cases around the world in which intact ecosystems had been converted for logging, farming, or fishing. The researchers estimated the value of water filtration, carbon absorption, and other ecological services and found them to far outweigh the financial gain from development in all five cases. Indeed, they argued that putting money into nature conservation would yield a 100-to-1 payoff. Extrapolating from their five cases, they estimated that a global system of marine and terrestrial nature preserves would cost about $45 billion a year but yield $4.4 to $5.2 trillion in ecosystem services each year. The scientists thus concluded that such nature conservation presents a compelling economic argument (Balmford et al. 2002).

The subject of social cost accounting has been taken seriously by at least some public officials in the United States as well as globally (Hecht 1999; Lutz 1993). For example, President Clinton directed the Bureau of Economic Analysis (BEA) in the Commerce Department to begin work on recalculating the U.S. GDP along greener lines.[27] Similarly, through its Design for the Environment Program, the EPA has worked with industry, academia, and the accounting profession to encourage a fuller and more accurate consideration of environmental costs. The United States, however, has not been among the world's leaders in advancing environmental accounting (Hecht 1999).

Government Purchasing Power

Another alternative to regulation is using the buying power of government to change existing markets. The federal government alone makes use of 500,000 buildings and buys more than $200 billion a year in goods and services. If added to purchases by state and local governments, the public sector accounts for about 18 percent of the nation's total economic output. Some simple changes can produce remarkable effects on the economy and on emerging green markets. Equally impressive opportunities are available for nonprofit organizations and industry to use their substantial purchasing power to change the way products are manufactured and used. Many already are doing so. For example, in 2002 Federal Express pledged to replace all of its fleet vehicles (44,000) with diesel-electric trucks that promise to increase fuel efficiency by 50 percent and to cut health-damaging emissions by some 90 percent (Mastny 2004).

A good example of using purchasing power involves computer equipment. Computers—including copiers, fax machines, and printers—have been the fastest growing energy users in commercial buildings (and colleges and universities) since the late 1980s. After 1994 all federal agencies were required to buy energy-efficient computers when they replace equipment. The EPA estimated at the time that purchase of the Energy Star–rated computers and printers would save the government some $40 million each year in electricity costs (National Performance Review 1993a). The federal government has accounted for only 3 to 5 percent of national computer sales. By guaranteeing a market for energy-efficient machines, however, the policy allowed manufacturers to shift to new technology. That change involved the minor redesign of monitor, printer, and computer circuits. Reduction in electricity use nationwide should be substantial.

The EPA's Energy Star program, managed cooperatively with the DOE, was extended by the late 1990s to a diversity of other products, including major appliances; home electronics such as televisions and videocassette recorders; windows, skylights, and doors; heating and cooling systems; and lightbulbs and lighting fixtures. As noted in Chapter 6, some states have expanded the concept to standards for new home construction.

Ecosystem Management

A more fundamental way to reform natural resource policies as well as pollution control efforts is through the use of ecosystem management. Historically, governments developed policies to deal with discrete elements of the environment such as forests, water, soil, and species, often through different federal agencies and without coordination among them. Since its founding in 1970, the EPA has dealt almost exclusively with public health and paid little attention to maintenance of ecosystem health. The agency also rarely has coordinated efforts across the separate media of land, water, and air.

These conventional approaches have contributed to ineffective and inefficient environmental policy.[28] They also have resulted in public policies that concentrate limited resources on small public health risks that bring few benefits at high cost while larger risks are ignored. The backlash against environmental policy in the 1990s—from industry, state and local governments, and the property rights and wise use movements—derived from these policy weaknesses as much as anything else.

The more comprehensive ecosystem management approach has gradually established a foothold (Cortner and Moote 1999). It reflects advances in ecological research that are beginning to build an understanding of ecosystem functioning. To some extent it also incorporates ideas of ecological rationality advanced by social scientists (Bartlett 1986; Costanza, Norton, and Haskell 1992; Dryzek 1987). Rather than focus on individual rivers and localized cleanup efforts, for example, emphasis has shifted to entire watersheds and the diverse sources of environmental degradation that must be assessed and managed (Daily 1997). As mentioned in Chapter 1, for instance, in a path-breaking decision, New York City chose in 1997 to protect its large upstate watersheds rather than construct an expensive water treatment plant. So far the effort has been successful, and it may become a model for other cities (Platt, Barten, and Pfeffer 2000).

Similarly, instead of trying to save individual endangered species, the new goal is the preservation or restoration of ecosystems themselves. The Florida Everglades restoration project is a case in point. Among other results, the restoration of habitat in the Everglades may save 68 endangered and threatened species under the South Florida Multi-Species Recovery Plan, the largest such plan ever in the United States. The plan demonstrates the feasibility of an ecosystem rather than single-species approach to wildlife protection (McKinley 1999b). An especially attractive feature of the plan is that it has been broadly embraced by diverse local stakeholders, from environmentalists to sugarcane growers, many of whom cooperated in the project's design (Cushman 1998f; McKinley 1999a).

New approaches to ecological risk assessment, although still in their infancy, promise to provide the necessary knowledge on which to base a broader, more holistic, and better focused attack on environmental problems. Such assessment can create a systematic process for clarifying risks and setting priorities (U.S. EPA 1992b), which is one of the purposes of the new program in biological resources in the Interior Department, as discussed in Chapter 6.

Following the devastating Mississippi River floods of 1993, attention focused on the extensive system of dams and levees along the river. The Clinton White House charged Secretary of Agriculture Mike Espy with reviewing flood control programs and recommending actions to prevent similar damage in the future. A key component of the secretary's report recommended restoration of natural hydrologic cycles that had been severely disrupted by eliminating wetlands in the river's basin. In this form of ecosystem management, the prevention or mitigation of flooding depends on preserving and restoring wetlands in addition to whatever maintenance of engineered flood control mechanisms is needed. Acting somewhat like a sponge, wetlands absorb excessive rain and release it slowly, thus limiting the risk of flooding. Wetlands perform other vital ecological functions as well (Cushman 1994d).

In a related decision announced in late 2002, the Bush administration revised guidelines for the Army Corps of Engineers for mitigating the loss of wetlands. The corps is to use a watershed-based approach in which the needs of an entire watershed are taken into account rather than the effects of a particular development project (for instance, a mall parking lot) on localized wetlands. Consistent with the argument earlier in the chapter for regular evaluation of environmental programs, the corps and other agencies involved with wetlands protection (the EPA and the Agriculture, Interior, Commerce, and Transportation Departments) are to produce an annual report on the program's effectiveness.[29]

■ CONCLUSIONS

Since the 1970s environmental policies have become highly complex, and their reach has extended to every segment of the economy and every corner of the nation. Their costs and impacts on society are much debated. They are also at the center of many political controversies over the role of government in protecting public health and managing the nation's natural resources. Evaluating their successes and failures helps inform these debates even if such studies cannot answer all questions or eliminate conflicts over the direction of environmental policy.

One of the best ways to ensure that new scientific knowledge and policy and program evaluations are brought to bear on policy choices is to design such studies into the policies themselves. The Montreal Protocol that governs international action to phase out ozone-depleting chemicals like CFCs offers one model for doing so. It integrates continuous assessment of changing environmental conditions with new policy actions. Congress has occasionally provided mechanisms of this kind for pollution control policies. In 1977 it created the National Commission on Air Quality and charged it with overseeing and evaluating the EPA's performance in implementing the Clean Air Act. The 1972 Clean Water Act created a National Commission on Water Quality to study technical, economic, social, and environmental questions related to achieving certain goals established by the policy. Its report guided Congress in revision of the act in 1977 (Freeman 1990).

Another imperative is rethinking the logic of policy design (Schneider and Ingram 1990, 1997). For a policy to work well, it must be based on an understanding not only of environmental conditions, but also of the institutions and people who implement the policy and those who have to comply with the regulations and other directives it produces. Analysts and policymakers can, and should, do a better job in the future. Citizens can help by learning about how well policies are working and participating in decision making at all levels of government that affect the reform and redirection of environmental policy.

DISCUSSION QUESTIONS

1. What is the best way to assess whether progress is being made with environmental protection or natural resource policies? For any particular program, how would you determine whether it has been successful or not?
2. Controversies continue over the use of cost–benefit analysis and risk assessment in environmental policy decisions. Are these methods helpful in deciding which policies and programs, or particular regulations, are justifiable? What other issues should be considered in such a judgment?
3. Should environmental organizations try to support their recommended actions with economic analyses, as many have done in recent years? Are their arguments on behalf of environmental protection or resource conservation likely to be more persuasive if they do so?
4. Among the most widely discussed alternatives to command-and-control regulation is the use of market incentives. Is their use a positive development or not? For what kinds of environmental or resource issues are market incentives most likely to be effective?
5. The imposition of higher user fees for access to public lands is often recommended as a way to reduce environmental degradation attributable to mining, ranching, agriculture, and timber harvesting. What are the advantages of raising such fees? The disadvantages?

SUGGESTED READINGS

Chertow, Marian R., and Daniel C. Esty, eds. *Thinking Ecologically: The Next Generation of Environmental Policy*. New Haven, CT: Yale University Press, 1997.

Mazmanian, Daniel A., and Michael E. Kraft, eds. *Toward Sustainable Communities: Transition and Transformations in Environmental Policy.* Cambridge, MA: MIT Press, 1999.

National Academy of Public Administration. *Environment.gov: Transforming Environmental Protection for the 21st Century.* Washington, DC: National Academy of Public Administration, 2000.

Sexton, Ken, Alfred A. Marcus, K. William Easter, and Timothy D. Burkhardt, eds. *Better Environmental Decisions: Strategies for Governments, Businesses, and Communities.* Washington, DC: Island Press, 1999.

ENDNOTES

1. See Felicity Barringer and Michael Janofsky, "G.O.P. Plans to Give Environmental Rules a Free-Market Tilt," *New York Times,* November 8, 2004, A14.

2. One measure that Congress was able to approve was the Small Business and Regulatory Enforcement Fairness Act of 1996 (PL 104-121). It allowed small businesses to seek legal redress when agencies such as the EPA or BLM failed to conduct an adequate study of the economic impacts of their regulations. See Allan Freedman, "GOP's Secret Weapon Against Regulations: Finesse," *CQ Weekly,* September 5, 1998, 2314–20.

3. Economists and analysts would respond by saying that economic methods for estimating environmental and resource values when there are no evident market values are fairly sophisticated and widely used. For a discussion of how benefits and other environmental values can be estimated and used in decision making, see Freeman (1993). For a contrasting perspective, see Sagoff (1993).

4. EPA maintains a National Center for Environmental Economics that conducts and oversees research of this kind. Other useful sites include the World Resources Institute (www.wri.org), Resources for the Future (www.rff.org), and the Commerce Department's Bureau of Economic Analysis (www.bea.gov/), which reports on pollution and abatement expenditures.

5. The study is entitled "Historic Economic Performance of Oregon and Western Counties Associated with Roadless and Wilderness Areas."

6. For a detailed economic assessment of the costs of highway salting, see Donald F. Vitaliano, "An Economic Assessment of the Social Costs of Highway Salting and the Efficiency of Substituting a New Deicing Material," *Journal of Policy Analysis and Management* 11 (1992): 397–418.

7. Estimates of economic impacts show a wide variance, depending on the methods and models used and on the economic indicators selected. Over the past decade, such studies indicate that the effect on inflation and productivity is probably between 0.1 and 0.4 of a percentage point. In one early accounting, the CEQ noted in its 1979 *Environmental Quality* report that the annual accruing benefits of all federal environmental programs were substantially greater than the total cost of compliance. It also found the effect of these programs on the economy to be marginal.

8. A detailed assessment of the environmental technology sector can be found in a 1998 study prepared for the Office of Technology Policy in the Commerce Department, *The U.S. Environmental Industry,* available at www.ta.doc.gov/Reports/Environmental/env.pdf. The California greenhouse gas emissions report can be found at http://calclimate.berkeley.edu/managing_GHGs_in_CA.html.

9. Several papers related to the project are available at Meyer's Web site: http://web.mit.edu/polisci/mpepp/environment_&_economy.htm.

10. Consistent with these findings from state-level analysis, Bezdek (1993) reports some evidence that nations with the most stringent environmental policies have the highest rates of economic growth and job creation.

11. The quotation comes from the EPA Web site for the Office of Environmental Justice.

12. The Office of Environmental Justice Web site has a description of the executive order and provides links to the federal guidance documents for its implementation, in addition to other pertinent material: www.epa.gov/compliance/environmentaljustice/index.html.

13. One of the limitations of such information provision strategies is that consumers are not always capable of using the information as well as the designers of such policies intend (Hadden 1986). With increasing reliance on such information provision in new laws dealing with pesticides in food products and the quality of local drinking water supplies, policymakers need to ask about how effectively consumer choices are being assisted.

14. The EPA began to make use of market incentives like this one in 1976. In addition to the offset and bubble policies for air pollution control, programs in which incentives were used included wetlands mitigation banking, the phaseout of lead in gasoline, an air toxics offsets program, scrappage of old cars ("cash for clunkers"), privatization of wastewater systems, and incentives for safer pesticides.

15. Unfortunately, even with the reduction in sulfur dioxide emissions, acid rain in the Northeast continues to exact damage. A report by the GAO raised questions about how effective the 1990 Clean Air Act has been in this regard. For example, sulfur levels have declined substantially in the threatened Adirondack Mountains of New York State, but nitrogen levels have continued to rise, damaging aquatic life. See James Dao, "Acid Rain Law Found to Fail in Adirondacks," *New York Times*, March 27, 2000, 1, A23.

16. See Gary Polakovic, "Innovative Smog Plan Makes Little Progress," *Los Angeles Times*, April 17, 2001, B1, 7.

17. On lead paint litigation, see Pam Belluck, "Lead Paint Suits Echo Approach to Tobacco," *New York Times*, September 21, 2002, A12.

18. Evelyn Nieves, "Court Overturns Jury Award in '89 Exxon Valdez Spill," *New York Times*, November 8, 2001, A10.

19. See Richard W. Stevenson, "Government Plan May Make Private up to 850,000 Jobs," *New York Times*, November 15, 2002, A1–21.

20. See Jo Thomas, "Suit Accuses Federal Contractors of Mishandling Cleanup at Nuclear Lab," *New York Times*, February 19, 2001, A10. See also Joel Brinkley, "Energy Dept. Contractors Due for More Scrutiny," *New York Times*, November 24, 2002. According to this report, the DOE has acknowledged its failure to supervise contractors. Moreover, an internal DOE report concluded that the department's program to clean up nuclear weapons production facilities (handled almost entirely by contractors) has been fundamentally mismanaged since its founding, with much of the $60 billion spent on the program wasted.

21. On the crop insurance subsidy, see Michael Grunwald, "Sowing Resentment over Crop Insurance," *Washington Post National Weekly Edition*, November 15, 1999, 29. Even the Agriculture Department watchdog has complained that the program suffers from waste and abuse, creating large profits for insurers.

22. For example, see the report "Welfare for Waste: How Federal Taxpayer Subsidies Waste Resources and Discourage Recycling," released in 1999. It was produced by the GrassRoots Recycling Network, Taxpayers for Common Sense, the Materials Efficiency Project, and Friends of the Earth. The report identifies 15 tax and spending subsidies for corporations that cost taxpayers $13 billion over a five-year period, or $2.6 billion per year (www.grrn.org/).

23. The GAO reported in 1994 that studies by agricultural economists suggest that higher water prices being instituted in western water projects will increase irrigation efficiency and conservation, and thereby reduce environmental degradation attributable to irrigation as well as free up water currently used for irrigation for other purposes (U.S. GAO 1994).

24. The Nature Conservancy's home page provides additional information on its activities: http://nature.org/.

25. See Krista West, "The Billionaire Conservationist," *Scientific American* (August 2002): 34–35; and Larry Rohter, "An American in Chile Finds Conservation a Hard Slog," *New York Times*, August 7, 2005, 4.

26. Descriptions of the programs and current statistics can be found at one of the USDA Web sites: www.ers.usda.gov/Features/farmbill/analysis/landretirement.htm.

27. By some accounts, these initiatives date back to proposals during the Ford administration. The Commerce Department began the new calculations in the last year of the George H. W. Bush administration.

28. The Conservation Foundation, now part of the World Wildlife Fund, for years sponsored research and issued position papers on cross-media pollution control as part of its Options for a New Environmental Policy Project. One element of that work was the development of a model environmental policy for the nation that incorporated these integrative principles. See Rabe (1986) and National Commission on the Environment (1993).

29. Katharine Q. Seelye, "U.S. Revises Guidelines on Wetlands Conservation," *New York Times*, December 28, 2002, A11.

Environmental Policy and Politics for the Twenty-First Century

Previous chapters have described the development and implementation of U.S. environmental policies, their effects, and alternative policy strategies that might improve their performance. Any assessment of environmental policy and politics also must identify longer-term trends and emerging needs that could change the way we appraise environmental problems and the solutions that are called for. This chapter focuses on selected environmental issues both domestically and internationally that are likely to be among the most important in the decades ahead. They illustrate an evolving agenda for environmental policy that is centered on the achievement of sustainable development and involves more global interaction than has prevailed since the modern environmental movement began in the late 1960s. These issues were first introduced in Chapter 1 as presenting a daunting array of challenges to policymaking in the early twenty-first century as Earth's population grows and aspirations for economic development soar.

This final chapter begins with an overview of the third generation of environmental policy and politics and compares it to the previous two generations that have dominated U.S. policy debate over more than three decades. It then traces the new focus on sustainability that emerged in the late 1980s. Today, such concerns are most evident within the United States in the rise of the sustainable communities movement and in efforts to deal with such local and regional issues as the consequences of urban sprawl and the maintenance of quality of life in urban areas. They are also apparent in nascent efforts by the business community to promote a sustainable economy.

Finally, the chapter turns to international environmental policy, which presents a different array of issues, institutions, and policy actions than discussed in earlier chapters. Global environmental issues reached a new level of importance and visibility in the aftermath of the 1992 Earth Summit, for which sustainable development was the key organizing principle. Discussion concentrates on the institutional and political factors that will affect the pursuit of sustainable development in the decades ahead through a diversity of international environmental agreements.

■ ENVIRONMENTAL GOALS AND POLICY CHOICES: DOMESTIC AND GLOBAL

Given the controversial nature of environmental problems and policies, it is no surprise that we find diverse perspectives among policymakers, analysts, and activists about what actions to take and the proper role of government. Some analysts and commentators, for instance, are technological optimists. They project a future of economic prosperity, continued advancement in technical prowess, and few environmental or resource problems that cannot be solved with human ingenuity and determination. Many of them also tend to express more confidence in free market solutions than in government planning and regulation (Bailey 1999; Huber 2000; Lomborg 2001; Simon 1995; Simon and Kahn 1984).

In contrast, other analysts and many environmental scientists are less sanguine about our collective capacity to address environmental problems. They believe that without significant changes in human behavior, the United States and the world face a perilous future. They characterized it as presenting multiple ecological and public health risks that threaten economic well-being, social equity, and world peace. Such observers often look to public policy initiatives domestically and internationally to try to reduce or eliminate those risks (Meadows, Randers, and Meadows 2004; Ophuls and Boyan 1992; Starke 2006; World Commission on Environment and Development 1987).

Such differences in estimates of human well-being and ecological health for the twenty-first century reflect at least one point of agreement: The future is not determined solely by demographic, technological, and environmental changes over which human beings have little control. It is influenced as well by our values and the way we think about and act toward the natural world. That is, to a large extent the human future will reflect what individuals and nations want it to be and the actions they take to help realize their visions. Of necessity, government decisions will be among the most important of such critical social choices.

With respect to uncertain future trends such as climate change, climatologist Stephen Schneider (1990) has argued that society might choose among three courses of action: (1) relying on technological fixes or corrective measures with little change in human behavior and institutions, (2) adapting to changing environmental conditions without attempting to counteract them, and (3) trying to prevent the adverse changes from occurring by altering the practices that cause them. Environmentalists almost always prefer preventive measures, which they believe are essential to avoid severe or irreversible consequences such as global climate change. Technological optimists, and many others, view adaptation as a realistic and less costly alternative, particularly if substantial uncertainty exists about the severity of environmental risks. Either way, however, citizens and policymakers make an explicit choice about their preferred policies. Such a choice is likely to be strongly affected by their perceptions of the relative risks, costs, and benefits of government action.

Environmental policies historically have been based on each of the three strategies that Schneider outlines, often in ill-defined combinations. In recent years, however, there has been an increasing emphasis on prevention of environmental degradation and the risks it often presents for public health. Even as conflict continues on policy issues at all levels of government, much agreement exists on the broader environmental agenda for the twenty-first century.

That agenda was considered at the 1992 Earth Summit and at the preparatory meetings that preceded it. Delegates at the summit explored at length the nature of the world's environmental and resource problems, especially in relation to the critical need for economic development in poor nations. Agenda 21, endorsed at that meeting, offered a blueprint for global sustainable development and for the institutional and policy changes it requires (United Nations 1993). Instituting those changes will preoccupy the nations of the world over the next several decades and very likely for most of the twenty-first century. How the United States and other countries respond to those challenges and how swiftly they formulate and implement suitable environmental policies and other reforms will significantly affect the quality of life in both developed and less developed nations in the future (Axelrod, Downie, and Vig 2005; Tobin 2006). The United States is slowly coming to terms with that reality in what is often called a third generation of environmental policy, but old ideas, policies, and practices will not be abandoned easily.

■ THREE GENERATIONS OF ENVIRONMENTAL POLICY AND POLITICS

The previous chapters recounted the adoption of the first generation of U.S. environmental protection and resource policies and their effects. Taken together, it is clear that they have produced significant gains since the 1960s and 1970s. For the most part, these policies promise to maintain, or even increase, improvements in environmental quality and human health and well-being as they are implemented in the future. It is equally evident, however, that these policies have exhibited serious weaknesses.

In response to the rising criticism, beginning around 1980 and continuing into the early twenty-first century, a second generation of environmental policies has been much discussed. The proposals have centered on reform of the statutes enacted in the previous decade more than their replacement. Emphasis here has been on promotion of efficiency, flexibility, cooperation between government and industry, and the use of market incentives, information disclosure, voluntary pollution reduction, and other nonregulatory and less intrusive policy tools. Increased devolution of responsibilities to the states and greater collaboration among stakeholders at state and local levels have also been part of this shift in thinking about how best to achieve environmental policy goals. Such collaboration presents increased opportunities for involvement by diverse stakeholders in environmental disputes, including interested citizens (Chertow and Esty 1997; National Academy of Public Administration 2000; Sexton et al. 1999). Controversy has swirled around many of these proposals, however, in part because environmentalists see them as a rolling back of environmental protection goals and many business representatives regard them as not going far enough to grant them the flexibility they seek (Durant, Fiorino, and O'Leary 2004; Kraft and Scheberle 1998; Marcus, Geffen, and Sexton 2002).

A third generation of environmental policy has been evolving since the late 1980s. It has not yet replaced the two earlier generations. Rather, it has built on them and incorporated new ways of thinking about environmental problems, policy goals, and the best means for achieving them. For example, there is likely to be more comprehensive and integrated analysis of the way in which human activities affect natural systems and, in turn, how human society depends on the healthy functioning of such systems, from the purification of air and water to the stabilization of climate (Daily 1997). A global as well as local, regional, or national perspective is also a key element in this new view of environmental policy.

The most distinctive characteristic of third-generation policy discussions is an emphasis on sustainability, or the imperative over time to reconcile the demands of human society with the capability of natural systems to meet its needs. At the beginning of the Clinton administration, the independent and bipartisan National Commission on the Environment, with solid representation by former EPA administrators, urged a national focus on sustainable development to underscore the inextricable linkage of environmental and economic goals. It endorsed a series of policy and institutional changes to achieve them (National Commission on the Environment 1993). By the end of the 1990s, the National Research Council (1999) issued a similar report calling for a "common journey" toward sustainability.

The implications of a shift to sustainability are profound. They range from the redesign of industrial processes to the promotion of sustainable use of natural resources such as agricultural land and forestland, surface water and groundwater, and energy. Substantial changes in human behavior would be called for as well, whether encouraged through regulation, provision of economic incentives, or public education. The need for new kinds of knowledge and new methods of analysis to promote sustainable development and help formulate public policies is equally important (Mazmanian and Kraft 1999; Parris 2003). Although the third generation of policy extends to global environmental problems and thus to international policy efforts, its advancement is perhaps most noticeable at local and regional levels, where many communities have begun to take sustainability seriously (Paehlke 2006; Portney 2003).

TOWARD SUSTAINABLE DEVELOPMENT?

The political process usually pushes policymakers toward preoccupation with short-term policy disputes and the tasks of reconciling diverse interests. Even when a general consensus exists on long-term goals such as sustainable development, both citizens and policymakers find it difficult to get a firm fix on how that abstract concept affects short-term decisions on controversial public policies. It does not help that governments, like most other organizations, tend to be deficient in their capacity to forecast the future and plan sufficiently for it. Instead, ordinarily policymakers muddle through, making incremental adjustments as needed. This time-tested strategy may work well when the rate of change is slow enough to permit such adaptation. Higher rates of change are problematic for governments as well as other organizations (Ophuls and Boyan 1992). That is especially true when decision makers must act without sufficient knowledge of the scope of change, the probable impacts on the environment and society, and the effectiveness of alternative strategies of response.

The United States and other nations find themselves in precisely this predicament in the first decade of the twenty-first century. Forecasts of changing environmental conditions offer little basis for complacency. Yet they also come with enough uncertainty that disputes over the facts and the logic of competing policy strategies may prevent agreement and action. These conditions suggest that the promotion of sustainable development will depend on improvements in scientific forecasts and their integration with decision making as well as on political skills in building public consensus. The Clinton administration's initiatives on sustainable development illustrate those needs, as do sustainable community initiatives of the last decade.

The President's Council on Sustainable Development

In June 1993 President Clinton created by Executive Order 12852 the President's Council on Sustainable Development (PCSD) to advise him on sustainability issues. He instructed the council to develop "bold, new approaches to achieve our economic, environmental, and equity goals." As discussed earlier, from the Brundtland Commission report of 1987, *Our Common Future*, to the Earth Summit's Agenda 21, environmentalists have pressed government to make sustainable development the central guiding principle of environmental and economic policymaking. The PCSD helped set the foundation for such a change in perspective and demonstrate how society could link short-term policy decisions to long-term environmental goals. To guide its work, the council adopted the Brundtland Commission's definition of sustainable development: "meeting the needs of the present without compromising the ability of future generations to meet their own needs" (43).

Throughout the 1990s the council functioned largely as an "envisioning" body to clarify the meaning and practical impact of sustainability. It brought together top corporate officials, leaders of environmental organizations, and administration officials, including members of the cabinet, to explore the connection between the environmental agenda and current policies. It also held hundreds of formal and informal meetings and hearings across the country during which its eight task forces gathered information about subjects such as population and consumption; eco-efficiency; sustainable agriculture; energy and transportation; and innovative local, state, and regional approaches. In early 1996 the council released its main report, *Sustainable America: A New Consensus for Prosperity, Opportunity, and a Healthy Environment for the Future*. The council's task forces issued their own recommendations, most of which can be found in a popular version of the council's work (Sitarz 1998).

Sustainable Development at State and Local Levels

The PCSD's activities during the 1990s reflected ongoing action by state and local governments in support of sustainable development and also encouraged them to innovate in new ways. In cooperation with industry and environmental organizations, many of these governments have recognized the need to formulate strategies for sustainable development. Some of them have been doing so under the banner of the sustainable communities movement or in the process of implementing new so-called smart growth initiatives that encourage or require local governments to develop long-term land use or growth management plans.

State and local governments are likely to play an especially crucial role in effective land use planning, a function historically handled at the local level. With encouragement and support from the federal government, states and localities can fashion land use planning policies that promise to protect environmentally sensitive areas such as wetlands and watersheds as well as biological diversity, encourage energy conservation and efficiency, sustain the productivity of agricultural land, select appropriate sites for locating industry and housing, and meet the many other environmental needs that fall within local jurisdictions. Public involvement in the formulation of such land use plans often helps ensure responsiveness to public needs and the requisite degree of public support for implementation of the plans (Knopman, Susman, and Landy 1999).

Control of urban sprawl has proven to be popular with voters in recent years, and thus many elected officials have endorsed it enthusiastically. As a notable example, former governor of New Jersey James E. McGreevey pledged to reshape the image of his state dramatically as a bastion of spreading subdivisions and clogged highways. Soon after his inauguration in 2002, the governor established a Smart Growth Policy Council to fight a "war on sprawl" that would go far beyond the actions of his predecessor, Christine Todd Whitman.[1] Similarly, in 1999 Georgia established a new Regional Transportation Authority with the power to halt development of new shopping malls in overly congested areas if road transportation is insufficient. The authority also can plan and build rail or bus systems to try to reduce traffic congestion. Sprawl in the Atlanta metropolitan area led to the initiative.[2]

The willingness to raise local taxes to pay for open space preservation and to halt the spread of cities and suburbs into surrounding countryside is especially noteworthy. Voters' preferences are understandable. According to New Jersey's Garden State Preservation Trust, an organization set up to administer the state's new program, development can reach a point of diminishing or negative returns. That is, new residential or commercial development might cost more in additional public services than it generates in new property taxes. The American Farmland Trust argues that the pattern holds in most states in which suburban growth has become a big issue.[3] Sprawl is also a leading contributor to the loss of farmland, and it results in the loss of billions of gallons of water as rainfall is washed away from impervious surfaces such as roadways and parking lots rather than filtering into the soil to recharge aquifers.[4]

The sustainable communities movement goes well beyond land use policies. Across the nation, many state and local governments have taken a keen interest not only in curbing urban sprawl and conserving open space, but in restoring damaged ecosystems and adopting innovative environmental policies on transportation, urban design, and other concerns (Mazmanian and Kraft 1999; Paehlke 2006; Press 2002). Often these kinds of decisions are made by using new and promising forms of collaborative decision making that can foster local consensus on action (John and Mlay 1999; Kraft and Johnson 1999; Shutkin 2000). For instance, during the late 1990s, hundreds of cities and towns began sustainable community initiatives that sought to reconcile environmental, economic, and social goals and improve the quality of community life. Many of them—for instance, in Portland, Oregon, and Chattanooga, Tennessee—were thought to be models of community action that demonstrated well the potential for cooperation and success at the local level.

According to political scientist Kent Portney, at least 25 major U.S. cities have "invested significant amounts of time, resources, and political capital in the development of initiatives to pursue some form of sustainability" (Portney 2003, ix). These cities include Portland, Seattle, San Francisco, Boulder, Tucson, Phoenix, Austin, Tampa, and Boston. Many more cities are considering similar actions.

Despite much evidence on progress within cities and states, there is a long way to go. It will not be easy to stimulate and maintain sustainable development or to foster a change in society's values that is as essential to achievement of environmental sustainability as is public policy. It would be useful to know more about what kinds of initiatives work well and what kinds do not, which actions are likely to receive public and policymaker support and which are not, and what conditions encourage (or discourage) successful policies and programs. The same questions apply to international efforts to encourage sustainable development, discussed later.

Business and the Environment

No matter how carefully designed and effective public policies might be, government activities are necessarily limited in their ability to change consumer behavior and industrial activities. Thus environmental sustainability depends as well on actions taken in the private sector, including those by business organizations. That realization both cheers and worries environmentalists.

Business and industry groups have often been active opponents of environmental policy, and pursuit of profit by private corporations and landowners is responsible for much of the abuse of natural resources in the United States and globally. Many leading business groups continue their efforts to weaken federal and state environmental laws and regulations that they believe are too costly and burdensome (Kamieniecki 2006; Kraft and Kamieniecki 2007). Yet some of the largest and best known U.S. corporations have demonstrated a new willingness to foster sustainable resource use, to support pollution prevention initiatives, and to develop and market green products (Fiorino 2006; Press and Mazmanian 2006).

The greening of industry is evident in many quarters, and it has been stimulated by federal environmental policies and changing market conditions. Pollution prevention as a strategy has proved to make good economic sense for many corporations. They save money by reducing or eliminating the production of wastes and pollutants rather than by disposing of them or cleaning them up. They use cleaner technologies, improved production processes, better controls and materials handling, and materials substitution. Corporate environmental management systems such as the chemical industry's Responsible Care program and the broader ISO 14001, a set of environmental standards established by the private International Organization for Standardization, have become increasingly common as well (Coglianese and Nash 2001; Potoski and Prakash 2005). Federal actions such as publication of the annual Toxics Release Inventory provide incentives for companies to minimize pollution and avoid public censure (Graham and Miller 2001; Hamilton 2005; Stephan 2002). Consumer demand for environmentally benign and energy-efficient products has also been important, although so far it has been uneven and often insufficient to encourage corporations to develop and market new products they fear will find too few buyers.

Such shifts in corporate behavior are most evident among progressive or socially conscious businesses where visionary CEOs such as Ray Anderson of Interface committed their corporations to achieving sustainability over time (Anderson 1999; Assadourian 2006; Hawken 1994).[5] Among automobile manufacturers, Honda has a similar reputation. It is the only major auto manufacturer that did not join the industry trade association in fighting tougher fuel efficiency and emissions standards, and its cars regularly set new standards for environmental performance.[6] Examples of a change to sustainable product design can be found among major chemical companies as well. For instance, the chemical giant DuPont announced in 2006 that it now allocates nearly 10 percent of its $1.3 billion annual research budget to a search for bio-based raw materials that might eventually replace its reliance on oil and natural gas for chemical stocks (Deutsch 2006). In documenting Web sites that cover these shifts in product design, Parris (2006, 3) found the trend widespread: "Some of the world's largest companies are working to integrate principles of sustainable product design." Even Wal-Mart, often criticized by consumer advocates and environmentalists for its practices, announced in 2005 that it would pursue sweeping environmental goals, including a doubling of its trucks' fuel efficiency, minimization of packaging, and reduction of energy use in its stores. It also said it would demand similar changes among the thousands of companies that supply it with goods and services (Barbaro and Barringer 2005).

Environmentalists have cooperated with industry leaders in some cases to propose new models of "natural capitalism" that they hope will appeal to corporations willing to rethink the way they do business (Hawken, Lovins, and Lovins 1999). For many corporations, however, their initial efforts have been far more limited. Sometimes the actions appear to be little more than public relations gimmicks and symbolic gestures, as when auto manufacturers and oil companies run glossy ads in national magazines touting their environmental credentials. Environmentalists deride such corporate actions as *greenwashing*, in which corporations highlight their positive contributions and ignore the environmental harm they cause. In other cases, corporations have made real and meaningful environmental progress that can be justified as economically beneficial, even in the short term.

Environmental groups have brought considerable pressure on many companies to improve their performance, sometimes with remarkable success. For example, a two-year campaign by the Rainforest Action Network in association with other groups led Home Depot, the largest retailer of old-growth wood products, to change its ways. It announced in late 1999 that by the end of 2002 it would stop carrying products made from old-growth forests. The company had been the target of demonstrations and protests around the world for carrying such products, some from British Columbia's endangered coastal rain forest (Mastny 2004).

Not all companies can adjust easily to new demands for environmentally responsible actions. Environmental protection policies may be especially burdensome on small businesses, many of which have narrow profit margins and little flexibility in product manufacturing or services. Dry cleaners are a case in point. Their use of perchloroethylene (or perc) pollutes the air and has contaminated groundwater. Thus it has become increasingly regulated. Southern California air quality officials, for example, decided to phase out the use of perc by 2020; all newly installed cleaning machines must use one of the new technologies for "green cleaning." These new methods include using water and biodegradable detergents, liquid carbon dioxide, and silicone-based solvents. Few of the nation's 33,000 dry cleaners have switched so far, in part because the new processes can take longer, raise labor costs, and sometimes shrink clothes or otherwise affect their quality. And it all comes at a time when the trend toward casual dress has reduced the demand for dry cleaning (Feder 2000).

Many small businesses face comparable dilemmas and depend on a combination of technological innovation, government assistance, and the willingness of consumers to pay higher prices for their goods and services.

Consumers can do much to motivate businesses to take environmental concerns seriously (Starke 2004). They can exercise their enormous financial power directly in the marketplace as well as through the vast sums they maintain in pension and other retirement accounts. In the last several years, some of the largest state pension funds have successfully pushed corporations in the direction of environmental sustainability. The case for more honest social accountability reporting by corporations received a big boost in the aftermath of scandals over failure of the Enron Corporation and indictment of its auditor, Arthur Andersen. Social reporting, including environmental audits, is now increasingly popular.[7]

Citizens and the Environment

As much as any other change in society, environmental sustainability depends on public attitudes, values, and behavior. Without a supportive public, governments are unlikely to enact and implement strong environmental policies that are perceived to constrain individuals' lifestyles, limit their rights, or raise their taxes. Nor will businesses market green products that are not otherwise economically defensible. An informed, environmentally committed, and active public provides the incentives that policymakers and the business community need to steer a course toward sustainability (Shabecoff 2000).

Helping the public become environmentally literate and participate effectively in decision-making processes, both public and private, is an essential part of any long-term environmental agenda. Recent trends in U.S. politics offer a sobering picture of the obstacles to citizen participation, but they also hint at the opportunities (Beierle and Cayford 2002; Shutkin 2000). For example, as discussed in Chapter 4, organized environmental groups do much to educate the public on the issues and to facilitate their participation in governmental processes. There also has been an enormous growth in the number of nongovernmental organizations both within the United States and worldwide, and they exert considerable influence on media coverage of environmental problems and on public policy decisions (McCormick 2005; National Research Council 2001).

One of the most encouraging trends is the rapid expansion of environmental information that is available to citizens, even if much of it is used far less than it might be. A vast quantity of data can be found on government agency Web sites, from the EPA to the Fish and Wildlife Service, as well as on the sites managed by nonprofit organizations and corporations. Yet recent surveys have found that the Internet remains relatively low on lists of "major sources" of environmental information on which Americans rely.[8] Moreover, many people remain disengaged from government and the political process, so they are unlikely to seek out information about environmental policy developments or even to inquire about environmental problems in their own communities (Putnam 2000; Skocpol and Fiorina 1999). The situation is hardly hopeless, however. The successful transformation of many cities suggests what can be done to motivate people to take more interest in local environmental conditions and to work toward creating more sustainable communities (Paehlke 2006; Portney 2003).

▓ INTERNATIONAL ENVIRONMENTAL POLICY AND POLITICS

If progress toward sustainable development has been slow and uneven within the United States, it has been even more difficult at the international level. This is despite its strong endorsement at the Earth Summit of 1992 and in countless documents, meetings, and speeches since that time. Recent counts point to more than 1,000 international legal instruments that focus on the environment in some fashion. Yet their implementation to date has been halting, and their effectiveness over time is by no means assured. Moreover, few rich nations have lived up to the commitments made at the Earth Summit to increase substantially their economic development assistance to poor nations.

Not all the news is so disappointing. Some international environmental treaties, most notably the Montreal Protocol to protect the stratospheric ozone layer, have been highly successful. The Convention on International Trade in Endangered Species (CITES) is another example of cooperative international action that has enjoyed considerable success. Under the right conditions, then, nations can join with one another to deal with global environmental threats. In this last section of the chapter, discussion focuses on some of the most important developments in international environmental policy and the factors that are likely to affect pursuit of sustainable development in the future.

Environmental Institutions and Policies

International environmental issues, much like their domestic counterparts, rose to prominence on government agendas during the 1960s and 1970s. As Lynton Caldwell noted so well, they presented nations with "new geophysical imperatives" with which most policymakers had no experience. That is because global environmental changes were "occurring on unprecedented scales" that were "not yet faced by modern society" (Caldwell 1990, 303). Without historical precedent, policymakers in the 1970s struggled to adapt conventional diplomatic approaches to the new problems. The search for new policy ideas and new political processes to build support for them continues today.

From Stockholm to Rio: 1972 to 1992   Symbolizing the emerging global concern for environmental problems at the time, the United Nations convened a Conference on the Human Environment in Stockholm in June 1972, attended by 113 nations. The conference theme of Only One Earth underscored the newly recognized importance of addressing global environmental problems through concerted international action. One outcome of this conference was establishment of the United Nations Environment Programme (UNEP) as a forum for discussing international environmental issues, joining other specialized UN agencies such as the World Health Organization (WHO) and the Food and Agriculture Organization (FAO).

In recognition of the role of developing nations in international affairs, UNEP was located in Nairobi, Kenya, far from other UN agencies. It also initially suffered from a small operating budget and staff. Over time, however, its budget and staff increased and it won respect and cooperation from established international agencies and nongovernmental organizations such as the World Conservation Union and World Wildlife Fund. It also began to exercise influence on environmental policy (Soroos 2005). Other international

TABLE 8.1

Selected International Environmental Policy Web Sites

Organization	Special Features and Links	Web Address
United Nations	Extensive links to UN organizations, conferences, and international activities.	www.un.org
UN Environmental Programme	Elaborate links to international environmental actions, scientific assessments, and key documents such as Agenda 21 and major environmental treaties.	www.unep.org
UN Development Programme	Links to activities and reports on economic development and environment.	www.undp.org
UN Population Fund	Funds population assistant programs worldwide, particularly family planning and reproductive health. Issues reports on population growth and its effects.	www.unfpa.org
UN Food and Agriculture Organization	One of the largest UN organizations, focusing on agriculture, forestry, fisheries, and rural development. Works to alleviate poverty and hunger worldwide.	www.fao.org
World Health Organization	A specialized UN organization focusing on health issues. Collects extensive data on the status of human health worldwide.	www.who.int/ en/
Commission on Sustainable Development	Established at the 1992 Earth Summit to follow up on recommended actions. Monitors implementation of international agreements.	www.un.org/ esa/sustdev/ csd.htm
World Bank	One of the largest sources of economic development assistance to developing nations.	www.world bank.org
International Monetary Fund	One of the largest sources of international funding for economic development.	www.imf.org
Global Environment Facility	Assists developing nations in funding sustainable development goals in biodiversity loss, climate change, international waters, ozone-layer depletion, land degradation, and persistent organic pollutants.	www.gefweb .org
European Union	The regional governing federation for Europe, with extensive environmental rules that apply to member states.	http://europa .eu.int/ index_en .htm
Intergovernmental Panel on Climate Change (IPCC)	The UN-sponsored scientific assessment panel that studies global climate change.	www.ipcc.ch
World Trade Organization (WTO)	The leading organization that oversees and enforces international trade.	www.wto.org

organizations, because of their size, experience, and prominence, have had greater effects on environmental and economic decisions, particularly on the direction of economic development. These organizations include the World Bank, whose assets and influence dwarf those of UNEP. Table 8.1 lists these and other organizations whose Web sites provide invaluable information about international environmental policy.[9]

On the 20th anniversary of the Stockholm conference, the world's nations convened in Rio de Janeiro for the United Nations Conference on Environment and Development (UNCED), better known as the Earth Summit. By 1992 there was a more palpable sense of urgency about global environmental problems such as climate change, degradation of agricultural land, water scarcity, lost of critical habitat, and threats to biological diversity, all of which were exacerbated by a growing human population. The conference organizers hoped that delegates would significantly strengthen international action and set a firm course toward sustainable development that could address the full range of environmental threats. These hopes were captured in the summit's slogan: Our Last Chance to Save the Earth.

Sustainable development provided the intellectual framework for the Rio conference, building on the Brundtland Commission report *Our Common Future* (World Commission on Environment and Development 1987). Most critically, that report and the summit itself defined environmental issues as integrally related to economic development. That is, environmental protection was seen as best achieved through the pursuit of sustainable development in decisions on agriculture, transportation, energy use, water development, and other sectors. Likewise, economic development that ignores environmental and resource constraints was thought unlikely to be successful over time.

As indicated at the beginning of Chapter 1, the Earth Summit was the largest international diplomatic conference ever held, and its activities and recommendations were much anticipated and closely watched. Among its most important actions were approval of (1) a Rio Declaration on Environment and Development that set out 27 broad principles to guide future actions; (2) a nonbinding Agenda 21, a long-term plan of action for achieving conference goals of environmentally sound development; (3) a nonbinding statement on forest principles that recommended action by nations to assess the impact of forest loss and to minimize loss; and (4) two international agreements, a Framework Convention on Climate Change and a Convention on Biological Diversity, both of which were considered to be legally binding documents (United Nations 1993). The climate change convention sought to reduce greenhouse gas emissions to 1990 levels by 2000 and eventually stabilize them at a level that would prevent human-caused climate change. The biodiversity convention requires nations to inventory plants and wildlife and develop plans to protect endangered species. It also mandates that nations signing the treaty share research, profits, and technologies with the countries that supply the genetic resources.

Agenda 21 is of obvious importance as the main plan of action to emerge from the meeting. Critics fault it as an 800-page treatise that merely points to general goals of sustainable development, with no commitments from developed nations for specific actions or economic assistance to poor nations. Yet as an official and broadly endorsed statement on the world's need for environmentally sensitive development, the document both reflects a new perspective on economic development and outlines a path for bold global action.

The World Summit on Sustainable Development   On the 10th anniversary of the Earth Summit in 2002, delegates from more than 100 of the world's nations met once again in Johannesburg, South Africa, for the World Summit on Sustainable Development. Few observers of international environmental policy believed the Johannesburg conference would match Rio in setting new directions for economic development, and the meeting itself received less attention in the news media despite the presence of some 40,000 participants (Speth 2003). For reasons discussed later, progress on the goals set in Rio had been too modest to expect more from the 2002 meeting.

Nonetheless, conference organizers saw considerable value in the meeting, as did independent observers. The organizers believed that the conference "reaffirmed sustainable development as a central element of the international agenda and gave new impetus to global action to fight poverty and protect the environment." They argued as well that "understanding of sustainable development was broadened and strengthened" by the summit, in particular "the important linkages between poverty, the environment and the use of natural resources."[10] Even the *New York Times* concluded that the meeting was "reasonably successful" because it offered a conceptual framework for integrating environmental protection and economic growth and produced a 65-page plan of implementation.[11] That plan was agreed to by more than 100 governments that pledged to work together to achieve environmental goals and to reduce world poverty. Few concrete plans emerged from the meeting, however, and the United States campaigned against specific timetables and goals.[12] The United Nations has continued to promote its goal of sharply reducing world poverty through its Millennium Development Goals, and development specialists such as Jeffrey Sachs, author of *The End of Poverty* (2005), have campaigned passionately to persuade policymakers to increase their commitment of funds for the effort.

International Environmental Agreements   In addition to prominent conferences at which international agreements are formulated, debated, and endorsed, environmental treaties emerge from discussions between two or more nations and through a variety of other meetings and forums for negotiations. Although, as noted earlier, environmental issues constitute a portion of perhaps a thousand international agreements, only about 230 agreements are predominantly environmental in character. The UN Environment Programme considers over 40 of these to be "core environmental conventions" (French 2002; Weiss and Jacobson 1999). Table 8.2 provides a select list of some of the most important of these along with their associated Web sites. Those sites offer a great deal of information about provisions of the agreements, actions taken, and progress made toward achievement of their goals.

Some environmental agreements focus on the establishment of regional institutions and policies. For instance, the European Union has moved to harmonize environmental regulations while also promoting freer trade among its member nations, and EU environmental standards are among the highest in the world (Vig and Faure 2004). The North American Free Trade Agreement (NAFTA) is an example that directly affects the United States. NAFTA established a regional trade liberalization program that was intended to promote economic trade among the United States, Canada, and Mexico. A supplemental environmental agreement negotiated by the Clinton administration created a Commission for Environmental Cooperation that was to oversee NAFTA's operation and resolve some disputes that arose. The trade agreement seeks to prevent any of the three nations from using environmental

TABLE 8.2

Selected International Environmental Agreements

Agreement	Key Goals and Objectives	Date of Adoption	Number of Parties	Web Site
UN Convention on the Law of the Sea (UNCLOS)	Establishes a framework to govern ocean use, designates 200-mile exclusive economic zones and includes provisions on conservation of living marine resources, protection of marine populations, and protection of the oceans from pollution.	1982	148	www.un.org .depts/los/
Convention on International Trade in Endangered Species of Wild Fauna and Flora (CITES)	Establishes a framework for protection of endangered species. Nations that agree to the convention implement national laws to ensure that international trade in specimens of wild animals and plants does not threaten their survival.	1975	169	www.cites .org
Montreal Protocol on Substances That Deplete the Ozone Layer	Requires the gradual phaseout of CFCs, halons, and other chemicals damaging the stratospheric ozone layer that protects life on Earth from harmful ultraviolet radiation. The protocol has been modified several times to reflect new scientific knowledge. Fewer nations have ratified the amendments adopted after 1987.	1987	189	www.unep .org/ozone
Basel Convention on the Control of Transboundary Movement of Hazardous Wastes and Their Disposal	Restricts international export of hazardous wastes from industrial to developing nations, unless the latter agree to import them. A 1994 amendment bans all hazardous waste exports to developing nations for final disposal and recovery.	1989	168	www.basel .int
Convention on Biological Diversity (CBD)	Establishes a framework for the conservation of biodiversity, sustainable use of biological resources,	1992	188	www.biodiv .org

Agreement	Key Goals and Objectives	Date of Adoption	Number of Parties	Web Site
	and fair and equitable sharing of the benefits of using genetic resources. A biosafety protocol of 2000 deals with the effects of transporting genetically modified organisms across national boundaries.			
Kyoto Protocol to the 1992 UN Framework Convention on Climate Change	Establishes a framework for addressing the release of greenhouse gases. Requires industrialized nations to reduce emissions of carbon dioxide by a specified amount within a particular time frame so as to meet the overall goal of stabilizing atmospheric concentration of gases that contribute to climate change.	1997	162	www.unfccc .int
Stockholm Convention on Persistent Organic Pollutants (POPs)	A global agreement to protect human health and the environment from persistent organic pollutants (POPs) such as dioxins and PCBs. Governments are to take measures to eliminate or reduce the release of POPs into the environment.	2001	50 (other nations continue to con- sider ratifica- tion)	www.pops .int

Sources: Adapted from Hilary French and Lisa Mastny, "Controlling International Environmental Crime," in Linda Starke, ed., *State of the World 2001* (Washington, DC: Worldwatch Institute), 169–70, and UN Environment Programme Web page (www.unep.org), as well as the Web pages for the individual agreements.

regulations to gain an economic advantage, but it does not override international agreements such as the Montreal Protocol or CITES. Experience to date suggests that NAFTA has helped strengthen Mexico's environmental policies and standards, but progress has been limited by Mexico's economic difficulties in recent years (Esty 2005; Vogel 2006).

Environmental organizations were sharply divided over NAFTA's adoption, and they continue to voice concern over the agreement's potential to weaken U.S. environmental regulations. They express similar concerns about the effect of economic globalization on the environment, and they have frequently protested decisions of the World Trade Organization. Over time, freer trade among nations is more likely to aid rather than weaken environmental protection. As poor nations develop economically, they are more likely to favor stronger environmental standards (Vogel 2006). In the short term, however, conflicts are certain to arise with economic growth in eastern Europe, Asia, Latin America, and Africa.[13]

There is increasing recognition that global environmental politics involves more than what critics call the top-down approach to planetary management that we see in UN conferences and the major treaties (Speth 2002, 2004). Supplementing this conventional approach are diverse efforts to deal with environmental threats, including economic development and social changes that are better characterized as forms of bottom-up problem solving. For instance, there has been much emphasis in recent years on management of critical natural resources by indigenous people, who have an obvious stake in the maintenance of productive forests, fisheries, and agricultural land. Some of these new perspectives were evident at the World Summit in 2002 as discussion focused less on new international treaties and more on pragmatic solutions for fighting environmental degradation and global poverty and including corporations and nongovernmental organizations (NGOs) in future meetings.

Institutional Capacity for Global Sustainable Development

The large body of international law established since the late 1960s helps govern the global environment, and numerous international institutions in addition to UNEP have been established to assist in their implementation (Caldwell 1996; Soroos 2005). International conferences that focus broadly on the environment and development, such as the Earth Summit, and more specialized meetings focusing on food, population, water, human settlements, and climate have defined the issues and spurred international agreements. Taken together, these activities have accomplished much (Axelrod, Downie, and Vig 2005; Starke 1990). Any assessment of additional requirements to protect the global environment and to assist nations in moving along a path of sustainable development, however, must be grounded in political realities that are less encouraging.

Institutions such as UNEP and the conference diplomacy that has characterized international environmental policy are necessarily limited in bringing about significant policy and institutional changes, particularly in the short term. UNEP, for example, has served primarily as a catalyst for environmental action by member states. International institutions such as the World Bank are well-staffed and powerful influences on the world's economic development. Yet as one striking example, the bank has a history of favoring large environmentally destructive development projects such coal-fired power plants and enormous dams to generate hydroelectric power. In recent years, it has promised more careful attention to the environmental impacts of its projects, but environmentalists remain skeptical of such pledges (French 1994, 2000; Soroos 2005).

However constrained global institutions such as UNEP and the World Bank have been in fostering sustainable development, environmentalists nonetheless remain hopeful that their capacity for future leadership can be enhanced. For instance, the World Summit in 2002 called for strengthening and streamlining the UN system's environmental agencies and programs and improving cooperation among the United Nations, the World Bank, the International Monetary Fund, and the World Trade Organization. It also sought to increase the availability of information on international issues and to promote greater involvement by NGO representatives. Perhaps not surprisingly, the summit delegates called on all nations to prepare and adopt national and local Agenda 21s, to ratify and implement environmental treaties, and to honor the funding pledges from Rio.

Implementing International Environmental Policy   Even with substantial improvement in global institutions, implementation of international agreements is likely to remain a stumbling block for a long time. Such agreements are invariably weaker than domestic environmental laws, and they apply unevenly to the world's nations. Only those nations signing the agreements are obliged to comply, and compliance is by no means automatic, any more than it is for domestic environmental policies. Moreover, no international institution has legal authority over nation-states comparable to their own governments, and each nation continues to define its interest based on well-entrenched concepts of national sovereignty (Downie 2005; Sands and Peel 2005). Only slowly are nations beginning to "green" the idea of sovereignty as it applies to international relations (Litfin 1998). Speth (2002) expressed the limitations well: "International environmental law is plagued by vague agreements, minimal requirements, lax enforcement, and underfunded support" (20). The treaties, he observes, are mostly frameworks for action; by themselves they do not drive change. Moreover, the process of negotiation that leads to approval of the treaties provides considerable leverage to countries that seek to protect the status quo. Thus the United States weakened the Kyoto Protocol on climate change and later withdrew from it anyway.

That said, international treaties and agreements such as the Montreal Protocol and CITES have had significant effects, respectively, on phasing out use of ozone-depleting substances and protecting endangered wildlife. For those agreements that have been studied closely, it is apparent that implementation and compliance have been improving. In part that is attributable to increased public concern for the environment, enhanced media coverage of the issues, and pressure from both national and international nongovernmental organizations (NGOs), such as environmental groups (DeSombre 2002; Weiss and Jacobson 1999). Environmental NGOs have been proliferating in recent years and have become influential political actors in shaping both policy adoption and implementation. They have contributed as well to the development of a global civil society in which human concerns the world over can be debated and acted on (Kamieniecki 1993; McCormick 2005; National Research Council 2001; Wapner 1996).

In situations in which compliance with international agreements is insufficient, several strategies may help: so-called sunshine methods (e.g., national reporting, on-site monitoring by NGOs, and media access), provision of positive incentives (e.g., financial and technical assistance and training programs), and coercive measures (sanctions and penalties). In short, much like domestic policies, specific actions may be taken to improve compliance with international environmental policies (Weiss and Jacobson 1999).

As an illustration of compliance difficulties, between 2003 and 2005, the Bush administration sought "critical use exemptions" from the Ozone Secretariat of UNEP for the pesticide methyl bromide. Under provisions of the Montreal Protocol, the chemical was to be banned from use after 2005. The administration was trying to help farmers, golf course operators, and others who want to continue using the pesticide on the grounds that no acceptable substitutes are available. Environmentalists objected that granting of too many exemptions will undermine the treaty and threaten damage to the ozone layer. They pressured the White House to minimize the requests for exemptions under the treaty. Final decisions on such exemptions are made by an expert advisory panel to the Ozone Secretariat.[14]

Despite these kinds of challenges, the Montreal Protocol is widely viewed as the most effective environmental agreement ever adopted. Experience with its formulation and implementation suggests how other global environmental issues might be addressed. In his assessment of the protocol, for instance, Benedick (1991) concluded that a number of features might be equally appropriate for other environmental treaties. Among them are the following: (1) a need to have scientists play an unaccustomed but critical role in negotiations, (2) the possibility that governments may have to act in the face of scientific uncertainty (the so-called precautionary principle), (3) the necessity of educating and mobilizing public opinion to generate pressure on governments and private companies to act, (4) the desirability of a leading country taking preemptive environmental protection measures in advance of a global agreement to help build international support, (5) sufficient recognition in an agreement of economic inequalities among countries, (6) employment of market incentives to stimulate technological innovation, and (7) the involvement of citizen groups and industry in diplomatic efforts to formulate and adopt such treaties.[15]

Political Commitment by Developed Nations   This experience speaks to what is needed to achieve the demanding goals of the Earth Summit's Agenda 21. In the early 1990s, the UNCED secretariat estimated that the cost of implementing Agenda 21 would be about $600 billion per year between 1993 and 2000. Developing nations were to provide most of those funds. The plan, however, called for the industrialized nations to contribute $125 billion a year beyond what they already provided under a variety of existing programs. The target aid level was 0.7 percent of GNP "as soon as possible." At the time, U.S. aid totaled about 0.2 percent of GNP, less than amounts contributed by 14 other nations.

The new spending, part of which was to be funneled through the Global Environment Facility (GEF), was roughly to double the levels of support then in existence. The GEF is an international financing mechanism originally established as a partnership involving the World Bank, the UN Development Programme, and UNEP to provide developing nations with the means to bypass polluting and wasteful technologies and move toward sustainable economic development. It was restructured after UNCED as a larger and better financed agency to assist in implementing international conventions on ozone depletion, biodiversity, and climate change as well as provisions of Agenda 21 (Soroos 2005). Such "financial transfer institutions" are increasingly viewed as essential for environmental protection in developing nations, but they are also problematic and not always effective (Keohane and Levy 1996).

The financial pledges from developed nations were an essential component of Agenda 21 and necessary to help poor nations make progress toward the economic development and environmental protection goals of the Earth Summit. Yet the developed nations have fallen short of those commitments. The United States has been among the worst performers. In one comparison of economic aid contributed by developed countries, it came in dead last, at least when viewed as a percentage of the overall size of national economies. In 2000 it contributed only 0.10 percent of its GNP in such assistance, or only half of the level it supported in 1992. France, Germany, Japan, and the United Kingdom were all above 0.27 percent of GNP. Of course, the total dollar amount contributed by the United States was still a sizable $9.5 billion in 2000 because of its large economy (French 2002). Consistent with these economic measures, a ranking of 142 nations on an index of environmental sustainability released in 2002 put the United States 51st. U.S. performance was considered to be uneven; the nation was highly ranked for water pollution control and promoting environmental policy debates. It lagged others, however, in controlling greenhouse gas emissions and in reducing waste. By 2005 the U.S. ranking had improved slightly; it was then 45th out of 146 nations that were compared. Total U.S. economic development assistance rose to nearly $19 billion by 2004, or more than twice that of any other developed nation, yet it remained low as a percentage of the nation's GNP (at 0.16 percent).[16]

In a similar assessment, the first report of the panel set up to monitor achievements following the Rio conference hinted at implementation problems ahead. In 1994 the United Nations Commission on Sustainable Development indicated that only slow progress was being made. The commission chair said that the international community had fallen "significantly short of expectations and requirements" in providing money and the technological expertise developing nations need to foster environmental sustainability. He called on the rich nations to do more to restrict their own environmentally harmful consumption patterns (P. Lewis 1994).

Later reports were not much more hopeful. In 1997, following a five-year review of Agenda 21's achievements, the United Nations concluded that global environmental conditions had worsened and that "overall trends remain unsustainable"; it urged more intensive action. In his comprehensive review of international action on Agenda 21, Bryner (1999) concluded that "relatively little changed during the first five years in the structure of the global community and its capacity to organize for sustainable development" (183). His views were echoed by many others. A decade after the Earth Summit, despite many initiatives by individual nations, international organizations, business, and NGOs to work toward sustainable development, progress has been modest at best, especially from the perspective of developing nations (Najam 2005).

In his review of events since Rio, Secretary-General Kofi Annan of the United Nations expressed similar disappointment that progress "has been slower than anticipated." Conservation measures, he argued, were "far from satisfactory," the environment is "still treated as an unwelcome guest" at discussions of finance and the world economy, and high-consumption lifestyles "continue to tax the Earth's natural life-support systems" (Annan 2002, 12). Annan was hopeful, however, that the Johannesburg summit would launch a major assault on global poverty that could pave the way for further progress on the environmental front. He looked especially to partnerships among governments, private businesses, nonprofit groups, scholars, and concerned citizens as "the most creative agents of change." As noted earlier, the new UN Millennium Development Goals are an expression of such hope.

U.S. Leadership on Global Environmental Issues   For the current ensemble of international institutions, agreements, and agendas to succeed in reaching the goal of environmental sustainability, strong public support, governmental commitment, and especially political leadership will be needed within each nation. There are good reasons to be skeptical that all will be forthcoming in the near term. Within the fragmented

U.S. political system, for example, leadership generally can come only from the White House. Yet it was largely absent under Ronald Reagan and George H. W. Bush, and it was much weaker under Bill Clinton than environmentalists had hoped to see.

The Clinton administration was supportive of the UNCED climate change and biodiversity agreements, and it took a strong stance on the need to reduce world population growth, as discussed later. Nonetheless, environmental groups criticized the administration for its lack of forceful leadership on climate change issues and for its positions on expanding international trade that might pose a threat to U.S. environmental standards (Vogel 2006). They were even more critical of the ineffective leadership of Congress on international environmental issues during the 1990s, particularly its refusal to sign the biodiversity and climate change conventions (Paarlberg 1999).

Under President George W. Bush, the United States withdrew further from its previous position as a global environmental leader, most notably on climate change issues. The administration maintained that climate science was too inexact to warrant demanding and costly national policies and, as discussed later, withdrew from the Kyoto Protocol. Because of its decision to abandon its long-standing leadership role on the environment, allies in Europe and elsewhere openly dissented from the U.S. position (Vig and Faure 2004). Bush declined to attend the World Summit, and when Secretary of State Colin Powell delivered a brief speech there, he was interrupted twice by hecklers who shouted "Shame on Bush!"

These disappointments notwithstanding, the goals and the processes that UNCED set in motion remain highly important. As UNCED organizer Maurice Strong observed, the 1992 meeting was a "launching pad," not a quick fix. The previously fuzzy concept of sustainable development was given a clearer form, and guiding principles and goals were set in place that will shape international economic and environmental decision making over the next several decades. The mutual dependency of environmental health and economic well-being was firmly established, and realization of such relationships set a new context for international politics and ethics in the twenty-first century.

What is needed over the next several decades is concerted action to build on the commitments made at Rio and Johannesburg. The choices are stark. The world will likely experience phenomenal economic growth over the next half century and more. That growth has a real potential to seriously erode environmental systems and make the world's people worse off in many ways. If the right choices are made, however, it also has the potential to restore damaged ecosystems, protect public health, and promote widespread prosperity. As James Speth (2002) stated recently, there "is still world enough and time for this century to see the coming of a future more wondrous, intimate, and bountiful than our scenarios can imagine. But this world will not be won without a profound commitment to urgent action" (24).[17]

■ POLITICAL CONFLICT AND GLOBAL ENVIRONMENTAL POLICY

Despite general agreement on the goals of sustainable development, international environmental policy and politics will be characterized by considerable conflict in the decades ahead. As discussed earlier, third-generation environmental issues such as climate change and loss of biodiversity are difficult to address given their global scale, scope, cost, uncertainties, and the necessity of a level of cooperation among nations that is never easy to achieve. As evident in declining support for economic assistance for poor nations just described, political leadership by the developed nations has not always been forthcoming. The United States in particular seems disinclined to play its historical leadership role on these issues. Commenting on climate change politics, for example, Lamont Hempel noted that although "unquestionably a world leader in many aspects of environmental protection, the United States is increasingly viewed as the world's leading laggard when it comes to global warming issues" (2006, 288).

A brief review of controversies that have surrounded three of the most important third-generation environmental issues helps illuminate both the potential and pitfalls of international environmental policy and politics. The descriptions focus on the linkages between domestic politics and international policy and also underscore the difficulty of addressing complex global environmental problems. In all three cases, the evidence points toward substantial achievements over the past three and a half decades in establishing long-term international environmental goals and public policies to help reach them. Yet as Speth suggested in the statement cited above, if the world is to make significant progress toward sustainable development, a much greater commitment by both citizens and policymakers will be needed in the future.

Climate Change

Climate change is widely considered to be the most significant environmental problem of the twenty-first century. It is a prototypical third-generation environmental issue, global in its scale, long term in its scope, and with substantial scientific uncertainty over the magnitude, timing, and location of its effects. Political conflicts over how to respond to the risks of climate change are anchored in the short-term costs of cutting back sharply on use of fossil fuels and the implications for economic development. Political support for action on climate change has been particularly lacking in the United States. In part it is because the issue fails to arouse much public concern and because climate change is perplexing to most people (Bosso and Guber 2006). Weak political support is also attributable to the influence of the fossil fuel, automobile, and other industries that might be adversely affected by policy action to curb emissions of greenhouse gases (Layzer 2007).

The Framework Convention on Climate Change was agreed to by 150 nations at the 1992 Earth Summit. Following a series of international meetings culminating in Kyoto, Japan, in December 1997, delegates approved the Kyoto Protocol, which set out country-by-country targets for reduced emission of greenhouse gases. Of special importance for the United States, the agreement called for 39 industrialized nations to reduce their emissions about 5 percent below 1990 levels by 2012. As noted in Chapter 2, the U.S. target was 7 percent below its 1990 level, in effect a reduction of about 30 to 35 percent from emissions that would otherwise occur (Hempel 2006). The protocol applies to all major greenhouse gases, not just carbon dioxide. At a follow-up meeting in Buenos Aires in November 1998, the Clinton administration signed the agreement, but the U.S. Congress remained opposed.

The Clinton White House tried to make the U.S. position more palatable to industry and Congress by proposing extensive use of emissions trading with developing nations to meet the U.S. reduction targets. Indeed, most of the cost of the administration's planned cutbacks in U.S. emissions depended on the use of such market-based incentives. Environmentalists argued strongly that the United States could and should do better through an intensive program of energy conservation and research and development in support of alternative energy sources. Reflecting those views, many states and communities have tried to further energy conservation based on concern for global climate change (Rabe 2004; Rabe and Mundo 2007). California and the states in the Northeast have been among the most innovative leaders.[18]

The Bush administration adopted a more skeptical stance on climate change than was prevalent throughout the 1990s. Most striking was its announcement in March 2001 that it would withdraw the United States from the Kyoto agreement. The White House said that the agreement would weaken the U.S. economy and create inequities by exempting developing nations from the treaty's requirements. In its place the administration called for additional scientific research and urged U.S. companies to set voluntary targets for reduction in greenhouse gas emissions. Environmentalists denounced both positions as inadequate and unjustified based on available scientific evidence of human effects on climate change (Gardiner and Jacobson 2002; Hempel 2006).[19] The administration also made clear that the United States would not be bound by the Kyoto Protocol or decisions made to implement it. As discussed in Chapter 6, at the same time the Bush administration made these decisions it was proposing a U.S. national energy policy grounded largely in expanded use of fossil fuels. That energy policy was approved by Congress in August 2005.

The Bush White House showed no sign of softening its position even when an EPA report to the United Nations released in mid-2002 underscored the dire consequences of climate change for the United States. They included an increase in stifling heat waves; threats to alpine meadows, coral reefs, and other vulnerable ecosystems; and public health threats from heat stress, air pollution, extreme weather, and diseases that spread more easily in a warmer climate. The report laid the blame for these health and environmental effects squarely on human actions, especially the burning of coal, oil, and natural gas.[20] Under fire from conservatives to distance himself from the report, President Bush said he read "the report put out by the bureaucracy" but remained opposed to the Kyoto treaty.[21] At about the same time, the administration sought to replace an American scientist, Dr. Robert T. Watson, who for six years had served as chair of the UN-sponsored Intergovernmental Panel on Climate Change (IPCC). Responding to pleas from energy and automobile industry lobbyists, the White House and State Department pressed for someone who was less outspoken on climate change issues.[22]

In subsequent years, the administration maintained the same stance on climate change and its skepticism on climate science. It continued to oppose the Kyoto Protocol, creating a profound rift between the United States and other industrialized nations during international meetings on climate change (Revkin 2005; Rohter 2004). By late 2005, however, there were many indicators that public and political support for more aggressive action on climate change was growing, in part because of increasingly convincing and well-publicized scientific evidence of human-caused warming (Flannery 2005). Several bills in Congress gained substantial backing, and the chair of the Senate Energy and Natural Resources Committee, Pete Domenici (R-New Mexico), previously a climate change skeptic, agreed with the need to take stronger steps. The Senate itself passed a nonbinding resolution in 2005 saying that to combat climate change the United States must turn to mandatory restrictions on greenhouse gases. Major corporations, such as DuPont, also began to recognize the reality of climate change and the need to deal with it (Kriz 2005; Schulte 2006). Even evangelical Christian groups took a surprising interest in the subject and pressed the Bush administration to act (Goodstein 2006).

Whatever position the United States takes on the Kyoto Protocol or any agreement that replaces it, the challenge of dealing with climate change is enormous. Implementation of climate stabilization policies and programs in the years ahead will depend heavily on the capacity of the world's nations to maintain these agreements and to foster cooperation between industrialized nations and developing nations such as China and India. That surely will not be easy. Moreover, conflicts over climate change policies at the Johannesburg conference in 2002 and at other meetings since then indicated plainly that the United States was by no means the only nation reluctant to approve strong provisions (Swarms 2002).

Protection of Biological Diversity

Any program of sustainable development also must include policies to halt the loss of biological diversity, restore ecosystem health, and maintain the ecological functions essential to long-term environmental sustainability. Within the United States, controversies over the Endangered Species Act attest to the obstacles in formulating and implementing policies and programs to achieve such goals. International policy for protection of biodiversity is a relatively recent development that depends largely on efforts within individual nations to inventory and protect species and the habitats in which they live. Almost no one believes that these tasks will be achieved easily in light of growing human demand for land and resources and short-term economic pressures—for instance, to harvest tropical forests—that often drive out concern for long-term ecosystem preservation (Tobin 2006). The UN Millennium Ecosystem Assessment, a four-year $24 million study of threats to the world's ecosystems, confirmed such fears. It found that 60 percent of global ecosystems are being degraded or used in an unsustainable manner, and that 10 to 30 percent of mammal, bird, and amphibian species may be threatened with extinction as a result.[23]

The chief international policy for biodiversity protection is the UN Convention on Biological Diversity (CBD). After a decade of formulation, it was approved at the 1992 Earth Summit and took effect in late 1993. As of early 2006, 188 nations had ratified the CBD and become parties to the agreement. The United States was not among them. The Clinton administration endorsed the CBD, but the Senate, whose approval is required under the U.S. Constitution, had reservations. Among them were the implications for intellectual property rights to biological and genetic resources, a source of conflict because most of the biodiversity resources are in developing nations but likely to be used most by industrialized nations.

The CBD is designed to slow the loss of Earth's biodiversity through adoption of national policies to conserve species and their habitats and to promote public awareness of conservation and sustainable uses of biological diversity. Parties under the treaty maintain their sovereign rights over biological resources within their countries, but they also assume responsibility for biodiversity conservation and sustainable use of biological resources. The CBD framework provides for an international forum, a series of meetings that bring together public officials, NGOs, academics, and others to discuss issues and review progress. The Conference of Parties, consisting of those nations that have ratified the treaty, constitutes a governing body for the CBD. It is charged with reviewing progress, identifying priorities, and setting work plans for members. Activities taken by developing countries in support of the convention are eligible for support through the Global Environment Facility (GEF), which pools money from donor nations.

The CBD commits parties to "fair and equitable sharing of the benefits arising out of the utilization of genetic resources." As is often the case in policy implementation, however, concern focuses on the details of such arrangements. Developed nations also are to provide developing countries with "new and additional financial resources" to enable them to meet expectations under the treaty. As shown earlier, however, such economic assistance has fallen short of expectations. Consequently, developing nations have lacked the resources to meet the treaty's goals.

In the early 2000s, the Bush administration argued that the United States remained committed to the objectives of the CBD both at home and abroad, and it defended its level of contribution to developing nations on behalf of biodiversity conservation. The administration emphasized reliance on partnerships between public and private actors, however, rather than on more formal government programs.[24] The administration also indicated it was reviewing the issue of treaty ratification.

Experience with the Convention on International Trade in Endangered Species (CITES) offered some hope that international public concern could be aroused and nations persuaded to adopt conservation policies. Yet the CBD faces much greater obstacles because its goals are more directly related to human pressures on the environment. Human society today uses more than 40 percent of global plant production and an estimated 50 percent of the world's freshwater runoff. As the population increases and economic growth continues, the potential for adversely affecting biodiversity is enormous. A prominent example is the destruction of Indonesian rain forests at the rate of about 4 million acres a year, or an area the size of Connecticut. By one estimate, 80 percent of Indonesia's timber trade is illegal, but intensive logging continues because of the desperate need for employment and economic gain, rampant corruption among government and military officials who profit from the timber industry, and strong demand around the world for prized tropical hardwood.[25]

Despite the obvious constraints on biodiversity conservation, some nations, including developing nations that often are considered to be too preoccupied with alleviation of poverty to exhibit any concern for environmental protection, have made remarkable progress. Two cases in point are Costa Rica and Bolivia, each of which has adopted innovative and highly successful policies and programs to conserve tropical biodiversity. These programs include establishment in Costa Rica of one of the best national park systems in the world and pioneering efforts in promotion of ecotourism and biodiversity prospecting. The nation also had a president who "made sustainable development the conceptual underpinning of his entire administration" (Steinberg 2001, 3). Bolivia created the world's first debt-for-nature swap in which a portion of national debt is exchanged for land to be set aside for conservation purposes. It also developed the world's largest forest-based climate change mitigation project, organized a national environmental endowment that serves as a model for nations in the region, and "established an effective, high-profile biodiversity conservation agency" (Steinberg 2001, 4).

Why are some nations so committed and successful in pursuit of biodiversity protection goals while others lag far behind? With the world's biodiversity conservation largely in the hands of individual nations, particularly developing countries, that is an important question. In his study of four decades of reform in Costa Rica and Bolivia, Paul Steinberg (2001) suggests that much depends on policy leadership within the nations. That is, biodiversity conservation does not come about solely because of decisions made by international organizations, efforts by scientists and other experts (what Peter Haas has called epistemic communities), media coverage, or public pressure. It is equally a result of domestic political activities that help build national commitment to conservation goals. Steinberg finds in particular that "bilateral activists," individual policy entrepreneurs who operate in both the domestic and international spheres, have been enormously influential. These activists include reformers within government as well as activists associated with NGOs. Given the many obstacles to success in global biodiversity conservation, the study's conclusions offer a hopeful perspective on how other nations might initiate comparable policies.

Population Growth and Economic Development

Stabilization of the human population is an essential component of sustainable development. Fortunately, rates of growth have slowed in recent decades, to a global average of about 1.2 percent per year by 2005 and an average for developing nations (excluding China) of 1.8 percent. Many reasons account for the slower growth rates, including economic development in poor nations, the availability of family planning and other health care services, and improvement in the status of women. Yet, as discussed in Chapter 2, the current rate of growth nevertheless translates into an increase in the world's population of about 80 million people annually and projections for a global population of over 9 billion by 2050. Population growth is likely to continue throughout the twenty-first century, reaching perhaps 10 billion by 2100, with important consequences for achieving economic development and environmental protection goals (United Nations 2005).

Population growth is perched precariously on the international political agenda. Like many other third-generation environmental issues the problem is global and long term, and it is nearly invisible to the average person. It is also difficult to appreciate how personal decisions on family size or national action on population policies that promote family planning can affect a range of environmental and economic conditions over time. In addition, population policy has been highly controversial because of perceived conflicts with cultural and religious values.

Individual nations have long had international population policies that were intended to fund family planning programs abroad. U.S. policies of this kind began in the early 1960s under President Lyndon Johnson, and they received strong bipartisan backing for two decades. The United States was a recognized leader in fostering family planning around the world and for years was the largest donor to the United Nations Fund for Population Activities (UNFPA), later renamed the United Nations Population Fund (Kraft 1994a). Following a UN conference on population in Mexico City in 1984, however, the Reagan administration ended all U.S. contributions to the UNFPA, the major multilateral funding agency for international family planning programs. The cutoff continued under President George H. W. Bush from 1989 to early 1993. The Reagan and Bush administrations took the position that the

United States needed no policy on either national or global population growth, neither of which was thought to be a significant problem. Both administrations sought to appease important conservative constituencies who were concerned about China's tough population policy as well as about moral issues related to both family planning and abortion.

Although the elimination of U.S. financial support for UN population programs lasted from 1986 to 1993, Presidents Reagan and Bush did maintain support for U.S. bilateral population assistance programs in which the nation directly supplies funds to other countries, largely to support family planning programs. Nevertheless, the shift in population policy under both presidents contributed significantly to the virtual disappearance of population issues on the national agenda.

As soon as he took office, President Bill Clinton reversed the so-called Mexico City policy of the Reagan and Bush administrations and reestablished support for the UN population program. He also boosted funding for the nation's bilateral family planning assistance programs. In 1993 the Clinton administration already had signaled it would reclaim the leadership position on world population issues that the United States held in the 1960s and 1970s. It did so at the 1994 International Conference on Population and Development (ICPD) in Cairo, where delegates debated a proposed action plan on global population stabilization. Most of the controversy at the ICPD focused on the issue of abortion, with the Vatican and many Muslim and Latin American nations objecting strenuously to provision of legal abortion as part of reproductive health care. Yet despite those disagreements, delegates to the historic meeting, including those representing the Vatican, demonstrated a remarkable consensus on the basic principles of population policy for the twenty-first century. Representing 180 nations, they approved a 20-year "program of action" that they believed could hold world population to below UN projections at the time of 7.5 billion by 2020 and 9.8 billion by the year 2050.

The 113-page declaration called for a tripling of the amount the world spends on population stabilization. Spending was to rise from the $5 billion spent in 1994 to $17 billion by 2000, with an even higher target of $22 billion by 2015. Delegates also expanded the concept of population policy well beyond traditional family planning programs. The action plan called for governments and donor nations to support education for girls to help promote gender equity, to provide women with a range of choices on family planning and health care issues, and to improve the status of women in developing nations to empower them to make decisions related to reproductive choice (Cowell 1994). By late 1999 at a "Cairo Plus Five" conference, however, such measures appeared to be falling well short of pressing world needs.[26]

In his second day in office in January 2001, President George W. Bush reinstated the Mexico City policy that withholds U.S. funds from international family planning programs run by overseas NGOs (largely those that include abortion-related services, medical referrals, research, or public information campaigns). The restrictions do not apply to financial grants to foreign governments. Family planning professionals argue that the effect of such restrictions on reproductive health services worldwide is significant because the United States is the largest single donor to international population assistance programs (Cincotta and Crane 2001).

In addition, the following year the president decided to end U.S. funding for the United Nations Population Fund despite pleas for such financial support from

Secretary of State Colin Powell. Powell had praised the UN agency for its "invaluable work," and a state department study appeared to absolve the agency from any participation in coercive family planning in China. Predictably, anti-abortion groups applauded the Bush decision and environmental and prochoice groups condemned it.[27] Under long-standing U.S. law, the UN program already is barred from using U.S. money in China or in support of abortion services. The UN agency spends about $270 million a year on reproductive health care and family planning programs, about $3.5 million of which goes to China. To underscore their disappointment with the Bush decision on funding cuts, UNFPA representatives asserted that the $34 million the president withheld from UN programs could result in 2 million unwanted pregnancies, 800,000 induced abortions, 4,700 maternal deaths, and 7,700 infant and child deaths worldwide.[28] The Bush administration continued to withhold the UNFPA funds in subsequent years. By 2006 it also proposed cutting U.S. spending on bilateral population assistance programs by 18 percent; the nation had been spending $425 million a year on such programs (Dugger 2006).

Continuing controversies over abortion-related language in official documents also led the administration to threaten to withdraw the United States from the landmark ICPD "program of action." According to press accounts, the U.S. position, announced at a population and development conference in Bangkok, Thailand, in November 2002, startled members of other national delegations attending the meeting. In addition, it drew sharp criticism from Chinese, Indian, and Indonesian officials, who complained that the U.S. action could undermine a global consensus on population policy. European and UN officials and members of the U.S. Congress who view reproductive health care programs as one of the most effective ways to help reduce global poverty expressed similar concerns.[29] Many of these apparent conflicts reflect posturing on the issues in an effort to appease particular constituencies at home. Yet they also remind us that environmental agreements often rest on a fragile political consensus that can weaken at any time.

Neither Republican nor Democratic administrations in the United States have taken seriously one of the most notable omissions in U.S. population policy: a failure to exhibit any concern for population growth in the United States itself and its implications for sustainable development at home and abroad. As noted in Chapter 2, the United States is growing as fast or faster than any other industrialized nation, at about 1 percent (or nearly 3 million people) a year. This is 10 times the rate that prevails in western European nations. Between 1990 and 2000, the U.S. gained 33 million people, and the latest Census Bureau projections put the U.S. population at about 420 million by 2050 (Kent and Mather 2002).[30] A larger U.S. population can dramatically increase demand for homes, automobiles, and other consumer products, as well as the energy and natural resources their production and use require. It also raises serious questions of equity in use of the world's resources (Mazur 1994; Postel 1994; Tobin 2006).

■ CONCLUSIONS

Environmental policy depends on advances on many fronts: scientific research, technological invention, reengineering of industrial processes and improvements in corporate management, enhancement of governmental capacities for policymaking and implementation, a more widespread embrace of environmental values, and increases in public knowledge and involvement. The early twenty-first century is a time of profound and unpredictable changes in these areas of human activity. It is also a difficult period for those who place their hope in government and political processes. Critics frequently disparage government and politics and thereby contribute to the prevailing public cynicism. The effects are to limit the collective power of citizens and to increase the influence of well-organized special interests that pursue political values at odds with those held by the public. An invigorated democratic politics is essential to any strategy for creating a just and sustainable society, and policymakers and activists could seek ways to make the political system more open to public participation and also more responsive to public needs.

The short-term environmental policy agenda for the early twenty-first century is clear and broadly supported. There also are signs of progress in achieving it despite continuing battles over environmental protection and natural resources policies in the United States and within international policy forums. Individuals will disagree over the interpretation of the latest data and studies and over the way policymakers should reconcile conflicting positions on the issues. Those who find the direction, form, or pace of policy and institutional changes deficient should consider entering the fray to fight for their views.

The longer-term agenda of sustainable development is less distinct, but it is becoming sharper as communities and nations struggle to define its meaning and shift programs and priorities to promote it both domestically and internationally. The challenges here are more daunting and demand more commitment than has been evident in either government or corporate circles. Citizens need to press both government and business to do a better job. They can help by building coalitions for environmental sustainability, articulating the social, economic, and political changes necessary, and devoting themselves to their realization.

DISCUSSION QUESTIONS

1. To what extent is the movement to take sustainability seriously in U.S. communities a success? What are the most important factors in encouraging citizens and communities to adopt and support sustainability initiatives such as preserving open space or improving a city's quality of life?

2. How seriously has U.S. industry begun to work toward sustainable development? Are the kinds of initiatives evident to date chiefly a form of greenwashing, or do they indicate a significant commitment to environmental goals? What would motivate companies to do more?

3. What is the potential for citizen involvement in environmental decision making, at any level of government? What might encourage a greater level of such "civic environmentalism"?

4. To what extent is the present array of international environmental institutions and policies capable of dealing with global environmental challenges? If they are not sufficient, what else is needed to deal effectively with global environmental threats and economic development over the next several decades?

5. Some international environmental treaties have been more successful than others. What factors most significantly affect the success of international agreements such as the Kyoto Protocol on climate change or the Convention on Biological Diversity?

SUGGESTED READINGS

Axelrod, Regina S., David Leonard Downie, and Norman J. Vig, eds. *The Global Environment: Institutions, Law, and Policy,* 2nd ed. Washington, DC: CQ Press, 2005.

Brown, Lester R. *Plan B 2.0: Rescuing a Planet Under Stress and a Civilization in Trouble.* New York: W. W. Norton, 2006.

Chasek, Pamela S., David L. Downie, and Janet Welsh Brown. *Global Environmental Politics,* 4th ed. Boulder, CO: Westview Press, 2006.

Desai, Uday, ed. *Environmental Politics and Policy in Industrialized Countries.* Cambridge, MA: MIT Press, 2002.

DeSombre, Elizabeth R. *The Global Environment and World Politics: International Relations for the 21st Century.* New York: Continuum, 2002.

Speth, James Gustave. *Red Sky at Morning: America and the Crisis of the Global Environment.* New Haven, CT: Yale University Press, 2004.

Steinberg, Paul F. *Environmental Leadership in Developing Countries: Transnational Relations and Biodiversity Policy in Costa Rica and Bolivia.* Cambridge, MA: MIT Press, 2001.

ENDNOTES

1. Andrew Jacobs, "New Jersey Governor Enlists Himself in 'War on Sprawl,' II" *New York Times,* January 2, 2003, A19.
2. David Firestone, "Georgia Setting Up Tough Anti-Sprawl Agency," *New York Times,* March 25, 1999, A18.
3. See John Maggs, "Local Taxes Make the Garden State Greener," *National Journal,* April 8, 2000, 1146–47. Arguments of this kind are common in proposals of sustainable communities, and Web sites focusing on those issues cover other studies. See, for example, the American Farmland Trust (www.farmland.org), the Smart Growth Network (www.smartgrowth.org), the Sprawl Watch Clearinghouse (www.sprawlwatch.org), the Sustainable Communities Network (www.sustainable. org), and the Land Trust Alliance (www.lta.org).
4. For information on the loss of farmland and water, see a study released in late 2002 by American Rivers, the Natural Resources Defense Council, and Smart Growth America: *Paving Our Way to Water Shortages: How Sprawl Aggravates the Effects of Drought,* available at www.americanrivers.org.
5. Interface's employees have been formally trained in the company's environmental principles, which were derived from The Natural Step, a Swedish organization dedicated to helping corporations become more environmentally responsible while maintaining profitability. Several Web sites are dedicated to these kinds of actions: The Natural Step (www.naturalstep.org), the World Business Council for Sustainable Development (www.wbcsd.ch), and the Coalition for Environmentally Responsible Economies (www.ceres.org). Anderson is now chairman of the board of Interface; others are responsible for day-to-day management of the company.
6. See Danny Hakim, "Honda Takes Up Case in U.S. for Green Energy," *New York Times,* June 2, 2002, C1–4.
7. Amy Cortese, "The New Accountability: Tracking the Social Costs," *New York Times,* March 24, 2002, Business section, 4. See also Bernd Kasemir, Andrea Süess, and Alexander J. B. Zehnder, "The Next Unseen Revolution: Pension Fund Investment and Sustainability," *Environment* 43 (November 2001): 9–19.

8. The data come from Roper's Green Gauge reports (www.roper.com). In the report released in December 2001, 63 percent of the public said that television was a major source of environmental information; 59 percent cited newspapers; 32 percent, radio; and 31 percent, environmental groups. Only 23 percent characterized Internet sources in the same way.

9. A helpful guide to UN Web sites that deal with the environment can be found in Thomas M. Parris, "Navigating the Environmental Sites of the United Nations," *Environment* 42 (October 2000): 3–4.

10. The statements come from "Key Outcomes of the Summit," on the summit Web page: www.johannesburgsummit.org.

11. Editorial in the *New York Times*, September 6, 2002, A24.

12. For an overview of the meeting, see Rachel L. Swarns, "Broad Accord Reached at Global Environmental Meeting," *New York Times*, September 4, 2002, A5; James Dao, "Protesters Interrupt Powell Speech as U.N. Talks End," *New York Times*, September 5, 2002, A8; and Andrew C. Revkin, "Small World After All," *New York Times*, September 5, 2002, A8.

13. For a review of Web sites related to international trade and the environment, see W. Christopher Lenhardt, "Green Trade on the Web," *Environment* 42 (November 2000): 3–4.

14. See Rebecca Adams, "Ozone vs. Food Supply, a Chemical Dilemma," *CQ Weekly*, September 5, 2005, 2291–92.

15. For an insightful discussion of how citizens and nations can learn from experience with the Montreal Protocol, see Hilary French, "Learning from the Ozone Experience," in *State of the World 1997*, ed. Linda Stark (Washington, DC: Worldwatch Institute, 1997).

16. The results for the Environmental Sustainability Index, a joint project of Yale University, Columbia University, and the World Economic Forum, can be found at www.ciesin.columbia.edu/indicators/ESI/. The 2005 report is described in Felicity Barringer, "Nations Ranked as Protectors of the Environment," *New York Times*, January 24, 2005, A9. For a comparison of environmental politics within industrialized nations that helps explain such differences in performance, see Desai (2002). The economic assistance figures for 2004 are taken from the OECD Web site: www.oecd.org.

17. There is no shortage of scientific assessments of the world's environmental ills and scenarios for the future. For a review of data sources for global environmental outlooks, see Thomas M. Parris, "A Crystal Ball for Sustainability," *Environment* 44 (September 2002): 3–4. One of the most useful is UNEP's series of state of the environment reports, the latest of which, the Global Environmental Outlook-3 report, was released in mid-2002. It takes an unusual look at the patterns of policy development and environmental impacts of the past three decades and then outlines four scenarios for the next three decades. None of the scenarios leads to a very positive outcome, in part because of the accelerating growth of large, poor, and unplanned urban development in poor nations. Over a thousand people from collaborating environmental research centers around the world contributed to the report.

18. Danny Hakim, "At the Front on Air Policy: California Is Moving to Set U.S. Standard," *New York Times*, July 3, 2002, 1, A12.

19. For an account of reactions to the Bush plan, see Andrew C. Revkin, "Bush Offers Plan for Voluntary Measures to Limit Gas Emissions," *New York Times*, February 15, 2002, A6.

20. The report is summarized in Andrew C. Revkin, "Climate Changing, U.S. Says in Report," *New York Times*, June 3, 2002, 1, A11, and it can be found in full online at the EPA Web site: http://yosemite.epa.gov/oar/globalwarming.nsf/content/ ResourceCenterPublicationsUSClimateActionReport.html. The climate report was consistent with other recent reports on the subject, including studies by the U.S. National Academy of Sciences and the Intergovernmental Panel on Climate Change. The IPCC reports are available at its Web site: www.ipcc.ch/.

21. Katharine Q. Seelye, "President Distances Himself from Global Warming Report," *New York Times*, June 5, 2002, A19.

22. See Andrew C. Revkin, "Dispute Arises Over a Push to Change Climate Panel," *New York Times*, April 2, 2002, A10.

23. The study's findings can be found at the project Web site: www.millenniumassessment.org.

24. The administration set out its positions in a statement to the sixth conference of parties in The Hague, Netherlands, in April 2002. The statement may be found at the State Department Web site: www.state.gov/g/oes/rls/rm/2002/9577.htm.

25. Raymond Bonner, "Indonesia's Forests Go Under the Ax for Flooring," *New York Times*, September 13, 2002, A3. For an assessment of the relationship between biodiversity conservation and poverty, see William M. Adams et al., "Biodiversity Conservation and the Eradication of Poverty," *Science* 306 (November 12, 2004): 1146–49.

26. For a brief news report on the assessment, see Paul Lewis, "Population Control Measures to Aid Women Are Stumbling," *New York Times*, April 11, 1999, 12. A fuller account can be found in the UN Population Fund's *The State of the World Population 1999: A Time for Choices*, released in October of that year and available at the agency's Web site. A recent assessment of family planning needs worldwide is Malcolm Potts, "The Unmet Need for Family Planning," *Scientific American* (January 2000): 88–93.

27. Todd S. Purdum, "U.S. Blocks Money for Family Clinics Promoted by U.N.," *New York Times*, July 23, 2002, 1, A6.

28. Barbara Crossette, "U.N. Agency on Population Blames U.S. for Cutbacks," *New York Times*, April 7, 2002, A11.

29. James Dao, "U.S. May Abandon Support of U.N. Population Accord," *New York Times*, November 2, 2002, A8. The United States was unsuccessful in pushing to amend conference resolutions that referred to "reproductive health services" and "reproductive rights." For a broader account of how anti-abortion groups have quietly pushed their agenda in international forums, see Gregg Sangillo, "Going Global," *National Journal*, January 11, 2003, 104–5.

30. Population estimates and projections can be found at the Census Bureau site: www.census.gov/.

References

Ackerman, Bruce A., and William T. Hassler. 1981. *Clean Coal/Dirty Air.* New Haven, CT: Yale University Press.

Adams, Rebecca, 2002a. "Not Even Rumblings of War Shake Loose an Energy Policy." *CQ Weekly,* October 5, 2570–73.

_____. 2002b. "Regulating the Rule-Makers: John Graham at OIRA." *CQ Weekly,* February 23, 520–26.

_____. 2006. "EPA Program Offers Too Much Carrot, Not Enough Stick." *CQ Weekly,* February 27, 528–30.

Allen, Mike, and Eric Pianin. 2002. "Cries of 'Timber!' in National Forests." *Washington Post National Weekly Edition,* December 6–22, 12.

Alliance to Save Energy, American Council for an Energy-Efficient Economy, Natural Resources Defense Council, and Union of Concerned Scientists. 1991. *America's Energy Choices: Investing in a Strong Economy and a Clean Environment.* Cambridge, MA: Union of Concerned Scientists.

Amy, Douglas J. 1987. *The Politics of Environmental Mediation.* New York: Columbia University Press.

Anderson, James E. 2006. *Public Policymaking: An Introduction,* 6th ed. Boston: Houghton Mifflin.

Anderson, Ray C. 1999. *Mid-Course Correction—Toward a Sustainable Enterprise: The Interface Model.* Post Mills, VT: Chelsea Green.

Anderson, Terry L., and Donald R. Leal. 1997. *Enviro-Capitalists: Doing Good While Doing Well.* Lanham, MD: Rowman and Littlefield.

_____. 2001. *Free Market Environmentalism,* rev. ed. New York: Palgrave Macmillan.

Andrews, Edmund L. 2006. "Vague Law and Hard Lobbying Add Up to Billions for Big Oil." *New York Times,* March 27, 2006, 1, A16.

Andrews, Richard N. L. 1999. *Managing the Environment, Managing Ourselves: A History of American Environmental Policy.* New Haven, CT: Yale University Press.

_____. 2006. "Risk-Based Decisionmaking: Policy, Science, and Politics." In *Environmental Policy,* 6th ed., edited by Norman J. Vig and Michael E. Kraft. Washington, DC: CQ Press.

Annan, Kofi A. 2002. "Toward a Sustainable Future." *Environment* 44 (September): 10–15.

Assadourian, Erik. 2006. "Transforming Corporations." In *State of the World 2006,* edited by Linda Starke. New York: W. W. Norton.

Axelrod, Regina. 1984. "Energy Policy: Changing the Rules of the Game." In *Environmental Policy in the 1980s,* edited by Norman J. Vig and Michael E. Kraft. Washington, DC: CQ Press.

Axelrod, Regina S., David Leonard Downie, and Norman J. Vig, eds. 2005. *The Global Environment: Institutions, Law, and Policy.* Washington, D.C.: CQ Press.

Ayres, B. Drummond, Jr. 1997. "San Diego Backs 'Model' Nature Habitat Plan." *New York Times,* March 30, A10.

Baber, Walter F., and Robert V. Bartlett. 2005. *Deliberative Environmental Politics: Democracy and Ecological Rationality.* Cambridge, MA: MIT Press.

Barbaro, Michael, and Felicity Barringer. 2005. "Wal-Mart to Seek Savings on Energy." *New York Times,* October 25, C1.

Bailey, Ronald, ed. 1999. *Earth Report 2000: Revisiting the True State of the Planet.* New York: McGraw-Hill.

Baish, Sarah K., Sheila D. David, and William L. Graf. 2002. "The Complex

Decisionmaking Process for Removing Dams." *Environment* 44 (May): 21–31.

Balmford, Andrew, Aaron Bruner, Philip Cooper, Robert Costanza, Stephen Farber, Rhys E. Green, et al. 2002. "Economic Reasons for Conserving Wild Nature." *Science* 297: 950–53.

Barnthouse, Larry, ed. 1998. *Sustainable Environmental Management*. Pensacola, FL: SETAC Foundation for Environmental Education (Proceedings of a Workshop at Pellston, Michigan, August 25–31, 1993).

Bartlett, Robert V. 1986. "Ecological Rationality: Reason and Environmental Policy." *Environmental Ethics* 8 (Fall): 221–40.

———. 1990. "Comprehensive Environmental Decision Making: Can It Work?" In *Environmental Policy in the 1990s*, edited by Norman J. Vig and Michael E. Kraft. Washington, DC: CQ Press.

———. 1994. "Evaluating Environmental Policy Success and Failure." In *Environmental Policy in the 1990s*, 2nd ed., edited by Norman J. Vig and Michael E. Kraft. Washington, DC: CQ Press.

———, ed. 1989. *Policy through Impact Assessment: Institutionalized Analysis as a Policy Strategy*. New York: Greenwood Press.

Bartlett, Robert V., and Charles R. Malone, eds. 1993. "Science and the National Environmental Policy Act." *The Environmental Professional* 15 (1): 1–149.

Baskin, Yvonne. 1993. "Ecologists Dare to Ask: How Much Does Diversity Matter?" *Science* 264 (April 8): 202–3.

Baumgartner, Frank R., and Bryan D. Jones. 1993. *Agendas and Instability in American Politics*. Chicago: University of Chicago Press.

Beardsley, Dan, Terry Davies, and Robert Hersh. 1997. "Improving Environmental Management: What Works, What Doesn't." *Environment* 39 (September): 6–9, 28–35.

Becker, Elizabeth. 2002. "U.S. Sets New Farm-Animal Pollution Curbs." *New York Times*, December 17, A28.

Behr, Peter. 2001. "On the Energy Roller Coaster." *Washington Post National Weekly Edition*, September 10–16, 18.

Beierle, Thomas C., and Jerry Cayford. 2002. *Democracy in Practice: Public Participation in Environmental Decisions*. Washington, DC: RFF Press.

Benedick, Richard E. 1991. *Ozone Diplomacy*. Cambridge, MA: Harvard University Press.

Bennear, Lori Snyder, and Cary Coglianese. 2005. "Measuring Progress: Program Evaluation of Environmental Policies." *Environment* 47 (March): 22–39.

Berke, Richard L. 1998. "Sierra Club Ads in Political Races Offer a Case Study of 'Issue Advocacy.'" *New York Times*, October 24, A12.

Berry, Jeffrey M. 1977. *Lobbying for the People: The Political Behavior of Public Interest Groups*. Princeton, NJ: Princeton University Press.

———. 1996. *The Interest Group Society*, 3rd ed. Glenview, IL: Scott, Foresman.

Berry, Jeffrey M., and Kent E. Portney. 1995. "Centralizing Regulatory Control and Interest Group Access: The Quayle Council on Competitiveness." In *Interest Group Politics*, 4th ed., edited by Allan J. Cigler and Burdett A. Loomis. Washington, DC: CQ Press.

Bezdek, Roger H. 1993. "Environment and Economy: What's the Bottom Line." *Environment* 35 (September): 7–11, 25–32.

Birkland, Thomas A. 1997. *After Disaster: Agenda Setting, Public Policy, and Focusing Events*. Washington, DC: Georgetown University Press.

Bosso, Christopher J. 1987. *Pesticides and Politics: The Life Cycle of a Public Issue*. Pittsburgh: University of Pittsburgh Press.

———. 1991. "Adaptation and Change in the Environmental Movement." In *Interest Group Politics*, 3rd ed., edited by Allan J. Cigler and Burdett A. Loomis. Washington, DC: CQ Press.

———. 2000. "Environmental Groups and the New Political Landscape." In *Environmental Policy*, 4th ed., edited by Norman J. Vig and Michael E. Kraft. Washington, DC: CQ Press.

_____. 2005. *Environment, Inc.: From Grassroots to Beltway*. Lawrence: University Press of Kansas.

Bosso, Christopher J., and Michael Thomas Collins. 2002. "Just Another Tool? How Environmental Groups Use the Internet." In *Interest Group Politics*, 6th ed., edited by Allan J. Cigler and Burdett A. Loomis. Washington, DC: CQ Press.

Bosso, Christopher J., and Deborah Lynn Guber. 2006. "Maintaining Presence: Environmental Advocacy and the Permanent Campaign." In *Environmental Policy*, 6th ed., edited by Norman J. Vig and Michael E. Kraft. Washington, DC: CQ Press.

_____. 2007. "Framing ANWR: Citizens, Consumers, and the Privileged Position of Business." In *Business and Environmental Policy*, edited by Michael E. Kraft and Sheldon Kamieniecki. Cambridge, MA: MIT Press.

Bowman, Ann O'M., and Mark E. Tompkins. 1993. "Environmental Protection and Economic Development: Can States Have It Both Ways?" Paper presented at the annual meeting of the American Political Science Association, Washington, DC, September 2–5.

Bradsher, Keith. 1999a. "Clinton Allays Criticism of New Pollution Rules." *New York Times*, December 22, A20.

_____. 1999b. "With Sport Utility Vehicles More Popular, Overall Automobile Fuel Economy Continues to Fall." *New York Times*, October 5, A18.

Brick, Philip D., and R. McGreggor Cawley, eds. 1996. *A Wolf in the Garden: The Land Rights Movement and the New Environmental Debate*. Lanham, MD: Rowman and Littlefield.

Brooke, James. 1998. "West Celebrates Mining's Past, but Not Its Future." *New York Times*, October 4, 16.

_____. 1999. "Environmentalists Battle Growth of Ski Resorts." *New York Times*, January 19, A10.

Brown, R. Steven. 2000. "The States Protect the Environment." Council of State Government's Web page www.sso.org/ecos.

The article appeared originally in *ECOStates* magazine, Summer 1999.

Browner, Carol M. 1993. "Environmental Tobacco Smoke: EPA's Report." *EPA Journal* 19 (October–December): 18–19.

Bryant, Bunyan, ed. 1995. *Environmental Justice: Issues, Politics, and Solutions*. Washington, DC: Island Press.

Bryant, Bunyan, and Paul Mohai, eds. 1992. *Race and the Incidence of Environmental Hazards: A Time for Discourse*. Boulder, CO: Westview Press.

Bryner, Gary C. 1987. *Bureaucratic Discretion: Law and Policy in Federal Regulatory Agencies*. New York: Pergamon Press.

_____. 1995. *Blue Skies, Green Politics: The Clean Air Act of 1990 and Its Implementation*, 2nd ed. Washington, DC: CQ Press.

_____. 1999. "Agenda 21: Myth or Reality?" In *The Global Environment*, edited by Norman J. Vig and Regina S. Axelrod. Washington, DC: CQ Press.

Bullard, Robert D. 1994. "Overcoming Racism in Environmental Decisionmaking." *Environment* 36 (May): 10–20, 39–44.

Bumiller, Elisabeth. 2006. "Bush's Goals on Energy Quickly Find Obstacles." *New York Times*, February 2, 1, A18.

Bumiller, Elisabeth, and Carl Hulse. 2005. "Bush Concedes Energy Bill Offers No Help on Gas Prices." *New York Times*, April 21, online edition.

Burger, Joanna, and Michael Gochfeld. 1998. "The Tragedy of the Commons: 30 Years Later." *Environment* 40 (December): 4–13, 26–27.

Burros, Marian. 1999. "High Pesticide Levels Seen in U.S. Food." *New York Times*, February 19, A12.

Cahn, Robert. 1993. "Report on Reports: Science and the National Parks." *Environment* 35 (March): 25–27.

Caldwell, Lynton Keith. 1970. *Environment: A Challenge for Modern Society*. Garden City, NY: Doubleday.

_____. 1982. *Science and the National Environmental Policy Act: Redirecting Policy through Procedural Reform.* Tuscaloosa: University of Alabama Press.

———. 1990. "International Environmental Politics: America's Response to Global Imperatives." In *Environmental Policy in the 1990s,* edited by Norman J. Vig and Michael E. Kraft. Washington, DC: CQ Press.

———. 1996. *International Environmental Policy: Emergence and Dimensions,* 3rd ed. Durham, NC: Duke University Press.

———. 1998. *The National Environmental Policy Act: An Agenda for the Future.* Bloomington: Indiana University Press.

Calvert, Jerry W. 1989. "Party Politics and Environmental Policy." In *Environmental Politics and Policy,* 2nd ed., edited by James P. Lester. Durham, NC: Duke University Press.

Camia, Catalina. 1994. "Severity of Job Loss at Issue in Mining Law Overhaul." *Congressional Quarterly Weekly Report,* January 8, 18–20.

Cantrill, James G., and Christine L. Oravec, eds. 1996. *The Symbolic Earth: Discourse and Our Creation of the Environment.* Lexington: University Press of Kentucky.

Carnegie Commission. 1992. *Environmental Research and Development: Strengthening the Federal Infrastructure.* New York: Carnegie Commission on Science, Technology, and Government.

———. 1993. *Risk and the Environment: Improving Regulatory Decision Making.* New York: Carnegie Commission on Science, Technology, and Government.

Catton, William R., Jr., and Riley E. Dunlap. 1980. "A New Ecological Paradigm for Post-Exuberant Sociology." *American Behavioral Scientist* 24: 15–47.

Cawley, R. McGreggor. 1993. *Federal Land, Western Anger: The Sagebrush Rebellion and Environmental Politics.* Lawrence: University of Kansas Press.

Chaffey, Douglas Camp. 1999. "Tribal Governments and Environmental Protection: The Emergent Federalism Triad." Chatham, PA: Chatham College, draft manuscript.

Chasek, Pamela S., David L. Downie, and Janet Welsh Brown. 2006. *Global Environmental Politics,* 4th ed. Boulder, CO: Westview Press.

Chertow, Marian R., and Daniel C. Esty, eds. 1997. *Thinking Ecologically: The Next Generation of Environmental Policy.* New Haven, CT: Yale University Press.

Chivian, Eric, Michael McCally, Howard Hu, and Andrew Haines, eds. 1993. *Critical Condition: Human Health and the Environment.* Cambridge, MA: MIT Press.

Cincotta, Richard P., and Barbara B. Crane. 2001. "The Mexico City Policy and U.S. Family Planning Assistance." *Science* 294 (October 19): 525–26.

Claiborne, William. 1999. "A Tree Grows on a Chicago Rooftop." *Washington Post National Weekly Edition,* December 13, 30.

Clarke, Jeanne Nienaber, and Daniel McCool. 1996. *Staking Out the Terrain: Power and Performance Among Natural Resource Agencies,* 2nd ed. Albany: State University of New York Press.

Clary, Bruce B., and Michael E. Kraft. 1989. "Environmental Assessment, Science, and Policy Failure: The Politics of Nuclear Waste Disposal." In *Policy through Impact Assessment,* edited by Robert Bartlett. New York: Greenwood Press.

Clines, Francis X. 2000. "Navigating the Renaissance of the Ohio River That Once Caught Fire." *New York Times,* January 23, 12.

Cobb, Clifford, Ted Halstead, and Jonathan Rowe. 1995. "If the GDP Is Up, Why Is America Down?" *The Atlantic Monthly,* October, 59–78.

Coglianese, Cary. 1997. "Assessing Consensus: The Promise and Performance of Negotiated Rulemaking." *Duke Law Journal* 46: 1255–1349.

Coglianese, Cary, and Laurie K. Allen. 2004. "Does Consensus Make Common Sense? An Analysis of EPA's Common Sense Initiative." *Environment* 46 (January): 10–25.

Coglianese, Cary, and Jennifer Nash. 2001. *Regulating from the Inside: Can*

Environmental Management Systems Achieve Policy Goals. Washington, DC: RFF Press.

_____. 2002. "Policy Options for Improving Environmental Management in the Private Sector." *Environment* 44 (November): 11–23.

Coglianese, Cary, and Lori D. Snyder Bennear. 2005. "Program Evaluation of Environmental Policies: Toward Evidence-Based Decision Making." In *Decision Making for the Environment: Social and Behavioral Science Research Priorities,* edited by Garry D. Brewer and Paul C. Stern. Washington, DC: National Academy Press.

Cohen, Joel E. 1995. *How Many People Can the Earth Support?* New York: W. W. Norton.

Cohen, Richard E. 1995. *Washington at Work: Back Rooms and Clean Air,* 2nd ed. New York: Allyn & Bacon.

Cohen, Steven. 1984. "Defusing the Toxic Time Bomb: Federal Hazardous Waste Programs." In *Environmental Policy in the 1980s,* edited by Norman J. Vig and Michael E. Kraft. Washington, DC: CQ Press.

Cohen, Steven, Sheldon Kamieniecki, and Matthew A. Cahn. 2005. *Strategic Planning in Environmental Regulation: A Policy Approach That Works.* Cambridge, MA: MIT Press.

Colborn, Theo, Dianne Dumanoski, and John Peterson Myers. 1996. *Our Stolen Future: Are We Threatening Our Fertility, Intelligence, and Survival?* New York: Dutton.

Cole, Leonard A. 1993. *Element of Risk: The Politics of Radon.* Washington, DC: AAAS Press.

Commission for Environmental Cooperation. 2001. *The North American Mosaic: A State of the Environment Report.* Montreal: Commission for Environmental Cooperation.

Cooper, Joseph, and William F. West. 1988. "Presidential Power and Republican Government: The Theory and Practice of OMB Review of Agency Rules." *Journal of Politics* 50 (November): 864–95.

Cooper, Mary H. (and the staff of *CQ Weekly*). 1999. "Energy Politics: What Next?" *CQ Outlook,* Supplement to *CQ Weekly,* March 20, 1–30.

_____. 2002. "Energy Security at Risk: How Vulnerable Is America's Energy System?" *CQ Outlook,* Supplement to *CQ Weekly,* February 23, 1–15.

Cortner, Hanna J., and Margaret A. Moote. 1999. *The Politics of Ecosystem Management.* Washington, DC: Island Press.

Costanza, Robert, ed. 1991. *Ecological Economics: The Science and Management of Sustainability.* New York: Columbia University Press.

Costanza, Robert, Bryan G. Norton, and Benjamin D. Haskell, eds. 1992. *Ecosystem Health: New Goals for Ecosystem Management.* Washington, DC: Island Press.

Costanza, Robert, Ralph d'Arge, Randolf de Groot, Stephen Farber, Monica Grasso, and Bruce Hannon. 1997. "The Value of the World's Ecosystem Services and Natural Capital." *Nature* 387 (May 15): 253–60.

Council on Environmental Quality (CEQ). 1980. "Public Opinion on Environmental Issues: Results of a National Public Opinion Survey." Washington, DC: CEQ.

_____. 1998. *Environmental Quality, Along the American River: The 1996 Report of the Council on Environmental Quality.* Washington, DC: CEQ.

_____. 1999. Environmental Quality: The 1997 Report of the Council on Environmental Quality. Washington, D.C.: CEQ. Available at the CEQ Web site: http://ceq.eh.doe.gov/nepa/reports/1997/index.html.

Council on Environmental Quality and Department of State. 1980. *Global 2000 Report to the President,* Vols. I, II, and III. Washington, DC: U.S. Government Printing Office.

Coyle, Kevin. 2005. *Environmental Literacy in America.* Washington, DC: National Environmental Education and Training Foundation, September.

Cowell, Alan. 1994. "U.N. Population Meeting Adopts Program of Action." *New York Times,* September 14, A2.

Cronon, William. 1983. *Changes in the Land: Indians, Colonists, and the Ecology of New England.* New York: Hill and Wang.

Crossette, Barbara. 1999. "Rethinking Population at a Global Milestone." *New York Times,* September 19, Week in Review, 1, 4–5.

Culhane, Paul J. 1981. *Public Lands Politics: Interest Group Influence on the Forest Service and the Bureau of Land Management.* Baltimore: Johns Hopkins University Press.

———. 1984. "Sagebrush Rebels in Office: Jim Watt's Land and Water Politics." In *Environmental Policy in the 1980s,* edited by Norman J. Vig and Michael E. Kraft. Washington, DC: CQ Press.

Cushman, John H., Jr. 1994. "Administration Plans Revision to Ease Toxic Cleanup Criteria." *New York Times,* January 31, 1, A7.

———. 1997. "Clinton Sharply Tightens Air Pollution Regulations Despite Concern Over Costs." *New York Times,* June 26, 1, A12.

———. 1998a. "The Endangered Species Act Gets a Makeover." *New York Times,* June 2, 2.

———. 1998b. "E.P.A. and States Found to Be Lax on Pollution Law." *New York Times,* June 7, 1, 17.

———. 1998c. "E.P.A. Dilutes Its Pamphlet on Pesticides." *New York Times,* December 30, A10.

———. 1998d. "In Colorado Resort Fires, Culprits Defy Easy Labels." *New York Times,* October 24, A11.

———. 1998e. "Record Pollution Fines Planned against Makers of Diesel Engines," *New York Times,* October 22, 1, A14.

———. 1998f. "U.S. Unveils Plan to Revamp South Florida's Water Supply and Save Everglades." *New York Times,* October 14, A12.

———. 1999. "Audit Faults Forest Service on Logging Damage in U.S. Forests." *New York Times,* February 5, A15.

———. 2002. "New Study Adds to Debate on E.P.A. Rules for Pesticide." *New York Times,* June 2, A21.

Daily, Gretchen C., ed. 1997. *Nature's Services: Societal Dependence on Natural Ecosystems.* Washington, DC: Island Press.

Daily, Gretchen C., and Katherine Ellison. 2002. *The New Economy of Nature: The Quest to Make Conservation Profitable.* Washington, DC: Island Press.

Dana, Samuel Trask, and Sally K. Fairfax. 1980. *Forest and Range Policy: Its Development in the United States,* 2nd ed. New York: McGraw-Hill.

Dao, James. 1999. "Study Sees Acid Rain Threat in Adirondacks and Beyond." *New York Times,* April 5, A19.

Davidson, Roger H., and Walter J. Oleszek. 2006. *Congress and Its Members,* 10th ed. Washington, DC: CQ Press.

Davies, J. Clarence, ed. 1996. *Comparing Environmental Risks: Tools for Setting Government Priorities.* Washington, DC: Resources for the Future.

Davies, J. Clarence, III, and Barbara S. Davies. 1975. *The Politics of Pollution,* 2nd ed. Indianapolis, IN: Bobbs-Merrill.

Davies, J. Clarence, and Jan Mazurek. 1998. *Pollution Control in the United States: Evaluating the System.* Washington, DC: Resources for the Future.

Davis, Charles, ed. 2001. *Western Public Lands and Environmental Politics,* 2nd ed. Boulder, CO: Westview Press.

Davis, David Howard. 1993. *Energy Politics,* 4th ed. New York: St. Martin's.

Davis, Thomas. 2000. *Sustaining the Forest, the People, and the Spirit.* Albany: State University of New York Press.

Deutsch, Claudia H. 2006. "DuPont Looking to Displace Fossil Fuels as Building Blocks of Chemicals." *New York Times,* February 28, C1, 15.

Desai, Uday, ed. 2002. *Environmental Politics and Policy in Industrialized Countries.* Cambridge, MA: MIT Press.

DeSombre, Elizabeth R. 2000. *Domestic Sources of International Environmental Policy: Industry, Environmentalists, and U.S. Power.* Cambridge, MA: MIT Press.

———. 2002. *The Global Environment and World Politics.* New York: Continuum Books.

De Saillan, Charles. 1993. "In Praise of Super-fund." *Environment* 35 (October): 42–44.

Deudney, Daniel H., and Richard A. Matthew, eds. 1999. *Contested Grounds: Security and Conflict in the New Environmental Politics*. Albany: State University of New York Press.

Douglas, Mary, and Aaron Wildavsky. 1982. *Risk and Culture*. Berkeley: University of California Press.

Dower, Roger. 1990. "Hazardous Wastes." In *Public Policies for Environmental Protection*, edited by Paul R. Portney. Washington, DC: Resource for the Future.

Downie, David Leonard. 2005. "Global Environmental Policy: Governance through Regimes." In *The Global Environment*, ed. Regina S. Axelrod, David Leonard Downie, and Norman J. Vig. Washington, DC: CQ Press.

Downs, Anthony. 1972. "Up and Down with Ecology: The 'Issue-Attention Cycle.'" *The Public Interest*, Summer, 38–50.

Dryzek, John S. 1987. *Rational Ecology: Environment and Political Economy*. New York: Basil Blackwell.

_____. 2005. *The Politics of the Earth: Environmental Discourses*, 2nd ed. New York: Oxford University Press.

Dryzek, John S., and James P. Lester. 1995. "Alternative Views of the Environmental Problematic." In *Environmental Politics and Policy*, 2nd ed., edited by James P. Lester. Durham, NC: Duke University Press.

Duffy, Robert J. 1997. *Nuclear Politics in America: A History and Theory of Government Regulation*. Lawrence: University Press of Kansas.

_____. 2003. *The Green Agenda in American Politics: New Strategies for the Twenty-First Century*. Lawrence: University of Kansas Press.

Dugger, Celia W. 2006. "U.S. Cuts Funds for Family Planning Overseas, Stirring Opposition." *New York Times*, February 15, A7.

Dunlap, Riley E. 1987. "Polls, Pollution, and Politics Revisited: Public Opinion on the Environment in the Reagan Era." *Environment* 29 (July/August): 6–11, 32–37.

_____. 1992. "Trends in Public Opinion Toward Environmental Issues: 1965–1990." In *American Environmentalism*, edited by Riley E. Dunlap and Angela G. Mertig. Philadelphia: Taylor and Francis.

_____. 1995. "Public Opinion and Environmental Policy." In *Environmental Politics and Policy* 2nd ed., edited by James P. Lester. Durham, NC: Duke University Press.

_____. 2004. "Bush and the Environment: Potential for Trouble?" Accessed at the Gallup Organization Web page: www.gallup.com, April 9, 2004.

Dunlap, Riley E., George H. Gallup Jr., and Alec M. Gallup. 1993. "Of Global Concern: Results of the Health of the Planet Survey." *Environment* 35: 7–15, 23–48.

Dunlap, Riley E., Michael E. Kraft, and Eugene A. Rosa, eds. 1993. *Public Reactions to Nuclear Waste: Citizens' Views of Repository Siting*. Durham, NC: Duke University Press.

Durant, Robert F. 1992. *The Administrative Presidency Revisited: Public Lands, the BLM, and the Reagan Revolution*. Albany: State University of New York Press.

_____, Daniel J. Fiorino, and Rosemary O'Leary. 2004. *Environmental Governance Reconsidered: Challenges, Choices, and Opportunities*. Cambridge, MA: MIT Press.

Durning, Alan. 1992. *How Much Is Enough? The Consumer Society and the Future of the Earth*. New York: W. W. Norton.

Eads, George C., and Michael Fix. 1984. *Relief or Reform? Reagan's Regulatory Dilemma*. Washington, DC: Urban Institute.

Eccleston, Charles H. 1999. *The NEPA Planning Process: A Comprehensive Guide with Emphasis on Efficiency*. New York: John Wiley and Sons.

Eckersley, Robyn. 2004. *The Green State: Rethinking Democracy and Sovereignty*. Cambridge: MIT Press.

Edelman, Murray. 1964. *The Symbolic Uses of Politics.* Urbana, IL: University of Illinois Press.

Egan, Timothy. 1993a. "Sweeping Reversal of U.S. Land Policy Sought by Clinton." *New York Times,* February 24, 1, A9.

———. 1993b. "Wingtip 'Cowboys' in Last Stand to Hold on to Low Grazing Fees." *New York Times,* October 29, 1, A8.

———. 1998. "Get Used to the New West, Land Managers Tell the Old West." *New York Times,* February 12, A10.

———. 2000. "Putting Some Space between His Presidency and History." *New York Times,* January 16, Week in Review, 3.

Ehrlich, Paul R., and Anne H. Ehrlich. 1996. *Betrayal of Science and Reason: How Anti-Environmental Rhetoric Threatens Our Future.* Washington, DC: Island Press.

Eisner, Marc Allen. 2004. "Corporate Environmentalism, Regulatory Reform, and Industry Self-Regulation: Toward Genuine Regulatory Reinvention in the United States." *Governance* 17 (April): 145–167.

Eisner, Marc Allen, Jeff Worsham, and Evan J. Ringquist. 2000. *Contemporary Regulatory Policy.* Boulder, CO: Lynne Rienner.

Ernst, Howard. 2003. *Chesapeake Bay Blues: Science, Politics, and the Struggle to Save the Bay.* Lanham, MD: Rowman and Littlefield.

Erskine, Hazel. 1972. "The Polls: Pollution and Its Costs." *Public Opinion Quarterly* 36 (Spring): 120–35.

Eskeland, Gunnar A., and Ann E. Harrison. 2003. "Moving to Greener Pastures? Multinationals and the Pollution Haven Hypothesis." *Journal of Development Economics* 70 (February): 1–23.

Esty, Daniel C. 2005. "Economic Integration and Environmental Protection." In *The Global Environment,* edited by Regina S. Axelrod, David Leonard Downie, and Norman J. Vig. Washington, DC: CQ Press.

Evans, Ben, and Joseph J. Schatz. 2005. "Details of Energy Policy Law." *CQ Weekly,* September 5, 2337–45.

Fairfax, Sally K., and Darla Guenzler. 2001. *Conservation Trusts.* Lawrence: University Press of Kansas.

Fairfax, Sally K., Lauren Gwin, Mary Ann King, Leigh Raymond, and Laura A. Watt. 2005. *Buying Nature: The Limits of Land Acquisition as a Conservation Strategy, 1780–2004.* Cambridge, MA: MIT Press.

Feder, Barnaby J. 2000. "Cleaning Up the Dry Cleaners." *New York Times,* February 15, C1–C16.

Feiock, Richard C., and Christopher Stream. 2001. "Environmental Protection versus Economic Development: A False Trade-off?" *Public Administration Review* 61 (May/June): 313–21.

Fiorino, Daniel J. 2006. *The New Environmental Regulation.* Cambridge, MA: MIT Press.

Fischbeck, Paul S., and R. Scott Farrow, eds. 2001. *Improving Regulation: Cases in Environment, Health, and Safety.* Washington, DC: RFF Press.

Fischer, Frank. 1990. *Technocracy and the Politics of Expertise.* Newbury Park, CA: Sage.

Flannery, Tim. 2005. *The Weather Makers: The History and Future Impact of Climate Change.* New York: Atlantic Monthly Press.

Flynn, James, James Chalmers, Doug Easterling, Roger Kasperson, Howard Kunreuther, C.K. Mertz, et al. 1995. *One Hundred Centuries of Solitude: Redirecting America's High-Level Nuclear Waste Policy.* Boulder, CO: Westview Press.

Foreman, Christopher H., Jr. 1998. *The Promise and Peril of Environmental Justice.* Washington, DC: Brookings Institution.

Foss, Philip O. 1960. *Politics and Grass.* Seattle: University of Washington Press.

Freedman, Allan. 1996. "Provisions: Safe Drinking Water Act Amendments." *Congressional Quarterly Weekly Report,* September 14, 2622–27.

———. 1998. "Law Sparks Another Round in Pesticides Battle." *CQ Weekly,* May 2, 1117–20.

Freeman, A. Myrick, III. 1990. "Water Pollution Policy." In *Public Policies for Environmental Protection,* edited by Paul R. Portney. Washington, DC: Resources for the Future.

_____. 2006. "Economics, Incentives, and Environmental Regulation." In *Environmental Policy,* 6th ed., edited by Norman J. Vig and Michael E. Kraft. Washington, DC: CQ Press.

Freemuth, John C. 1991. *Islands under Siege: National Parks and the Politics of External Threats.* Lawrence: University of Kansas Press.

French, Hilary F. 1994. "Rebuilding the World Bank." In *State of the World 1994,* edited by Linda Starke. New York: W. W. Norton.

_____. 2000. "Coping with Ecological Globalization." In *State of the World 2000,* edited by Linda Starke. New York. W. W. Norton.

_____. 2002. "Reshaping Global Governance." In *State of the World 2002,* edited by Linda Stark. New York: W. W. Norton.

Friedman, Benjamin M. 2005. *The Moral Consequences of Economic Growth.* New York: Alfred A. Knopf.

Furlong, Scott R. 1995a. "The 1992 Regulatory Moratorium: Did It Make a Difference?" *Public Administration Review* 55: 254–62.

_____. 1995b. "Reinventing Regulatory Development at the Environmental Protection Agency." *Policy Studies Journal* 23 (Fall): 466–82.

_____. 1997. "Interest Group Influence on Rulemaking." *Administration and Society* 29 (July): 325–47.

_____. 2007. "Businesses and the Environment: Influencing Agency Policymaking." In *Business and Environmental Policy,* edited by Michael E. Kraft and Sheldon Kamieniecki. Cambridge, MA: MIT Press, in press.

Gaddie, Ronald Keith, and James L. Regens. 2000. *Regulating Wetlands Protection: Environmental Federalism and the States.*

Albany: State University of New York Press.

Gardiner, David. 1994. "Does Environmental Policy Conflict with Economic Growth?" *Resources* 115 (Spring): 20–21.

Gardiner, David, and Lisa Jacobson. 2002. "Will Voluntary Programs Be Sufficient to Reduce U.S. Greenhouse Gas Emissions?" *Environment* 44 (October): 24–33.

Gelbspan, Ross. 2004. *Boiling Point: How Politicians, Big Oil and Coal, Journalists, and Activists Are Fueling the Climate Crisis—and What We Can Do to Avert Disaster.* New York: Basic Books.

Gibbs, W. Wayt. 2001. "On the Termination of Species." *Scientific American* 227 (November): 40–49.

Giltmier, James W. 1998. "Evolution of an Agency." *Forum for Applied Research and Public Policy* 13 (Summer): 6–10.

Global Strategy Group. 2004. "The Environmental Deficit: Survey on American Attitudes on the Environment." New York: Global Strategy Group and Yale University School of Forestry and Environmental Studies, May. Available at www.yale.edu/forestry/downloads/yale_enviro_poll.pdf.

Gonzalez, George A. 2001. *Corporate Power and the Environment: The Political Economy of U.S. Environmental Policy.* Lanham, MD: Rowman and Littlefield.

Goodstein, Laurie. 2006. "Evangelical Leaders Join Global Warming Initiative." *New York Times,* February 8, online edition.

Goodwin, Craufurd D., ed. 1981. *Energy Policy in Perspective.* Washington, DC: Brookings Institution.

Gormley, William T., Jr. 1989. *Taming the Bureaucracy: Muscles, Prayers, and Other Strategies.* Princeton, NJ: Princeton University Press.

Gottlieb, Robert. 1993. *Forcing the Spring: The Transformation of the American Environmental Movement.* Washington, DC: Island Press.

_____. 2001. *Environmentalism Unbound: Exploring New Pathways for Change.* Cambridge, MA: MIT Press.

Gould, Lewis L. 1999. *Lady Bird Johnson: Our Environmental First Lady*. Lawrence: University of Kansas Press.

Graham, Mary, and Catherine Miller. 2001. "Disclosure of Toxic Releases in the United States." *Environment* 43 (8): 8–20.

Greenhouse, Linda. 2000. "Court Backs 'Citizen Suit' to Clean Up Ailing River." *New York Times,* January 13, A20.

Greve, Michael S., and Fred L. Smith Jr., eds. 1992. *Environmental Politics: Public Costs, Private Rewards*. New York: Praeger.

Gruenspecht, Howard K., and Robert N. Stavins. 2002. "New Source Review under the Clean Air Act: Ripe for Reform." *Resources* 147 (Spring): 19–23.

Grunwald, Michael, and Juliet Eilperin. 2006. "A Smorgasbord with Mostly Pork: Oil and Gas Firms Win Big in the New Energy Bill." *Washington Post National Weekly Edition,* August 8-14, 18.

Guber, Deborah Lynn. 2003. *The Grassroots of a Green Revolution: Polling America on the Environment*. Cambridge, MA: MIT Press.

Hadden, Susan G. 1986. *Read the Label: Reducing Risk by Providing Information*. Boulder, CO: Westview Press.

———. 1989. *A Citizen's Right to Know: Risk Communication and Public Policy*. Boulder, CO: Westview Press.

———. 1991. "Public Perception of Hazardous Waste." *Risk Analysis* 11 (1): 47–57.

Hager, Carol J. 1994. *Technological Democracy: Bureaucracy and Citizenry in the Germany Energy Debate*. Ann Arbor: University of Michigan Press.

Hall, Bob, and Mary Lee Kerr. 1991. *1991–92 Green Index: A State-by-State Guide to the Nation's Environmental Health*. Washington, DC: Island Press.

Halley, Alexis A. 1994. "Hazardous Waste Disposal: The Double-Edged Sword of the RCRA Land-Ban Hammers." In *Who Makes Public Policy? The Struggle for Control between Congress and the Executive,* edited by Robert S. Gilmour and Alexis A. Halley. Chatham, NJ: Chatham House.

Hamilton, Michael S., ed. 1990. *Regulatory Federalism, Natural Resources, and Environmental Management*. Washington, DC: American Society for Public Administration.

Hamilton, James T. 2005. *Regulation Through Revelation: The Origins, Politics, and Impacts of the Toxics Inventory Release Program*. New York: Cambridge University Press.

Hardin, Garrett. 1968. "The Tragedy of the Commons." *Science* 162 (December 13): 1243–48.

Harrington, Winston, Richard D. Morgenstern, and Peter Nelson. 1999. "Predicting the Costs of Environmental Regulations: How Accurate Are Regulators' Estimates?" *Environment* 41 (September): 10–14, 40–44.

Harrington, Winston, Richard D. Morgenstern, and Thomas Sterner, eds. 2004. *Choosing Environmental Policy: Comparing Instruments and Outcomes in the United States and Europe*. Washington, DC: RFF Press.

Harris, Hallett J., and Denise Scheberle. 1998. "Ode to the Miner's Canary: The Search for Effective Indicators." In *Environmental Program Evaluation,* edited by Gerrit J. Knaap and Tschangho John Kim. Champaign: University of Illinois Press.

Harris, Richard A., and Sidney M. Milkis. 1996. *The Politics of Regulatory Change: A Tale of Two Agencies,* 2nd ed. New York: Oxford University Press.

Harrison, Kathryn. 1995. "Is Cooperation the Answer? Canadian Environmental Enforcement in Comparative Context." *Journal of Policy Analysis and Management* 14 (Spring): 221–44.

Harrison, Neil E., and Gary C. Bryner, eds. 2004. *Science and Politics in the International Environment*. Lanham, MD: Rowman and Littlefield.

Hawken, Paul. 1994. *The Ecology of Commerce: A Declaration of Sustainability*. New York: Harper Business.

Hawken, Paul, Amory B. Lovins, and L. Hunter Lovins. 1999. *Natural Capitalism:*

Creating the Next Industrial Revolution. New York: Little, Brown.

Hays, Samuel P. 1959. *Conservation and the Gospel of Efficiency.* Cambridge, England: Cambridge University Press.

———. 1987. *Beauty, Health, and Permanence: Environmental Politics in the United States, 1955–1985.* New York: Cambridge University Press.

Hecht, Joy E. 1999. "Environmental Accounting: Where We Are Now, Where We Are Heading." *Resources* 135 (Spring): 14–17.

Heilbroner, Robert L. 1991. *An Inquiry into the Human Prospect: Looked at Again for the 1990s.* New York: W. W. Norton.

Hempel, Lamont C. 1996. *Environmental Governance: The Global Challenge.* Washington, DC: Island Press.

———. 2006. "Climate Policy on the Installment Plan." In *Environmental Policy,* 6th ed., edited by Norman J. Vig and Michael E. Kraft. Washington, DC: CQ Press.

Herzog, Antonia V., Timothy E. Lipman, Jennifer L. Edwards, and Daniel M. Kammen. 2001. "Renewable Energy: A Viable Choice." *Environment* 43 (December): 8–20.

Higgs, Robert, and Carl P. Close, eds. 2005. *Re-Thinking Green: Alternatives to Environmental Bureaucracy.* Oakland, CA: The Independent Institute.

Hill, Stuart. 1992. *Democratic Values and Technological Choices.* Palo Alto, CA: Stanford University Press.

Hird, John A. 1994. *Superfund: The Political Economy of Risk.* Baltimore: Johns Hopkins University Press.

H. John Heinz III Center for Science, Economics and the Environment (Heinz Center). 2002. *The State of the Nation's Ecosystems: Measuring the Lands, Waters, and Living Resources of the United States.* New York: Cambridge University Press.

Hockenstein, Jeremy B., Robert N. Stavins, and Bradley W. Whitehead. 1997. "Crafting the Next Generation of Market-Based Environmental Tools." *Environment* 39 (May): 13–20, 30–33.

Hogan, William H. 1984. "Energy Policy." In *Natural Resources and the Environment,* edited by Paul R. Portney. Washington, DC: Resources for the Future.

Holusha, John. 1988. "Bush Pledges Aid for Environment." *New York Times,* September 1, 9.

———. 1995. "Cities Redeveloping Old Industrial Sites with EPA's Aid." *New York Times,* December 4, 1, A10.

Hosansky, David. 1996a. "Drinking Water Bill Clears; Clinton Expected to Sign." *Congressional Quarterly Weekly Report,* August 3, 2179–80.

———. 1996b. "Provisions: Pesticide, Food Safety Law." *Congressional Quarterly Weekly Report,* September 7, 2546–50.

———. 1996c. "Rewrite of Laws on Pesticides on Way to President's Desk." *Congressional Quarterly Weekly Report,* July 27, 2101–4.

Huber, Peter. 2000. *Hard Green: Saving the Environment from the Environmentalists (A Conservative Manifesto).* New York: Basic Books.

Hunt, Suzanne, C., and Janet L. Sawin (with Peter Stair). 2006. "Cultivating Renewable Alternatives to Oil." In *State of the World 2006,* edited by Linda Starke. New York: W.W. Norton.

Hunter, Susan, and Richard W. Waterman. 1992. "Determining an Agency's Regulatory Style: How Does the EPA Water Office Enforce the Law?" *Western Political Quarterly* 45: 403–17.

———. 1996. *Enforcing the Law: The Case of the Clean Water Acts.* Armonk, NY: M. E. Sharpe.

Idelson, Holly. 1992a. "After Two-Year Odyssey, Energy Strategy Clears." *Congressional Quarterly Weekly Report,* October 10, 3141–46.

———. 1992b. "National Energy Strategy Provisions." *Congressional Quarterly Weekly Report,* November 28, 3722–30.

Inglehart, Ronald. 1990. *Culture Shift in Advanced Industrial Society.* Princeton, NJ: Princeton University Press.

Ingram, Helen, and Steven Rathgeb Smith, eds. 1993. *Public Policy for Democracy.* Washington, DC: Brookings Institution.

Ingram, Helen M., and Dean E. Mann. 1983. "Environmental Protection Policy." In *Encyclopedia of Policy Studies,* edited by Stuart S. Nagel. New York: Marcel Dekker.

Intergovernmental Panel on Climate Change (IPCC). 2001. *Climate Change 2001: The Scientific Basis,* edited by J. T. Houghton, Y. Ding, D. J. Griggs, M. Noguer, P. J. van der Linden, and D. Xiaosu. New York: Cambridge University Press. A summary for policymakers and others is available on the IPCC Web site: www.ipcc.ch/.

Jalonick, Mary Clare. 2004. "Healthy Forests Initiative Provisions." *CQ Weekly,* January 24, 246–47.

Janofsky, Michael. 2005. "Big Refiner Is Fined and Will Spend $525 Million to Improve Air." *New York Times,* January 18, A17.

John, DeWitt. 1994. *Civic Environmentalism: Alternatives to Regulation in States and Communities.* Washington, DC: CQ Press.

John, DeWitt. 2004. "Civic Environmentalism." In *Environmental Governance Reconsidered,* edited by Robert F. Durant, Daniel J. Fiorino, and Rosemary O'Leary. Cambridge, MA: MIT Press.

John, De Witt, and Marian Mlay. 1999. "Community-Based Environmental Protection: Encouraging Civic Environmentalism." In *Better Environmental Decisions,* edited by Ken Sexton, Alfred A. Marcus, K. William Easter, and Timothy D. Burkhardt. Washington, DC: Island Press.

Johnson, Kirk. 1993. "Reconciling Rural Communities and Resource Conservation." *Environment* (November): 16–20, 27–33.

———. 2006. "Out of Old Mines' Muck Rises New Reclamation Model for West." *New York Times,* March 4, A8.

Jones, Charles O. 1975. *Clean Air: The Policies and Politics of Pollution Control.* Pittsburgh: University of Pittsburgh Press.

———. 1984. *An Introduction to the Study of Public Policy,* 3rd ed. Monterey, CA: Brooks/Cole.

Kady, Martin II, with Isaiah J. Poole. 2004. "Record Gas Prices Immune to Any Legislative Magic." *CQ Weekly,* June 12, 1388–96.

Kahn, Joseph. 2001. "Cheney Promotes Increasing Supply as Energy Policy." *New York Times,* May 1, 1, 18.

Kamieniecki, Sheldon, ed. 1993. *Environmental Politics in the International Arena: Movements, Parties, Organizations, and Policy.* Albany: State University of New York Press.

———. 1995. "Political Parties and Environmental Policy." In *Environmental Politics and Policy,* edited by James P. Lester. Durham, NC: Duke University Press.

———. 2006. *Corporate America and Environmental Policy: How Often Does Business Get Its Way?* Stanford, CA: Stanford University Press.

Kamieniecki, Sheldon, David Shafie, and Julie Silvers. 1999. "Forming Partnerships in Environmental Policy: The Business of Emissions Trading in Clean Air Management." *American Behavioral Scientist* 43 (September): 107–23.

Karkkainen, Bradley C., Archon Fung, and Charles Sabel. 2000. "After Backyard Environmentalism: Toward a Performance-Based Regime of Environmental Regulation." *American Behavioral Scientist* 44: 690–709.

Kates, Robert W., William C. Clark, Robert Corell, J. Michael Hall, Carlo C. Jaeger, Ian Lowe, et al. 2001. "Sustainability Science." *Science* 292 (April 27): 641–42.

Kawachi, Ichiro, Graham A. Colditz, Frank E. Speizer, JoAnn E. Manson, Meir J. Stampfer, Walter C. Willett, and Charles H. Hennekens. 1997. "A Prospective Study of Passive Smoking and Coronary Heart Disease. *Circulation* 95: 2374–79.

Kellert, Stephen R. 1996. *The Value of Life: Biological Diversity and Human Society.* Washington, DC: Island Press.

Kempton, Willett, James S. Boster, and Jennifer A. Hartley. 1996. *Environmental Values in American Culture.* Cambridge, MA: MIT Press.

Kent, Mary M., and Mark Mather. 2002. "What Drives U.S. Population Growth." *Population Bulletin* 57 (December): 1–40.

Kenworthy, Tom. 1992a. "Federal Projects Are Not Endangered." *Washington Post National Weekly Edition,* March 9–15, 37.

———. 1992b. "It's No Day at the Beach for the National Park Service." *Washington Post National Weekly Edition,* April 13–19, 34.

Keohane, Robert O., and Marc A. Levy, eds. 1996. *Institutions for Environmental Aid: Pitfalls and Promise.* Cambridge, MA: MIT Press.

Kerr, J. B., and C. T. McElroy. 1993. "Evidence of Large Upward Trends of Ultraviolet-B Radiation Linked to Ozone Depletion." *Science* 262 (November 12): 1032–34.

Kerr, Richard A. 1998. "Acid Rain Control: Success on the Cheap." *Science* 282 (November 6): 1024–27.

Kerwin, Cornelius M. 2003. *Rulemaking: How Government Agencies Write Law and Make Policy,* 3rd ed. Washington, DC: CQ Press.

Kettl, Donald F. 1993. *Sharing Power: Public Governance and Private Markets.* Washington, DC: Brookings Institution.

———, ed. 2002. *Environmental Governance: A Report on the Next Generation of Environmental Policy.* Washington, DC: Brookings Institution Press.

Kingdon, John W. 1995. *Agendas, Alternatives, and Public Policies,* 2nd ed. New York: Longman.

Klyza, Christopher McGrory. 1996. *Who Controls Public Lands? Mining, Forestry, and Grazing Policies, 1870–1990.* Chapel Hill: University of North Carolina Press.

Knaap, Gerrit J., and Tschangho John Kim, eds. 1998. *Environmental Program Evaluation: A Primer.* Champaign: University of Illinois Press.

Koontz, Tomas M. 2002. *Federalism in the Forest: National Versus State Natural Resource Policy.* Washington, DC: Georgetown University Press.

———. 2005. "We Finished the Plan, So Now What? Impacts of Collaborative Shakeholder Participation on Land Use Policy." *Policy Studies Journal* 33 (2005): 459–81.

Koontz, Tomas M., Toddi A. Steelman, JoAnn Carmin, Katrina Smith Korfmacher, Cassandra Moseley, and Craig W. Thomas. 2004. *Collaborative Environmental Management: What Roles for Government?* Washington, DC: RFF Press.

Knopman, Debra S., Megan M. Susman, and Marc K. Landy. 1999. "Civic Environmentalism: Tackling Tough Land-Use Problems with Innovative Governance." *Environment* 41 (December): 24–32.

Koplow, Douglas N. 1993. *Federal Energy Subsidies: Energy, Environmental, and Fiscal Impacts.* Lexington, MA: Alliance to Save Energy.

Kraft, Michael E. 1981. "Congress and National Energy Policy: Assessing the Policy Process." In *Environment, Energy, Public Policy,* edited by Regina S. Axelrod. Lexington, MA: Lexington Books.

———. 1984. "A New Environmental Policy Agenda: The 1980 Presidential Campaign and Its Aftermath." In *Environmental Policy in the 1980s,* edited by Norman J. Vig and Michael E. Kraft. Washington, DC: CQ Press.

———. 1994a. "Population Policy." In *Encyclopedia of Policy Studies,* 2nd ed., edited by Stuart S. Nagel. New York: Marcel Dekker.

———. 1994b. "Searching for Policy Success: Reinventing the Politics of Site Remediation." *The Environmental Professional* 16 (September): 245–53.

———. 1995. "Congress and Environmental Policy." In *Environmental Politics and Policy,* 2nd ed., edited by James P. Lester. Durham, NC: Duke University Press.

———. 1996. "Democratic Dialogue and Acceptable Risks: The Politics of High-Level

Nuclear Waste Disposal in the United States." In *Hazardous Waste Siting and Democratic Choice*, edited by Don Munton. Washington, DC: Georgetown University Press.

————. 2000. "Policy Design and the Acceptability of Environmental Risks: Nuclear Waste Disposal in Canada and the United States." *Policy Studies Journal* 28 (1): 206–18.

————. 2006. "Environmental Policy in Congress." In *Environmental Policy*, 6th ed., edited by Norman J. Vig and Michael E. Kraft. Washington, DC: CQ Press.

Kraft, Michael E., Bruce B. Clary, and Richard J. Tobin. 1988. "The Impact of New Federalism on State Environmental Policy: The Great Lakes States." In *The Midwest Response to the New Federalism*, edited by Peter Eisinger and William Gormley. Madison: University of Wisconsin Press.

Kraft, Michael E., and Scott R. Furlong. 2007. *Public Policy: Politics, Analysis, and Alternatives*, 2nd ed. Washington, DC: CQ Press.

Kraft, Michael E., and Bruce N. Johnson. 1999. "Clean Water and the Promise of Collaborative Decision Making: The Case of the Fox–Wolf River Basin in Wisconsin." In *Toward Sustainable Communities*, edited by Daniel A. Mazmanian and Michael E. Kraft. Cambridge, MA: MIT Press.

Kraft, Michael E., and Sheldon Kamieniecki, eds. 2007. *Business and Environmental Policy: Corporate Interests in the American Political System*. Cambridge, MA: MIT Press.

Kraft, Michael E., and Denise Scheberle. 1998. "Environmental Federalism at Decade's End: New Approaches and Strategies." *Publius: The Journal of Federalism* 28 (Winter): 131–46.

Kraft, Michael E., and Diana Wuertz. 1996. "Environmental Advocacy in the Corridors of Government." In *The Symbolic Earth*, edited by James G. Cantrill and Christine L. Oravec. Lexington: University of Kentucky Press.

Kriz, Margaret. 1993. "Quick Draw." *National Journal*, November 13, 2711–16.

————. 1994a. "Cleaner Than Clean?" *National Journal*, April 23, 946–49.

————. 1994b. "How the Twain Met." *National Journal*, June 4, 1291–95.

————. 1999. "Call of the Wild." *National Journal*, October 23, 3038–43.

————. 2000. "Testing the Waters at the EPA." *National Journal*, April 22, 1286–87.

————. 2005. "Heating Up." *National Journal*, August 6, 2504–8.

Kriz, Margaret, and James A. Barnes. 2002. "How Green Is Our Electorate." *National Journal*, April 27, 1256–57.

Kruger, Joseph A., and William A. Pizer. 2004. "Greenhouse Gas Trading in Europe." *Environment* 46 (October): 6–23.

Krupnick, Alan J. 2002. "Does the Clean Air Act Measure Up?" *Resources* 147 (Spring): 2–3.

Kusler, Jon A., William J. Mitsch, and Joseph S. Larson. 1994. "Wetlands." *Scientific American* 220 (January): 64–70.

Lacey, Michael J., ed. 1989. *Government and Environmental Politics: Essays on Historical Developments since World War II*. Baltimore: Johns Hopkins University Press.

Ladd, Everett Carll, and Karlyn H. Bowman. 1995. *Attitudes Toward the Environment: Twenty-Five Years after Earth Day*. Washington, DC: American Enterprise Institute.

Landy, Marc K., Marc J. Roberts, and Stephen R. Thomas. 1994. *The Environmental Protection Agency: Asking the Wrong Questions*, 2nd ed. New York: Oxford University Press.

Layzer, Judith. 2007. "Deep Freeze: How Business Has Shaped the Legislative Debate on Climate Change." In *Business and Environmental Policy: Corporate Interests in the American Political System*, edited by Michael E. Kraft and Sheldon Kamieniecki. Cambridge, MA: MIT Press.

League of Conservation Voters. 1999. "What the Polls Say." *LCV Insider*, March.

Lee, Gary. 1994. "A Potential Killer's Modus Operandi." *Washington Post National Weekly Edition,* June 20–26, 38.

Leopold, Aldo. 1970. *A Sand County Almanac.* New York: Oxford University Press, 1949. Expanded ed., with additional essays from *Round River.* Reprint: New York: Ballantine Books (page references are to reprint edition).

Leshy, John D. 1984. "Natural Resource Policy." In *Natural Resources and the Environment,* edited by Paul R. Portney. Washington, DC: Resources for the Future.

Lester, James P., ed. 1995. *Environmental Politics and Policy: Theories and Evidence,* 2nd ed. Durham, NC: Duke University Press.

Lewis, Daniel. 1999. "The Trailblazer." *New York Times Magazine,* June 13, 50–53.

Lewis, Martin W. 1994. *Green Delusions: An Environmentalist Critique of Radical Environmentalism.* Durham, NC: Duke University Press.

Lewis, Paul. 1994. "U.N. Panel Finds Action on Environment Lagging." *New York Times,* May 29, 6.

Lichter, S. Robert, and Stanley Rothman. 1999. *Environmental Cancer: A Political Disease?* New Haven, CT: Yale University Press.

Lindblom, Charles E., and Edward J. Woodhouse. 1993. *The Policy-Making Process,* 3rd ed. Englewood Cliffs, NJ: Prentice Hall.

Lindzen, Richard S. 1992. "Global Warming: The Origin and Nature of the Alleged Scientific Consensus." *Regulation: Cato Review of Business and Government* 15 (Spring): 87–98.

Litfin, Karen T., ed. 1998. *The Greening of Sovereignty in World Politics.* Cambridge, MA: MIT Press.

Lomborg, Bjørn. 2001. *The Skeptical Environmentalist: Measuring the Real State of the World.* New York: Cambridge University Press.

Lowi, Theodore J. 1979. *The End of Liberalism,* 2nd ed. New York: W. W. Norton.

Lowry, William R. 1992. *The Dimensions of Federalism: State Governments and Pollution Control Policies.* Durham, NC: Duke University Press.

———. 1994. *The Capacity for Wonder: Preserving National Parks.* Washington, DC: Brookings Institution.

———. 2003. *Dam Politics: Restoring America's Rivers.* Washington, DC: Georgetown University Press.

———. 2006. "A Return to Traditional Priorities in Natural Resource Policies." In *Environmental Policy,* 6th ed., edited by Norman J. Vig and Michael E. Kraft. Washington, DC: CQ Press.

Lubchenco, Jane. 1998. "Entering the Century of the Environment: A New Social Contract for Science." *Science* 279 (January 23): 491–97.

Lubell, Mark. 2004. "Collaborative Watershed Management: A View from the Grassroots." *Policy Studies Journal* 32: 341–61.

Luke, Timothy W. 1997. *Ecocritique: Contesting the Politics of Nature, Economy, and Culture.* Minneapolis: University of Minnesota Press.

Lutz, Ernst. 1993. *Toward Improved Accounting for the Environment.* Washington, DC: The World Bank.

MacNeill, Jim, Pieter Winsemius, and Taizo Yakushiji. 1991. *Beyond Interdependence: The Meshing of the World's Economy and the Earth's Ecology.* New York: Oxford University Press.

Mangun, William R., and Daniel H. Henning. 1999. *Managing the Environmental Crisis: Incorporating Competing Values in Natural Resource Administration,* 2nd ed. Durham, NC: Duke University Press.

Mann, Dean E. 1986. "Democratic Politics and Environmental Policy." In *Controversies in Environmental Policy,* edited by Sheldon Kamieniecki, Robert O'Brien, and Michael Clarke. Albany: State University of New York Press.

Marcus, Alfred A. 1992. *Controversial Issues in Energy Policy.* Newbury Park, CA: Sage.

Marcus, Alfred A., Donald A. Geffen, and Ken Sexton. 2002. *Reinventing Environmental*

Regulation: Lessons from Project XL. Washington, DC: RFF Press.

Mastny, Lisa. 2004. "Purchasing for People and the Planet." In *State of the World 2004,* edited by Linda Starke. Washington, DC: Worldwatch Institute.

Mazmanian, Daniel, and David Morell. 1992. *Beyond Superfailure: America's Toxics Policy for the 1990s.* Boulder, CO: Westview Press.

Mazmanian, Daniel A. 1999. "Los Angeles' Transition from Command-and-Control to Market-Based Clean Air Policy Strategies and Implementation." In *Toward Sustainable Communities,* edited by Daniel A. Mazmanian and Michael E. Kraft. Cambridge, MA: MIT Press.

Mazmanian, Daniel A., and Michael E. Kraft, eds. 1999. *Toward Sustainable Communities: Transition and Transformations in Environmental Policy.* Cambridge, MA: MIT Press.

Mazmanian, Daniel A., and Jeanne Nienaber. 1979. *Can Organizations Change? Environmental Protection, Citizen Participation, and the Corps of Engineers.* Washington, DC: Brookings Institution.

Mazmanian, Daniel A., and Paul A. Sabatier. 1983. *Implementation and Public Policy.* Glenview, IL: Scott, Foresman.

Mazur, Laurie Ann. 1994. *Beyond the Numbers: A Reader on Population, Consumption, and the Environment.* Washington, DC: Island Press.

McAvoy, Gregory E. 1999. *Controlling Technology: Citizen Rationality and the NIMBY Syndrome.* Washington, DC: Georgetown University Press.

McClure, Robert, and Andrew Schneider. 2002. "Shafting the West." *OnEarth* (Spring): 33–36.

McConnell, Grant. 1966. *Private Power and American Democracy.* New York: Knopf.

McCool, Daniel. 1990. "Subgovernments as Determinants of Political Viability." *Political Science Quarterly* 105 (Summer): 269–93.

McCormick, John. 1989. *Reclaiming Paradise: The Global Environmental Movement.* Bloomington: Indiana University Press.

———. 2005. "The Role of Environmental NGOs in International Regimes." In *The Global Environment,* 2nd ed., edited by Regina S. Axelrod, David L. Downie, and Norman Vig. Washington, DC: CQ Press.

McKinley, James C., Jr. 1999a. "Sugar Industry's Pivotal Role in Everglades Effort." *New York Times,* April 16, 1, A19.

———. 1999b. "U.S. Unveils Plan to Aid 68 Species in Everglades." *New York Times,* May 19, A18.

McSpadden, Lettie M. 2000. "Environmental Policy in the Courts." In *Environmental Policy,* 4th ed., edited by Norman J. Vig and Michael E. Kraft. Washington, DC: CQ Press.

Meadowcroft, James. 2004. "Deliberative Democracy." In *Environmental Governance Reconsidered,* edited by Robert F. Durant, Daniel J. Fiorino, and Rosemary O'Leary. Cambridge, MA: MIT Press.

Meadows, Donella, Jørgen Randers, and Dennis Meadows. 2004. *Limits to Growth: The 30-Year Update.* White River Junction, VT: Chelsea Green Publishing Group.

Melnick, R. Shep. 1983. *Regulation and the Courts: The Case of the Clean Air Act.* Washington, DC: Brookings Institution.

Meyer, Stephen M. 1993. "Environmentalism and Economic Prosperity." Cambridge, MA: MIT Department of Political Science.

Michaelis, Laura. 1993. "Calls for Pesticide Reform Linked to New Report." *Congressional Quarterly Weekly Report,* July 3, 1730.

Milbrath, Lester W. 1984. *Environmentalists: Vanguard for a New Society.* Albany: State University of New York Press.

———. 1989. *Envisioning a Sustainable Society: Learning Our Way Out.* Albany: State University of New York Press.

Miller, Kenton R., Walter V. Reid, and Charles V. Barber. 1991. "Deforestation and Species Loss: Responding to the Crisis." In *Preserving the Global Environment,* edited by Jessica Tuchman Mathews. New York: W. W. Norton.

Misch, Ann. 1994. "Assessing Environmental Health Risks." In *State of the World 1994*, edited by Linda Starke. New York: W. W. Norton.

Mitchell, Robert Cameron. 1984. "Public Opinion and Environmental Politics in the 1970s and 1980s." In *Environmental Policy in the 1980s*, edited by Norman J. Vig and Michael E. Kraft. Washington, DC: CQ Press.

———. 1989. "From Conservation to Environmental Movement: The Development of the Modern Environmental Lobbies." In *Government and Environmental Politics*, edited by Michael Lacey. Baltimore: Johns Hopkins University Press.

———. 1990. "Public Opinion and the Green Lobby: Poised for the 1990s?" In *Environmental Policy in the 1990s*, edited by Norman J. Vig and Michael E. Kraft. Washington, DC: CQ Press.

Mitchell, Robert Cameron, Angela G. Mertig, and Riley E. Dunlap. 1992. "Twenty Years of Environmental Mobilization: Trends Among National Environmental Organizations." In *American Environmentalism*, edited by Riley E. Dunlap and Angela G. Mertig. Philadelphia: Taylor and Francis.

Moe, Terry M. 1980. *The Organization of Interests: Incentives and the Internal Dynamics of Political Interest Groups*. Chicago: University of Chicago Press.

Morgenstern, Richard D. 1999. "An Historical Perspective on Regulatory Decision Making: The Role of Economic Analysis." In *Better Environmental Decisions*, edited by Ken Sexton, Alfred A. Marcus, K. William Easter, and Timothy D. Burkhardt. Washington, DC: Island Press.

———, and Paul R. Portney, eds. 2004. *New Approaches on Energy and the Environment: Policy Advice for the President*. Washington, DC: RFF Press.

Morgenstern, Richard D., William A. Pizer, and Jhih-Shyang Shih. 1999. "Jobs versus the Environment: Is There a Trade-off?" Washington, DC: Resources for the Future. RFF Discussion Paper 99–01.

Mullins, Brody. 1999. "Will Superfund Reform Be Dumped Again?" *National Journal*, October 30, 3139–40.

Munton, Don, ed. 1996. *Hazardous Waste Siting and Democratic Choice*. Washington, DC: Georgetown University Press.

Myers, Norman. 1997. "The World's Forests and Their Ecosystem Services." In *Nature's Services*, edited by Gretchen C. Daily. Washington, DC: Island Press.

Myers, Norman, and Jennifer Kent. 2001. *Perverse Subsidies: How Misused Tax Dollars Harm the Environment and the Economy*. Washington, DC: Island Press.

Myerson, Allen R. 1998. "U.S. Splurging on Energy after Falling Off Its Diet." *New York Times*, October 22, 1, C6–C7.

Najam, Adil. 2005. "The View from the South: Developing Countries in Global Environmental Politics." In *The Global Environment*, edited by Regina S. Axelrod, David Leonard Downie, and Norman J. Vig. Washington, DC: CQ Press.

Nash, Roderick Frazier. 1990. *American Environmentalism: Readings in Conservation History*, 3rd ed. New York: McGraw-Hill.

National Academy of Public Administration. 1987. *Presidential Management of Rulemaking in Regulatory Agencies*. Washington, DC: National Academy of Public Administration.

———. 1994. *The Environment Goes to Market: The Implementation of Economic Incentives for Pollution Control*. Washington, DC: National Academy of Public Administration.

———. 1995. *Setting Priorities, Getting Results: A New Direction for EPA*. Washington, DC: National Academy of Public Administration.

———. 2000. *Environment.gov: Transforming Environmental Protection for the 21st Century*. Washington, DC: National Academy of Public Administration.

National Acid Precipitation Assessment Program. 1990. *Background on Acidic Deposition and the National Acid Precipitation*

Assessment Program and Assessment Highlights. Washington, DC: NAPAP.

National Commission on the Environment. 1993. *Choosing a Sustainable Future: The Report of the National Commission on the Environment.* Washington, DC: Island Press.

National Journal. 1990. "Opinion Outlook: Views on the American Scene." *National Journal,* April 28, 1052.

National Performance Review. 1993. *Accompanying Report of the National Performance Review,* multiple reports. Washington, DC: Office of the Vice President. (Released in 1994.)

National Research Council. 1990. *Forestry Research: A Mandate for Change.* Washington, DC: National Academy Press.

———. 1996. *Understanding Risk: Informing Decisions in a Democratic Society.* Washington, DC: National Academy Press.

———. 1999. *Our Common Journey: A Transition toward Sustainability.* Washington, DC: National Academy Press.

———. 2001. *The Role of Environmental NGOs: Russian Challenges, American Lessons.* Washington, DC: National Academy Press.

———. 2004. *Valuing Ecosystem Services: Toward Better Environmental Decision-Making.* Washington, DC: National Academies Press.

Nelson, Gaylord (with Susan Campbell and Paul Wozniak). 2002. *Beyond Earth Day: Fulfilling the Promise.* Madison: University of Wisconsin Press.

New York Times. 1994. "U.S. Issues New Rules on Protected Species." *New York Times,* June 15, 7.

Norse, Elliott A. 1990. "What Good Are Ancient Forests?" *The Amicus Journal* (Winter): 42–45.

O'Brien, Mary. 2000. *Making Better Environmental Decisions: An Alternative to Risk Assessment.* Cambridge, MA: MIT Press.

O'Leary, Rosemary. 1993. *Environmental Change: Federal Courts and the EPA.* Philadelphia: Temple University Press.

———. 2006. "Environmental Policy in the Courts." In *Environmental Policy,* 6th ed., edited by Norman J. Vig and Michael E. Kraft. Washington, DC: CQ Press.

———, and Lisa B. Bingham, eds. 2003. *The Promise and Performance of Environmental Conflict Resolution.* Washington, DC: RFF Press.

Olson, Mancur. 1971. *The Logic of Collective Action.* Cambridge, MA: Harvard University Press.

O'Malley, Robin, and Kate Wing. 2000. "Forging a New Tool for Ecosystem Reporting." *Environment* 42 (April): 21–31.

Ophuls, William, and A. Stephen Boyan Jr. 1992. *Ecology and the Politics of Scarcity Revisited.* New York: W. H. Freeman.

Ostrom, Elinor. 1990. *Governing the Commons: The Evolution of Institutions for Collective Action.* New York: Cambridge University Press.

———. 1999a. "Coping with Tragedies of the Commons." In *Annual Review of Political Science,* vol. 2, edited by Nelson W. Polsby. Palo Alto, CA: Annual Reviews.

———. 1999b. "Institutional Rational Choice: An Assessment of the Institutional Analysis and Development Framework." In *Theories of the Policy Process,* edited by Paul A. Sabatier. Boulder: Westview Press.

Ostrom, Elinor, Thomas Dietz, Nives Dolšak, Paul C. Stern, Susan Stonich, and Elke U. Weber, eds. 2002. *The Drama of the Commons.* Washington, DC: National Academy Press.

O'Toole, Randall. 1988. *Reforming the Forest Service.* Washington, DC: Island Press.

Ott, Wayne R., and John W. Roberts. 1998. "Everyday Exposure to Toxic Pollutants." *Scientific American* 224 (February): 86–91.

Paarlberg, Robert L. 1999. "Lapsed Leadership: U.S. International Environmental Policy since Rio." In *The Global Environment,* edited by Norman J. Vig and Regina S. Axelrod. Washington, DC: CQ Press.

Paehlke, Robert C. 1989. *Environmentalism and the Future of Progressive Politics.* New Haven, CT: Yale University Press.

_____. 2000. "Environmental Values and Public Policy." In *Environmental Policy,* 4th ed., edited by Norman J. Vig and Michael E. Kraft. Washington, DC: CQ Press.

_____. 2004. *Democracy's Dilemma: Environment, Social Equity, and the Global Economy.* Cambridge, MA: MIT Press.

_____. 2006. "Environmental Sustainability and Urban Life in America." In *Environmental Policy,* 6th ed., edited by Norman J. Vig and Michael E. Kraft. Washington, DC: CQ Press.

Parris, Thomas M. 2003. "Toward a Sustainability Transition: The International Consensus." *Environment* 45 (January/February): 13–22.

_____. 2006. "Internet Resources for Sustainable Product Design." *Environment* 48 (March): 3.

Parry, Ian W. H. 2002. "Is Gasoline Undertaxed in the United States?" *Resources* 148 (Summer): 28–33.

Perlez, Jane, and Kirk Johnson. 2005. "Behind Gold's Glitter: Torn Lands and Pointed Questions." *New York Times,* October 24, 1, A10.

Peskin, Henry M., Paul R. Portney, and Allen V. Kneese, eds. 1981. *Environmental Regulation and the U.S. Economy.* Baltimore: Johns Hopkins University Press.

Pirages, Dennis, and Ken Cousins, eds. 2005. *From Resource Scarcity to Ecological Security: Exploring New Limits to Growth.* Cambridge, MA: MIT Press.

Platt, Rutherford H., Paul K. Barten, and Max J. Pfeffer. 2000. "A Full, Clean Glass? Managing New York City's Watersheds." *Environment* 42 (June): 6–20.

Pope, Charles. 1998. "National Parks, Private Funds: Trouble in Paradise?" *CQ Weekly,* October 31, 2938–41.

_____. 1999a. "Political Ground May Be Shifting under Mine Operators." *CQ Weekly,* September 11, 2111–14.

_____. 1999b. "Suburban Sprawl and Government Turf." *CQ Weekly,* March 13, 586–90.

_____. 2000. "Clean Water: The Next Wave." *CQ Weekly,* March 18, 585–86.

Porter, Michael E., and Claas van der Linde. 1995. "Green and Competitive: Ending the Stalemate." *Harvard Business Review* 73 (September/October): 120–34.

Portney, Kent E. 2003. *Taking Sustainable Cities Seriously: Economic Development, the Environment, and Quality of Life in American Cities.* Cambridge, MA: MIT Press.

Portney, Paul R. 1990. "Air Pollution Policy." In *Public Policies for Environmental Protection,* edited by Paul R. Portney. Washington, DC: Resources for the Future.

_____. 1994. "Does Environmental Policy Conflict with Economic Growth?" *Resources* 115 (Spring): 21–23.

_____. 1995. "Beware of the Killer Clauses Inside the GOP's 'Contract.'" *Washington Post National Weekly Edition* (January 23–29): 21.

_____. 1998. "Counting the Costs: The Growing Role of Economics in Environmental Decisionmaking." *Environment* 40 (March): 14–18, 36–38.

_____. 2000. "EPA and the Evolution of Federal Regulation." In *Public Policies for Environmental Protection,* edited by Paul R. Portney and Robert N. Stavins. Washington, DC: RFF Press.

_____. 2002. "Penny-Wise and Pound-Fuelish? New Car Mileage Standards in the United States." *Resources* 147 (Spring): 10–15.

_____, ed. 1984. *Natural Resources and the Environment: The Reagan Approach.* Washington, DC: Urban Institute Press.

Portney, Paul R., and Katherine N. Probst. 1994. "Cleaning Up Superfund." *Resources* 114 (Winter): 2–5.

Portney, Paul R., and Robert N. Stavins, eds. 2000. *Public Policy for Environmental Protection,* 2nd ed. Washington, DC: Resources for the Future.

Postel, Sandra. 1988. "Controlling Toxic Chemicals." In *State of the World 1988,* edited by Lester R. Brown. New York: W. W. Norton.

_____. 1994. "Carrying Capacity: Earth's Bottom Line." In *State of the World 1994,* edited by Linda Starke. New York: W. W. Norton.

Potoski, Matthew, and Aseem Prakash. 2005. "Covenants with Weak Swords: ISO 14001 and Facilities' Environmental Performance." *Journal of Policy Analysis and Management* 24: 745–69.

Powell, Mark R. 1999. *Science at EPA: Information in the Regulatory Process.* Washington, DC: Resources for the Future.

Presidential/Congressional Commission on Risk Assessment and Risk Management. 1997. *Risk Assessment and Risk Management in Regulatory Decision-Making.* Final Report, Vol. 2. Washington, DC: Commission offices. (The report and other studies and commentary on risk are available at www.riskworld. com.)

President's Council on Sustainable Development. 1996. *Sustainable America: A New Consensus for Prosperity, Opportunity, and a Healthy Environment for the Future.* Washington, DC: U.S. Government Printing Office.

Press, Daniel. 1999. "Local Open-Space Preservation in California." In *Toward Sustainable Communities,* edited by Daniel A. Mazmanian and Michael E. Kraft. Cambridge, MA: MIT Press.

_____. 2002. *Saving Open Space: The Politics of Local Preservation in California.* Berkeley: University of California Press.

Press, Daniel, and Daniel A. Mazmanian. 2006. "The Greening of Industry: Combining Government Regulation and Voluntary Strategies." In *Environmental Policy,* 6th ed., edited by Norman J. Vig and Michael E. Kraft. Washington, DC: CQ Press.

Probst, Katherine N., and Adam I. Lowe. 2000. *Cleaning Up the Nuclear Weapons Complex: Does Anybody Care?* Washington, DC: Resources for the Future.

Probst, Katherine N., and Michael H. McGovern. 1998. *Long-Term Stewardship and the Nuclear Weapons Complex: The Challenge Ahead.* Washington, DC: Resources for the Future.

Probst, Katherine N., and David M. Konisky (with Robert Hersh, Michael B. Batz, and Katherine D. Walker). 2001. *Superfund's Future: What Will It Cost?* Washington, DC: RFF Press.

Putnam, Robert D. 2000. *Bowling Alone: The Collapse and Revival of American Community.* New York: Simon & Schuster.

Rabe, Barry G. 1986. *Fragmentation and Integration in State Environmental Management.* Washington, DC: Conservation Foundation.

_____. 1999. "Sustainability in a Regional Context: The Case of the Great Lakes Basin." In *Toward Sustainable Communities,* edited by Daniel A. Mazmanian and Michael E. Kraft. Cambridge, MA: MIT Press.

_____. 2004. *Greenhouse and Statehouse: The Emerging Politics of American Climate Change.* Washington, DC: Brookings Institution Press.

_____. 2006. "Power to the States: The Promise and Pitfalls of Decentralization." In *Environmental Policy,* 6th ed., edited by Norman J. Vig and Michael E. Kraft. Washington, DC: CQ Press.

_____, and Philip A. Mundo. 2007. "Corporate Interest in the American Political System." In *Business and Environmental Policy: Corporate Interests in the American Political System,* edited by Michael E. Kraft and Sheldon Kamieniecki. Cambridge, MA: MIT Press.

Rahm, Dianne. 1998. "Controversial Cleanup: Superfund and the Implementation of U.S. Hazardous Waste Policy." *Policy Studies Journal* 26 (Winter): 719–34.

Randel, William J., Richard S. Stolarski, Derek M. Cunnold, Jennifer A. Logan, M. J. Newchurch, and Joseph M. Zawodny. 1999. "Trends in the Vertical Distribution of Ozone." *Science* 285 (September 10), 1689–92.

Reid, Walter V. 1997. "Strategies for Conserving Biodiversity." *Environment* 39 (7) (September): 16–20, 39–43.

Renner, Michael. 2000. "Creating Jobs, Preserving the Environment." In *State of the World 2000,* edited by Lester R. Brown, Christopher Flavin, and Hilary French. Washington, DC: Worldwatch Institute.

Revkin, Andrew C. 2002. "Law Revises Standards for Scientific Study." *New York Times,* March 21, A24.

_____. 2005. "Glacial Gains on Emissions." *New York Times,* December 11, 1, 14.

Riebsame, William. 1996. "Ending the Range Wars?" *Environment* 38 (May): 4–9, 27–29.

Ringquist, Evan J. 1993. *Environmental Protection at the State Level: Politics and Progress in Controlling Pollution.* Armonk, NY: M. E. Sharpe.

_____. 1995. "Evaluating Environmental Policy Outcomes." In *Environmental Politics and Policy,* 2nd ed., edited by James P. Lester. Durham, NC: Duke University Press.

_____. 2006. "Environmental Justice: Normative Concerns, Empirical Evidence, and Government Action." In *Environmental Policy,* 6th ed., edited by Norman J. Vig and Michael E. Kraft. Washington, DC: CQ Press.

_____, and Carl Dasse. 2004. "Lies, Damned Lies, and Campaign Promises? Environmental Legislation in the 105th Congress." *Social Science Quarterly* 85 (June): 400–19.

Ripley, Randall B., and Grace A. Franklin. 1991. *Congress, the Bureaucracy, and Public Policy,* 5th ed. Pacific Grove, CA: Brooks/Cole.

Robbins, Jim. 2004. "Critics Say Forest Service Battles Too Many Fires." *New York Times,* February 8, A14.

Rohter, Larry. 2004. "U.S. Waters Down Global Commitment to Curb Greenhouse Gases." *New York Times,* December 19, 6.

Roodman, David Malin. 1996. "Paying the Piper: Subsidies, Politics, and the Environment." Worldwatch Paper 133. Washington, DC: Worldwatch Institute.

_____. 1997. "Getting the Signals Right: Tax Reform to Protect the Environment and the Economy." Worldwatch Paper 134. Washington, DC: Worldwatch Institute.

Rosenbaum, Walter A. 1987. *Energy, Politics, and Public Policy,* 2nd ed. Washington, DC: CQ Press.

_____. 2006. "Improving Environmental Regulation at the EPA: The Challenge in Balancing Politics, Policy, and Science." In *Environmental Policy,* 6th ed., edited by Norman J. Vig and Michael E. Kraft. Washington, DC: CQ Press.

Rothenberg, Lawrence S. 2002. *Environmental Choices: Policy Responses to Green Demands.* Washington, DC: CQ Press.

Rowland, F. Sherwood. 1993. "The Need for Scientific Communication with the Public." *Science* 260 (June 11): 1571–76.

Ruckelshaus, William D. 1990. "Toward a Sustainable World." In *Managing Planet Earth,* edited by Scientific American. New York: W. H. Freeman.

Rushefsky, Mark. 1986. *Making Cancer Policy.* Albany: State University of New York Press.

Russell, Clifford S. 1990. "Monitoring and Enforcement." In *Public Policies for Environmental Protection,* edited by Paul R. Portney. Washington, DC: Resources for the Future.

Russell, Milton, E. William Colglazier, and Bruce E. Tonn. 1992. "The U.S. Hazardous Waste Legacy." *Environment* 34: 12–15, 34–39.

Saar, Robert A. 1999. "Tracking Ground Water's Unwelcome Guests." *New York Times,* November 23, D8.

Sabatier, Paul A., ed. 1999. *Theories of the Policy Process.* Boulder, CO: Westview Press.

Sabatier, Paul A., and Hank C. Jenkins-Smith. 1993. *Policy Change and Learning: An Advocacy Coalition Approach.* Boulder, CO: Westview Press.

Sabatier, Paul A., Will Focht, Mark Lubell, Zev Trachtenberg, Arnold Vedlitz, and Marty Matlock, eds. 2005. *Swimming Upstream: Collaborative Approaches to*

Watershed Management. Cambridge, MA: MIT Press.

Sagoff, Mark. 1988. *The Economy of the Earth.* Cambridge, England: Cambridge University Press.

_____. 1993. "Environmental Economics: An Epitaph." *Resources* 111 (Spring): 2–7.

Sachs, Jeffrey D. 2005. *The End of Poverty: Economic Possibilities for Our Time.* New York: Penguin Press.

Samet, Jonathan M., and John D. Spengler, eds. 1991. *Indoor Air Pollution: A Health Perspective.* Baltimore: Johns Hopkins University Press.

Sands, Philippe, and Jacqueline Peel. 2005. "Environmental Protection in the Twenty-First Century: Sustainable Development and International Law." In *The Global Environment,* edited by Regina S. Axelrod, David Leonard Downie, and Norman J. Vig. Washington, DC: CQ Press.

Sanger, Davie E., and Sam Howe Verhovek. 1999. "Clinton Proposes Wider Protection for U.S. Forests." *New York Times,* October 14, 1, A16.

Savas, E. S. 2000. *Privatization and Public-Private Partnerships.* New York: Chatham House.

Sawin, Janet. 2004. "Making Better Energy Choices." In *State of the World 2004,* edited by Linda Starke. Washington, DC: Worldwatch Institute.

Schattschneider, E. E. 1960. *The Semi-Sovereign People: A Realist's View of Democracy in America.* New York: Holt, Rinehart and Winston.

Scheberle, Denise. 2004. *Federalism and Environmental Policy: Trust and the Politics of Implementation,* 2nd ed. Washington, DC: Georgetown University Press.

_____. 1998. "Partners in Policymaking: Forging Effective Federal–State Relations." *Environment* 40 (December): 14–20, 28–30.

Schlozman, Kay Lehman., and John T. Tierney. 1986. *Organized Interests and American Democracy.* New York: Harper & Row.

Schneider, Anne L., and Helen Ingram. 1990. "Policy Design: Elements, Premises, and Strategies." In *Policy Theory and Policy Evaluation,* edited by Stuart S. Nagel. Westport, CT: Greenwood Press.

_____. 1997. *Policy Design for Democracy.* Lawrence: University of Kansas Press.

Schneider, Keith. 1991. "Ozone Depletion Harming Sea Life." *New York Times,* November 16, 6.

_____. 1992. "Administration Tries to Limit Rule Used to Halt Logging of National Forests." *New York Times,* April 28, A7.

_____. 1994a. "EPA Moves to Reduce Health Risks From Dioxin." *New York Times,* September 14, A8.

_____. 1994b. "Exxon Is Ordered to Pay $5 Billion for Alaska Spill." *New York Times,* September 17, 1, 9.

Schneider, Stephen H. 1990. "The Changing Climate." In *Managing Planet Earth,* edited by Scientific American. New York: W. H. Freeman.

Schoenbrod, David. 2005. *Saving Our Environment from Washington: How Congress Grabs Power, Shirks Responsibility, and Shortchanges the People.* New Haven, CT: Yale University Press.

Schulte, Bret. 2006. "Turning up the Heat: A Surprising Consensus Is Transforming the Complex Politics of Global Warming." *U.S. News and World Report,* April 10.

Schwartz, John. 2006. "Experts See Peril in Reduced Monitoring of Nation's Streams and Rivers." *New York Times,* April 11, D3.

Sclove, Richard E. 1995. *Democracy and Technology.* New York: Guilford Press.

Seelye, Katharine Q. 2001. "South's Forests Seen Hurt by Sprawl." *New York Times,* November 27, A10.

_____. 2002. "Administration Approves Stiff Penalties for Diesel Engine Emissions, Angering Industry." *New York Times,* August 3, A9.

Sexton, Ken. 1999. "Setting Environmental Priorities: Is Comparative Risk Assessment the Answer?" In *Better Environmental Decisions,* edited by Ken Sexton, Alfred A. Marcus, K. William Easter, and Timothy D. Burkhardt. Washington, DC: Island Press.

Sexton, Ken, Alfred A. Marcus, K. William Easter, and Timothy D. Burkhardt, eds. 1999. *Better Environmental Decisions: Strategies for Governments, Businesses, and Communities.* Washington, DC: Island Press.

Shabecoff, Philip. 1993. *A Fierce Green Fire: The American Environmental Movement.* New York: Hill and Wang.

_____. 2000. *Earth Rising: American Environmentalism in the 21st Century.* Washington, DC: Island Press.

Shaiko, Ronald G. 1999. *Voices and Echoes for the Environment: Public Interest Representation in the 1990s and Beyond.* New York: Columbia University Press.

Shanley, Robert A. 1992. *Presidential Influence and Environmental Policy.* Westport, CT: Greenwood Press.

Shapiro, Michael. 1990. "Toxic Substances Policy." In *Public Policies for Environmental Protection,* edited by Paul R. Portney. Washington, DC: Resources for the Future.

Sheaffer, John R., J. David Mullan, and Nathan B. Hinch. 2002. "Encouraging Wise Use of Flood Plains with Market-Based Incentives." *Environment* 44 (January/February): 33–43.

Shogren, Jason F., ed. 2004. *Species at Risk: Using Economic Incentives to Shelter Endangered Species on Private Lands.* Austin: University of Texas Press.

Shipan, Charles R., and William R. Lowry. 2001. "Environmental Policy and Party Divergence in Congress." *Political Research Quarterly* 54 (June): 245–63.

Shrader-Frechette, K. S. 1991. *Risk and Rationality: Philosophical Foundations for Populist Reforms.* Berkeley: University of California Press.

_____. 1993. *Burying Uncertainty: Risk and the Case against Geological Disposal of Nuclear Waste.* Berkeley: University of California Press.

Shutkin, William A. 2000. *The Land That Could Be: Environmentalism and Democracy in the Twenty-First Century.* Cambridge, MA: MIT Press.

Sigman, Hilary. 2000. "Hazardous Waste and Toxic Substance Policies." In *Public Policies for Environmental Protection,* 2nd ed., edited by Paul R. Portney and Robert N. Stavins. Washington, DC: RFF Press.

Simendinger, Alexis. 1998. "The Paper Wars." *National Journal* (July 23): 1732–39.

Simon, Julian L. 1995. *The State of Humanity.* New York: Basil Blackwell.

Simon, Julian L., and Herman Kahn, eds. 1984. *The Resourceful Earth: A Response to "Global 2000."* New York: Basil Blackwell.

Sinclair, Barbara. 2001. *Unorthodox Lawmaking: New Legislative Processes in the U.S. Congress,* 2nd ed. Washington, DC: CQ Press.

Singer, Paul. 2005. "Beyond a Catchy Slogan." *National Journal,* December 10, 3792–96.

Sitarz, Daniel, ed. 1998. *Sustainable America: America's Environment, Economy, and Society in the 21st Century.* Carbondale, IL: EarthPress.

Skocpol, Theda, and Morris P. Fiorina, eds. 1999. *Civic Engagement in American Democracy.* Washington, DC: Brookings Institution.

Slovic, Paul. 1987. "Perception of Risk." *Science* 236: 280–85.

_____. 1993. "Perceived Risk, Trust, and Democracy." *Risk Analysis* 13: 675–82.

Smardon, Richard, and Brenda Nordenstam. 1998. "Adirondacks and Beyond: Understanding Air Quality and Ecosystem Relationships." *Environmental Science and Policy* (special issue) 1, 3: 139–267.

Smil, Vaclav. 2003. *Energy at the Crossroads: Global Perspectives and Uncertainties.* Cambridge, MA: MIT Press.

Smith, Eric R. A. N. 2002. *Energy, the Environment, and Public Opinion.* New York: Rowman and Littlefield.

Smothers, Ronald. 1994. "Group Urges Tough Limits on Logging." *New York Times,* May 27, A9.

Solomon, Barry D., and Russell Lee. 2000. "Emissions Trading Systems and

Environmental Justice." *Environment* 42 (October): 32–45.

Soroos, Marvin. 2005. "Global Institutions and the Environment: An Evolutionary Perspective." In *The Global Environment*, 2nd ed., edited by Regina S. Axelrod, David L. Downie, and Norman J. Vig. Washington, DC: CQ Press.

Speth, James Gustave. 2002. "A New Green Regime: Attacking the Root Causes of Global Environmental Deterioration." *Environment* 44 (September): 16–25.

———. 2003. "Perspectives on the Johannesburg Summit." *Environment* 45 (January/February): 24–29.

———. 2004. *Red Sky at Morning: America and the Crisis of the Global Environment.* New Haven, CT: Yale University Press.

Starke, Linda. 1990. *Signs of Hope: Working Towards Our Common Future.* New York: Oxford University Press.

———, ed. 2004. *State of the World 2004.* New York: W. W. Norton.

———, ed. 2006. *State of the World 2006.* New York: W. W. Norton.

Stavins, Robert N. 1991. *Project 88—Round II, Incentives for Action: Designing Market-Based Environmental Strategies.* Washington, DC: A public policy study sponsored by Senator Timothy E. Wirth and Senator John Heinz.

Stein, Bruce A. 2001. "A Fragile Cornucopia: Assessing the Status of U.S. Biodiversity." *Environment* 43 (September): 11–22.

Steinberg, Paul F. 2001. *Environmental Leadership in Developing Countries: Transnational Relations and Biodiversity Policy in Costa Rica and Bolivia.* Cambridge, MA: MIT Press.

Stephan, Mark. 2002. "Environmental Information Disclosure Programs: They Work, But Why?" *Social Science Quarterly* 83 (March): 190–205.

Stevens, William K. 1993. "Scientists Confront Renewed Backlash on Global Warming." *New York Times*, September 14, B5–B6.

———. 1994. "Money Grow on Trees? No, But Study Finds Next Best Thing." *New York Times*, April 12, B12.

———. 1999. "Putting Things Right in the Everglades." *New York Times*, April 13, D1–D2.

———. 2000a. "Conservationists Win Battles but Fear War Is Lost." *New York Times*, January 11, D5.

———. 2000b. "U.S. Found to Be a Leader in Its Diversity of Wildlife." *New York Times*, March 16, A18.

Stewart, Barbara. 2001. "ExxonMobil to Pay Big Fine for Lying About Poison Waste." *New York Times*, December 14, A28.

Stone, Deborah. 2002. *Policy Paradox: The Art of Political Decision Making*, rev. ed. New York: W. W. Norton.

Stone, Richard. 1994. "California Report Sets Standard for Comparing Risks." *Science* 266 (October 14): 214.

Stroup, Richard L., and John A. Baden. 1983. *Natural Resources: Bureaucratic Myths and Environmental Management.* San Francisco: Pacific Institute for Public Policy Research.

Swarms, Rachel L. 2002. "U.S. Is Not the Only Nation Resisting a Strong Pact at the Summit Meeting on Global Warming." *New York Times*, August 31, A4.

Swartzman, Daniel, Richard A. Liroff, and Kevin G. Croke, eds. 1982. *Cost–Benefit Analysis and Environmental Regulations: Politics, Ethics, and Methods.* Washington, DC: Conservation Foundation.

Switzer, Jacqueline Vaughn. 1997. *Green Backlash: The History and Politics of Environmental Opposition in the U.S.* Boulder, CO: Lynne Rienner.

Taubes, Gary. 1993. "The Ozone Backlash." *Science* 260 (June 11): 1580–83.

Terborgh, John. 1999. *Requiem for Nature.* Washington, DC: Island Press.

Thomas, Craig W. 2003. *Bureaucratic Landscapes: Interagency Cooperation and the Preservation of Biodiversity.* Cambridge, MA: MIT Press.

Tierney, John, and William Frasure. 1998. "Culture Wars on the Frontier: Interests, Values, and Policy Narratives in Public Lands Politics." In *Interest Group Politics*,

5th ed., edited by Allan J. Cigler and Burdett A. Loomis. Washington, DC: CQ Press.

Tietenberg, Tom. 2006a. *Environmental and Natural Resource Economics*, 7th ed. Reading, MA: Addison-Wesley-Longman.

———. 2006b. *Emissions Trading: Principles and Practices*, 2nd ed. Washington, DC: RFF Press.

Tilman, David. 1997. "Biodiversity and Ecosystem Functioning." In *Nature's Services*, edited by Gretchen C. Daily. Washington, DC: Island Press.

Tobin, Richard J. 1990. *The Expendable Future: U.S. Politics and the Protection of Biological Diversity*. Durham, NC: Duke University Press.

———. 2006. "Environment, Population, and the Developing World." In *Environmental Policy*, 6th ed., edited by Norman J. Vig and Michael E. Kraft. Washington, DC: CQ Press.

Tong, Rosemarie. 1986. *Ethics in Policy Analysis*. Englewood Cliffs, NJ: Prentice Hall.

Uchitelle, Louis, and Megan Thee. 2006. "Americans Are Cautiously Open to Gas Tax Rise, Poll Shows." *New York Times*, February 28, A14.

United Nations. 1993. *Agenda 21: The United Nations Programme of Action from Rio*. New York: United Nations.

———. 2005. *State of the World Population 2005: The Promise of Equality: Gender, Equity, Reproductive Health and the Millennium Development Goals*. New York: United Nations Population Fund. Available at: www.unfpa.org/.

U.S. Department of Energy (U.S. DOE). 1998. *Energy in the United States: A Brief History and Current Trends*. Washington, DC: Energy Information Administration.

———. 2005. *Annual Energy Review 2004*. Washington, DC: DOE, Energy Information Administration. Available at: www.eia.doe.gov/emeu/aer/contents.html.

U.S. Environmental Protection Agency (U.S. EPA). 1987a. "Congressional Hearings Held, 1984, 1985, 1986." Washington, DC: EPA, Office of Legislative Analysis.

———. 1987b. *Unfinished Business: A Comparative Assessment of Environmental Problems*. Washington, DC: EPA, Office of Policy, Planning, and Evaluation.

———. 1990a. *Environmental Investments: The Cost of a Clean Environment: Report of the Administrator of the Environmental Protection Agency to the Congress of the United States*. Washington, DC: EPA.

———. 1990b. *Reducing Risk: Setting Priorities and Strategies for Environmental Protection*. Washington, DC: EPA, Science Advisory Board.

———. 1992a. *Environmental Equity: Reducing Risk for All Communities*, 2 vols. Washington, DC: EPA, Office of Policy, Planning, and Evaluation.

———. 1992b. *Framework for Ecological Risk Assessment*. Washington, DC: EPA, Office of Research and Development.

———. 1997a. *Community-Based Environmental Protection: A Resource Book for Protecting Ecosystems and Communities*. Washington, DC: EPA, Office of Policy, Planning, and Evaluation.

———. 1997b. *EPA Strategic Plan*. Washington, DC: EPA, Office of the Chief Financial Officer.

———. 2002a. *Latest Findings on National Air Quality: 2001 Status and Trends*. Washington, DC: U.S. EPA, Office of Air Quality Planning and Standards, September. Available at the EPA Web site: www.epa.gov/oar/aqtrnd01/.

———. 2002b. *National Water Quality Inventory: 2000 Report to Congress*. Washington, DC: EPA, Office of Water Quality, August. Available at the EPA Web site: www.epa.gov/305b/.

———. 2003. *Latest Findings on National Air Quality: 2002 Status and Trends*. Washington, DC: U.S. EPA, Office of Air Quality and Standards, August.

———. 2005. "Air Emissions Trends—Continued Progress Through 2004." Washington, DC: U.S. EPA Office of Air and Radiation, 2005. Accessed online January 26, 2006.

_____. 2006. "Drinking Water and Health: What You Need to Know." Washington, DC: U.S. EPA. Accessed online at www.epa.gov/safewater/dwhealth.html, January 27, 2006.

U.S. Government Accountability Office (U.S. GAO). 1992. *Environmental Protection Issues, Transition Series*. Washington, DC: U.S. Government Printing Office.

_____. 1997a. *Department of Energy: Contract Reform Is Progressing, But Full Implementation Will Take Years*. Washington, DC: GAO.

_____. 1997b. *Land Management Agencies: Major Activities at Selected Units Are Not Common Across Agencies*. Washington, DC: GAO.

_____. 2002. *DOE Contractor Management: Opportunities to Promote Initiatives That Could Reduce Support-Related Costs*. Washington, DC: GAO, GAO-02-1000.

_____. 2003. *Forest Service: Information on Appeals and Litigation Involving Fuels Reduction Activities*. Washington, DC: GAO, GAO-04-52, October 24.

_____. 2005a. *National Energy Policy: Inventory of Major Federal Energy Programs and Status of Policy Recommendations*. Washington, DC: GAO, GAO-05-379.

_____. 2005b. *Nuclear Waste: Better Performance Reporting Needed to Assess DOE's Ability to Achieve the Goals of the Accelerated Cleanup Program*. Washington, DC: GAO, GAO-05-764).

_____. 2005c. *Observations on EPA's Cost-Benefit-Analysis of Its Mercury Control Options*. Washington, DC: GAO, GAO-05-252.

_____. 2006. *Endangered Species: Time and Costs Required to Recover Species Are Largely Unknown*. Washington, DC: GAO, GAO-06-463R.

U.S. Office of Management and Budget. 2003. *Informing Regulatory Decisions: 2003 Report to Congress on the Costs and Benefits of Federal Regulations and Unfunded Mandates on State, Local, and Tribal Entities*. Washington, DC: Office of Information and Regulatory Affairs, OMB.

U.S. Office of Technology Assessment. 1988. *Are We Cleaning Up? 10 Superfund Case Studies*. Washington, DC: U.S. Government Printing Office.

_____. 1991a. *Complex Cleanup: The Environmental Legacy of Nuclear Weapons Production, Summary*, OTA-0-485. Washington, DC: U.S. Government Printing Office.

_____. 1991b. *Improving Automobile Fuel Economy: New Standards, New Approaches, Summary*, OTA-E-508. Washington, DC: U.S. Government Printing Office.

Vaughn, Jacqueline. 2004. *Environmental Politics: Domestic and Global Dimensions*, 4th ed. New York: Thomson Wadsworth.

_____, and Hanna Cortner. 2004. "Using Parallel Strategies to Promote Change: Forest Policymaking under George W. Bush." *Review of Policy Research* 21: 767–82.

Verhovek, Sam Howe. 1999. "An Expensive Fish." *New York Times*, March 17, A14.

Vig, Norman J. 1994. "Presidential Leadership and the Environment: From Reagan and Bush to Clinton." In *Environmental Policy in the 1990s*, 2nd ed., edited by Norman J. Vig and Michael E. Kraft. Washington, DC: CQ Press.

_____. 2006. "Presidential Leadership and the Environment." In *Environmental Policy*, 6th ed., edited by Norman J. Vig and Michael E. Kraft. Washington, DC: CQ Press.

Vig, Norman J., and Michael G. Faure, eds. 2004. *Green Giants? Environmental Policies of the United States and the European Union*. Cambridge, MA: MIT Press.

Vig, Norman J., and Michael E. Kraft, eds. 1984. *Environmental Policy in the 1980s: Reagan's New Agenda*. Washington, DC: CQ Press.

_____. 2006. *Environmental Policy: New Directions for the Twenty-First Century*, 6th ed. Washington, DC: CQ Press.

Vogel, David. 2006. "International Trade and Environmental Regulation." In *Environmental Policy*, 6th ed., edited by Norman J. Vig and Michael E. Kraft. Washington, DC: CQ Press.

Wackernagel, Mathis, and William Rees. 1996. *Our Ecological Footprint: Reducing Human Impact on the Earth*. Gabriola Island, BC, Canada: New Society Publishers.

Wald, Matthew L. 1992. "U.S. Finds Energy Industry Subsidies Are Small." *New York Times*, December 14, C2.

———. 1993. "After 20 Years, America's Foot Is Still on the Gas." *New York Times*, October 17, E4.

———. 1997. "A California Utility's Contract May Make Solar Power Cheaper." *New York Times*, May 19, A10.

———. 1999a. "Court Overturns Air Quality Rules." *New York Times*, May 15, 1, A10.

———. 1999b. "Cruise Line Pleads Guilty to Dumping of Chemicals." *New York Times*, July 22, A10.

———. 1999c. "An Ill Wind Blows at Vacation Sites." *New York Times*, August 6, 1, A11.

———. 2002. "Court Says Agency Can Tighten Smog Rules." *New York Times*, March 27, A18.

Wang, Jinnan, Jintian Yang, Chazhong Ge, Dong Cao, and Jeremy Schreifels. 2004. "Controlling Sulfur Dioxide in China: Will Emissions Trading Work? *Environment* 46 (June): 28–38.

Wapner, Paul. 1996. *Environmental Activism and World Civic Politics*. Albany: State University of New York Press.

Wargo, John. 1998. *Our Children's Toxic Legacy: How Science and Law Fail to Protect Us from Pesticides*, 2nd ed. New Haven, CT: Yale University Press.

Warrick, Joby, and Juliet Eilperin. 2004. "Big Energy in the Wild West: The Bush Administration's Land-Use Decisions Favor Oil and Gas." *Washington Post National Weekly Edition*, October 4–10.

Weber, Edward P. 1998. "Successful Collaboration: Negotiating Effective Regulations." *Environment* 40 (November): 10–15, 32–37.

———. 1999. *Pluralism by the Rules: Conflict and Cooperation in Environmental Regulation*. Washington, DC: Georgetown University Press.

———. 2003. *Bringing Society Back In: Grassroots Ecosystem Management, Accountability, and Sustainable Communities*. Cambridge, MA: MIT Press.

Weiss, Edith Brown, and Harold K. Jacobson. 1999. "Getting Countries to Comply with International Agreements." *Environment* 41 (July/August): 16–20, 37–45.

Wengert, Norman. 1994. "Land Use Policy." In *Encyclopedia of Policy Studies*, 2nd ed., edited by Stuart S. Nagel. New York: Marcel Dekker.

Wenner, Lettie M. 1982. *The Environmental Decade in Court*. Bloomington: Indiana University Press.

Whitaker, John C. 1976. *Striking a Balance: Environment and Natural Resources Policy in the Nixon–Ford Years*. Washington, DC: American Enterprise Institute.

Wildavsky, Aaron. 1988. *Searching for Safety*. New Brunswick, NJ: Transaction Books.

———. 1995. *But Is It True? A Citizen's Guide to Environmental Health and Safety Issues*. Cambridge, MA: Harvard University Press.

Wilson, Edward O. 1990. "Threats to Biodiversity." In *Managing Planet Earth*, edited by Scientific American. New York: W. H. Freeman.

Wilson, James Q. 1980. "The Politics of Regulation." In *The Politics of Regulation*, edited by James Q. Wilson. New York: Basic Books.

Wines, Michael. 1993. "Tax's Demise Illustrates First Rule of Lobbying: Work, Work, Work." *New York Times*, June 14, 1, A11.

Wondolleck, Julia M., and Steven L. Yaffee. 2000. *Making Collaboration Work: Lessons from Innovation in Natural Resource Management*. Washington, DC: Island Press.

World Commission on Environment and Development. 1987. *Our Common Future.* New York: Oxford University Press.

World Wildlife Fund. 1994. "Old-Growth Forests, Ecosystem Management, and Option 9." *Conservation Issues* 1 (May/June): 5–8.

Yaffee, Steven Lewis. 1994. *The Wisdom of the Spotted Owl: Policy Lessons for a New Century.* Washington, DC: Island Press.

Yandle, Bruce. 1999. *The Market Meets the Environment: Economic Analysis of Environmental Policy.* Lanham, MD: Rowman and Littlefield.

Yoon, Carol Kaesuk. 1999. "Report on Acid Rain Finds Good News and Bad News." *New York Times,* October 7, A22.

Yosie, Terry F. 1993. "The EPA Science Advisory Board: A Case Study in Institutional History and Public Policy." *Environmental Science and Technology* 27: 1476–81.

Index

Johannesburg summit. *See* World Summit on
Sustainable Development
Johnson, Lyndon B., 89, 265
Johnson, Stephen, 107, 135

Katrina (hurricane), and climate change, 44
Kyoto Protocol, 43–44, 64, 107, 169, 255t,
261–263. *See also* UN Convention on
Climate Change

Labeling, green, 224
Land(s), public
administration of, 179–182
current status, 110n3, 176–179
distribution of, 87–88
management of. *See* Natural resource policies
privatization of, 232–242
protection of, 106
use vs. preservation of, 175–179
user fees for, 232
Land and Water Conservation Fund Act (1964),
89, 177, 180t, 203n23
Land ethic, 9
Land systems, federal, 189–190
Land trusts, 233
Land use, 175–176
development vs. preservation, 175–179,
185–186, 188
planning, 245–247
Landfills, 40–41, 123–124
Lands Legacy initiative, 186, 203n23
Lead, 27, 29, 36, 125, 143t, 144t, 218, 239n17
League of Conservation Voters, 73, 85,
103–104, 109n1
Leavitt, Michael, 107, 135
Legislation. *See also specific laws*
influence of states on, 80–81
list of major laws, 92t, 113t, 180–181t
litigation and, 79–80
Legitimation, policy, 59, 66–67
Leopold, Also, 9
Litigation,
citizen suit provisions, 156n12
on Clean Water Act, 119
on Endangered Species Act, 193–194
by environmentalists, 79–80
on land use, 160
on National Environmental Policy Act, 198
prevalence of, 148, 160
provisions for, 119
tort law and, 229–230
Local governments
energy initiatives, 172–174
policy alternatives, 227–228
role in policymaking, 70, 80–81
sustainable development and, 245–247
Logging, 182–183, 184–186, 218
Love Canal, 38

Mainstream environmental organizations, 95–96
Man and Nature, 86
Marketplace
government purchasing in, 234–235
incentives, 225t, 226–227, 239n14
regulation of, 10
Membership of environmental organizations,
93–94, 95–96
Methyl tert-butyl ether (MTBE), 171
Millennium Ecosystem Assessment, 47, 263
Mining fees, 232
Mobilization of bias, 72
Montreal Protocol, 19, 31, 237, 250, 254t,
257–258, 270n15
Motor vehicle(s)
air pollution from, 26–27
alternative-fuel, 167–168, 172
emission standards for, 27, 68, 114–116, 140,
145–146, 211
fuel economy standards for, 164, 167–169,
202n8, 202n10
market incentives for, 226
Motor Vehicle Air Pollution Control Act (1965),
114
Motor vehicle manufacturers
energy policy and, 167, 169
innovative products from, 169, 172
Multiple use of lands, 187–188
Multiple Use-Sustained Yield Act (1960), 180t,
182
Muskie, Edmund, 91

National Acid Precipitation Assessment Program,
30
National Agenda for Clean Water, 121
National Ambient Air Quality Standards, 114,
142, 144t
National Commission on the Environment, 4
National Energy Act (1978), 164
National Energy Strategy, 65
National Environmental Performance Partnership
System, 137
National Environmental Policy Act (1969),
66–67, 166, 177, 180t, 196–199, 204n35
National Forest Management Act (1976), 181t,
182–183
National monuments, 106, 186
National Oceanic and Atmospheric Administra-
tion, 136, 190
National Park Service, 88, 110n3, 179, 181,
188–191, 212
National Park System, 189, 212
National parks, 28, 87–88, 175, 181, 188–191,
212, 264
National Parks Omnibus Management Act, 191
National Pollutant Discharge Elimination System,
119
National Priorities List, 20, 38, 129–130